Lotus
-Eating
Days

Dear Christina,
best wishes,
Caroline

Lotus -Eating Days

From Surrey to Singapore, 1923–1959

The Letters, Diaries and Recordings of Theresa Repton
(née Pang Kim Lui) and Geoffrey Christopher Tyrwhitt Repton

CAROLINE REPTON

The Book Guild Ltd

First published in Great Britain in 2022 by
The Book Guild Ltd
Unit E2, Airfield Business Park
Harrison Road
Market Harborough
Leicestershire, LE16 7UL
Tel: 0116 279 2299
www.bookguild.co.uk
Email: info@bookguild.co.uk
Twitter: @bookguild

Typeset in 11pt Minion Pro

Printed and bound in the UK by TJ Books LTD, Padstow, Cornwall

ISBN 978 1914471 100

British Library Cataloguing in Publication Data.
A catalogue record for this book is available from the British Library.

For Mum and Dad, with fondest love

Contents

Family Trees   viii

Cast List   xiii

I Was Born Number 13 (1923–1941)   1

Gather Ye Rosebuds While Ye May (1934–1939)   4

A Hot Sun in a Cloudless Sky (1940)   37

Lotus-Eating Days (1941)   88

It Was Touch-and-Go (1942–1945)   114

Rather Trying at Times (1942–1945)   118

I Am Now Free and in Safe Hands (1945)   127

I Had to Make Up Words Sometimes (1945–1950)   165

The World Has Been Forgetting (1946–1947)   168

There's One Damn Good Chance for You (1948–1949)   200

There is Something About Asia (1950–1952)   251

He Went Back to His Own Funny Steps (1953–1956)   327

Through the Silvery Olive Grove (1953–1956)   336

I Miss You Most in the Morning (1957–1959)   375

The Backstory   441

Historical Notes   453

Epilogue   459

Bibliography   461

Acknowledgements   462

Pang Family Tree - 1st to 8th Brother

Pang How Yew — John (b. 1877, m. 1899, d. 1960) & **Yao Kwee Choo — Mary** (b. 1882, d. 1958)

1st Brother
- **Pang Tong Soon Moses** (d. 1942)
- Spouse: **Lim Quee Liang Mary** (b. 1910, d. 1987)
- Children / Spouses:
  - Pang Seow Guan Benedict (b. 1928) — Oh Mui Keow Theresa (b. 1931)
  - Pang Pheck Choon Theresa (b. 1929) — Ho Kim Chong Joseph
  - Pang Seow Hong Joaquim
  - Pang Seow Cheam Thomas (b. 1939) — Lim Poh Sieck (b. 1941)

2nd Brother
- **Pang Tong Hak John** (b. 1911, d. 1973)
- Spouse: **Tay Agnes** (b. 1911, d. 1973)
- Children / Spouses:
  - Pang Seow Teck Benedict (b. 1934) — Quek May Ann Christina (b. 1936)
  - Pang Seow Cheng Francis (b. 1936) — Choi Jek Lam Florence (b. 1939)
  - Pang Pheck Eng Mary — Goh Kok Siew

3rd Brother
- **Pang Tong Kuan**
- Spouse: **Teo Kim Neo**
- Children / Spouses:
  - Pang Seow Huat Gregory — Ah Nia Irene

4th Brother
- **Pang Tong Yong Joseph** (b. 1913, d. 1990)
- Spouse: **Lee Hak Tiang** (b. 1926)
- Children / Spouses:
  - Pang Pheck Tor Joanna — Low Anthony
  - Pang Seow Kee Andrew (b. 1947)
  - Pang Seow Keng Michael (b. 1949) — Pat Lilian (b. 1948)
  - Pang Pheck Gek Margaret (b. 1950) — Lim Jit Kiang Jeffrey (b. 1948)
  - Pang Seow Chye Matthew (b. 1952) — Siek Ah Choo Betsy (b. 1955)
  - Pang Pheck Hian Rose (b. 1964) — Lek Whi Kok Daniel (b. 1962)

5th Sister
- **Pang Kim Keow Mary** (b. 1914, d. 1993)
- Spouse: **Cheng Yong Nghee Joseph** (d. 1969)
- Children / Spouses:
  - Cheng Gueh Eng Lucy (b. 1941) — Lim Khiow Mong Damien (b. 1940)
  - Cheng Gueh Liang Catherine Nam (b. 1942) — Kwok Kien (b. 1939)
  - Cheng Gueh Meng Agnes (b. 1947) — Yeo Kian Heng David (b. 1942)
  - Cheng Poh Chye Eloisius (b. 1951, d. 2019) — Lau Puay Gek (b. 1952)
  - Cheng Gueh Im Rosalina (b. 1952) — Kho Su Kia Richard (b. 1948)
  - Cheng Poh Wan Sebastian (b. 1957)

6th Brother
- **Pang Tong Khiam John** (b. 1917, d. 1998)
- Spouse: **Chew Cheok Eng Teresa** (b. 1929, d. 2015)
- Children / Spouses:
  - Pang Seow Ngiap (b. 1947) — Wang Swee Gek (b. 1950)
  - Pang Seow Chew Anthony (b. 1948) — Chia Guat Hong Daphne (b. 1958)
  - Pang Peck Thor Veronica (b. 1950, d. 1973)
  - Pang Peck Lan Agatha (b. 1952)
  - Pang Seow Hung Gabriel (b. 1958)
  - Pang Seow Kwan Peter (b. 1960) — Tan Yak Hwee Martina (b. 1963)
  - Pang Peck Hia Elizabeth (b. 1963) — Lim Gerard Keith (b. 1962)

7th Brother
- **Yeo Kim Khian Joseph** (Adopted cousin, d. 1989)
- Spouse: **Lee Swee Lan Maddalene** (d. 2003)
- Children / Spouses:
  - Ngoo Ah Moy Cecilia — Hui Shoon Seng Francis
  - Yeo Anthony — Ng Maria
  - Yeo Martin
  - Yeo John — Ng Theresa
  - Yeo Elizabeth — Ng Peter
  - Yeo Lucy — Lim Kit Hock
  - Yeo Margaret
  - Yeo Joseph — Loh Catherine
  - Yeo Chye Huat
  - Yeo Soon Huat John — Yeo Sherry

8th Brother
- **Pang Tong Jin Andrew** (b. 1919, d. 1986)

5th Sister Pang Kim Keow Mary

Children	Spouses	Grandchildren	
Cheng Gueh Eng Lucy m.1967	Lim Khiow Mong Damien	Lim Hwee Miang Lydia b.1971	Lim Choon Kiat Joseph b.1972
Cheng Gueh Liang Catherine Nam m.1966	Kwok Kien	Kwok Su-Mei Karen b.1972	
Cheng Gueh Meng Agnes m.1971	Yeo Kian Heng David	Yeo Choon Poh Aidan b.1972 m.2001	Yeo Su Shan Davina b.1975 m.2005
Cheng Poh Chye Eloisius d.2019	Lau Puay Gek	Cheng Yeow Kiang Clement Kenneth b.1977 m.2005	Cheng Yao Jie b.1985
Cheng Gueh Im Rosalina m.1982	Kho Su Kia Richard	Kho Guan Guo (Xu Guanguo) b.1984 / Kho Jia Her (Xu Jiahe) b.1993	Kho Jia Yi (Xu Jiayi) b.1994
Cheng Poh Wan Sebastian			

6th Brother Pang Tong Khiam John

Children	Spouses	Grandchildren	
Pang Seow Ngiap Augustine m.1975	Wang Swee Gek	Pang Nghee Kheem Brendan b.1977 m.2007	Pang Nghee Thena Aaron b.1981 m.2013
Pang Seow Chew Anthony m.1986	Chia Guat Hong Daphne	Pang Wei En Joan b.1992 / Pang Su En Jeanette b.1993	Pang Li En Marie-Therese b.1994 / Pang Sze En Marjorie b.1995
Pang Peck Thor Veronica d.1973			
Pang Peck Lan Agatha			
Pang Seow Hung Gabriel			
Pang Seow Kwan Peter m.1991	Tan Yak Hwee Martina		
Pang Peck Hia Elizabeth m.1991	Lim Gerard Keith	Lim Yu Michelle Caroline b.1995 / Lim Wei Jeremy Philip b.1997	Lim Juin Damien Gerard b.1998

Pang Family Tree - 9th Sister to 16th Brother

Pang How Yew John b. 1877, m. 1899, d. 1960
Yeo Kwee Choo Mary b. 1882, d. 1958

Main sibling row

Sibling	Spouse
9th Sister: Pang Kim Kee Maria	Tan Tat Kwang
10th Brother: Pang Tong Chew	Ang Poh Luang
11th Brother: Pang Tong Hui Peter, b. 1921, d. 1984	
12th Sister: Pang Kim Heok Elizabeth, b. 1922, m. 1947, d. 2016	Chua Wee Heng John, b. 1911, d. 1986
13th Sister: Pang Kim Lui Theresa, b. 1923, m. 1959, d. 2020	Repton Geoffrey Christopher, b. 1918, d. 1998
14th Sister	
15th Sister: Pang Kim Wha Agnes, b. 1926, m. 1943, d. 2016	Toh Chai Seng Ignatius, b. 1918, d. 2009
16th Brother	

9th Sister: Pang Kim Kee Maria

Children	Spouses
Tan Gek Sit	Lim Hun Siang
Tan Teck Heng	Hoo Siew Ching
Tan Siok Muay	Lee Boon Ho
Tan Teck Seng	Lee Sok Heok
Tan Teck Kee	Goh Bee Siew, b. 1960

10th Brother: Pang Tong Chew

Children
Pang Peck Noi Helen
Pang Seow Kee Francis
Pang Peck Hong Dorothy (Dolly)
Pang Magdalene
Pang Seow Heng Joseph

Grandchildren:
- Pang Peck Hoon Jeanette, b. 1960
- Pang Peck Hwang Josephine

13th Sister: Pang Kim Lui Theresa

Children	Spouses
Repton Caroline Mary, b. 1960	Carter Colin Ex-partner, b. 1962
Repton Angela Frances, b. 1962	Jordan Andrew, b. 1959

15th Sister: Pang Kim Wha Agnes

Children	Spouses
Toh Chee Seng Francis, b. 1943, d. 2021	Seow Ah Moi Anne, b. 1950
Toh Gek Kheng, b. 1944, d. 1944	
Toh Eng Kee, b. 1945, d. 1945	
Toh Chui Hua Elizabeth, b. 1952	Chua Chong Hock, b. 1949
Toh Chui Hoon Christina, b. 1956	Ong Kay Guan Gerrard, b. 1954
Toh Chui Hong Bernadette, b. 1958	
Toh Chui Ling Anne, b. 1961	Tan Yong Swee Ignatius, b. 1961

12th Sister: Pang Kim Heok Elizabeth — Spouse: Chua Wee Heng John

Children	Spouse
Chua Hong Chye John, m. 1978, d. 2005	Lim Sai Guek Annie
Chua Sok Cheng Theresa	
Chua Hong Chuan Alphonsus	

Grandchildren:

Chua Eng How Justin, b. 1980, m. 2010	Chua Su Ling Rebecca, b. 1984, m. 2005

15th Sister: Pang Kim Wha Agnes

Children	Spouses	Grandchildren	
Toh Chee Seng Francis, m. 1971	Seow Ah Moi Anne, d. 2006	Toh Wei Kiat Dominic, b. 1972	Toh Tee Hian Angelina, b. 1973
Toh Gek Kheng, d. 1944			
Toh Eng Kee, d. 1945			
Toh Chui Hua Elizabeth, m. 1980	Chua Chong Hock	Chua Wei Ping Cheryl, b. 1988, m. 2018	Chua Wei Shi Claire, b. 1989
Toh Chui Hoon Christina, m. 1979	Ong Kay Guan Gerrard	Ong Eng Soon Calvin, b. 1982; Ong Eng Huat Shaun, b. 1988	Ong Eng Leong Jonathan, b. 1990
Toh Chui Hong Bernadette			
Toh Chui Ling Anne, m. 1988	Tan Yong Swee Ignatius	Tan Jie Ru Andrea, b. 1993	Tan Jun Jie Timothy, b. 2003

13th Sister: Pang Kim Lui Theresa

Children	Spouses	Grandchildren	
Repton Caroline Mary, m. 1986	Carter Colin Ex-partner	Carter Yen Mei Madeleine, b. 1994	Carter Yen Lian Alice Ruth, b. 1997
Repton Angela Frances	Jordan Andrew	Jordan Robin David, b. 1991, m. 2019	Jordan Thomas Benjamin, b. 1995

Compiled by Anne Toh, youngest daughter of Theresa's 15th sister Agnes

Repton Family Tree c.1720 to 1864

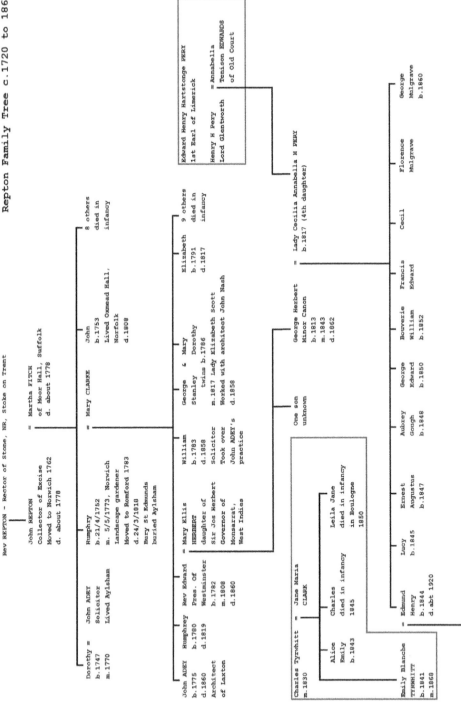

Rev REPTON - Rector of Stone, NR, Stoke on Trent

John REPTON
Collector of Excise
Moved to Norwich 1762
d. about 1778
= Martha FITCH
of Moor Hall, Suffolk
d. about 1778

Mary CLARKE

Dorothy =
b.1747
m.1770

John ADEY
Solicitor
Lived Aylsham

Humphry
b.21/4/1752
m. 5/5/1773, Norwich
Landscape gardener
Moved to Romford 1783
d.24/3/1818
Bury St Edmunds
buried Aylsham

John
b.1753
Lived Oxmead Hall,
Norfolk
d.1808

8 others
died in
infancy

John ADEY
b.1775
d.1860
m.1819
Architect
of Laxton

Humphrey
b.1780
d.1819

Rev Edward
b.1782
m.1808
d.1860
Pres. Of
Westminster
= Mary Ellis
HERBERT
daughter of
Sir Jos Herbert
Governor of
Monsarrat,
West Indies

William
b.1783
d.1858
Solicitor
Took over
John ADEY's
practice

George   &   Mary
Stanley   Dorothy
twins b.1786
m.1817 Lady Elizabeth Scott
Worked with architect John Nash
d.1858

Elizabeth
b.1791
d.1817

9 others
died in
infancy

Edward Henry Hartstonge PERY
1st Earl of Limerick
= Annabella
Tenison EDWARDS
of Old Court

Henry H Pery
Lord Glentworth

George Herbert
Minor Canon
b.1813
m.1843
d.1862
= Lady Cecilia Annabella H PERY
b.1817 (4th daughter)

One son
unknown

Charles Tyrwhitt = Jane Maria
m.1830   CLARK

Alice
Emily
b.1843

Charles
died in infancy
1845

Leila Jane
died in infancy
in Boulogne
1850

Emily Blanche
TYRWHITT
b.1841
m.1868

Edmund
Henry
b.1844
d.abt 1920

Lucy
b.1845

Ernest
Augustus
b.1847

Aubrey
Gough
b.1848

George
Edward
b.1850

Bouverie
William
b.1852

Francis
Edward

Cecil

Florence
Mulgrave

George
Mulgrave
b.1860

X

Repton Family Tree 1865 to 2021

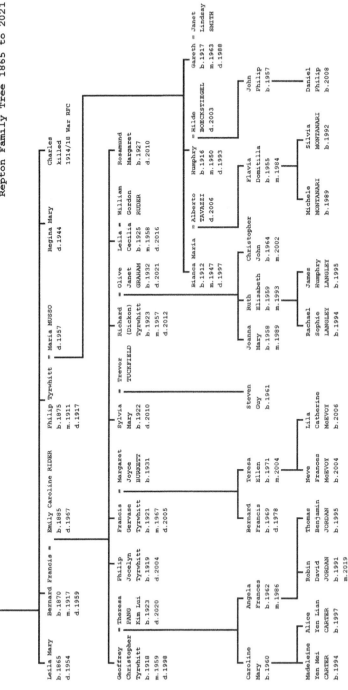

This is a section of the family tree compiled by Mr. G. Cope-Cartledge, genealogist, between 1964 and 1971, who traced the ancestry of Humphry Repton the famous landscape gardener back to 1520. Later additions are by family members.

Cast List

Pang Family

Theresa Theresa Repton (née Pang Kim Lui), known as 'Number 13' or thirteenth sister/aunt to her family, and Terry to friends. Born in Singapore on the 13th July 1923.

Agnes Fifteenth sister/aunt, or 'Small Sister'. Theresa's younger sister and the youngest in the family.

Ignatius Toh Chai Seng Agnes's husband.

Elizabeth Twelfth sister/aunt. Theresa's sister closest in age to her.

Mary Fifth sister/aunt, known as 'Big Sister'. Theresa's eldest surviving sister.

Joseph Cheng Yong Nghee Mary's husband, also known as 'CID Man'.

Second Brother Theresa's eldest surviving brother, John Pang Tong Hak.

Sixth Brother John Pang Tong Khiam.

Daisy Pang Sye Noi Theresa's second cousin on her father's side.

Dick and Amy Pang Second Brother's elder son and his wife.

Repton Family

Christopher (C.)	Geoffrey Christopher Tyrwhitt Repton, firstborn of Bernard and Caroline, known as Christopher to his family and Chris to friends. Born in Montreal on the 3rd December 1918.
Bernard	Bernard Francis Charles Repton, known as 'Pop' or 'Dadda' (pronounced 'Dair-da') to his offspring. Christopher's father.
Caroline	Emily Caroline Repton (née Rider). Christopher's mother.

Christopher's younger siblings, from eldest to youngest

J.	Jocelyn.
G.	Gervase.
S.	Sylvia.
D.	Dickon.
L.	Leila.
R.	Rosamund.

Extended family

'Big Leila'	Aunt Leila.
Ina (Regina)	Aunt Ina.
B.	Bianca (cousin).
H.	Humphry (cousin).
G.	Gareth (cousin).
Aunt Nell and Uncle Reg	Christopher's maternal aunt and her husband, Dr Reginald Riches.
Aunt Mary and Aunt Belle	Christopher's unmarried maternal aunts who lived together.

Pets

Peter	The family's dog in the 1930s.
Marcus	Rosamund's dog in the 1940s.

Other correspondents

Perpetua Watkin	Friend of Christopher and the Repton family.
Christopher (Dom A. Watkin)	Friend from St. Edmund's primary boarding school.
Arthur E. Field	Friend from St. Edmund's primary boarding school.
Mr A. W. Goodfellow	Christopher's first employer at his accountancy firm in the City of London.
Paddy Ellison	Friend of Sylvia's.
June	Friend of Sylvia's.
Connie Braham	Christopher's colleague at the United Nations Relief and Rehabilitation Administration (UNRRA), and fiancée in the late 1940s.
John A. Millward	Christopher's acquaintance from on board the *Trafalgar*.
Maria (M.)	A girlfriend Christopher met in London in 1951.
John Harold Phillips	Theresa's boss at Turquand Youngs.
Margaret Ross (aka Bond)	Mutual friend of Christopher and Connie.
Hu Chye Neo	A friend of Theresa's who had moved to London.

Christopher's former teachers/monks from Blackfriars School, Laxton
Fr Henry
Fr Dominic Atkinson
Fr Gerald Meath
Fr Aelwin

Christopher's fellow POWs
Jack Shuttle
Leo Lavender
'Hooky' Walker
Ron
Bill Mill
Dan Moriarty
Don (from India)
Ray Caward
G. W. Lehle
Bill 'Charlie' Charlton
George Schultz (Dutchman)
Pat

Christopher's friends from UNRRA

Gilbert ('Gillie') Brown
Pamela ('Pam') Brown
Peggy
Dorothy ('Dee')
Robert H. ('Robbie') Robertson
George Price

Christopher's friends/acquaintances from P. & T. Lands

Roy and Stella Coulson-Gilmer
Paddy Knights
Peter Briggs
Bobby Cox
Gerald W. Champney

Christopher's friends from Turquand Youngs

Walter Bellam
Trevor and Jean Brown
Willie Lochhead
Colin Coey

Time and Love[1]

I

When I have seen by Time's fell hand defac'd
The rich proud cost of outworn buried age;
When sometime lofty towers I see down-ras'd,
And brass eternal slave to mortal rage;

When I have seen the hungry ocean gain
Advantage on the kingdom of the shore,
And the firm soil win of the wat'ry main,
Increasing store with loss and loss with store;

When I have seen such interchange of state,
Or state itself confounded to decay;
Ruin hath taught me thus to ruminate,
That Time will come and take my love away.

This thought is as a death, which cannot choose
But weep to have that which it fears to lose.

1   Shakespeare's Sonnets 64 & 65, from Christopher's favourite book of poetry, *The Golden Treasury*, compiled by F. T. Palgrave.

II

Since brass, nor stone, nor earth, nor boundless sea
But sad mortality o'er-sways their power,
How with this rage shall beauty hold a plea,
Whose action is no stronger than a flower?

O, how shall summer's honey breath hold out
Against the wrackful siege of batt'ring days,
When rocks impregnable are not so stout,
Nor gates of steel so strong, but time decays?

O fearful meditation! where, alack,
Shall time's best jewel from time's chest lie hid?
Or what strong hand can hold his swift foot back?
Or who his spoil of beauty can forbid?

O, none, unless this miracle have might,
That in black ink my love may still shine bright.

(William Shakespeare)

ONE

I Was Born Number 13

1923–1941

Theresa Pang Kim Lui ('Golden Bud')

There were sixteen of us altogether: nine boys and seven girls. I was born number thirteen of the family on the 13th July 1923. We all lived in the shop-house at 62 Rochore Road[1], Singapore, where my father kept a shop selling chickens and ducks bought from the countryside. Later he changed his trade to that of a grocer. After my parents died, my second, fourth and tenth brothers took over the running of the shop.

My parents left China in the early 1900s and emigrated to Singapore after my father quarrelled with his brother. They converted to Catholicism in China before leaving. They had to travel by boat all the way from Swatow in southern China, near Fujian province[2], sleeping on the deck. It was not an easy journey.

Most of us were born in Singapore, except for my fifth sister, Mary. She was born in China, because in 1913 my parents went back to see my grandmother, who was very ill. My eldest sister – who would have been First Sister – had been born in China too, but she drowned in a pond while trying to save a chicken[3].

---

1   The spelling of the road name was later changed to Rochor Road.
2   Swatow is a port city in Guangdong province, about five hundred kilometres south of the border with Fujian province, from where they came.
3   The eldest daughter's name and dates of birth and death are unknown. She was omitted from the parents' numbering of the children who were born afterwards, and hence from the family tree. However, the seventh brother was included, despite being an adopted nephew of Theresa's mother.

When I was three years old, I had an accident. My left hand was scalded when my second brother left a pot of boiling tea on the table – I spilled it, and this resulted in the contraction of three fingers on my left hand. But I was able to use the hand later in life, and I was able to type.

When I was born, a doctor and his wife, friends of the family, wanted to adopt me. But my second brother hid me so that I was not found. Later he would be responsible for sending me to an English school, St. Anthony's Girls' School in Middle Road, where I was educated. I remember walking to and from school every day with my brothers and sisters, on the shady side of the street to shelter from the hot sun.

My parents were very religious people. They used to go to the early morning Mass at 6.30, then come back and wake us all up for the eight o'clock Mass. We had to sleep on the floor, except for my sister Mary, who had a bed. Somehow, we did not mind, and we were very happy together.

My school classmates Mary Boey (Yoke Chee), Kuan Yang Chew ('Double') and Joyce Chia were my close friends. The four of us used to go out to the cinema on Saturday mornings, and we saw each other quite frequently. Double was given her nickname by Mary Boey because if you asked to borrow money from her, she would say, "I'll charge you double!" Yoke Chee never got married because she didn't like men. She didn't like anybody to control her; she was very private. We used to take her out on her birthday to the Peking Restaurant for dinner and dancing.

I was in love with a Chinese man, Morgan Hu. He was a friend of my tenth brother – I was eighteen and he was a bit older. As he was the eldest son, his mother refused to let him become a Catholic, as she was a staunch Buddhist. So we never got engaged, and the friendship ended. He was fond of mynah birds. Aloysius[4] was also friends with him, because they both kept birds and fish, and they lived in Serangoon Gardens. He used to come over to look at my father's mynah bird that talked. His mother was very kind; I liked her. But his aunt found a girlfriend for him, and they soon got married and had twins. It was just before the Japanese came in.

The war in Europe started in 1939, and it came to Singapore on the 8th December 1941, when the first bombs were dropped on Boat Quay, where my eldest sister was living. Pearl Harbor was bombed a few hours before that. At that time, we were still doing our senior Cambridge examinations.

---

4   Theresa's sister Mary's elder son.

The centre was the Convent of the Holy Infant Jesus, and it was the last two subjects – history on the morning of the 8th. We managed to sit out the exam while the air raid was going on. The following day we had to go back for arts. After that, it was very difficult to know what was happening, because the Japanese were marching down from Malaya very fast, and there was a lot of shelling going on.

TWO

Gather Ye Rosebuds While Ye May

1934–1939

Glossary

A ha'porth: (pronounced 'hay-perth') a halfpenny's worth, i.e. a little bit.

Early/late: early/late Mass.

Eight: eight o'clock Mass.

71 in the shade: All temperatures are in Fahrenheit, e.g. 71° = 22° Celsius, 24°F = –4°C, 32°F = 0°C, 70°F = 21°C, 85°F = 29°C, etc.

10.30: 10.30 a.m. Mass.

To free-lib *v*.: to visit the Free Library.

To park *v*.: to take a walk in the park, presumably the nearby St. Ann's Hill.

The Lodge: St. Ann's Lodge, the house in Chertsey, Surrey, where Christopher's parents, Bernard and Caroline, lived with their seven children during the 1930s.

Topers: drunks.

1934

Christopher and his brothers were sent to boarding school from the age of nine or ten. They used to write home to their parents every week.

St Ann's Lodge, Chertsey

Blackfriars
Laxton
11th Nov.

My dear Mother and Father,

I hope you are very well. There was no match yesterday and we had a cinema show in the evening. Today the place is crowded with 'old boys'. We played them at rugger today and lost 17–0. We all enjoyed the trip to Oxford. The journey took over three hours each way. I went round Christ College and Pembroke College. You are allowed to go anywhere in the colleges except upstairs. We had dinner at the Dominican Priory in silence. A special section of Lyons[5] was engaged for us to have tea. The match was good. Oxford weren't beaten too badly. It was very cold watching the match though. We haven't got any more holidays till Dec. 8th now.

One of the old boys here lives at Amersham and knows Mrs. Newton. His name is Young. I'm afraid I can't think of much more to say now. Please excuse the smudges.

Love from Christopher
xxxxxxx
Please give my love to the others.

---

5   Teahouse/café.

1935

Blackfriars
Laxton
27th Jan.

My dear Mother and Father,

I hope you are very well. In the last few days we have had quite a bit of snow, but it does not seem to stay long. It is snowing at this moment. Have you had any yet? Don't you think it would be a good idea to send us a book of stamps instead of sending one or two each week? It was not much use sending me that free ticket to the cinema from Weybridge, for I will not be able to use it. It was from the *Treasure Island* thing which Jocelyn and I did at King George's Cinema, Weybridge. I am sending it back in case Aunt Ina or Leila would care to use it.

Yesterday the 1st XV played Wyggeston Sc. II[6] away at Leicester and won 18–0. A howling blizzard prevented those left from playing rugger. My heel is almost better now. I went to Matron on Wednesday and got some medicated plaster put on it and got leave off rugger for a few days. I have not played rugger at all yet. It is almost certain that we come home after Easter. I'm quite glad in a way because it means that we shall get half of May for the Easter Hols.

The play is called *The Crooked Billet*; we saw it done by the Divines at St. Edmund's. It is a crook play. I am not in it but Jocelyn is – he takes the part of the heroine.

We were very glad of the cake we brought back. I rather wish we'd taken them both back now. Thank you for the clothes. Please could you send two of my ties that I have left behind? They are both fairly new, and will most probably be in the chest of drawers in our room. We got quite a pile of letters yesterday. Doesn't Humphry write mad things?

Best love from Christopher
xxxxxxxx

---

6   Wyggeston Grammar School for Boys, which Sir David Attenborough attended in 1937-44, closed down in 1976, a century after it was founded, when comprehensive schools were introduced. It then became Wyggeston and Queen Elizabeth I College.

Blackfriars

Laxton

Feb. 17

My dear Mother and Father,

I hope you are very well. Thank you for your letter.

Today there is the usual fortnightly film show. This year the annual retreat comes just before St. Thomas's Day (March 7th), so we will have rather a slack time as regards classes. Talking of slack times, the last part of this week has been a very slack period for our form, for our two principal masters have been unable to take us: Fr. Henry is, as I told you last week, down with flu at Oxford, and then Fr. Aelwin caught flu and has been in bed since Wednesday evening; I think he is getting up on Monday though.

On Wednesday, the Woodland Pytchley Hunt[7] came all the way from Brigstock and met outside the school specially for the purpose of allowing the boys to follow the hounds. We had dinner at 11.30, and so got off the last two classes. Then the hunt started at 12.15. Practically everybody turned out, all changed into rugger things. We had to wait about a bit at first, then we followed the hounds into Wakerley Woods where there were several long waits. The hounds took a long time to find the scent, and people were beginning to despair of ever finding a fox, but at last, about 2 hours after the start, there was a noise of barking – the hounds had found. Everybody rushed madly after them. Many got left behind. In the end 14 boys and Fr. Aelwin reached a disused iron quarry at Wakerley where the fox had got to earth. The hole was too narrow and deep for the hounds, and the fox terriers weren't on the spot. Then the hunt tried two spinneys near Wakerley, but the hounds drew blanks. Then we walked home, very tired, and got back at about 3.40.

There are still about four chaps in bed with flu, and now there is a rumour (it is really more than a rumour but has not been

---

7   A famous traditional fox hunt, the Woodland Pytchley Hunt split from the Pytchley Hunt in 1930, as agreed by Lord Spencer of Althorp. The Pytchley Hunt was founded in 1750 in the village of Pytchley, Northamptonshire. The UK government banned fox hunting in 2004. But the Pytchley with Woodland Hunt, merged again in 2020, continues to this day, as, under legal exemptions, certain wild animals can be hunted with dogs for birds of prey to eat.

announced definitely) to the effect that one of the chaps down with flu has got German measles. I do not think any of us are likely to get it, though we have all had colds and coughs. I will tell you for certain next week. Nine weeks today it will be Easter Sunday. It has been quite warm this week, but there has been a strong sou'west gale. There was no match yesterday, although there should have been one with Ratcliffe, but it was scratched.

Best love,
Christopher
xxxxxx

1938

While living with his family at St. Ann's Lodge, Chertsey, the nineteen-year-old Christopher wrote a diary nearly every day during the year between leaving school and starting a job. The following are some selected entries.

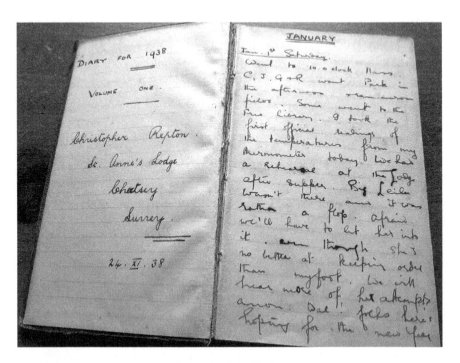

Christopher's 1938 diary

Saturday 1ˢᵗ January
Went to 10 o'clock Mass. C., J., G. & R. went to Park in the afternoon and ran across fields. Some went to the Free Library. I took the first official readings of the temperature from my thermometer today. We had a rehearsal at the Lodge after supper. Big Leila wasn't there, and it was rather a flop. Afraid we'll have to let her into it even though she's no better at keeping order than my foot. We will hear more of her attempts anon. Wal! Folks, here's hoping for the New Year.

Wednesday 26ᵗʰ January
Yes! I was right – the display that we saw in the sky last night was the Aurora Borealis which was seen all over England. Many thousands (Bianca was one of the herd) thought something was on fire and rang up, or nearly rang up, the brigade. Today's weather was exactly the reverse of yesterday's (Boreas' baleful influence?). A fine morning changed to a wet noon. I began refilling the greenhouse with soil and went on with the clearing of orchard. Mother and I planted 50 tulip bulbs. Aunt Leila came to lunch. Shortish Park walk in 'noon. Listened to Prokofiev and the *Eroica* after supper. A fine, slightly frosty night. Let's hope we're in for a cold spell.

Monday 31ˢᵗ January
A drizzly morning. Letter from Thake asking if we'd like to buy the house for £2,000. I had the last pipe out of my Balkan tin. Spent most of the morning clearing brambles from the south side of the orchard. Aunt Leila came to lunch and went down to Chertsey afterwards. Peter sick. Before the walk I completely cleared the smaller quince tree of brambles. Mother wrote three letters – one to P.&O., one to Cunard-White Star and one to Mr. Barton. Ran across both fields on walk. Gales and heavy rain after supper. January's the month for gales.

Wednesday 2ⁿᵈ February
Candlemas. Weather not quite 'fine & fair' but more inclined to be that than 'wet & foul', so quite possibly 'the half of winter's to come and mair'. In the morning I re-dug the plot below the redcurrants and then sowed two rows of broad beans there – the first sowing of the year – whilst Mother went on with the herbaceous border and J. cleared up the woodyard. I dug the carrot-

patch-to-be after lunch. Concert in the evening – Mozart piano concerto and Handel. Pop didn't want the Elgar. Ina writes to say she has given up all drink because the spectacle of the 'topers' in the club is so nauseating. I read Bianca's suggested Shaw[8] play. Unhelpful letter from P.&O. A day almost summery in its mildness. The first daffodil in the orchard has been in flower for several days now. I spotted a snowdrop – fully out – in the orchard this afternoon. In the morning all three of us had a go at Ina's garden – what a job! I had a pipe (the first after its soaking in whisky) and so for some time I was unable to work much. In the afternoon I dug a large new strip in the kitchen garden. Aunt Leila went to see *Victoria the Great*. S., L. & R. late for supper because of *Mikado* dress rehearsal. S. rather annoyed at supper because I spoke of Veronica as being large. Listened to Chopin recital – not Moiseiwitsch[9] but Orloff. Pop's joke: Moiseiwitsch is all off!

Monday 7th February

A full day. Pop called me at 7.15 – an uncivilised hour. I went down to the station with the girls in the car. Caught the 8.55. Another man and myself both told a girl (she was in service) when she asked if it stopped at Surbiton, that it did do so. I felt rather shamefaced when it whizzed right through Surbiton as if it hadn't noticed the beastly place. I'll bet the other chap did too. On the other hand, I was glad it didn't stop there as it eliminated the possibility of Mr. Dyer getting into the same carriage as me, which, though the odds were against it, would have been rather awkward for me if it had happened. Went to the Bank[10] by the City railway. Luckily, I saw in time a notice which said, 'Fares paid on the train' and I did not ask where the booking office was. If I had done so in such a vast queue as there was, I should probably have been made to feel like one of H. M. Bateman's[11] adverts.

Still, it doesn't really matter. I found Mr. Barton's place after enquiring of a policeman and two other men, the last being most helpful, walking along with me in order to point out a shortcut to St. Botolph's Church. After waiting some time in Mr. Barton's waiting room, I was conducted to his

---

8   George Bernard Shaw, who wrote *Pygmalion*, upon which *My Fair Lady* was based.
9   Benno Moiseiwitsch (1890–1963), a Ukraine-born British pianist who was awarded a CBE in 1946 for his services to music during World War II, after performing countless concerts for servicemen and charities.
10 Underground station near the Bank of England in the City of London.
11 Popular cartoonist during the first half of the twentieth century.

room where he gave me an interview lasting about half an hour. Afraid we didn't really get anywhere. Still, he did all he could (which wasn't much). Then, after leaving him I proceeded to Pop's office. He told me to kill time and then return and have lunch with him. If J. turned up, he also would come to lunch. But J. didn't turn up. He had gone up by a later train than mine and then gone by the City Railway to a shipping office in Leadenhall Street: he too did not have much luck.

Meantime, I went east up Oxford Street and, finding myself near the British Museum, went in. I asked several attendants where the Roman coins were as I wanted to see those that had been found on the cricket field at Laxton, but I couldn't locate them. Returned to Pop's office – J. hadn't turned up; he had wandered round the City, bought some rock-plants, then gone home. I went to lunch with Pop at the Restaurant des Gourmets. Unfortunately, Emil, his favourite waiter, wasn't there. I had *escalope de veau Milanaise*, two lagers and a *pêche Melba* followed by coffee – Pop didn't object to me smoking a Player afterwards. Edouard, the head waiter, kept coming to our table and asking if everything was all right. "*Ça va?*" he said to me, and when I replied in English, he and Pop exchanged anecdotes illustrating the Englishman's horror of speaking foreign languages. Went back to the office just in case J. had turned up in our absence. Finding he hadn't, Pop came with me to the Carlton to see *The Buccaneer* and I believe he quite enjoyed it, although he did leave just before the end. Fredric March was good as Jean Lafitte and I liked the little Dutch girl, in spite of her habit of turning up continually in places where she wasn't wanted. It was really quite moving when she had to walk the plank – though, needless to say, she was rescued in time. I saw the beginning of the film round again. A phosphorescent skull and crossbones shone out hugely in the darkness to the accompaniment of music from Mendelssohn's 'Fingal's Cave'.

Sunday 6ᵗʰ March

Yet another heavenly day – even more so than yesterday as there was no early morning mist to delay the sun's appearance. I regretted not having gone to 'early' [Mass] on such a lovely day when we had to listen for half an hour to one of Fr. Hawarden's Lenten sermons. Its theme was that favourite tag of his, 'Here today and gone tomorrow', but not 'Gather ye rosebuds while ye may' – rather do penance. Lamb instead of beef for lunch, to my annoyance. Bianca could not come for a Sunday walk because of a cold and

11

it being Ina's last Sunday with her before the proposed American trip. S., J. and I therefore went for a bike ride, through Addlestone for a start, by Pyrford church, through Wisley Woods and the Portsmouth Road to Ripley. S. was rather annoyed that I chose to go by the shorter Portsmouth Road way to Newlands Corner because it was 'trafficky'. Newlands Corner was so crowded out by motorists attracted into the open air by the first warm Sunday of the year that we could not enjoy it. I should like to have that place to myself one day – that was why I got a really good impression at Blackdown. The Silent Pool at Shere was also full up, so we climbed the steep bank that flanks the water, in order to get away from the crowds, rather to the surprise of those following us. Returned through Merrow, Woking and the allotments. Pop was rather annoyed at our lateness. Still, it was a good ride and worth the minor row that followed. During the ride we noticed many trees covered with white and pink blossom. Had a pipe at the Cottage after supper.

Monday 14th March

What amazing weather we're having! Today's sun shone in a brilliant blue sky without a single cloud from dawn to setting. I was awoken by its rays shining through our east window at 6.45. The frosty air made it glow red just above the horizon. The roofs and fields sparkled white. It seemed too early to get up then, but I wish I had done so as I love a frosty morning and at this time of year the frost thaws very quickly. The first two or three flowers of the cherry blossom are out now on the southernmost tree. I finished filling the greenhouse so that J. was able to formaldehyde the soil after lunch, and then I did more work on my border. Mother insisted on planting the first two or three plants in it – Canterbury bells etc. I sowed two rows of cabbages under the wall after lunch. Smoked three pipes today – if I go on like this it won't have been much use giving up fags. Ina thanked the Cottage for our Pont[12] telegram. The European situation is, I believe, very tense – I hope Ina doesn't start a war by insulting the Germans on her ship. Amusing letter from Gareth.

Tuesday 22nd March

The threat of rain has passed and today we had yet another beautiful day.

---

12 Pont (Graham Laidler) was a popular cartoonist for Punch magazine in the 1930s and early 1940s, sending up the quintessential British character, with all its eccentricities and 'stiff upper lip'.

L. & R. again stayed away from school but did not seem very bad as they were playing in the garden most of the day. Fortified with the knowledge that I acquired from Reg yesterday, I pruned the standard roses in the herbaceous border. J. too pruned other roses. After lunch I dug and fertilised the rose-bed (hot work) and later sowed a row of spinach. I did not meet S. Aunt Leila came to tea. After tea S., J. and I parked, reminisced about Middleton. Pop has a sprained finger. We could not listen to Brahms from Frankfurt as all German stations were speechifying.

Christopher's Uncle Reg

Friday 1st April

April came in as March went out; the weather gave us no sign that a new month had begun. But we cannot hope for another month like the one just ended – rather sad because fine weather would have been particularly appreciated during the lads' holidays. We had a letter from Dickon this morning intimating that he was feeling alright now and describing the treatment that has been and shall be given to his teeth. Found ourselves rather at a loose end as regards gardening today. Most of the heavy jobs are over with the winter, and such things as the sweeping of paths and tidying up are too boring to keep one occupied for long; they can only be done in short shifts. However, after lunch I found a sweaty job, viz. mowing the lawn. It had not been mown properly on Monday and so I cut it fairly close, and did I get hot? I'll say I did! The sweat poured off me as if it had been a summer's day – as it really was with the temperature at 71 in the shade. The work going on in the road outside is very disturbing now.

Saturday 2nd April

Today the weather was not so fine, though it did not rain. I never thought we should be wanting rain so soon after last Friday's fall. I have had a cold bath every day of the week so far – I find it very exhilarating after it. I rode this morning to Weybridge where I went to Confession and then bought six packets of Carter's vegetable seeds, viz. cabbage, cottager's kale, Brussels sprouts, lettuce, marrow and ridge cucumber. S., J. & I parked when I returned. After lunch S. went with Aunt Leila and Bianca to *I Met Him in Paris* at the Playhouse. I sowed hardy annuals on prepared parts of my border. Pop, rather surprisingly, did a bit of gardening. We ate Leila's mustard & cress for tea. The spikes of J.'s sweetcorn are just beginning to poke up. Some of the potatoes that we put in on March 1st are beginning to show up. S., J. and I went to the Free Library. The gardens are looking lovely now with the young green and the white blossom of the fruit trees overhanging the fish ponds. Their prunus tree, before the entrance to the library, is fully out now – before ours. Their sweet williams and Canterbury bells look better than ours.

Sunday 3rd April

Apparently, it rained a bit in the night as I noticed several puddles on the way to 8 o'clock Mass, but the ground looked as dry as ever in the garden. Bianca & S. also went to eight as Humphry was expected to be cycling down – again, however, he did not turn up. I pricked off the first seedlings in the greenhouse – bar J.'s *Stachys* – after breakfast. After lunch when H. had finally been given up, S., B., J. & I went for a long field walk, striking out on a new line. We explored the marsh and spinneys between Almners and the 2nd crossroads. In the process Sylvia got both her feet wet above the ankles while attempting to cross a large stream, but she needn't have done so as I discovered a bridge a few yards further south. She walked back along the Lyne & Egham road without shoes or stockings and became the cynosure of many eyes. After tea Bianca & Sylvia attempted to give J. & me dancing lessons. J. got fed up after the waltz, but I carried on with the quickstep. The tunes on the record were terrible.

Monday 4th April

Breaking-up day for S., L. & R. They went in the morning to hear 'marks' but came back in time for lunch. Leila, I believe, was first in her class and looking as pleased as Punch, but S. & R., who were both something like last in theirs, were silent and morose. Sylvia's surliness at times like this is very 'un-girl-like'. I expect she picks it up from the boys of the family. It was quite a fine day again, although much cooler than of late. Everything is looking very dry still – there could only have been very little rain on Saturday night, and I did some watering most evenings. Before lunch, Mother, J. & I sticked three rows of peas and then I sowed a row of beetroot. After lunch I pricked off more flower seedlings – tobacco plants especially as they are very congested. My cauliflowers in the greenhouse are coming along well now. Sowed another row of onions afterwards. S., J. & I parked after tea – the young larches look beautiful near the badgers' earth. We were extremely 'het up' after supper at the curtailment of a concert of Beethoven's Fifth relayed from Berlin because they wanted to get on with dance music. It was partly the Germans' fault through starting the concert late, but it was nothing short of criminal of the BBC to cut off in the middle of that wonderful scherzo. There was also a short breakdown in the andante! It's frosty tonight.

Wednesday 6th April
I still bear rancour towards the BBC for their disgraceful performance on Monday night. I hope to see many letters of protest in the *Radio Times* […]

Thursday 7th April
Another wonderful day – clear sky most of the time and really hot in the sun. For this reason, Mother, Sylvia and 'the little ones' were not to be envied their trip up to London to see the film *Snow White*. However, they enjoyed it seemingly, and after the film did a bit of gadding around. S. got a coat and skirt somewhere and was quite thrilled about it when she returned. They went, amongst other things, to Kensington Gardens and 'rounded' the Round Pond. J. & I were left at home by ourselves, although we had Leila to lunch. Medd had said last night that he would ring us up re. the canoe, but as he did not do so we made no move. I went on with the clearing up of the border this morning; also dug more of the marrow bed and my border, in which I planted more gladiolus bulbs. After lunch I got busy on the tennis court. I located and put on all the corner places by means of Pop's tape-measure. Then I started erecting the bottom and lower side nettings – still Pop has not objected, and that means 'Go ahead.' I was glad to see that there were two letters in the *Daily Telegraph* today calling attention to the BBC's unpardonable behaviour on Monday last.

Sunday 8th May
Went to 10.30 Mass. A bishop was present and there was a long and complicated service. Last night was indeed cold. The temperature fell to 24

degrees and most of our potatoes were blackened, and fruit blossoms were amongst other things to suffer. The day was fine, and about noon, or rather later, when the sky seemed still, the wind at last changed round from the cold quarter to the warm south. This happened while I was reading *Crome Yellow* under the big old apple tree and chuckling to myself over Scogan, and B. & G. were fighting out a singles,[13] which B. won. I joined them, and with Pop we had a foursome. Good walk after supper. G. burnt a hole in his pocket with a box of matches just after the first crossroads. We discovered Tanglewood for the first time – at least it was for me. Its floor was carpeted with bluebells which looked gorgeous in the gathering dusk. Altogether, I was charmed by the place. Went back via Thorpe where we stopped at the Red Lion for half-pints and cheese biscuits.

Sunday 15th May
Rosamund's birthday, but she was not quite so cock-a-hoop as I thought she would be. Mother, S., L. & R. went to eight. Bright periods in the morning, clouding up in the middle of the day but it became quite sunny in the evening, but yesterday's heatwave did not continue as the wind was stronger. Rosamund received various presents during breakfast: a pencil-box and tiny penknife from J. & me, then the tortoises – Hitler & Mussolini (pro tem, perhaps 'per saecula') – were duly exhibited to her on the lawn. The Mission father preached a short sermon at the 10.30 Mass. Fr. Bolton said Mass very quickly – Fr. Hawarden is a bit out of the limelight these days. Argentine beef for dinner. Afterwards we went to Tanglewood – J., S., L. & R. walking, with Peter, Bianca and I biking. We found it less charming than usual because of the presence (noisy at that!) of several undesirable lads. Birthday tea went off quite mildly – the usual girl's cake was eaten; a sticky mass of chocolate. Tennis after tea; a very slow foursome but Bianca and I ended up with a good singles. Then S., B., J. & I climbed on the roof and ate Snocreems.[14]

Tuesday 14th June
A real scorcher of a day, in spite of the wind being in the north-west. My thermometer reached 85 in the afternoon – topped 80 for the first time this

---

13 Tennis match.
14 Wall's ice cream.

year. First day of Ascot. I started on a bit of gardening in the morning but, finding it too hot, I got J. and we went for a bathe in the river – the first this year. I did not find it at all cold, but J. did, judging by the time he took to take the plunge. Sunbathed and swum across in the second dip. Pop did not go up to London today and he had dinner with us; it made the meal seem rather strange. The interest has gone from the Test Match now Bradman is stonewalling. Had a lazy afternoon reading Compton Mackenzie's *The Old Men of the Sea*. I was violently sick both before and after tea (first time since I was at St. Edmund's). I don't really know why – quite possibly it was slight sunstroke as Mother said, because I did expose the back of my neck down at the river. The funny thing is that S. was also sick in the evening and Ros. later. Also J. was sick last Sunday evening. It cooled off considerably in the evening and much hosing was done by J. and Mother.

Saturday 18th June

We're over halfway through June and I haven't yet visited Tanglewood in the early morning – I must do so soon. It should have been a hot day today. It was, in fact, close, but the sun never came out properly and there were even a few specks of rain in the afternoon. As I write I hear the distant booming of the Aldershot Tattoo guns. I went with S. in the morning, and after leaving her I smoked a pipe of Gold Block down by the river. Had my hair cut – I don't like those two barbers – and then went to Confession. Made up bed and sowed seeds of white marrow afterwards. Pop didn't get up for lunch. Ina was wearing her blue trousers in the garden. I said, "Lovely pyjamas", and she said, "What do you mean, pyjamas? They're breeks." Played no tennis this afternoon. Later I put out five tomato plants […], having removed my frame. Free-libbed after tea. Gardens looking lovely, especially spiraea, roses and sweet williams (darn Ina for getting us only two kinds). Peas from garden for supper; only a few. I had a tiff with S. re. picking them. More witticisms dropped from the lips of the park-keeper when we went up after supper. They have planted out kochia.

Wednesday 22nd June

It was cloudy and close today – unlike yesterday's fine and clear weather. There was even a sprinkling of rain in the afternoon, but just a 'ha'porth'. It's now a warm June night as I write. Sowed runner beans on my border. Re-planted Mother's tomatoes away from my onions, hoed between rows and planted out kale. J. sprayed beans with fresh Katakilla and clipped the herbaceous border box hedge. The border is now a picture, today's tidying by Mother and J. vastly improving it. Delphiniums at their height of beauty are now its chief glory, especially the dark blue seven-footer at the south end. Lupins in their second crop of spikes are good but not what they were. Salmon and crimson sweet williams and nemesia of varying shades of red and orange provide a splash of vivid colour to the front of the upper border, while pink, yellow and red antirrhinums blaze in the lower one. Other flowers now out are white pinks, geums, anchusa, day lilies, masses of pink Canterbury bells vying with the sweet williams and nemesia, pansies, star of Bethlehem, a few pyrethrums, early stocks, foxgloves and others. The first clarkia blossom is out now in my border.

Sunday 31ˢᵗ July

Sunday 31ˢᵗ July

A hot and fairly fine day – perhaps the hottest day of the year so far. I swelter as I write. The temperature, I think, reached 85. We either went to 8 or 10.30, I forget. The morning was not sunny till lateish, but the clouds were only heat clouds and devilish warm – it was 74 degrees before the sun appeared. Yes, we went to 10.30, I remember distinctly, and I don't think any tennis was played before lunch. I may be wrong though. I retired to the orchard after lunch, but G. soon routed me out to play a sweaty 'singles'. Further tennis followed. Good tea. I played a bit more tennis after tea and then retired to my deckchair under the walnut tree to read Rose Macaulay's *Orphan Island* and sip a lemon (gin, a little and soda). At 9ish we managed to collect ourselves and we five and Bianca went for a walk. It was across the marshes to the spinney where Dickon had an unlucky accident – he fell into the stream and wore Sylvia's coat back. As we emerged onto the road by Glenn's Farm a strange man in a white hat told us we were trespassing, but we settled him. Lovely starlit night now. When we got up to bed it was so warm that I 'windowed'. Then the brilliant idea of sleeping out of doors came to me. G. caught on and we got out onto the roof with blankets and eiderdowns. J. caught on too and he brought our blankets and pillows for us. We got silently down via the pantry window, then went out to the hay pile in the orchard and prepared our couches. I got a nasty hay splinter in my foot and it took some time to extract it. Then we tried to sleep under the stars. G. got to sleep quite soon. J. gave up after one hour. I stayed but did not sleep all night. Before dawn I got up and wandered across to my deckchair under the walnut tree and then went to the greenhouse and ate a tomato. The dew was colossal; it was in great swathes of mist. I returned and smoked a good 'fag'. Saw Prim (Ina's cat) stalking by the mulberry tree. Woke G. to see the sunrise. Funny birds in the cherry tree. Then at 6ish I slept.

Humphry & Christopher hiking c.1930s

Monday 8th August

Start of walking tour. Various articles were brought from all parts of the house and stuffed into the rucksacks until both were full and heavy. Testing them in the garden and contrasting them with the haversack and tent valise plus two army capes, we were under the impression that they were lighter than the latter, but we soon found out our error this afternoon. Edith (maid) gave us the address of her sister at East Grinstead before we started. Lunched at 12.45 and then after a short fag and rest we went to the Cottage and said "goodbye" to Aunt Leila. "Expect to see us coming back through the fields ten or fourteen days hence," we said… In error J. & I allowed G. & D. to carry the heavy rucksacks while we took the tents and army capes and haversacks – that stretch to Box Hill was the first and last time that D. carried a rucksack on the whole tour…

We moved on again, deciding, and feeling rather jubilant about our decision, to make Leith Hill our camping ground for the night, instead of the Weald to the east of it. We had got out of the town and were just beginning our climb when Dickon spotted a Wall's man and slipped off to buy a Snocreem. J. & G. decided to share one, but I didn't want one myself.

Hereupon occurred our most amazing piece of luck. A decent, quiet-voiced, academic-looking fellow stopped in a good-looking car and asked us if we'd care for a lift up to Coldharbour, and of course we jumped at the offer. J., G. & D. filed in at the back (with all the baggage) and sucked their ices, whilst I sat in front with our new-found friend. On hearing that we intended to camp on Leith Hill he considered awhile and then suddenly offered to let us camp in the field he rented next to his house. I gladly accepted and thanked him sincerely. A great load was taken off my mind – and the others', if they heard in the back what he said. At Coldharbour he turned the car left by the church and went down a little way – past his house, Mountview, pointing out, as we passed, a small pool that he said we might use if we wanted a bathe – till we came to the field that we were to camp in. What a lovely prospect it was for our first night; a fine evening with little cloud except on the southern horizon (ominous note in minor key amidst delightful pastoral melodies). Large, shady beech trees stood at the top of the field which sloped in an easterly direction down towards the Weald of East Surrey and Kent, there stretching before our eyes with the friendly Downs to the south. Lower down the field was bathed in the light of the westering sun. Here, with baggage and tents, we made our way, after all thanking our benefactors very much and being given instructions where we might get water and bathe and where was the farm for the morning...

Tuesday 9th August

Woke up soon after midnight to see that the moon was now obscured by clouds. Slept again, and then was woken by the fell sound of raindrops rattling on canvas. This must have been about 4 a.m. J. got out of his tent and loosened the guy ropes – very noble of him, because a fine spray was coming through the stretched pores of the canvas. It was a thoroughly unpleasant experience. I put the hood of the sleeping bag over my head to keep it off my face but that was not adequate. Groans were heard from each tent. Jocelyn's "Oh, good Lord!" changed, when the rain's battering became harder, to "Oh, good Lord!" A solitary boom of thunder increased our sensation of doom. The rain eased off for a bit and I think I dozed fitfully, then it came on harder and the spray came through again, wetting the sleeping bags and everything in the tents. All were awake now and talked in despairing fashion. Shortly before 7 a.m. it stopped, more or less... so we decided to get up, tired and worn out as we were. What a scene greeted our eyes. Great swathes of misty rain hung over the Weald, and the smoke from a Horsham chimney stack floated still from the south-east. Further rainclouds seemed to hang around, and there were but few chinks in the heavy mantle of cloud that covered us. We dressed quickly and damply, put on army capes and felt like pioneers encountering hardships. The effect of being up and about, however, was bracing, and now that the rain seemed to have stopped our spirits rose...

Thursday 11ᵗʰ August

Jocelyn: We left Hurstpierpoint in an easterly direction heading for Ditchling – which had a certain interest for us due to an Old Laxtonian, Conrad Pepler, being involved in the Ditchling Press, and we also wanted to start our westward trek along the Downs at Ditchling Beacon, which is one of the more pronounced hills in the range…

We got permission to camp in a field high up on Truleigh Hill from a farm on the road lower down where we got our milk etc. in the morning. I can't remember much about the day's walk except that we were on the crest of the Downs for a long stretch, and there is a photograph of C., G. & D. walking towards the magnificent clump of beech trees which is Chanctonbury Ring – I think it has Ancient Briton connections…

Friday 23ʳᵈ September

G. & D. went back to school. Very hot day for the season – 80 in some parts. It was sunny in the morning but became overcast and muggy p.m. The day was usual as regards work. I lunched with Miss W. I had to ask Pearce to let me ring up Bianca at 11 as I suddenly realised that we had misunderstood each other when arranging to ring up at lunch. Left leisurely and walked up to Marble Arch. Had to wait some time at the Tube station. Serious-looking headlines about the Czech affair, 'Russia warns Poland', etc. Humphry appeared at last, and we walked to Langham Place. We paid 2/- (H., myself, Bianca and a chap we had just met) for stools in the queue at Queen's Hall. We adjourned with this chap, who appeared to be a decent sort of bloke, to an ABC[15] and ate poached eggs. Did crosswords when we returned till H. appeared with Bianca. Moved into the hall soon after – pretty crowded. I shamed H. & B. by sitting on the floor before it began. The first part of the concert was very good, especially the 'Emperor'. We adjourned to the bar for drinks in the interval. Listened to the second part in the passage – not very good. Just caught the 10.27 – raining when we got to Chertsey.

Monday 26ᵗʰ September

A fateful day! The brooding sky and close, damp weather, together with

---

15   The ABC (Aerated Bread Company) had dozens of tea shops across London in the early 20ᵗʰ century, serving tea, bread, cakes and hot meals at moderate prices. They started off in the late 19ᵗʰ century by mass-producing bread, patenting a new method using carbon dioxide instead of yeast.

the effect of the coppery, heatless sun at noon, combined to aid the general impression of impending catastrophe. For me it was quite an eventful day visiting Scammell Lorries at Watford – but that is of secondary importance and will be dealt with elsewhere. The question of the hour is now not "IS WAR COMING?" but "CAN WAR BE AVOIDED?" It is not customary for me to deal with political matters in these columns, wherefrom you will be able to gather in some measure the gravity of the situation. Let us hope that, in looking back in days to come on what I have written, I shall be able to say, "What unnecessary pessimism and anxiety – it's all the fault of the press and the scaremongers", but Hitler's speech, which we heard translated a few hours ago, does not increase the possibility of this ever happening, although I, and I suppose millions of others, keep saying to myself, "War cannot come." I have moments when I realise how near it is and how terrible it will be if it does come. That speech of Hitler's was vile. Its furious lashings of poor Beneš,[16] "who sits in Prague and does evil", were in ill accord with the occasional pleas that he – Hitler – wanted peace. Altogether it gave the impression of being a form of self-justification – trying to place all the blame on Beneš' shoulders – before launching into action.

For the rest of the day – we had a visit to Watford Scammell Lorries p.m., so I asked Slee if he could give me a lift a.m. and he said O.K. We knocked off at 12 and lunched at the pub. I lost 1/6 in bets on the gambling machine and then a further 2d to Grierson as we betted on his 'whizzing clock' on a bar-room table to the clink of money. This was soon stopped by the landlord, Mr. Phillips. "Gentlemen, gentlemen, you'll get me to lose my licence..." We started about 1 o'clock. Good journey. I'm getting to know Harford a bit better – Hughman is, of course, a bit of a noodle. After a little misdirection and consequent 'gadding around' we got to the factory first. The other 8 arrived [within] twenty minutes. Penfold supervising complete with 'slip' [clipboard?]. One chap to take us all round – not good enough! I had a hell of a cold and soon a headache through the din and glare of the electric welders, but I managed to be impressed by some of the heavy vehicles and the display of couplings we

---

16 Edvard Beneš, then President of Czechoslovakia, had been Council Chairman of the League of Nations between the wars and opposed efforts by Austria and Germany to unite, as this would have threatened his country's existence. He was forced to surrender to German Chancellor Adolf Hitler's demands to take over the Sudetenland in September 1938. Beneš resigned on the 5th October 1938 and went into exile until after the war.

were given. Tea was eminently welcome. Managed to avoid seeing anything else by Slee's astute "I'd like to, but I've got to get these fellows home", and drive he did – flickered between 60 and 70[17] on the Watford bypass; plenty of traffic too. Had to put the hood up just before Hampstead because of rain. Slee took us into his flat at Hampstead and gave us another tea. Did not see his mother as she was ill, but were entertained by his mother's friend, a vivacious old lady – not very old really. Slee then drove us to Baker Street; very decent of him really. I travelled with Hughman to Charing Cross, just caught the 6.57 myself.

Tuesday 27th September

Cornwell rang up Pop to be excused from the office for A.R.P.[18] work. My train from Oxford Circus was late and was actually the first for over 20 minutes – believed to be secret preparations going on. Messrs Forsyth & Carton did not turn up today – called up? – though Rosenthal did turn up. Trenches being dug in Hyde Park. Ex-schoolmaster saw four anti-aircraft guns up near Marble Arch in the Park. Mr. Pitman and Mr. Maddox unable to appear to give their lectures. Gareth has been called up for a ground job in his branch of the Air Arm. Aunt Belle rang up, very worried – she, as a nurse, must report to HQ. Gas masks being issued everywhere, and now, according to Belle, on the third news which she heard but we missed, Hitler has given the Czechs until 2 p.m. tomorrow to decide instead of Saturday. Work went on as usual, although all received a note from Parry Thomas that the basement was going to be made bomb– and gas-proof in case of 'certain eventualities'.

Sunday 9th October

Very little rain apart from a little last night and a few 'spittings' during the day. It was warm for the season – 64 – and again S.W. wind. Poor Pop still has his cold and again today did not get up until the afternoon. All went to 10.30 Mass. Beef for lunch and garden cabbage – very good. Sunday walk after lunch as per usual for the season. Similar start to a fortnight ago – down allotments,

---

17 Miles per hour.
18 Air Raid Precautions – the ARP, run by local government, liaised with the emergency services during the 1920s and '30s to protect civilians from air raids. From September 1939 ARP wardens supervised the 'blackout', whereby all households had to close dark curtains at night so that buildings were invisible to enemy bombers. The wardens managed the air-raid sirens, had first aid kits and guided people into air-raid shelters during the Blitz from 1940-1941. In 1941, the ARP expanded as the Blitz intensified and became the Civil Defence Service.

through Silverlands Woods (Alsatians)[19] and out by Lyne church, crossed to salient, then crossed Chobham Common road higher than when H. came (a little further on, he and J. lured Bianca into a foot of black slime). Struck a little new lane just before Accommodation Road. Crossed it and into a field of cows that suddenly made a dirty dive at us. We legged it for the side of the field, but the cows had split our forces. S. & I got to the top of the field all right, but we had to wait there nearly ten minutes while B. & J. made a lengthy tour. Passed Flutters Hill House and into pine woods. Turned south-east at the ornamental duck pond and crossed heather and young pines until we reached Stanners Hill road. Crossed it and into another heather part which evidenced the damage suffered in a fire this year. Got to Ottershaw by the Chobham road, caught the 5.24 bus and got back in time for tea. Adrian Boult concert at 9; first of the season. Nice evening now with full moon. I think fine weather is coming.

Tuesday 25th October

Awful, foggy day – cold and dank and smoky. The temperature last night did not fall below 31.5 at 9 p.m. In London, the fog did not clear all day, although around noon a red, heatless sun glimmered faintly. Major Bullen to Pearce re. filing from 10 to 11 – "A judicious use of the waste-paper basket does away with a lot of the trouble of filing – W.P.B. as we called it in the army." I caught the 8.17 this morning against the fog and arrived at 9.30. The 'old fellow' and I were the first arrivals. I lunched (2/7d) with Short at the Crown; nice and hot. Heard results of book-keeping test – I was sixth with 72%. Rosenthal got a cheer at 3 p.m. when he entered the common room, apparently because he had last been seen floundering among a bevy of dames. Pearce came down to ask what the row was about and got an arch "It's very cold in here" from Forsyth.

Tuesday 15th November

Still rather foggy weather – strange after Sunday's gale, but the reason is a ridge of high pressure over us at the moment. Went by the 8.55 with Bianca; the Northern Line was all right today. Pop travelled to Oxford Circus with me as he had last-minute qualms about what J. & I had arranged for tonight. Four hours of Pearce today. Had my interview with Pitman at 11.30. Gave him various details about uncles and aunts etc. and got him to write down

---

19 This may be a reference to a wood where they saw some Alsatians previously.

names of two or three of firms on his list. He, like Pearce, said he thought I might have done better but I think he was influenced a lot by a Y^{20} in my accounts that should never have been there. I told Harrison about it afterwards and at 3 he told me it had been put right – rather late though. Anyhow, I got Pitman to agree to meet Pop in the near future. Slee's old co-luncher Hind appeared in the pub today and lunched with us. Apparently, he had been dismissed from a private secretarial job after three weeks. Met J. at Piccadilly at 5.15. He had had a haircut, got a new suit, and seen King Carol of Rumania's arrival on State visit along the road to Buckingham Palace. We had tea at Lyons. Went into the Plaza at 6.15. Very comfortable seats. Film *If I Were King* very good, especially Basil Rathbone. Nothing much else in programme. Tipped chap who parked our coats 6d. Had beer at Waterloo and caught 9.27. Mother went to Hanwell today to see Nell & Reg.

Sunday 27th November

Yes! Woke to see the first real frost of the season covering the roofs and fields etc. It was not very severe and thawed quickly. All went to 10.30 – First Sunday of Advent and Pastoral Letter. I played a little golf before lunch.

The morning was fine, but it clouded over during lunchtime and soon after 3.30 came on to rain fitfully, thus giving us another rainy Sunday walk. We usual four went: started by allotments, Bianca having previously had a tiff with Leila re. wearing a mac, then Silverlands, Lyne churchyard, Chobham Common road, Foxhills, water tank – disappearing trick by Bianca – pigeon woods, Accommodation Road, then along Stanners Hill road past Barley Mow Common. Rainy and gloomy now – getting near Chobham so cut left across fields (wet, but not for me) to aerodrome, then across Miss Gordon's meadows by footpath to 'Bleak House'. Caught the 5.15 bus home. Got back halfway through tea. The study dismantled for re-papering. Sung carols after tea and helped L. & R. with homework.

Saturday 3rd December

Fairly fine day: a rather chilly wind in west with a bit of north in it which accounts for its freezing now – 29.5 degrees – with a waxing moon shining on the hoar frost. My birthday – I got £1 (good, eh!) from Dad, socks from Aunt Leila and Bianca, a pipe and tobacco from Mother, J., S., L. & R., more

---

20   This may refer to an incorrect marking.

tobacco from H. & G., and a letter from Gervase (asking for a loan! It was a decent letter though). Got a reply from the City Appointments Bureau stating that an interview was necessary. Parked a.m. and met S. after lunch. S. & I went to film [*The Adventures of*] *Marco Polo* and a poor second film, *Love, Honor and Behave.* J. again obstinately would not come. Did not have a great birthday tea as we were late back from film. Went up to the Cottage after supper – Aunt Leila is uncheckable with her theatrical experiences.

Thursday 22nd December

We awoke to a transformed world – snow, thicker than I can ever remember, covered everything; the trees looking especially lovely. Unfortunately, however, a slight thaw – it may only be temporary – set in about noon and the trees began to shed a lot of their snow. Max. temp. 34, min. 28.5. It has fallen again now (10 p.m.) to 32.5, so maybe the roads will be icebound tomorrow; the bulk of the snow is still as it fell. Went up to the fields a.m. and tried to toboggan but not very successful. J., D. & I then parked. Ponds still frozen but a bit slushy on top. In the afternoon J. & S. biked, and G. & I walked to Chertsey where we bought a good many presents. Foster's lad very 'familiar' when we bought darts. Ina returned in the evening – I haven't seen her yet. Many of us have colds, Mother and me included. Lot of fuss about nothing tonight re. money spent on Christmas presents.

Sunday 25th December

Christmas Day. Started by going to Midnight Mass – J., S., G. & myself on foot and Bianca and Aunt Leila by car. Same carols as usual. Rather a cold and cloudy night as we walked and slid back home. Pop did not come down when we returned, and we were able to have a pleasant and undisturbed glass of sherry and cake with a fag in the kitchen. Retired soon after 2 a.m. and were routed out soon after 9 a.m., though S. didn't rise until after 11. When we got up late Pop said something about asking Fr. Hawarden to stop Midnight Mass, as it was such a disorganiser of households. Had a moderate breakfast, then G. & I took steps to find H. & G.[21] We had hardly started down the road to meet them when we saw them by the Grange. We slid down to meet them – yes, the roads were frozen all day – cars have flattened the snow on

---

21 Christopher and his brother Gervase went to look for their cousins Humphry and
    Gareth, who were staying in the Cottage.

the roads, and the top crust, which was thawed on Thursday and slightly on Saturday, froze over again. The temperature did not rise above 30 degrees today. They were slightly frozen on Saturday when G. & I tobogganed with Medd but today they were really good, and we had great fun sliding on them before lunch. My experimental slide on the herbaceous border path was nothing like so good. The sky was very gloomy and yellow before lunch – or rather dinner – and looked like more snow. Neither H. nor G. nor any of the Cottage came to dinner. Ina was piqued at our getting H. & G. down in spite of her arranging the opposite, and so wouldn't let anybody come down. It rather spoilt the meal but, as someone said, there was more to eat. Finished off wrapping and enveloping a few presents after dinner, which was pretty good, and then collected the Cottage as L. & R. were getting impatient. They broke the news to G. & me of their present to us of tickets to *These Foolish Things*. O.K., said we. H. & G. came down and we sang a carol or two, and then Bianca (but not Ina or Leila) came, and the Christmas tree ceremony began. The best surprise for J. & me was the electric shaver from H. & G. Soon a great fog was created by the smoke of many pipes trying out the Christmas tobacco, which was plentiful. Aunt Leila joined us for tea, previous to which we had a little tobogganing on the hill (the road outside) with a toboggan constructed by J. After tea we played Murder – pretty rough – and then Hunt the Slipper. Had a really good supper with plenty of drink circulating, but again Ina didn't come. Perhaps it was a good thing as she might have got too tipsy; at any rate we were all feeling pretty merry when we started up a sing-song which lasted for about two hours after supper. Pop joined in the merriment, admirably.

1939

A. W. GOODFELLOW & CO.
CHARTERED ACCOUNTANTS
3 Great Winchester Street
London E.C. 2
18th January 1939

G. C. T. Repton, Esq.
St. Anne's Lodge
Chertsey
Surrey
Dear Sir,

I have much pleasure in engaging you as a clerk in my office, to commence on January 30th subject to your references being satisfactory. I will let you know immediately I have heard from Mr. Brettell.

Yours faithfully,
A. W. Goodfellow

INTENSIVE BUSINESS COURSE AND MARLBOROUGH
GATE SECRETARIAL COLLEGE

Telephone: Paddington 3320
Sir Isaac Pitman & Sons Ltd.

61 and 62 BAYSWATER ROAD
(68 yds. west of Lancaster Gate
Tube Stn.)
LONDON W. 2
20th February 1939

G. C. T. Repton, Esq.
St. Anne's Lodge
St. Anne's Hill
Chertsey
Surrey

Dear Mr. Repton,

We have not heard from you since Mr. Pitman saw you and your father at the end of last year, and I am wondering whether you have yet made a start in business.

We shall be very much interested to hear what you are doing and how you are getting on.

Yours very truly,
Dorothy Parry-Thomas
Secretary

SIR ISAAC PITMAN & SONS LIMITED
TELEPHONE: HOLBORN 353839   PARKER STREET

TELEGRAMS: IPANDSONS   LONDON W.C. 2
WESTCENT   LONDON

28th February 1939

Christopher Repton, Esq.
St. Anne's Lodge
St. Anne's Hill
Chertsey

Dear Repton,

Miss Parry-Thomas has sent me your letter of February 23rd. I will certainly keep my eyes open for something for you, but if I were you I should not count too much on that.

Seeing that your father has such good connections in the film industry, he will be the best person to advise you on the question of changing your present job. At first sight, to me, the value of the experience you are getting at present seems to be better than the repetitive work of the contemplated position.

Yours sincerely,
I. J. Pitman[22]

Fairmead
Chichester Road
Dorking
6th August 1939

Dear Christopher,

How are you? Please excuse this letter being typed. I am too lazy to write anything by hand nowadays! I have got a job. It is as Assistant to the Almoner at the Hospital of St. John and St. Elizabeth; I get £2 a week, and lunches and teas which count for another 10/-. But the money is gone practically in one swoop when I pay my bill at the Hostel, which depresses me considerably! I resent having to work hard just to live! But I suppose it can't be helped, and Mummy

---

22   According to an article in the *Sunday Times* on the 15th November 2020, Isaac Pitman presented his shorthand system in 1837; therefore the I. Pitman whom Christopher met must have been one of his descendants.

is to the good as she has to give me very little now! The job is not too bad on the whole, but really hard work! My hours are from 9.30 – 5.30 and I have to work on Saturday mornings too! I have to keep registers of everybody in the Hospital with exact details of their ailments! The other day I saw the following on the casualty list:-

J. J. M—, aged 25. B.I.D.

I thought for ages but could not make out the 'B.I.D.', so I asked and was told quite airily, "Oh, that means 'Brought in dead'"!! So, my work is cheerful, if nothing else!!

What are you doing now? Still working in London, or with the Militia[23]? I hope not the latter or you will probably have pneumonia under the present weather conditions! I hear that Dickon came over here one day this week to see Chris.[24] I saw Chris last Sunday; he was looking very fit and seemed to be enjoying his holiday. He cycled from Bath to Worth in one day – 140 miles, it would have killed me!

Mummy has been away in Norfolk, but she comes back on the 16th. We have got some friends of Teresa's staying here who have brought a FOUL dog with them that attacks poor Ben in a brutal fashion with intent to kill. So, Ben has to go and stay in kennels while I am in London, and I have to keep him a prisoner in my room during the weekend – it is too bad, and in Ben's own house too! How are all the guinea pigs?? Also, your corn-on-the-cob? It was more successful than ours was last year, but we have planted more this year.

Well, I must write some more letters I suppose, so I must stop.

Yours affectionately,
Perpetua

Ben sends tail-wags to your dog and hopes he is well.
In September 1939 war was declared between Britain and Germany, and Christopher enlisted in the army. He joined the Queen's Royal Regiment and started military training at Stoughton, near Guildford.

---

23 Perpetua may be asking Christopher whether he has joined the army.
24 Perpetua's brother.

Stoughton Barracks
Oct. 17th

My dear Father and Mother,

This is just to let you know that I have got a pass for this weekend – 50% of the company have got leave this weekend and the other 50% next weekend. I should be home in time for lunch on Saturday if it is fine enough to cycle. It is really time that I wrote to Gervase as he has sent me two nice long ones and I owe him one, but will you ask him if he can wait until next week as I have a lot of letters to write this week – I got two letters on Monday when I was expecting none: one from Gareth and one from Perpetua. Have you heard from Gareth? There goes 'Last Post', which means lights out in 15 minutes, so I must pack up for tonight…

Wednesday evening

I am overwhelmed by excessive work tonight. All I have done so far is to 'blanco' my equipment; when it is dry the brass on that has to be cleaned and polished; my rifle must be cleaned and the barrel 'pulled-through'; all our kit has to be marked – one person's at a time as there is only one 'stamp'; then all kit must be folded and prepared for tomorrow's weekly kit inspection. This kit inspection is always a business, because every article must be laid out just so, and then Major Pain comes round, gives it one glance and passes on – it seems a little ridiculous to me. Still, you know what the army's like for red tape and such.

In the midst of all this work I am somehow contriving to write to you. I was pleased to get your letter this morning. I must write to Aunt Nell soon and thank her for those apples, and to Ina for her birthday! And to Gareth etc. But tomorrow I shall probably go out for the first time this week into Guildford – couldn't go last night as we had night operations for an hour – possibly go to a film. I got back at 3 minutes to 11 the other night. The rain stopped after Chertsey.

Yes, the umbrella was the cause of much merriment. The N.C.O.s[25] in the guardroom declared that I was "improperly dressed" but said they would enter me up as O.K. It was a great joke for them. And in the morning when our Sergeant saw it hanging up in the barrack-room, he nearly threw

---

25   Non-commissioned officers.

*Christopher's tobacco
case, Lamb & Flag
army cap badge*

a fit. Asked me if I thought this was the Stock Exchange. I knew it would cause a bit of fun, that's why I took it. Well, there's little more to say now, as I saw you last weekend, so:

Best love to all from Christopher

Stoughton Barracks
Nov. 9th

My dear Father and Mother,

You asked me to drop you a line during the week, so here we are; a bit late though. I thank you very much for the cake which arrived in very good condition yesterday; in fact, it is a particularly good example of what a cake should be.

Awful weather this week, isn't it? The mud around here is becoming very bad and it makes cleaning boots quite a job. Let's hope it gets dry by this weekend.

I cannot work out at present whether we are moving to 'B' Co. this Saturday or the following Wednesday…

There I broke off last night. It is now Friday evening, and everything is in bustle. We are moving tomorrow, but, as far as I can make out, only to the school just below us, and then on Wednesday we move again to Edgeborough School, a freshly commandeered building right in Guildford. All kit and equipment has to be packed exactly in the army fashion and it takes some time. What I'm going to do with the umbrella and suitcase I don't know!

I have not time for a long letter, but I am trying to get this off tonight in case I don't see you on Sunday. It may not be possible to get home on this Sunday because of the move, and also because we may be required for some ceremony in connection with Armistice Sunday. Still, don't be surprised if I do turn up for lunch.

They gave us a very strenuous day to end up with today – something to remember 'A' Company by, perhaps. Started after breakfast with our half-an-hour's drill on the square. Then in place of P.T. we had a four-mile run along roads. Following that we had a two-hour march in battle dress up the Worplesdon road and back along the Woking road, during which we got soaked by rain – no capes with us. After lunch, no rest because of parade, from which we went straight on to another hour's drill on the square. Then to finish us off we had two hours' 'fieldcraft' out on Rydes Hill and the common beyond, west of the barracks; fortunately, the rain had by then stopped. Tea at 4 p.m. was very welcome after all this.

Was Gervase very late the other night? I arrived 10 minutes late as my train was late at Woking, but nothing was said. Conditions down at the school, as regards getting in and out, should be a lot easier.

Well, I suppose I had better get on with this packing as I do intend to get out later this evening. How are the medlars? Hoping I may see you Sunday.

Love to all from Christopher

You know my address
Tuesday Dec. 19th

My dear Father and Mother and all at home,

Just a short letter to let you know that I am all right. I am writing this in a moving train somewhere in France. Yes, we are going by the route which I told you was probable, though our port of arrival, where we spent most of yesterday, was not what I had anticipated. The train has just stopped with a tremendous jerk (it always does), and now perhaps I can write a little less shakily for a while – I have fortunately managed to find a carriage to myself for the time being. I did manage to sleep during the night, and the night before, though how I know not. We have started again, by the way. Yesterday was quite fun and I had plenty of opportunity for using my French; I will tell you more about it later perhaps.

The voyage was fairly pleasant. I admit the east wind was bitingly cold, but it was warm and comfortable down below – not much room perhaps, but that was only to be expected.

Will you thank Nell for the camera? Also, I am very grateful to Jocelyn for bringing it over. What did he think of our school? I'm glad to be out of it, but I may be going to a worse place yet. This perpetual travelling is not too pleasant. The French country that we have seen is far from interesting: flat and rather treeless, and now it is dark again, so one can see nothing. I don't fancy another night in the train, but there we are.

How did Gervase enjoy his weekend up at Laxton? I suppose he is now at Epsom. I am sorry I am not going to be home for Christmas, but I suppose it would not have been the same this year in any case. I will write to you fairly often to let you know how I am getting on, but now I think I shall stop as there is not much more I can say without risk of offending the censor.

So love to all,
From Christopher

Somewhere at sea
Wednesday Dec. 27th (day after
Boxing Day; doesn't seem like it.)

Dear J., G. & D.,

As this is coming with another letter, I am writing it to you this time. Actually, that other letter should have been well on its way to you now, as mail was collected on Christmas Eve and somehow handed over to our destroyer escort which left on that night with our sister ship and left the mail at a certain place (I will not mention its name but it was where Mike Gardner was stationed last year!), but unfortunately I had not finished my letter when they were collected, so this is the result.

Today it is pleasantly sunny and warm after two cloudy and rather rough days. The blue waters have calmed down considerably now, and the ship is riding fairly evenly. Christmas and Boxing Day, however, particularly Christmas night, were quite disturbed days – nothing like an Atlantic swell, of course, but enough to make quite a few people seasick. It did not worry me though, and I was able to enjoy our Christmas dinner, which consisted of two roast chickens between eight of us – it was actually six, as two didn't want any. They were very well cooked for the army, and were followed by a species of Christmas pudding with rum sauce, the latter being O.K. Save for this, there was not much to remind one of Christmas at home. No drink at all – some of us were given vouchers for a free pint of beer after dinner, but the beer issue place closed before dinner and did not open again that day! The irony of it did not worry me much as the beer on board is pretty rotten. Still, it was damnable to realise that the officers were getting as much as they liked, and probably more, while we had to go dry, on Christmas Day too.

I don't think I have ever spent a more empty Christmas. Everyone was fed up and annoyed with one another and the spirit of 'peace and goodwill amongst men' was far from evident. How was your Christmas? If there is anything to tell, tell it in full when you write, and I expect a long letter from each of you soon, mind. I don't care how long you make them. I will not get bored. I must say I wish we were back in the old days again, before I had to join the army, but on the other hand, this will, I suppose, be an experience to look back on, and I should not mind roughing it after my present struggle for existence.

It is not so bad up on deck; in fact, we few had found a pleasant corner with a roof, protection from the wind, and a deckchair for the first arrival, and had been occupying it for several days, only to be told yesterday by the ship's Sergeant-Major that we were not allowed there as it was a second-class deck – still, we usually manage to find a fairly reserved place. A lot of troops get on one's nerves; I never feel one of them.[26]

Down below, however, in our Mess[27] deck, is where conditions are most unpleasant. It is hot and stuffy (the portholes cannot be opened after dusk), with very little room to move about in, and our table where we eat – and also read or write when there is room – is right beneath where we sleep in hammocks. Yes, I long to get back to civilisation, though it should be a bit better where we are going. I shall be satisfied if I can get a locker in which to keep my belongings instead of having them knocking about all over the place like they are here.

---

26 Christopher initially finds it hard to fit in with the other soldiers, after his sheltered upbringing.

27 Army term for accommodation.

Don't get the idea, though, that I am terribly depressed and would desert if I could. I am getting used to it and making the best of a bad business. In any case, I should have eventually had to go somewhere, perhaps to a worse place than whither we are going.

You will soon be starting too, I expect, Jocelyn, and if I know anything about it you should be a lot better off where you are starting than me. The only snag is that you will probably be unable to get the frequent weekends home that I had at Stoughton. Let me know about it.

Tomorrow we are stopping a few hours at a port you should guess, and instead of being allowed off as one likes, there is a sort of route march (I ask you!). Still, anything to tread on 'terra firma' again. We've been five days at sea now, but it's hard to keep an account of the time.

Now I find that we of the Queen's[28] have been picked as guards on the march tomorrow, and while the other troops walk free and easy, we have to carry rifles and wear equipment. That's the worst of belonging to the Queen's – hundreds of other regiments and they choose us because of our good reputation. Well, well, I suppose one ought to be proud of the honour, but I can't say that I am.

Well, it's nearly 4 p.m. now and the letters are supposed to be handed in then. So I'll try and finish. I saw, in the little news sheets that we sometimes get handed round, that frost and fog delayed London Christmas traffic; did you have one like last year, then? I cannot imagine it here. Well, I'd better pack up now. Tell Sylvia I'll write to her next.

Cheerio, Christopher

---

28 The Queen's Royal Regiment (West Surrey) was the senior English infantry regiment of the British Army, dating from 1661.

THREE

A Hot Sun in a Cloudless Sky

1940

On board H.M.T. *Nevasa*
Somewhere at sea
Jan. 1st 1940, 3 p.m.

My dear Mother & Father & all at home,

I wish you rather belatedly a Happy New Year and look forward to a return of greetings in my first letter from you, which will not arrive, I suppose, till late in January. Write frequently once you've started, won't you? I also wish you many very happy returns of the day, Mother, and am sorry that is all. This letter should arrive round about that date as I am in the tropics now.

We stopped for about nine hours last Thursday at rather an obvious port. It was a marvellous day; a hot sun in a cloudless sky but a breeze cool enough to make it pleasant. Soon after we had anchored a multitude of swarthy rascals clad in black and grimy rags swarmed over the ship. I believe they were supposed to be helping in the coaling, which was done in an unique way, but all they seemed to do was beg for English cigarettes. Others, less ragged, came alongside in small boats and tried, often with success, to sell all kinds of things.

Unfortunately, we were not allowed ashore freely, but a route march (rather short and easy) was organised in the morning and we were able to stretch our legs at the same time, seeing something of the colour and brilliance of this port.

It has been hot since we left there – very hot down below because the blackout is still observed, and the portholes are therefore shut at night (the blackout was lifted while we were in the last port and while we were in enclosed waters the same night after leaving it; it was a most welcome relief but did not last long). It would be almost as hot on deck but for the breeze.

I am getting used to the conditions on board now, though the heat does not make it any easier down below. Topees[29] and tropical suits are being worn generally now and sleeping on deck is allowed – allowed because there would probably be a riot otherwise. Although it has been fine, the seas have been rather heavy the last two days, so much so that when we opened our porthole for fresh air at breakfast yesterday, an exceptionally large wave poured in, throwing us back and swamping the place out. The portholes have been closed since. I shall be glad when we eventually land, though even then we have got a long and probably uncomfortable train journey before us. Most of all, I am waiting for news from you. Do not spare yourselves in writing, please.

Did you hear Lord Haw-Haw's[30] report that this ship (*Nevasa*) had been sunk? (It was rumoured that he had done so.) So far, at any rate, he is wrong.

I cannot give you much more news as there is none, or very little. Life is fairly lazy and uneventful. The ship's library was a boon, but they have stopped loaning books from today for an indefinite period. Nobody seems to play chess, though pontoon is very popular; in that, however, I have wisely not participated. By the way, if you can possibly manage it, would you send me a little cash sometime, as I am rather short now, and will be for several weeks to come? I must not go on much longer as the letters are being collected at six and it

---

29 Pith helmets worn by European troops serving overseas in hot countries.
30 'Lord Haw-Haw' was the nickname of William Joyce, a British fascist who broadcast Nazi propaganda from Germany to Britain during World War II. After the war he was arrested, extradited to Britain and hanged for treason.

is nearly that now. Although the sun is still shining brightly while I write on deck.

Some rocky islets are in sight; the first land since Friday, when we could see land all day. This ship is pretty slow really. I believe she averages 12 to 13 knots, which works out at a little over 300 miles per full day, so you can understand why we are so long travelling. The crew is mainly Lascar,[31] but they are quite pleasant men, unlike those who boarded us last week.

I don't suppose you will get another letter from me for at least a fortnight, as our stop tomorrow is our last before we disembark. However, it is time to sign off, I fear.

Love to all from Christopher

H.M.T. *Nevasa*
Somewhere at sea
Friday Jan. 5th, 6 p.m.

My dear Mother and Father and all,

We are on the last lap of the voyage now, and all things being well, should dock late on Sunday or early on Monday. It will be a great relief to get off this ship, whatever the alternative. It seems that we have been on her for weeks, though it is but a fortnight.

Every day now the sun shines almost continuously, but there is a pleasant breeze, so it is by no means unbearable. Here there are about eleven hours of daylight compared to your eight. I saw the sun rise at 7 a.m. this morning, and it has just set now at 6.10 p.m. That is the equivalent of an early March day in England, but the sun is very much hotter now than it is there in England.

One rises now at half past five, breakfast at half past six, and at seven P.T., which is rather a farce. The captain (he is not a genuine naval Captain) makes his rounds from 10 a.m. till 10.30ish, which is our only parade. The rest of the day is free, unless one is on sentry guard, which consists of four two-hour shifts as an informal sentry in 24 hours. Rather arduous when one is woken at 3 a.m. to go on

---

31   Indian sailors.

till 5, but mainly just boring. We are doing our second guard on the voyage today. Little else disturbs one unless one is fool enough to get caught for a fatigue. Yet for all this monotony the days seem to slip by, just as the sea slips by as one gazes at it.

The sea has little to offer in the way of interest. Less blue than it was ten days ago and decidedly calm. Many strange-coloured jellyfish are visible on the surface, if one cares to look, and for the more patient, a flying fish will now and again skim over the waves, looking like a drab swallow. Some say that the phosphorescent streaks that can be seen near us at night denote sharks, but I am sceptical about that as there are so many of these streaks, whereas I have not yet seen a shark in daylight. A few days ago, before we turned the corner[32], we saw, fairly near, a large waterspout, which brought the only rain I have seen for days.

Yes, I shall be glad when we finally arrive at our destination, but it seems that there are many things that one has to be very careful about there. Heat brings its attendant discomforts and dangers, though I could put up with the heat alone.

When you get this, you will know that I have arrived, as this cannot be posted until we get there. You never thought that it was going to be so soon after that two weeks' leave I had, did you? My estimation was that I should get there late in January, and it seems that I shall be a bit out. I cannot concentrate now so I will stop now and continue tomorrow when, I hope, my brain may be more fertile…

Saturday
Hore-Belisha[33] has resigned, I see, but not much else has happened according to our bulletins. The substitute, Stanley, doesn't seem to be an improvement. I don't see much chance of a sudden end to this war, do you?

---

32 Christopher may be referring to when their ship rounded the southernmost tip of the Arabian Peninsula, crossing from the Red Sea into the Gulf of Aden. Due to heavy wartime censorship, troops were not allowed to mention place names in their letters, especially not when travelling.

33 Secretary of State for War Leslie Hore-Belisha was dismissed by Prime Minister Neville Chamberlain in January 1940, reportedly because of his attempts to reform the army, or possibly due to anti-Semitism, Belisha being Jewish.

We had a short and interesting stop at our most southerly point on the voyage (nearly) last Tuesday afternoon. It looked a very arid place, this harbour and port: little or no vegetation, and naked brown crags towering over the strange-looking houses built in terrace fashion up the lower slopes. It was pleasant to see land, especially a place called the Crescent Hotel, even though it had no glass in its windows, like all the other houses there. It was nice to see lights twinkling too as we moved out at dusk. We picked up a new escort then[34] […] as you see it, some distance away, in the daytime, you would never suspect that it was around; but we had a close-up in the harbour and saw its […] torpedo-tubes, anti-aircraft guns, searchlights, aircraft detectors,

Christopher writes home from India, January 1940

machine-guns etc., and its R.N.[35] complement. All the same, I would prefer a destroyer because of its mobility, wouldn't you? However, we arrive early Monday, and it should not be long before I hear from you now. I am sorry for this skimpy letter, but I think I'd better pack up now, so:

Love to all, Christopher

'D' Co., 1st Battalion
Queen's Royal Regiment
MacPherson Barracks
Allahabad
India
Sunday Jan. 28th, 11 a.m.

Dear J., G., S. & D.,

For a change I will address this letter to you. I feel like writing as I have a lot of time on my hands today, being on guard. But I

---

34 The page has holes cut out, with a note: 'Sorry I had to cut so much out. C. S. D., Censor.'
35 Royal Navy.

still think that I should have had some sort of a letter by now – it is nearly three weeks since my arrival – possibly you have not thought of using the air mail; we get it twice a week.

Yes, I have got rather an unpleasant Sunday before me. We who have just arrived here struck it unlucky. You see, almost the entire battalion is away, either at camp or at the fort (5 miles), and, there being so few left here, we are called upon to do our share of these 24-hour guards as well as our ordinary month's training. The two guards we had on the voyage were bad enough, but here they are much worse. One spends nearly the whole of the afternoon and evening of the previous day in cleaning up for the guard. A high polish must be applied to boots. Drill shorts and jacket must be sent to the laundry to be starched and pressed. Equipment must be 'blancoed' and the brasses on it made to gleam. Leather chin-straps on the topee must glisten like glass and all buttons must be well-polished. Actually, I was fortunate yesterday. A 'bearer' did all my equipment for 8 annas.[36] One of our draft lent me his highly polished boots and an old soldier did my chin-strap for me, so I was able to sit back and rest. You've no idea what a high standard of smartness is demanded on the nine o'clock inspection before we mount guard. It seems ridiculous in wartime and even for peace a bit overdone, but the Queen's always have been like it.

Till about 9.30 a.m. tomorrow I am stuck in the guardroom with four stretches on duty from 1 p.m. to 3 p.m., 7 p.m. to 9 p.m., 1 a.m. to 3 a.m. and 7 a.m. to 9 a.m. The rest of the time is one's own, but if you want to sleep, you must do so fully dressed in boots and equipment. So, it's not exactly a pleasant time! Still, the battalion returns on Wednesday and we shan't have to do anymore. Also, this week, the next draft from Guildford arrives. It will be interesting to hear of their reactions to the troop ship and to get more recent news of England. The Indian newspapers do, of course, contain a lot of up-to-date home news, and we get the genuine English papers about 3 weeks to a month after publication.

I don't suppose you will get this letter till about the end of February or later, as I cannot afford air mail this week, so many happy returns of the day, Gervase, and buy a tin of tobacco for

---

36   Eight annas = half a rupee.

yourself from me! I must say I am longing to hear how things are going on at home, whether Jocelyn has been called up yet and how S. is getting on at Barton's, and most important, whether we are staying on at Chertsey or whether the house is going to be broken up. I shall be very sorry if I have to come back to a place other than St. Ann's Lodge, so I hope some unexpected luck has 'turned up'.[37] However, at the rate this war is progressing, I don't know when I shall be back – excuse my writing, but it's someone else's cheap pen – perhaps before the end of the year, perhaps in four years' time.

If I remember, you will possibly find some photographs enclosed. I have written on the backs where and what they are. You will see that it is quite a good camera by the fact that all have come out pretty well. The impersonality of most of them may, however, make them rather dull for you. I bought a second reel on the *Nevasa* and took one or two snaps of Bombay, including a close-up of our escort, the *Rauchi*. There are three more films to be taken; if I can get them taken and developed in time, I may enclose these too.

From what little news of English weather that is obtainable I gather that you have had another wintry Christmas and New Year with a lot of snow. I certainly miss the good old east wind; there was one blowing up when we crossed the Channel.

I am finding Dickon's *Highways and Byways in Sussex* by E. V. Lucas very interesting and an agreeable reminder of home. I expect there's quite a fine to pay on it now! We certainly must celebrate Peace (when it comes) by another walking tour, with H. & G. as well. Sussex again, as it is a more friendly county than Wiltshire for all its Savernakes etc.

Monday

It was a pleasant surprise to come off guard this morning and find a letter – the first I've had – waiting for me. It was Mother's, postmarked the 3rd Jan., so it only took 25 days by sea; not too bad. I am glad to say it had not been censored, though several people did get censored letters this morning. Did you know that it is possible to send letters by air mail from England? I was thinking that the one I sent by air from Port Said on the 28th Dec. should

---

37   Christopher is worried his family may have to move out of their beloved St. Ann's
       Lodge, as his parents can no longer afford nor need to stay in such a large rented
       house, with most of their offspring away in the armed forces.

have reached you before Mother's letter of the 3rd was posted. Perhaps the censorship held that up too – just fancy, ten days from central France to reach you! If you have not yet received a letter that I posted by air mail from here about the 17th Jan. it must be that the censor has stopped it because I included too much information about our journey. I hope not because it was a long letter and quite an effort to write. I suppose I should have written earlier since then, but all this time without getting a letter made me feel sort of *Well, why should I keep on writing without getting an answer?* However, I'll try and write a short letter by air mail on Friday and send that at the same time by sea. Photographs would make an air letter too heavy, you see.

Yes, your letter confirms the news of the hard winter in England. It seems to have been cold enough when Mother wrote, but this morning's Calcutta paper tells how you have just emerged from the coldest spell for 46 years, the Thames being frozen over, and 25 degrees and frost being recorded in London. I wish I'd been at home for it, if only to see my thermometer creep down! I hope you noted its minimum.

I'm sorry you didn't have much of a Christmas, but we knew it wasn't going to be much, didn't we? However, for all that, it must have been much more like a real Christmas than mine on the Mediterranean, as you may have gathered, if you have got my previous letters.

If I am writing rather a poor letter it is because I feel pretty tired after last night; being on guard duty as I told you, I only managed to snatch about 2 hours' sleep in bits. If nothing else, I should return home tougher from this place. I am already acquiring quite a summer tan; it seems funny to think of you freezing at home. I don't know how the drafts that are going home (the first goes this Saturday) will enjoy the English weather after their 5, 6, 7 etc. years in India! The idea is, I believe, eventually to replace the majority of the regulars out here with militia and 'terriers'. If we're lucky we'll get sent up to the hills in a few months' time and escape the really hot weather (it is, we are told, unbearably hot here in the summer, the temperature rising to 118 degrees F and more in the shade); some places up there are, I believe, quite pleasant and European.

Thursday morning, 1st February
Here I am on guard again! Just my luck to get Sunday and Thursday, our two days off. I shall probably finish this letter today and send it tomorrow. I have not taken the remaining 3 films of my second reel, so only the first reel will be enclosed.

I got another letter yesterday, from Aunt Dolly.[38] It should have reached me the day before I left, only she had addressed it 'Edgeborough School, Epsom, Guildford', so that it had (so I saw by the postmark) been to Epsom, stayed there for five days, gone to Guildford and then to me. I had no idea who it was from when I saw a Bournemouth postmark.

The next draft are not arriving till tomorrow (Friday) morning, and the batch of regulars leave for home, and probably later France, on Saturday. I might send this by one of them so as to avoid any possible censorship. Tell me when you write if that long air mail letter I sent you from here was interfered with at all.

The bulk of the battalion arrived back from camp this morning after a forced march of 32 miles. I have seen one or two of them limping about the place already. They will probably go to bed for the rest of the day.

How is everyone at home? I hope that the cold has not caused a flu epidemic. For my part, I feel pretty fit now. The second week we were here I felt rather rotten with a very bad throat (many of us got one, probably because of the dust we are unaccustomed to), a flu feeling and the effects of vaccinations. However, that has all gone now.

I am always feeling hungry here. It's probably because the food is modified to suit the climate. It is a standing joke that everything here is "modified for India". It is a fact, though, that in most respects we are 2 or 3 years behind England. The battle suit, which we wear sometimes in the evening, causes quite a lot of amusement.

The jackals still make a horrible noise with their nightly choruses, but apart from them and the kite-hawks and hideous vultures there is little wildlife apparent; so Rosamund, I fear, must be disappointed of her tiger-cub.

The 'regimental talkies', as the cinema is called, are not too bad. I saw my first the other night – a Warner Bros. programme (most films are American), *The Man Who Dared*, and a few amusing shorts.

Well, I must end this rather straggly letter now, so in parting let me remind you to ask anyone who might do so to write to me, as letters are a godsend here, and please ask Mother to send one or two letters by air mail at first.

Love from Christopher

---

38   Christopher's mother's youngest sister; the artistic one, who died young in 1949.

P.S. I am sending this by one Corporal Law who is returning with the first draft home. He may turn up at St. Ann's Lodge, as I asked him to. If he does, give him a good welcome – don't mind if he's a bit rough (that's 6 or 7 years in India), for he's a very decent chap.

Attached 'C' Company, 1st Battalion
Queen's Royal Regiment
MacPherson Barracks
Allahabad
Monday 19th February, 5 p.m.

My dear J. & G.,

I have just received your long-awaited letters of the 9th and 8th January, and you can realise my joy at getting two such long and interesting letters at the same time (don't start patting yourselves on the back because I'm buttering you up; it was about time), though how Sylvia's got here before yours is a mystery. Gervase says optimistically, 'Just think, this takes three whole weeks to reach you' – it has taken more than twice as long.

I am sitting down right now to reply as I believe it is good to strike while the iron is hot. Doubtless my mood of enthusiasm will expire before this letter is finished and it will drag on for a week or two before it is posted. I wish you would use the air mail. I know it is rather more expensive but judging by others' letters it is more reliable. I cannot really afford it on five rupees[39] a week, which is all we are getting until our accounts come through from England, but I have managed to send you several letters that way. However, a letter is a letter, and you must excuse my reproach. You, Gervase, will have to send this on to Jocelyn, as I do not yet know his new address. Still, enough of this carrying on about the 'whys' and 'wherefores' of letters; it seems to be taking the place of train discussions for me. By the way, Gervase, I was surprised to hear of your Woking adventure; you should have acquired more 'train-sense' than that by now!

You do not, either of you, make much comment on the extraordinary severity of your winter, and yet some bloke got a

---

39 Approximately seven shillings.

letter today with newspaper cuttings enclosed showing pictures of the Thames frozen at Kingston, Sunbury and other places. It must have been a hell of a 'snap' and I'm very sorry I missed it. I'll bet you missed my wise observations on the state of the weather and my midnight visits to the thermometer to see if it had fallen to a record level.

I'm afraid an interruption is coming now as it is supper time, and after that I intend to go and see *Indianapolis Speedway* (if you've ever heard of the film) at the 'local'. On Saturday I saw *Tail Spin* with Alice Faye, Constance Bennett and Nancy Kelly, but for all the imposing feminine cast it was rather a futile film. *Au revoir* then till tomorrow, when I promise to try and devote a whole evening to this, over in the peace of the library.

Tuesday

I shall write for a short while now, and then must stop till later in the evening as we have an hour's night operations from 6.30 till 7.30 – rather senseless as there will be a bright moon. The days have been somewhat hotter just lately with the temperature well into the eighties, and there has been a consequent increase in flies and mosquitoes; as yet, however, it is quite bearable. For a change it has clouded over rather greyishly this evening, perhaps meaning another pleasant day of rain (we've had two days with a little rain in six weeks). In England, you remember, I used to get very worried if one tiny white wisp of cloud marred the blue vault of a fine day. Here, my weather interest is practically nil – only a pleasurable anticipation if the sky looks the least bit like rain. One quite takes the sun for granted.

I have returned from my little night stunt and hope to settle down again. I had thought there was no beauty in the evenings out here, but tonight it was rather lovely out in the scrub, which is the best way of describing the land just outside the barrack area. There was some cloud to provide a short but pleasing sunset, and the feathery trees looked prettier in the moonlight than they do by day. The air was cooling off and from the soil rose that pleasant memory-stirring smell of damp stubble – you often find it in England in burnt fields on dewy nights – that always recalls to me our evening walks at Middleton. I say this because I thought that there was little beauty in India so appealing as that of the country at home and of the long summer evenings; I still think the same, but tonight one could enjoy the evening. The familiar stars can be seen. Orion's Belt is high up, almost in the zenith where it souths, and the Plough is upturned low in the north. On the voyage out here, I saw the famous Southern Cross once or twice in the hours before dawn.

That voyage I shall always remember. For all the hardships (which after all were not too bad for wartime), it had its high spots, such as the moon as we lay in Marseille harbour, the Christmas Eve sing-song on deck at night, the bright morning we arrived at Port Said, above all the heavenly night we went down Suez, and later the tropical nightfalls and swift dawns. That is all over and life is quite different now, but it seemed a lifetime while we were at sea. You ask how the mighty oceans and the rolling plains affect me, but remember that wherever you go the horizon is always there! You might be in the Pacific or the Straits of Dover, but you couldn't tell the difference by looking at the size of the sea.

You touched a soft spot in mentioning the South Downs and glorious Sussex. I cannot tell you how much I enjoyed reading Lucas's *Highways and Byways in Sussex* in my first weeks here. However long I may be out here, Wolstanbury and Firle, Chanctonbury and Ditchling and all that wonderful 'chain of mountains' (so says Gilbert White) will be my Mecca, the part I think of when I think of England. Do you know I am more at ease writing to you of Sussex than I am describing India; telling you of India I can improve little on the guide-book or encyclopaedia unless I exaggerated, and most of what I tell you will be of little interest to you. To talk of Sussex, that we both love, is far pleasanter. My return, as I seem to remember saying in a previous letter, must be celebrated with a third tour of that loveliest of counties. Peaceful Midhurst and its cattle meadows by the Rother; the high, lovely Downs from Cocking to Littleton and Duncton and on to Bignor and Bury; Swanbourne Park that commands South Stoke and the Arun Valley; Arundel itself, the centre and heart of Sussex, so it seemed; Chanctonbury and old-world Steyning (notice I miss the less popular Rackham and Kithurst Hills); and across the Arun to East Sussex with Newtimber Down, and above Truleigh Hill and Fulking Down; sparkling Brighton in the south and, higher up, Ditchling Beacon and its town, Hurstpierpoint. So on in like vein could I talk of Sussex to let you know that my memory is not short, but it grows late, so I must pause again. I've started writing both sides of the paper, for which I'm sorry. Goodnight, then.

Thursday – our midweek day of rest

I seem to have been babbling to you of Sussex, my reason being, I suppose, to prove to you that I still think of those Downs as before, and that on our railway journey here I saw nothing to touch them.

Yes, that will be the day, when I return, with peace restored, I hope. The day seems remote now, but it might easily be before next Christmas. I should most like to arrive in March or April to catch the spring and a quick return to warm weather. When that time comes, I hope we shall not be all too scattered.

In a little over a year, if war continues, you will have to register, won't you? Perhaps you would prefer the army to accountancy, but it is, in the ranks anyway, a singularly unintellectual life. When I get out of it all, my mind will be very backward, I expect. I can understand you not liking the work at Barton's. I, myself, was glad to get a job when I started at Goodfellow's, but I never enjoyed the 'ticking', which is all it consists of for the first year or two. That was just drudgery. The more advanced stages of book-keeping, such as Trial Balance, Profit & Loss Accounts, Balance Sheets and so on, I found pretty interesting when I touched on them at Pitman's, but in practice you rarely come into contact with the more interesting work until you get higher up. You must regard Barton's as only a temporary means of making money until you are called up, unless you intend in the meantime to take up some other work which will give you exemption from the army. If possible, though I don't quite see how you can do it now, this would be a good idea, as both Jocelyn and myself are already in the forces, and nowadays we don't believe in all those heroics as "I must fight for my country…" The only thing is that when you see everyone else joining up, you want to do the same yourself. It's a beastly problem, isn't it?

I don't think I have got much chance of applying for training for a commission now – I don't take soldiering seriously enough. To become an officer from the ranks you have got to be pretty hot. It is quite different for the man who, on leaving school, goes straight to Sandhurst or some such place – he may be quite unintelligent; that is why one sees so many callow young subalterns.[40] In any case, my only reason for wanting to become an officer would be that I could associate with people of my own class for a change. Put yourself in my position, as one who is not particularly keen on

---

40   Officer in the British Army below the rank of captain.

the army, and then think how difficult it is if Dad asks why I am not working hard to try and get a commission.

As a matter of fact, there is a possibility that when our training is over, I shall get transferred to Brigade HQ at Lucknow on a clerical job there. If it came off that wouldn't be so bad, as Lucknow is a much more civilised place than Allahabad. However, we shall see what we shall see. Life has changed so much for me in the past few months that many stranger things can still happen. Perhaps I shall be home before the summer is out. Perhaps we will be sent back home and then to France after some months' experience – a rumour spread by the second draft (I am in the first), but it seems to me unreasonable and without foundation; why have unnecessary troop movements in wartime? Such a possibility seems quite pleasant now but would probably be the opposite when we reached France. Again, perhaps we shall move up to the N.W. Frontier in September. This is based on more than a rumour, but now I hear that it is not so likely because so many regulars are being sent home from the battalion – there are 140 (3 drafts) militia here now and more to come, who are replacing them.

Saturday

I received Mother's parcel of newspapers on Thursday but no letter, which I should have preferred. Still, it was interesting looking through the *Daily Sketche*s even though they were 7 weeks old.

I am sorry to hear that Humphry has lost his job. What are his plans now? To join up? Will you tell him that I have started a letter to him but do not know when it will be completed, so if he likes to write to me first it will be all the better for me? He seems to have bucked up your Christmas a lot – as for you asking what our 'drunken revelry' was like at Christmas, let me state that all I managed to get, which was more than most, was a half-glass of whisky and the same of gin from a couple of second-class civilian passengers; just enough to recognise the taste! Still, I told you of our Christmas, such as it was, in my previous letters – and afterwards, the descriptions that both of you give of the Deanna Durbin evening sound very good. Sylvia too told me about it. Where is Gareth now? If you could get him and anybody you can think of, such as B. and Napper Young, to write I should be 'bucked'.

Time slips by quickly here; probably because the weekends are less well defined than at home. Soon it will be summer and unbearably hot – it is quite warm enough already in the afternoons.

I meant to enclose another letter with this especially to Mother and Father, but I am afraid that will bring it over the ½ ounce now, so that must be next week; however, I expect this will be passed round as a general letter and no one will mind it being addressed to you. I hesitate to write by sea mail now that I know how long it takes, and I can afford only one air mail a week, so, you see, my letter-writing is somewhat limited. I don't like asking, however, for any cash now that times are going to be so bad, but if you could mention to Reg and Nell that I am in low water, perhaps they could help me with a little till things get straightened out.

I am hoping to hear from you today, Monday.[41] It is hot today and a dusty wind is blowing. We spent this morning firing on the open ranges – first time – and our training ends this week. Well, I'm sorry I have said so little and yet written such a long letter. Remember to write again soon and let me know all the news.

Cheerio then.
Love to all from Christopher

c/o Lucknow District HQ
Ranikhet
United Provinces
India
Wednesday June 12th

My dear Father and Mother,

I wish you many happy returns of the day, Dad, but I'm afraid I'm a little late… Owing to moving up here, you see (note my new address) and settling in, I have not been able to write for the last few days. Next year I hope I shall be at home to wish you a happy birthday, though the sky is dark now. Yes, I have left Allahabad now, perhaps fortunately, though that remains to be seen.

I told you in my last letter, didn't I, that the C.O.[42] had interviewed

---

41 Christopher started this letter two days previously. He usually spent several days, or even weeks composing a letter home during wartime, in order to write a good long letter that was worth sending. Postage was costly on his meagre wages and letters would take months to reach England from the Far East by ship in those days.

42 Commanding officer.

me about my getting a job as a clerk at District HQ? Well, from the above you may see that the job has actually materialised. I was informed last Friday that I would be moving the following afternoon, which was rather short notice. However, there was not much packing to do, as I've now got a large trunk-type box, which I got from a bloke who was going overseas, in exchange for one of my kit bags, and found it easy to stow all my stuff into that and a kit bag. Had a few drinks that night with two or three of the blokes I've been 'in with' since I joined the army, in case we didn't meet again. The next day there was quite a lot to do before I left. There were my outstanding bills at the tailors etc. to be paid – fortunately, they didn't amount to much – railway warrants and documents to be collected from the orderly room, instructions to be obtained and various articles of equipment to be handed in. The biggest load off my mind was handing in my rifle – no more trouble with that for some time, I hope. As it was, it happened to be a little oily when the Colour Sergeant[43] inspected it for checking purposes and he nearly had a fit.

I got a 'tonga'[44] to take me down to the station at 3 o'clock in the heat of the afternoon and had to pay a rupee for it; I told the 'tonga wallah' I thought it a lot, but he wouldn't bargain, so to save arguing, I paid up. At Allahabad station I had to pay 'coolies'[45] to carry my luggage into the train, and the smaller of the two started worrying me for more because I paid the other man more than him. I pointed out to him that he was only a 'chico' (kid) and so entitled to less, and in the end he went. Throughout the whole journey I must have disbursed over two rupees on coolies who carried my luggage. Still, they were a necessity.

I had a reserved bunk in a second-class compartment and travelled up with a Staff Sergeant of the R.A.O.C.[46] from the Fort Allahabad, though he was not in charge of me; I was in fact a detachment of my own.

---

43   Non-commissioned officer ranked above sergeant and below warrant officer.
44   Light, horse-drawn two-wheeled vehicle used in India.
45   Unskilled native labourers in Asia.
46   Royal Army Ordnance Corps.

Tuesday June 18th

Nearly a week ago I started this, but the delay is accounted for by a most discouraging piece of news, namely the cancellation of the air mail. We might as well stop writing to each other now, since mail takes six weeks via the Cape and I shall have been here nearly eight weeks before you know of it.[47] However, I shouldn't like to go so far as that; you should hear from me and I from you regularly again after this enforced gap. Anyhow, it will be cheaper, and Gervase need not worry about cutting down his letters on account of weight!

Let us hope that we shall have turned the corner in this war by the time you get this, for it is truly terrible now, isn't it? With Italy joining in like a jackal when we are hard-pressed, Norway given up, the Maginot Line being vacated and the French brought almost to their knees, and most tragic of all – Paris, the jewel of France, in the hands of Germany, worse than ever happened in the last war. It seems inevitable that the French Army will have to surrender if the Germans continue their present rate of advance much longer, what do you think? And then where shall we be, without a battlefield on which to finally defeat Germany? With France beaten, Hitler will be able gradually to subdue the British Empire, and then life will not be worth living. Although the idea of an ignominious peace, dictated to us by Germany, seems incredible, it is now a definite and terrifying possibility, isn't it?

Thursday June 20th

To continue – Gervase's air mail letter (the last I shall get for a long while, I fear) was forwarded to me from Allahabad and I got it last Friday, the 14th. It was posted on the 4th. Yesterday your parcel of newspapers, dated the 5th May, arrived – all about Norway, but that's a forgotten phase of the war now, isn't it?

I was telling you, some pages back, how I came up here, I believe. It was not a very pleasant journey. The train left Allahabad at 4.30 and the 5½ hour

---

47   Although this letter has an airmail sticker, it must have been sent via sea, being
     postmarked 'Southampton, 12th May 1941'. It is addressed to St. Ann's Lodge, but
     Christopher's parents had moved so it was forwarded, first to Dr Riches (Uncle Reg)
     care of his workplace at St. Bernard's Hospital, Southall, then to the family's new
     address in Hinchley Wood. Someone wrote on the envelope, 'Rec'd 19th May 1941', so
     the letter took nearly a year to arrive.

journey from there to Lucknow, across the flat Ganges Plain, was almost intolerable through the heat – opening the windows only seemed to make the air more stifling. I have never seen such deadly country as on that 150-mile run, monotonously flat all the way, the land an arid yellowish-brown colour, the fields marked out with low mud walls, thirstily ready to catch the coming rains, not a blade of grass to be seen, the only green being that of the regular groups of trees. And what made the journey more boring was that we kept stopping at footling little stations where crowds of natives kept up a babel of noise about seemingly nothing. Although it was 10 p.m. when we reached Lucknow, the station resembled Waterloo on a Bank Holiday – where the seething mass thought they were going, I don't know. Managed to get some tea and toast – as a matter of fact, tea and toast three or four times was all I had from when I left Allahabad till the evening of the next day – and after army tea it was really enjoyable; reminded me of the tea at home.

Out here there is quite a different idea of salesmanship to that in England. The Indians come round persistently asking you if you want their wares, probably because there is so much competition among them and they are afraid of being unobserved. The tea, or whatever it is, is brought round, right to the carriage, on a tastefully arranged tray. But such service is only obtainable, of course, from the big catering contractors, and they are the only people from whom it is considered safe to buy eatables. If you happened to want tea and toast at 10 o'clock at night at some big station in England, you'd have to get out of the train, search for the buffet and in the end the girl behind the counter would probably give you a look as much to say, *What do you want such a thing at this time for?*

At Lucknow the Sergeant and I were unlucky, for a couple of Indians got into our compartment for the night. Mind you, they were fairly high-caste and clean, being second-class travellers, but one was a great mountain of a man, greasy with strong-smelling unguents. However, I managed to get a good night's sleep and woke at 6 o'clock at Bareilly, where one has to change onto the narrow-gauge railway for the hills. From Bareilly to Kathgodam, the terminus of the railway, is a run of about 60 miles, but it took four hours, from 8 till noon, as the train kept halting and slowing down. The country here, where the plains meet the hills, was still flat but much greener. There was no moderation in the heat yet. At Kathgodam I saw written beneath the name of the station, '1,691 feet above sea level', though we did not seem to have climbed much and the air was still as hot as ever.

The rest of the journey – some 50 miles to Ranikhet – has to be covered by bus. It cost me nearly 5 rupees because my railway warrant, through some oversight, only took me as far as Kathgodam. This last 4 hours or so was the best part of the journey. The little bus took us ever up and up and round and round, for the road is a succession of bends, many of them hairpin, to modify the steepness. After about half an hour of climbing it was possible to look down at some gorge far below, now fed with a mere trickle of water, and to feel deliciously cool breezes, of the rarer air, wafting in now and again. The luxuriance and greenness of the vegetation was a great contrast to that of the dry plains, and when we had climbed some thousands of feet, I caught the glorious smell of pines – they do not grow over most of India, of course – and saw great numbers of them, but no silver birch. When we had covered half the distance and were about 5,000 feet up, the road dropped right down, and for some miles we followed along a river valley. Saw quite a few monkeys of different sorts in the woods by our side; creatures that it is not possible to see in Allahabad. For the last 15 miles or so, however, we climbed steadily and by the time I was dropped at Ranikhet, at the offices of District HQ, I was some 6,200 feet above sea level. It was a lovely evening, about 5 o'clock, and to me, just off the plains in an open-neck shirt, the fresh air was almost cold, but at the same time invigorating.

The offices were all shut, it being a Sunday, and I had no idea where to go, but with the help of some coolies who carried my luggage and seemed to know the place I would be living in, the rest of the ascent, and very steep it was, was covered. Amongst the several bungalows (up here they are true bungalows with only one storey), I hit upon the right one first time, namely the District Clerk's. This year Ranikhet is not a hill station for troops in training. There is merely what is called a British Attached Section up here, consisting of us clerks, a wireless transmitting section, some Signallers and R.A., and a few blokes who stay here while on leave at Ranikhet. There are not more than 25 of us, and in consequence everything is very 'cushy'. Discipline is practically non-existent – no Orderly Corporals or Sergeants, no checking in at night, so that you could stay out till dawn if you so wished, no official reveille or lights-out, no bugles, no mosquito nets needed at night – in fact, very few of the unpleasant things of army life.

I usually get up about a quarter to eight! Have breakfast at quarter past and then scramble an unpleasant 200 yards or so down the steep hillside to reach the District offices shortly before 9 o'clock. My work at present is entirely different from that at Goodfellow's, so that my auditing experience there does not give me superior qualifications to anybody else who might have applied for the job. It just happened that J. B. Coates (Coates of cotton fame), our C.O., had one or two talks with me and decided that I had a better chance of getting on in the army at office work than otherwise – that remains to be seen, of course, but under ordinary peacetime conditions in the District offices, those who do all right usually get promoted to the rank of Paid Acting Sergeant after a year or two, jumping L/Cpl and Corporal; only last week a chap who had been here a year or two got his transfer to Army HQ Simla and, automatically, immediate promotion to the rank of P.A.S. – he was a Private like myself before that. The next step is to Staff Sergeant and transfer to the Indian Army Corps of Clerks after another year or so. Next, according to seniority, comes the rank of Sub-Conductor, then comes Conductor – the highest non-commissioned rank – and finally, the ambition of all those chaps who've been on the staff for years, the jump to full Lieutenant. Of course, it's a long business becoming a commissioned Staff Officer, as I've explained. Though wartime conditions may accelerate promotion, as I've not been in the racket long enough – in any case, I hope I'm not out here so long as to start thinking of it as a definite possibility – I'm quite content as I am at present, for it's a great relief to be away from the battalion and 'all its works'.

There are several different branches in District. The main ones are 'Q' – troop movements etc. and the more secret matters; 'G' – discipline, orders, etc.; 'Establishments' – a small branch dealing with the District staff itself; and 'A', the branch I am in. We are concerned mostly with pensions, allowances, budgets, claims, upkeep of Indian units and all that sort of thing – rather dull subjects in themselves but there are sometimes amusing letters from Indian followers or ex-soldiers or their families begging for pensions, etc. They have got some idea that the authorities can be flattered into giving them what they want.

I have got several hundred files under my care at present, all dealing with such closely connected matters that the working of the various cases that come in is rather confusing for me at the moment. My predecessor, now shifted to another branch, used to send out much of the correspondence without consulting anyone, but being new to the job, I have to get a rough draft from the branch superintendent for most of the letters, and a great deal of my work consists in typing out these letters. I have got no speed at typing, as you know of course, but in an army office that does not seem to matter. I find typing quite an interesting pastime, now that my fingers are getting used to it, but I should not like it as a career.

The great difference between an army office and that of a thriving London business, for example, is that we never seem to be 'pushed'. Just work on at your own pace, and if there is a lot of correspondence to be dealt with at the end of the day, just leave it till the next day. No last-minute rush to finish off. The official hours are 9 [a.m.] till 1 p.m. and 2 [p.m.] till 4 p.m. with half-days on Thursdays and Saturdays, and Sunday, of course, all day off. In addition to the ordinary work, though, one catches all-night duty every ten days. It is only a matter of receiving telegrams and wireless messages, entering them up on a schedule, and if it is an urgent message or a cipher, ringing up the officer concerned. One usually gets a fairly good night's sleep.

I've written so many pages that I think I'll start writing on the backs after this sheet; for, after all, there must be a limit to what can be sent by sea.

It's Tuesday 25th June (a year ago tomorrow, Humphry, Gareth and I started on our memorable walking tour[48] – hasn't time swept on?!) and a fine night. By the way, there's no electric light up here so I'm writing this by oil-lamp. Last night and this morning it rained heavily, so heavily that we thought that the monsoons had arrived; there have been intermittent heavy thunderstorms since I've been up here, but this was continuous and heavy, with the sky leaden as it often is in England, and as I have seldom seen it out here. It stopped in the middle of the morning, and as we 'climbed up' to lunch, it was possible to see the wet, billowy clouds in the valleys below us.

The rain must have cleared the air well, for it was a brilliant evening and the surrounding hills stood out marvellously in detail. For the first time since I have been up here, I saw the snow peaks of the Himalayas. They were a wonderful sight, with the evening sun shining on their snow and ice. At first when I looked, clouds obscured them and only a peak or two were visible above the clouds, appearing, through their whiteness, almost a part of them. But then the clouds settled down into the valleys and the great range could be very clearly seen in the north, stretching many miles either way – a magnificent prospect, with Nanda Devi (26,000 feet) and the Pindari Glacier prominent. One could imagine that they were five miles away instead of seventy, so clearly

---

48   Christopher went hiking with his cousins in June 1939 across the Sussex Downs.

featured were the spurs and pinnacles, the small dark patches and the great white patches of snow. I at once got the feeling that I should straightaway like to make for them and attempt an ascent, however I contented myself by merely taking a photograph, which will probably fail to reproduce the mountains as I used no filter. Still, it was a gamble worth taking.

By the way, that was a good photograph Gervase enclosed in his last letter. I am sorry all six were not sent, for it's a long time to wait now. Sylvia looked very winning in her breeches and I thought Dickon by her side abnormally sleek. The lupins, one saw, were in prime condition. You've been having a wonderful summer so far, then? And no one in the mood to appreciate it. How is Jocelyn? Must be at sea now. I'm terribly sorry I've not written to him all this time; please tell him when you next write. Gareth, too, where is he now? I heard from him at the beginning of March, but I'm afraid again that I did not answer. I wrote Humphry a long letter some while ago, but I haven't yet received his promised description of life in the army.

Well, I think that should be all for tonight. As inspiration is gradually running dry, it looks as though this letter may eventually come to an end. Goodnight – I shall be thinking of you at home. I long to be home again but have been out here so long now that I am used to it.

Friday June 28th

Where was I? Nowhere in particular, I think. How this letter's dragging out, but it makes no difference, for at the moment I've not even got the money to buy a stamp. Actually, I've been in low water for the past week or so. Before I left Allahabad, I drew my pay for the month in advance – R. 50, but somehow, what with settling Allahabad bills, a celebration on the night before I left, travelling expenses and a couple of visits to Ranikhet when I first arrived, it all seemed to evaporate within a week or so. However, I can get cigarettes on credit and down the hill there's the Lucknow District Club where I have got a certain amount of credit for beer etc. if required, so I shall manage to scrape along till next week. I can't grumble really, for it must be pretty bad at home now, with the price of everything going up. We don't really feel the war out here, though every day there's something in the paper about India's growing war-consciousness. They've even got an A.R.P. organisation in Karachi and a blackout took place the other day, and, too, a Maharajah of somewhere has presented the money to the government to buy one whole fighter plane.

I expect it's becoming a bit worrying for you now that Germany is starting air raids on Britain. It sadly looks as if the war is going to turn into an air one now that France has capitulated. Honestly, do you think there is any chance of our defeating Germany now? People here still talk about us being bound to win in the end, and the other day an office note was passed round saying that it has come to the notice of higher authority that some men had been spreading false rumours about the state of the war and talking in a defeatist-like manner; against such, action would in future be taken. That's all very well, but this continual affirming that we are bound eventually to crush Germany doesn't seem to have got us anywhere. I don't know what to think of it all. You who are right in the heart of things now must be worrying a great deal, and it will be months before I hear from you, unless they bring back the air mail service.

Yes, it is very pleasant up here after Allahabad. The weather is very like that of an English summer. Perhaps on the average a little warmer, but just lately it has rained quite a lot and there have been frequent thunderstorms. Out here, however, the thunder does not seem to have that full-blooded roar that it has in England; perhaps we haven't had a real storm yet.

Another parcel of newspapers of the week from May 6th–13th arrived on Wednesday. It seems funny finishing off (or rather attempting to do so) the crosswords that Dad has started, with those thousands of miles between us; just as if he had said, as in 'the old days', "There, I can't do anymore. Christopher, see if you can finish it off."

I'm not sure what will happen to me if the Queen's move up to the N.W. Frontier in the autumn. Probably get recalled, I suppose, which would, I expect, be rather a shock after some months of acclimatisation to the physically easy life here. This HQ moves down to Lucknow, its winter base, in October, and I should like to stay there, for Lucknow is about the best city in the United Provinces, being the present capital and residence of the Governor. If I'm out here long enough and manage to save enough, I shall get a fortnight's leave or so and spend it at Calcutta, I think. Several blokes have done so, and it is said that Calcutta is the nearest it is possible to get to civilisation in the East. Still, perhaps I'll be home before I have time to do so. I hope so. Well, I've carried on so long with this letter that I think the time has now come to give it a short, sharp end, so goodbye for a week or so.

Your loving son,
Christopher

HQ Lucknow District
Ranikhet
United Provinces
August 4th

My dear Mother and Father and all at home,

Yesterday I received the largest mail for weeks – two parcels of newspapers, the latest June 19th, a letter from Mother, and Gervase's letter of the 17th June. It was good to hear from you again after such a long break, even though the letters were six weeks old. I reproach myself now for having written so rarely during this intervening period. My last letter to you from Allahabad was posted, I believe, about the end of May; I didn't send another till the end of June, so there will have been a gap of over 2 months between those two letters. I am sorry, but it was so discouraging when the air mail ceased that I lost heart to write for a while. This will be my third letter to you since I have been up in the hills – eight weeks now. The photographs were very good, especially the one of Jocelyn standing up against the rhododendrons, but I've got one complaint – Rosamund still refuses to put on a natural face. I also notice that it is some time since Gervase last mowed the lawn. Any other photographs you may take will be very welcome. I had a full film in my camera when I came up here, but so far I have taken only three pictures, all of them impersonal and an ambitious attempt to capture the evening sun's light on the distant snows of the Himalayas; it will probably be a failure, as a yellow filter is really necessary for such photographs.

Well, these days life is quite bearable, almost pleasant at times. No militarism or military duties or officious N.C.O.s to annoy one; a nice climate – the temperature is almost ideal: never too hot and never too cold – though rather wet and damp at present. Plenty of work, and interesting work at that, to keep one's mind active. Lovely country around – not lovely in the sense that Sussex is; perhaps a better word would be 'fine' – and bracing air. The food is good for the army and I always seem to have an appetite for it, and there is quite a bit to do in the evenings. In fact, what more could one want except to be back in England?

Yes, we are very busy at present, and have been for the last few weeks. I think my hours are longer now than when I was at Goodfellow's – 9 a.m. till nearly 6 with just a ¾ hour break for lunch, nearly every day even on Thursdays and Saturdays, which are officially half-days. I usually do two or three hours' work after lunch, and once or twice I have had to go down to the office on a Sunday morning. Mind you, there is no compulsion, but I have to do it for my own sake, for if I get behind with my work, I am responsible, and for all that I am in one of the easiest branches. In one or two of the others, blokes sometimes work till 8 or 9 at night. Still, it's all in a good cause, I suppose – at least one hopes it is.

As a matter of fact, if I'm lucky I may be a paid Temporary Sergeant in a few days' time. Eastern Command wired down urgently for recommendations a fortnight ago and I was one of those recommended. The matter has now gone up to Army Headquarters, Simla, and the result should be known at the end of this week. It is expected that the recommendation will be sanctioned all right, as they were asked for urgently to fill vacancies, not submitted by this HQ for approval. Still, I'm not banking on it, but if it does come off, I shall be a temporary member of the I.A.C.C. (puzzle it out)[49] and shall no longer wear the badge of the Queen's. The pay is R. 210 a month, which, being the equivalent of nearly £4 a week, is not to be laughed at. On that rate of pay, I should be able to help you a little at home, so let us hope it does come off. These promotions, if they come off, may mean that those of us who are so temporarily appointed Sergeants or Staff Sergeants, or whatever it is, will be moved shortly. But I mustn't say more as, being on District HQ, I cannot help but know something of what is going on and if I were not careful, I might let out some news that I ought not to, which would have very serious results for me if the censor got hold of it.

Jocelyn may be surprised to hear that I went to see Deanna Durbin last Saturday in *That Certain Age*. The film was very light and enjoyable, especially the Melvyn Douglas scenes. Deanna was good too, but I did not catch the 'Durbin fever' – has Jocelyn tired of her now? There was another good film on last Friday: Claudette

---

49   Indian Army Corps of Clerks.

Colbert and James Stewart in *It's a Wonderful World*; this I also saw.

Last week I went over to the Military Hospital, Ranikhet, where most of the chaps I joined up with and came out to India with are acting as sort of guards on two military prisoners [who are] at present ill while awaiting court martial. I realised how much better off I now am after seeing them. One of the blokes I always used to get on well with, called Clifford Peake – he was in several of the photographs I sent home a while ago – has been lucky enough to get his transfer to the I.A.O.C. (Ordnance) and he is moving down from Dulikhut tomorrow to go to Allahabad Fort. He gets the rank of Sergeant after a month in the Corps. I don't know whether I told you, but Allahabad Fort is also an arsenal of sorts, which is the reason why there are Ordnance people there. As he has only been up here a week, I have not had time to see him and now probably shall not see him again.

When I first joined up there were five of us who rolled up to the Stoughton Barracks in a van together. This initial shoving up against each other made us stick more or less together in our first months in the army, since when we have been gradually separated. First, one preferred to wait and go to France rather than come out here, and another did not volunteer until the second batch, as he wanted to spend Christmas at home. This caused him to land up in a different company to us remaining three when he came to Allahabad, and now we see very little of him. Then I came up to District, which left only Graham and Smith. Now Peake is going into the Ordnance and we are all scattered. But one meets new friends. There are some very good blokes here on the wireless station, out of the Signals mostly, who consider themselves the elite of private soldiers – the Royal Corps of Signals, that is – and we have some good nights down at the club, especially as one of them has taken over the bar. There are two bottles of Devonshire sloe gin in the 'cellar', which we mean to broach when it can be afforded.

A new Secretary has taken over the club and has started a campaign to liven it up. As a part of this scheme a 'big night' was held last Wednesday which lasted from about 7.30 p.m. till 4.30ish a.m. so far as I can recall. The reason it went on so late was that it was arranged to hold a darts competition, but the organisers did not realise how long it would take to play off a knock-out competition with about 30 entrants. As a matter of fact, it was about 3.30 a.m. when I played the final with Conductor Wodehouse, the chief superintendent. I have never been so surprised as when I ended up the winner, for I can't say I've ever taken a great interest in darts, especially the game that was played, viz. '101 up' and '301 up' in the final. The prize was a singularly small silver cup – so small that I don't suppose it would be worth pawning, even! It was quite a good evening, or perhaps I should say night. There's another one tomorrow (Wednesday) and the Secretary has been sending round for suggestions. I suggested a whist drive, but the general opinion was that it wouldn't go down well, and a few, I believe, thought I was a 'shark', trying to get hold of further prizes.

But all this must seem a great contrast to life in England at present. Here are we leading a peaceful existence, never seeing an aeroplane and never listening to a news bulletin, no air-raid wardens coming round to see our lights are out at night or 'local defence volunteers', as you call them, scouring the countryside with ancient shotguns in search of German parachutists – I am sure Pont must have produced a joke on the subject – and there are you now in the thick of it at home. I hope the air raids are not getting too terrible. Every day one reads about them in the *Statesman*, but the localities bombed are seldom specified. I repeat what I said in my last letter to Gervase: if things get really bad, send me a telegram to say that you are all right. I suppose you must worry rather about Jocelyn and Gareth now, as they are both in the most active arms of the services.[50]

But the army, too, must have suffered pretty severely, judging by the casualty lists that have been appearing almost daily in the papers for the last weeks. Many of those Queen's men who went back in February and March when we relieved them were killed, I am afraid. That bloke who took that letter home for me in February never wrote, so perhaps he was unlucky too. I asked him to go and see you but apparently, he found it too much of an effort.

---

50 Jocelyn was in the navy; Gareth in the air force.

I am glad you are going to send my whites, though the need for them is not so urgent now. As a matter of fact, if Gervase is not wearing my blue suit, that would be more acceptable under my present circumstances as 'civvies' are almost a necessity up here. In fact, last week I went so far as to order a suit on the 'pay what you can when you can' basis. It's only costing R. 25/- so I don't suppose it will be of very good quality, but later on if I do get a Sergeant of the I.A.C.C.'s pay I shall be able to afford something better. However, for the rest of this month I shall be rather 'high and dry' through investing in this suit. Don't change your mind about sending the whites, though, for if I am still in District in September or October when we move down to Lucknow, they will be useful for playing tennis, which, I believe, one can get there.

The monsoon is still pretty active and there is a heavy shower or two most days, but I must have come to the wrong place, for it is nothing like I thought it would be. How's your summer going – still beautifully fine as you tell me it was in April and May and the first part of June? This time last year, if you remember, the rain never seemed to stop, and all the cricket matches were washed out over the Bank Holiday weekend. Oh, to be in England, now that August's there! There's my sentiments at present. I hope Gervase is having or has had a good holiday, and that you are not working too hard, Dad. Now, having reached my set limit, I must close. Please give love and best wishes to Reg and Nell, Leila and Ina, Bianca and H. & G. and everyone else, to whom I have not written for so long.

Your loving son,
Christopher

HQ, 8th Ind. Inf. Bde.
Bareilly
U.P.
Sept. 6th

My dear Father and Mother and all at home,

I am afraid that it is some time since I last wrote, but it is difficult to write regularly these days. I told you, I believe, in my last letter that I had been promoted to Temporary Sergeant of the I.A.C.C.; well now, as you may see from my above address, I have been moved again – to 8th Brigade Headquarters at Bareilly. I was really sorry to leave Lucknow District. It was very pleasant up in the hills (except, of course, for the steep climbing that had to be done every day), and really bracing. I had got into the work there, at least the particular job that I was doing, and had really got to know some good blokes up there. Yes, it grieved me when I was told that I was down for a transfer.

Still, Bareilly is not such a bad place as I had thought. Mind you, it is very hot after the cool hills. The max. temp. is daily between 90 and 95 degrees and the minimum seldom much below 80, so that it is at night that one feels it most. Up at Ranikhet, two blankets were usually necessary at night, but here, even with a fan going all night, one sheet's the most that one needs. Of course, the heat is nothing like it was in Allahabad before the monsoon. According to the newspapers, Bareilly has had over 40 inches of rain since June 1st, but since the date of my arrival here (which funnily enough was on the anniversary of the outbreak of the war), there has been no sign of rain. Everything looks very green and fresh though, and, in fact, the country here is quite attractive, which is remarkable for the plains.

Saturday Sept. 14th

A week has passed since I broke off 2 lines above, and we have had some rain – on Sunday night last.

News of the air raids that you have been going through lately has sounded so bad that this afternoon I decided to take advantage of the new E.F.M.[51] telegram service – special reduced rates to the U.K. for members of H. M. Forces; it only cost me R. 2/13/– for 10 words. Even now, perhaps, the message is hurtling over the cable between Bombay and London; on the other hand they are just as likely to hold it up a couple of days at Bombay if there is excess traffic. It was rather a bald telegram and I had to sign it 'Repton'; one of the conditions for these special telegrams is that the sender signs his surname only. I hope for a reply very shortly.

---

51 Expeditionary Forces Message.

I said in a previous letter that if I were promoted to the I.A.C.C., I should be able to send some of my pay home each month to help you; however, I am afraid I shall not be able to start until next month, owing to the fact that my pay has been coming in in driblets this month.

The change-over to the India Unattached List rather complicates one's accounts, for they have to be taken over by the C.M.A. (Controller of Military Accounts – incidentally an Indian), with whom one deals direct for the future. When I had to leave Ranikhet my I.A.C.C. pay for August, due on the 1st September, had not come through from the C.M.A., such change-overs being rather lengthy affairs. So, all I was to receive was the final balance of my account with the Queen's and a sum of R. 30/– which I was allowed to draw in advance as I was being transferred. The total of this was about 85/–, of which I received, after various bills and stoppages had been deducted, including a somewhat ponderous bar bill accounted for by the functions every Wednesday and the expensive night on which promotion was celebrated, the magnificent sum of R. 2/8/–. Of course, I had to tap the Chief Clerk for a further advance of R. 30/–, which, after some arguing, he gave me unofficially. Today the remainder of my pay came through from the C.M.A., amounting to something over R. 100/–. But after I have repaid the Chief Clerk his advance of R. 30/– and settled various other debts, bought some of the necessaries I require and sent off some letters, I shall not be too well off, which is why I can't quite manage to send any this month. But next month, i.e. the 1st October, I shall do so without fail. I am sorry I have failed to be of any use this month.

Sunday 15th

Today is the anniversary of that day (memorable to me) when I first entered the 'prison gates' of Stoughton Barracks, and there is not a single militiaman here with whom one can celebrate the date. Shall I still be in the army this time next year, I wonder? Life is a hundred times more bearable now, but I would still give anything to be home again; India can be quite pleasant, in fact it improves with acquaintance, but there is only one England.

As there are no British troops in Bareilly now, only odd members of the Ordnance Corps or Brigade HQ or M.E.S. (military engineering) or the Supply Corps, those of us who are unmarried or cannot afford to occupy a separate bungalow have quarters in the R.I.A.S.C.[52] Sergeants' Mess. It is a bit lonely having rooms of one's own after a year spent in various barrack rooms, but it is a definite improvement really, especially in that it is possible to get peace when one wants it. The food, too, is extraordinarily good after what I have been used to, and is served up quite luxuriously, but there is a 'catch', namely that one is stung for quite a large Mess bill at the end of the month. Every day, we have porridge and eggs and bacon for '*chota hazri*' (breakfast), curry and some other dish for lunch, and a three-course supper of soup, savoury and another dish – quite stylish living for the army, isn't it? And I fear it may make you, who are now being rationed so severely, a little envious.

I have managed to keep my bar bill fairly well down this month, as there are not so many occasions for 'having a quick one' as there were up at Ranikhet. At the only big 'do' we have had in the Mess here so far, given as a sort of farewell party to certain units and parts of units who were about to leave Bareilly permanently and were going on a long journey (!), all the drinks and refreshments were free, as we paid for the expenses out of some grant or other. It was quite a riotous evening and ended up with general singing of old and new songs.

There's only one cinema here, so if one is a fairly discriminating picture-goer, as I think (with all due respect to Sylvia) I may call myself, one does not go very often. I saw a very good one my first night here – William Powell and Myrna Loy in *Another Thin Man*. I've also seen Deanna Durbin in *It's a Date* while I've been here, making that my third Deanna film! The best film I've seen lately, though, is *The Wizard of Oz*, which I saw up at Ranikhet about a month ago. I found it really fascinating – you've seen it, perhaps? If *Snow White* was as good, I'm sorry I missed it, but I did overhear someone say that it wasn't half as good.

I've had my watch mended this week, after leaving it torpid for 3 months; at first it didn't seem to have been mended properly for it kept stopping, but I think it's all right now. I keep meaning to finish off the reel in my camera, with a view to sending you some more snaps, but somehow one never seems to get the opportunity. There is still the same film in it with which I went up to Ranikhet, and only 5 pictures taken. Some of the snaps you've sent me recently have been very good. The one of Jocelyn on guard made him

---

52   Royal Indian Army Service Corps.

look every inch a 'blue jacket' but was not much like the Jocelyn one used to know. I am still meaning to write to him; please tell him to expect a letter soon.

Yes, I am sorry I was not at home to help you dispose of the wonderful crop of raspberries that you have apparently had this year. I fear, too, that I shall not be at home this winter to help eat the pounds and pounds of jam that you have made. Sad, isn't it? My estimate of when the war will finish is about next May or June, and the earliest I could expect to be home after that would be about the following January, i.e. 1942 – even that is putting it conservatively, don't you think? A year or two, though, seems very little out here after one has been some time in contact with men of the I.A.C.C. and the Ordnance Corps etc. who've been out here 15 years or more.

On my last Sunday at Ranikhet three of us went for a long afternoon walk up and down and round the '*cuds*' (hills). It was my first really long walk in the wilds there, and up till then I had not realised quite how beautiful the place could be. After many days of rain and plenteous cloud, it was one of those bright, sunny afternoons with enough cloud to make the sky interesting. We went through thick pine forests which reminded me of those at home, and passed orange groves and apple orchards. At the bottom of the valley was a young stream, captivating in its windings and the sparkle of its waters as they passed over the rocks. It was a miniature torrent after the rains, and quite difficult to cross. The pines darkened it enough to make it interesting, for they came right down to the edge. The climb up from this valley bottom was very arduous, though, and I found myself sadly out of training. Near the summit we stopped at a dairy and refreshed ourselves with two or three pints of fresh milk. Yes, after that walk I wished I had gone out of my way to see more of Ranikhet's surrounding country but somehow one was always working too late on weekdays, and on Sundays a rest seemed called for.

As I travelled down in the bus from Ranikhet to Kathgodam, I noticed how greatly the monsoon had changed the country. Everywhere the trees were a dark green and thick with foliage and all vegetation was overgrown and luxuriant. Passing through the villages, one saw great melons and marrows and swelling gourds overflowing onto the road from the small gardens, where gigantic sunflowers reared their heads. The monsoon certainly does bring life to India – it is the same down here in Bareilly, which is now quite a lovely place.

The funny part about my coming down here was that after 3 months spent up in the comparative cool of the hills, during which time I felt nearly always fit and had not a single cold, one of my first actions at Bareilly was to catch a nasty chest cold; I suppose this can be accounted for by the unhealthy mixture of getting very hot and then sitting under an electric fan – I'm O.K. now though.

Lately I've had quite a few letters and the papers have been arriving, though in a very irregular manner. Anything posted by sea mail seems to take between eight and ten weeks to reach me; of course an extra few days is caused by letters having to chase round the United Provinces for me – first Allahabad, then up to Ranikhet, then down again to Bareilly. Yesterday (Sept. 21st)[53] your letter of July 21st arrived, posted at the same time as Gervase's air mail, as you said. Gervase's letter arrived nearly a month ago. So there is still a substantial difference. I also received two letters this week from Mr. Allwark and one from Perpetua. The latest parcel of papers from you was July 29th's.

Congratulations to Jocelyn on his being offered a commission – please convey mine pending a letter from me – he certainly seems to have found his feet all right. It makes me feel rather ashamed that I have not got on the same. Of course, I made a mistake in the first place in blindly joining the Infantry, and again in putting in for India. There are such things as Emergency Commissions out here, but at present I should find it rather difficult to put in for one. It is impossible, of course, for me to obtain a commission in the I.A.C.C., as this goes by seniority. So it seems best to hang on till the situation is clearer. This Brigade, you see, has been receiving all sorts of conflicting orders about moving. We are quite likely to move overseas, but there is nothing definite given out yet. You understand, don't you, that I've got to be very careful in what I say about movements now, as I know a lot more about what's happening than I did, and therefore if I give anything away and am found out by the censor, I am liable to be dropped in much more severely? They return 'offending' letters to units for 'disciplinary action', you know.

I am sorry to hear of the serious turn that has taken place in the financial situation; I do hope you'll be able to carry on and that Mr. Price will be able to help. Gervase did not mention it in his letter. As long as I am on my present pay, I will do my best to help a little each month, from now on.

---

53 Christopher wrote this letter sporadically over 15 days, being busy moving to Bareilly and after his promotion to Sergeant and answering letters from home which took a long time arriving.

I have still a lot to say, but have reached my limit, so I will continue in a letter to Gervase. I intend to send this, if possible, by the Hong Kong-America air route and Gervase's letter-to-be by the other air route, both on the same day, and you can tell me which is the shorter. I am sorry that this letter has been so long in the writing and that I have taken so long since I last wrote. It's hateful being so far away from you all at home now that you are having such a hard time to make ends meet, and on top of that those terrible air raids – no reply to my wire yet. Well then –

Best love to all from Christopher

Bareilly

U.P.

22nd Sept.

My dear Gervase,

    This is in continuation of a long letter to Mother and Dad that I have just finished, to enable me to say some of the things that I did not have room to say in that letter. I don't think it must be quite so long as I want to get both letters posted tomorrow. If one letter goes via Hong Kong, the other via S. Africa, between them they will have encircled the world.

    I must thank you for your letter of July 21st which reached me up at Lucknow District about Aug. 25th. The long letter telling of your holiday, I mean. It sounded an interesting nomadic holiday, full of variety. You certainly seem to have made my previous day's record for a cycle ride of 66 miles (to Blackdown and back) look silly; so also has Dickon with his trips to Basingstoke and Henley. I was fascinated with your description of the visit of Jocelyn and yourself to Hayling and all its old spots. Were you able to recapture the old atmosphere of our Portsmouth walks, or was the war too present? I suppose that one annoying thing about a cycling holiday was that you kept being stopped by police and L.D.V.s[54] and ordered to produce your identity card. Is it possible to escape absolutely

---

54   Local Defence Volunteers, known as the Home Guard – civilian militias formed from May 1940 to defend Britain against Nazi invasion, immortalised in the BBC comedy series *Dad's Army*.

from the war atmosphere anywhere in the English countryside now, like it was when you, Sylvia, Dickon and myself went for that ride to Leith Hill last year about a week after the opening of the war?

I still have the old love for Sussex and faith in another walking tour over its Downs when this frightful business is over. I suppose its coast must be pretty heavily scarred by the ravages of German bombers now. In the news the other day I heard something about a raid on Brooklands and damage caused there – you must have seen something of it, I presume. A strange and terrible world, isn't it?

Monday Sept. 23rd

Yesterday I had my first swim since early May, when I had one or two dips in the miniature swimming bath at Allahabad. My swim yesterday evening was in the Garrison Sergeants' Mess Bath, which is now almost deserted owing to the very few British soldiers here. Quite a decent size with a sprung diving board which I failed to try – must learn to dive one of these days.

We've got a tennis court by the Mess here and every night the native 'ball boys' put up the nets and get everything ready, but it is seldom that anyone plays. If I could but get hold of a racket somewhere there is a bloke who would play me. That's the trouble with being away from a regular army unit – one gets little or no sport unless it's of one's own making. I suppose I must be badly in need of exercise, for I don't even do any walking down here; just go back and forth from the office – in fact, back and forth from anywhere – on a bicycle.

I produced my pocket chess set the other day and found a bloke who could play. We had a game and now, I fear, I've started him on a craze for it, as he wants me to play every evening. We tried to get a decent set down at the bazaar and in the city, but so far have had no luck, only Indian-style sets having been discovered, which we do not want.

The weather's beginning to cool off now and soon will be really pleasant. We have had one or two heavy falls of rain just lately and now the skies are more English-looking, with a variety of cloud and occasional threats of a shower – not the monotonous perpetuity of clear blue sky and glaring sun that we usually get. This place gets very cold in the winter – if we're here then (!)

This afternoon I wore army boots and puttees[55] for the first time since early June – ordinarily one wears shoes and stockings in the office, and up in the hills we wore 'slacks' and shoes – did they feel queer! All Brigade staff and many others had to turn out for a lecture and demonstration on the working of a 'field ambulance', one of which is encamped here at present. It was quite comic and the old Medical Colonel who was giving the lecture didn't really seem to know what he was talking about. It was supposed to be a parade of sorts, but very different from those I remember at Allahabad.

I had rather a bitter disappointment the other day. A cipher telegram from Lucknow District came in, ordering us to despatch one Temporary Sergeant for overseas within 48 hours of receiving a letter containing detailed instructions which would follow. As there were only two T/Sgts in the Brigade, myself and another chap who's been here some years, I guessed I should be sent, and in fact it was almost certain that I was going, until the next day arrived another telegram sanctioning the promotion to T/Sgt of a learner clerk (like I was classified at Ranikhet at first) who had been recommended about a month before. At the end of the message was this cogent sentence – 'This man may be detailed for the appointment notified in my No. So-and-So' (the cipher I spoke of yesterday). This put paid to my chances of going, as they did not seem to want to lose me after I had just been posted here to make up the establishment and just as I seemed to be getting into the work. Yes, it was a disappointment, and now that lucky bloke is on his way to the 'collecting camp' for the overseas force that he's going with. I don't think I've divulged any information above that might be of use to the enemy, do you? I was down at the station the other night seeing off some fellows (all one seems to do in this place is see people off somewhere!) – we were actually seeing them off in the 1st-class refreshment room and bar, when who should walk in but an old pal of mine from Ranikhet. They say that, in spite of its size, you can't go far in India without meeting someone you've met before. Which seems to be fairly true. Of course, further celebration was called for and in the end the train was only caught by racing up the platform. I believe several glasses and bottles of beer got carried on to Delhi.

We were supposed to be moving down to Jhansi next month for Brigade Training Exercises – from there we might have moved somewhere else – but that was cancelled a short while ago. Now we may do the training

---

55 Strips of cloth wrapped round the legs from ankles to knees.

here. All the Indian battalion and supporting troops in the Brigade are fully mechanised, but only just lately so that accidents are rather frequent, these Indian drivers being undependable. One of them nearly killed myself and the Head Clerk as we were travelling in a truck the day I arrived here.

I doubt whether we shall spend Christmas in Bareilly, but one can never tell these days. I should have liked to have seen a bit of Lucknow this winter, for this place is very quiet. After all the varying rumours I see that the Queen's are moving up to the Frontier this autumn. I think I'm glad on the whole not to be going up there! You do hear some people say that the Frontier is the best and healthiest part of India and that they enjoyed their time there more than anywhere else. At Razmak, where the Queen's are supposed to be going, one is 7,000-odd feet above sea level, and there is thick snow in the winter. However, every regiment that goes up there suffers a certain amount of casualties from sniping and the occasional ambushes of these tribesmen. One lives inside a barbed-wire compound and seldom moves out except for patrols. Always one must be on guard. I don't think I should enjoy life there very much […]

No answer to my telegram yet. I'm beginning to get a little worried. Out here I can't really imagine what these air raids must be like. I suppose you have been kept awake by them night after night like the others one reads of, or don't you bother to take shelter in Chertsey? I see that many important streets and buildings of London have been damaged. I expect you are glad in some ways that Dad is not working in London at present, although I'm afraid you must be having a very hard time with no money coming in. Let us pray that something will happen to change our luck. I would hate to return to any other place than St. Ann's Lodge, Chertsey. Just shows you how we have come to look upon it as our permanent home, doesn't it?

How is your job getting on? Still rather boring, or don't you mind it so much now? I was thinking, the other day, how well represented the varying branches of the services are by Reptons – Jocelyn in the navy, Humphry and myself in the army, Gareth in the R.A.F., Dickon in the Home Guard (don't you fancy that now?), Bianca in the A.T.S.[56] and Sylvia in the Land Army. By the way, has Sylvia started on a farm yet? I would very much like a letter from her, so get on to her, will you? I've really written two to her now, but one of mine went down in the *Hannibal*. I think the others might write a bit

---

56 Auxiliary Territorial Service; the women's branch of the army during World War II.

more often too, for after all there's only one of me at this end to keep up the correspondence, whereas you are many.

A minor tragedy has occurred – I believe I've lost *Highways and Byways in Sussex*. I carried it loose to read on the train, and I know it got as far as Bareilly, but since then I've not seen it. Tell Dickon not to worry.

We've got a good wireless in the Mess here – very like, in fact, almost identical with one at home, but of course it's harder to get stations as there are few in the vicinity. We get the news from Daventry quite well, though Z— [illegible] is a far stronger station. Since I've been in India, though, I've never heard any real music. Still, if one ever hears them again, Beethoven and Brahms and the rest of them will be fresh again.

Well, it looks as if I must peter out – sorry this isn't one of my best letter-writing efforts, but you shall have another soon. Remember me to Fr. Gerald and others.

Best love from Christopher

HQ 8th Indian Infantry Brigade
Bareilly
United Provinces
Sun Oct. 13th

My dear Mother and Father and all at home,

I am so sorry that my letter-writing has been so infrequent these past months, but in the coming weeks I shall try to atone for the deficiency. One letter a week seems to be the limit of my output these days, and so the trouble is that when that letter is to someone else, I fail to write to you.

This will, I fear, be only a short letter, as I have not got much time! Time for what, you may ask, and that I will leave to your imagination except to say that in future my address will be as above, but instead of 'Bareilly, U.P.', you must put 'c/o Sub-Postmaster, New Delhi'. One reason for this is that it would prevent the letter chasing round India after me – the chasing will probably be increased now that my former regiment has moved up to the N.W. Frontier; yes, after all the contrary rumours that's where they've ended up. So that if you were still unaware of my move to Lucknow District last June, your letters might go first to Allahabad, then up to Razmak, then east again, possibly to Ranikhet if my regiment forgot that Lucknow District had moved down to the plains, then down to Lucknow itself and finally up to Bareilly. Thus, the letter would have travelled nearly 3,000 miles round India in search of me. Quite such a long journey as that is, however, unlikely. Of course, there is another reason for addressing me c/o Sub-Postmaster, but as I said before, I'll leave that for you to figure out.

Your answer to my wire arrived on the morning of Oct. 1st, nearly 3 weeks after I wired you. I did not think it would take so long. The reason for my sending a telegram at all was that the air raids appeared to be becoming very bad and I wanted to make sure that you were all all right. When you addressed me by my Regiment, were you under the impression that they had moved to Bareilly? I said, 'Am transferred Inf. Bde. Bareilly', hoping that you would understand that it meant 'HQ, Bareilly Infantry Brigade'. 'Repton, Inf. Bde., Bareilly, India' would have been sufficient. However, you didn't have to pay for the address, did you? I didn't.

On October 3rd I sent £5 by telegraphic M.O. which I hope you have now received. I sent it that way because your letter of Aug. 10th told me how bad things were becoming and I knew that if I sent it by registered letter it would take weeks and weeks. I know it is only a little, but from now on I am going to try to send home something to help each month. I do hope that Mr. Price will be able to help in some way. Of course, on account of this change-over that I've been hinting at, it's going to be rather difficult to send the money unless I can manage to arrange for an allotment of pay, which I'm afraid I've left rather late. It would be far simpler that way, of course, but might take some time as it's got to go through the C.M.A. (Command Paymaster) to the M.A.G. (Military Accountant General) and thence to the India Office. A lengthy business in these times of half-severed communications.

I shall be enclosing one or two photographs with this letter – none very good, I'm afraid. The 5 taken up at Ranikhet were sadly disappointing. One failed to come out, in the one of myself wearing civvies the light has ruined the picture, and the somewhat ineffectual study in white is my abortive attempt to 'snap' the snow peaks of the Himalayas; if you get hold of a magnifying glass you might be able to discover some trace of them, I didn't. The other two, though quite clear, seem purposeless and give no idea of the true grandeur and beauty of the mountain scene; you might note, however, that the nearest of the dun hills visible is over 5 miles away. The two best pictures, of myself and another bloke (he's a Sergeant in the Ordnance Workshops) up against a military vehicle, were taken here, just outside the garrison Mess in which we live. I enclose the negative of mine, in case it is worth enlarging.

The weather is cooling off beautifully now; in fact, it becomes definitely 'chilly' at night, though judged by English standards 65 degrees is not cool for a night temperature. Hasn't this summer raced by, and now while you anticipate with dread the long drear winter nights and the added misery of the war, I welcome the relief that winter brings. Sorry, I don't mean the German 'Winter Relief Fund'.

My weapon is now not a rifle, but a revolver, and I have been having some practice lately in the early mornings. It's amazing how inaccurate one can be with the thing, even at 10 yards' range. It's a very dangerous weapon too, and I don't fancy carrying it about with me all the time as I'll have to latch on; there's no safety catch on a service revolver, you see.

Christopher in Allahabad, January 1940. 'On the roof of D co. barracks, cookhouse behind me'

I've not been very hard-worked since I've been down here; was much busier at Ranikhet.

How is Sylvia getting on in the Land Army? Has she started somewhere else after her plum-picking in Lincolnshire? And Dickon is working at Vickers, is he? He must find it very strenuous with the present armaments speed-up in progress. Are Leila and Ros still at St. Maur's? I was just wondering how I should get used to all the changes that have taken place at home since I left when I return. I say when, for there does not appear to be any likelihood of my doing so for a long time yet.

Went to a dance last night at the R.K. Railway Institute but did not dance much or find it very amusing. As it was in aid of the War Fund and East India Fund for Spitfires, they charged the exorbitant price of R. 2/– for admission. The trouble with these Railway Institute dos is that there are too many Anglo-Indians present. The Anglo-Indian question is always a difficult one.

Well, it looks as if I shall have to stop here. I hope that all are well and that air raids are becoming less severe.

Your loving son,
Christopher

Somewhere at sea
Tuesday Oct. 22nd

My dear Father and Mother and all at home,

My above 'address' unfortunately prevents me from telling you much in this letter on account of the strict censorship of all mails.[57] For the present you must remain in the dark as to what I am doing on the sea and why, and where I am going and whence.

---

57 Christopher spent two months intermittently writing this letter. He started it in October while sailing from India to Malaya, and didn't finish it until December, after travelling overland from the west coast of peninsular Malaya to Kota Bharu on the north-east coast, where his brigade was based. Aware of censorship, especially during troop movements, he omitted place names while in Malaya. The letter arrived in Chertsey on the 12th February 1941.

I want to send you this short letter, however, informing you of my present situation, as my last letter from ****** must have been rather puzzling to you – that is, if you have yet received it.

In contrast to the last time I voyaged the oceans, accommodation is excellent, and I have no complaints. Actually, myself and the other British soldiers on board, being on our own, have been lucky enough to get a 1st-class cabin between us, although in other respects we are travelling 2nd class. Even in 2nd class the food is excellent, and we get a very varied menu.

However, the blackout regulations, which have to be rigorously complied with, are a 'bugbear' to us. At night the saloon is only dimly lit with blue lights and it is impossible to read or write, and with the portholes tightly shut the temperature of one's cabin is worse than that of a hot-house – fortunately there are electric fans, but even they do not really allay the heat. Still, war is war, one must agree.

By the way, in case you've got the wrong idea, I am not on my way back to England. It is unlikely that I shall return now until about six months after the cession of hostilities, which brings us to about the middle of December 1941. (You must excuse my bad writing, but I have still not got used to this pen.)

The voyage has been uneventful so far, and the sea pretty mild. I could wish it would liven up a bit.

I am afraid that it's going to be months before I get a letter from you again, with all this forwarding business. You've not succeeded in getting up to date with my changing addresses since May, have you? I shall pause awhile now to taste the cool oceanic breezes and think of more matter for this letter…

October 27th, Sunday
Still at sea – and apparently at a loss for further news, or was it the blackout?

Nov. 6th
On land (for a week now) and to be more explicit, 'somewhere in Malaya', which is, I am given to understand, the most that I am allowed to give away concerning my actual address.

Dec. 7th

I think the time I have taken writing this must be a record – even for me. I am terribly sorry that I have written so few letters in the last month or two, but since the beginning of October everything seems to have been one long rush – well, perhaps not a rush but one hasn't been able to settle down anywhere, if you see what I mean. I sent off a letter to Gervase from our last resting place, unfortunately by sea mail as I wasn't very well at the time. I intend to send off a cable to go from here as soon as I can get down to the Post Office. The last letter I had from you was dated about the middle of August, as far as I remember, and reached me at Bareilly at the beginning of October. I hope you got the money that I sent all right – I am going to try and send off some more quite soon. I would have done so earlier, but with all this moving around the system of payment has been very irregular.

It seems hardly worthwhile picking up the threads of this letter again after such a long interval, but I thought you might like to see what I wrote during the voyage. I'm always wondering how you all are, not having heard from you for so long, but on the other hand, 'no news is good news'; you've been able to send me one telegram and I know that if anything did happen you would wire me at once.

At the present time (and probably for many months to come) we are more or less in the wilds. Have a good look at the stamps on this letter and then consult an atlas, and if you can't deduce where I am, you're not very cute. The camp (actually it's not a camp in the sense that one ordinarily means, but a hutted camp) is situated in a palm grove and coconuts are for the taking, though I haven't yet reached the stage of being able to swarm up a tree and get one.

Before the rest of the Brigade reached So-and-So – our station previous to coming up here – I had quite an easy time for a week or so; no work, as we hadn't established an HQ anywhere, and a good Mess. But when everybody arrived, they moved straight into a tented camp, some way outside the city, and of course we of the advance party had to move in too. It was rather an unpleasant contrast, for the weather immediately broke and everywhere in the camp there was mud, and inside tents it was so damp that nothing could be kept dry. And when they arrived the mail started coming in and the work started, but the conditions were far from suitable for work, with a downpour every morning and the wind and rain pouring into the tent.

However, we'd only been in there about ten days when we came up here by train, through the jungle and rubber forests – entirely different from India, the country out here – only to find after a day or so that the weather was far worse. Jove! Does it rain or does it rain, as we used to say! Puts India's monsoon, which I only saw in the hills of course, in the shade. Funny, isn't it? I've just finished seeing out one monsoon in India and now I land up in what seems to be a far worse one. They get two monsoons a year here, the S.W. and the N.E. This is the N.E. and it sure comes in from the sea. Can hear the sea roaring during the heavy weather, but I haven't been down to see it yet. May do tomorrow (Sunday) if it keeps fine and have a swim.

One doesn't feel the heat too much here; the temperature's pretty even all the time. It's a bit sticky of course, but not so bad as Bombay. The mosquitoes are very plentiful and annoying, but I haven't had malaria yet.

Well, here it is nearing my second Christmas away from home and no sign of my returning yet. In fact, I seem to be still further away than ever, and you more inaccessible.

The mail comes out here twice a week by fast train and we go down to the office to sort it out – that is, officers and Privates. Eagerly, I look for one from you but no luck yet; perhaps tomorrow – Sundays and Wednesdays it comes, and I suppose you too are wondering what's happened to my letters. Tell me in your next letter how Humphry's getting on. I haven't heard from him since he joined up. And Gareth and Jocelyn and all the far-flung members of the family. Don't forget to address here, HQ 8th Ind. Inf. Bde., Malaya, and not c/o Sub-Postmaster, New Delhi, as I told you from India, as the old Sub-P.M. or whatever he is seems to have [illegible] letters for months. Well, I think I've written enough for tonight and will try to finish tomorrow.

Next day

Did not go swimming this afternoon as I was on duty but heard from those who did that it was very good. Not possible to swim as the rollers are too big and powerful, but good sport.

At the moment there are 17 of us in a combined Sergeants' Mess made up from various units of the Brigade HQ – Signals, Engineers, Ordnance (mainly for vehicle repair) and Medical. Apart from the officers, some of whom are Indian and a few R.A.M.C.[58] orderlies, that is the sum total of British troops in the Brigade. Near the camp there's a small air force station with about 5 blokes there on their own. Sometimes we go over to this place and sometimes they come over to ours. The only other British soldier on the spot is a Sergeant-Major of the Royal Sussex (didn't you say Humphry had been transferred to them?), long separated from his regiment and apparently more or less in charge of the local Malay Volunteer Force. We went over to his place the other night too and had a few glasses of beer.

We are just beginning to settle down now and have started the Mess going quite well. We are getting the field service scale of rations, which is quite good and plentiful as regards such items as cheese, bacon, butter, jam, meat, etc. (sorry, I was forgetting that you can scarcely get such things now), but we started the system of everybody paying a few cents extra per day and supplementing the rations with things that are not ordinarily issued.

When we first arrived here it was pretty awful – nothing ready, the rations not turning up, and tons of work to do with only a makeshift office to work in, and to confuse matters still more, half our HQ stayed behind in So-and-So to see the rest of the Brigade off, so one didn't quite know where one was. Now we are functioning pretty smoothly, though there's far more work than one is ordinarily supposed to get on field service – actually we're neither the one thing nor the other at present.

It's not rained for two or three days now, which is a wonder, but at the beginning of the week it came down in torrents for two or three days and the roads, which are not exactly good at ordinary times, were flooded in parts with over a foot of water. All the native houses are built on stilts six feet or more above the ground, which gives one an idea what to expect when the rain really gets into its stride.

It's rather difficult to get down to the town, such as it is. It's too far to walk and there's no bus service, so the only way to get down is to get hold of one of our military trucks, which is not too easy. We're all supposed to learn to drive in the Brigade but so far there has not been the opportunity. I am rather looking forward to doing so.

I daresay that when I dropped you the hint, at Bareilly, that I was going overseas, you thought I was going to Egypt. Actually, I believe we were intended for there, for I know there was a big change in plans towards the end of September.

---

58   Royal Army Medical Corps.

Four of us who were together at Lucknow District have all left now. One went up to the Records Office at Army Headquarters, Simla, and I had the surprise of meeting the others down at Bombay; one was doing an embarkation course which, as far as I could see, consists of sitting peacefully down at the docks and watching people get on and off the ships.

As yet I have not decided whether I prefer this country to India. The climate is certainly more like England's – in summertime – and there are no extremes. The luxuriant forest and vegetation everywhere is, too, in great contrast to the vast, arid monotony of the plain of India. One thing about India, though: the newspapers did arrive regularly first thing in the morning; here we have to be content with two-day-old newspapers. The railways are not so well developed, you see.

Well, I think it's time to say goodbye now, so a Merry Christmas, a Happy New Year and a pleasant Easter to all.

Best love,
Christopher

6092414 Sgt. C. Repton
I.A.C.C.
HQ 8th Ind. Inf. Bde.
Malaya
18th November

My dear Gervase,

I am afraid that it is over a month now since I wrote any sort of letter. My last one was posted (I hope) from our port of embarkation and was only a short one with little news in it, so you must be wondering by this time where I am and how I am getting on.

Of course, what I can tell you of my movements and whereabouts is strictly limited by the censorship which is in general application here; in India I never received a censored letter from you, nor, I conclude, did you from me, but in Malaya we are supposed to be at war.

At the present time we are under canvas for a short while, prior to moving to a wilder and more uncivilised part of the country, and I am writing this in one of our marquee-offices.

I, myself, travelled here with the advance party that was sent, and until the arrival of the main body lived quite comfortably in another unit's Mess. The change to camp conditions came as rather a rude shock and I expect that the main body, who were dumped here straight from the ship, felt it even more after the five-course lunches etc. and the cosy bunks with reading lamps and the luxuries installed.

The food that we are getting in camp at the moment is about the worst that I have experienced since the voyage I made out to India. Of course, our Indian cooks are rather handicapped by the rain falling into the fire and into the soup and in fact into everything that it can possibly manage to fall into, and by the customary non-arrival of rations until the time of the meal. The meals we used to have on our walking tours seemed like banquets, you remember, but even living in the open air here has no power to make the food seem other than what it is.

Apart from that, the camp's not too bad; of course it rains somewhat heavily every day now, and 'lake' would be a better word than 'morass' to describe the state of the ground, but that's only a minor matter: nothing is ever dry, but we like it that way – it prevents one from getting too hot.

Seriously though, it does show you that we soldiers out East are having too easy a time, that we should even notice the fact that we are sleeping under canvas. It is difficult to realise out here that there is a terrible war going on in and around Europe, and I don't suppose one ever will until something happens to wake things up a bit in this part of the globe. You recall how little we thought about air raids and the grimness of modern war until war was actually declared, and even then, we did not worry much in the first months of the war. But now you are really going through it, I'm afraid, and facing the music for the rest of the Empire. Of course, I don't know what your general outlook towards the war is like now, but I should imagine that it is very changed from the casual attitude that we all affected, even up to the time I left. From what one reads in the papers it is to be gathered that everyone is standing up to the attack with stoical calm and determination; this is not difficult to believe. But I guess it must take some getting used to before one overcomes one's natural terror at the sound of bombs falling close at hand. You must all have had some harrowing experiences by this time, I expect. However, I am thankful to know that all was well with you at the end of September (your telegram), since when the raids on London and the South do not appear to have been quite so severe, though Coventry's just had a very terrible day, I see.

When I went to a cinema the other day, I saw a newsreel showing some of the damage that had been done to London. It shook me to see how Oxford Street had suffered; John Lewis gutted by fire and almost a ruin, Peter Robinson's and the other buildings round Oxford Circus smashed and crumbling, and Selfridge's too badly damaged. How's Chertsey getting on? Has it taken any knocks yet?

I had hoped to come back to a normal England and to pick up all the old threads again, but it seems that everything will be changed – the old traditions, modes of living, amenities, class distinctions, music, literature and above all, people. Even under normal conditions, the soldier who does 3 or 4 years' service in India or some other distant corner of the Empire, without leave, is utterly lost when he eventually finds his way home. But with this war changing the mentality of the people in England from day to day, I'm bound to be thoroughly out of my depth when I do get home, which will be only heaven knows when.

I am longing to get a letter from you for it is nearly two months since I had your last, but now I've put still more time between us. Did you ever, by the way, get that letter that I posted from India via Hong Kong? It's supposed to be a quick route but is rather expensive, especially here, where it is 2 dollars 60 (a Straits dollar is said to be worth 2/4 in sterling; but actually it hasn't got that purchasing power except for drinks and smokes in canteens and Messes where stuff may be obtained at N.A.A.F.I.[59] prices, free of all duty – there is a N.A.A.F.I. organisation out here although there is none in India, whence they were ousted by the Indian Canteen Contractors forming themselves into a syndicate.

---

59   Navy, Army and Air Force Institutes; a company set up by the British government in
     1920 to provide recreational facilities and sell goods to servicemen and their families.

Nov. 20th

It sure does rain in this place. Every day for the past week great black clouds have rolled up about 11 a.m. and there has been a terrific downpour, leaving everything soaked, and now this morning, it was raining when I got up and still is from a leaden sky, steadily and more in the stately English manner than usual.

Of course, this constant rain makes the country very pretty – everything green and luxuriant, and everywhere grow palm trees (coconut). Nowhere is the fierce aridity of India to be met with. Actually, I prefer the dry heat of India, which is healthier than the humid, exhausting heat generally experienced here, where the temperature never rises above 95 degrees but seldom falls below 70.

I think I'll finish this letter here and write you a longer and 'newsier' one when I've got more time, and better conditions under which to write. Write me often as you can as I shall be wanting letters in days to come. Hope all are well.

Love,
Christopher

HQ, 8th Indian Infantry Brigade
MALAYA
December 1940

My dear Gervase,

As it happens to be my tour of duty at the HQ office and there's not much work on, I'm taking this opportunity of starting to type a letter to you – I say 'start' as I may never finish it.

You must think I'm very thoughtless for having written so few letters during the past three or four months. I can offer no excuses except to say that the longer one is away from home, the harder it becomes to write. However, I posted a long air mail letter off on Monday which should reach you in a couple of months' time. I also wired some money which should be well on its way to you now. I hope it will bring a wire back from you.

I wonder how you are getting on now without me! Probably much less Gervasian than you were. I'm not sure yet whether you've joined the 'Parashots', as they call them, or not; Mother said something about you and Dickon joining the L.D.V.s, but I'm uncertain whether she said you were thinking of joining or had joined. It must be quite fun for you. Actually, I've not held a rifle in six months, and we're supposed to be at war. When I knew the Brigade was going overseas, I rather hoped that it would be Egypt, as I'd like to be able to say that I'd seen something of the war when it's all over – if it ever is! However, there's very good news from Greece and Egypt now, isn't there? It looks as if the Italians in Libya will soon be packing in. Then I suppose the next step, when Italy's given in, is that Germany will stage another invasion to protect her 'ally' from the ravages of Britain, unless, that is, we have the boldness to get in first, and with a man like Churchill at the helm such a course is far from improbable.

Are you fed up and bored with the war now or has your spirit changed, as the newspapers seem to imply that everyone else's has, to one of steadfast resistance and determination to see the thing through? You must remember that I left at a time when things were pretty quiet and most people were rather bored with the whole affair, so that it is difficult for me to realise how much the general outlook of people has changed. For all I know, this letter coming from a more or less peaceful corner of the Empire may be so out of place as to jar on you.

Here I am sitting in our office hut amid the coconut palms, and gloomy grey clouds are scudding overhead just like an autumn day in England; I'm forgetting, though, it's winter now, isn't it, and your thoughts must be turning towards Christmas, a little wistfully perhaps, like mine. I don't suppose there'll be a very large gathering at St. Ann's Lodge this year. Perhaps next year we'll have the happy reunion; that is, one hopes that it will be happy. Just now, though, it seems about the most unattainable thing in the world to me – no, there's one thing more so, because it's more delightful, and that's another walking tour in Elysium, or if you like to give it its proper name, Sussex, county of one's dreams. What think you, my "vasian heen', as we used to say?

In the meantime, I suppose, one has got to make the best of it wherever one is and at the moment I have not much to grumble about, as I had when I first went out to India if you remember. I suppose that was merely due to the fact that I didn't like the strangeness of the East at first, and the strangeness of the army in the East.

There's a lovely beach about three or four miles from here, almost deserted except for a few primitive native dwellings nearby, and on Tuesday three or four of us went down in a truck (Military Lorry) and had a swim. The palm trees come right down to within a few yards of the sea – there is only a very narrow strip of sloping, sandy beach – and the place is almost exactly like one used to imagine a desert island appeared, except for the ferocity of the 'breakers' at present. There is a sort of monsoon on, you see, and they come rolling in very powerfully; although it's great fun fighting them they're almost too much for one, and when the tide's going out there's a very strong undercurrent – gave me quite a scare the other day when I thought it was too strong for me to get back to the shore. One ordinarily thinks of the tropic seas as serenely blue and calm, doesn't one? But these are very muddy-looking, which is, I believe a characteristic of the China Seas. Still, it's delightful having such an Arcadian beach so near.

On Wednesday December the 18th your letter of Sept. 15th arrived – over 3 months by air mail! But then it went all over India before coming out here, from G.P.O., London to Razmak on the N.W. Frontier, thence to Lucknow, then 400 miles north again up to Bareilly, from there down to Bombay again via the Sub-Postmaster, New Delhi, and so here. I cannot tell you how pleased I was to receive it after a silence of nearly three months; however I can go no further now as the light is so poor that I cannot see the keys, so *au revoir* till tomorrow or the next day…

FOUR

Lotus-Eating Days

1941

January 4th 1941

Here we are again after a pause of nearly 3 weeks. Bad show! But still – Christmas is over and forgotten, and what a strange Christmas it was, even stranger than last one which I spent in a rough sea on the Mediterranean, when we did at least sing a few carols on deck under the moon on Christmas Eve. Christmas Day here was about the warmest and finest that I can remember. After our Christmas dinner of duck and tinned puddings I went down to the beach with one or two others and found the sea the calmest yet and wonderful for swimming. The sea is about the best thing about this place; otherwise it is singularly devoid of amusements of any description.

This morning I received a telegram from Perpetua wishing me a Happy Xmas and saying that all the family (you) were well. I wrote a letter from Bareilly in reply to hers in which I mentioned that I should probably be going overseas in a short while but I did not say anything about Malaya, so I can only conclude that she is staying with you or you with her, as she gave the exact address (Sgt Repton, I.A.C.C., 8th Infantry Brigade, Malaya) that I gave in my telegram of the beginning of December, from which, of course, I also conclude that you have received that telegram. On the other hand, though, she may have merely rung you up to find out my correct address and then sent off the Greetings telegram; this does seem the more probable.

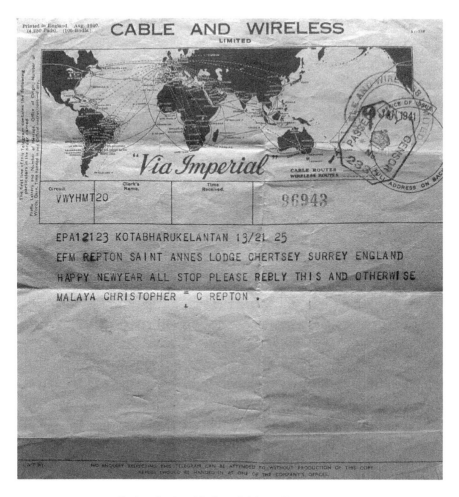

Christopher's cable from Malaya, January 1941

At first it gave me rather a shock and I thought that possibly St. Ann's Lodge or Fairmead had been destroyed and you were staying with her or her with you. A queer idea but I had rather a realistic dream the other night about air raids; I remember being in some big street like Oxford St. and suddenly seeing the panic as the sirens went off. Then I took shelter in the porch of some big shop and heard almost terrifyingly realistically the whine and thud of the falling bombs. It was only a dream, mind you, and I've no idea what an air raid is really like (shame on me!), but it seemed to me in the dream just like it would be. However, let's change the subject as it's really most tactless of me to talk to you, who are going through it, of such things. Fancy a bomb dropping only 70 yards from Dickon; it must have given him a terrible shock. Have they smashed Vickers and Brooklands aerodrome to bits or is it still carrying on? Actually, you know, if the censor had seen that in your letter it would never have got passed. The strict censorship for us here puzzles me. Everyone knows that 'substantial reinforcements', as they put it, have arrived in Malaya, in fact it was in the papers – English too, I believe, and I think Churchill mentioned it in one of his speeches; at any rate we're part of them.

I wonder when all this terrible, strange business will be over. Sometimes, even now after all the time I've been away, I get thoroughly fed up and long to be back at home again with the whole war over and done with, but even when the war's over it's going to be far from easy, isn't it? Very soon you'll be called up, won't you, and then you'll have to go through that strange period of getting used to the army and its life like I had to so long ago – as it seems now. Or have you ideas of joining the navy or air force instead?

It's a queer country, this Malaya. Doesn't seem to have any of the permanence or traditions of India, which I can look at more objectively now that I am out of it. I've been reading *The Rains Came* – I don't know whether you've ever read it but if not it's worth reading – and it has made me understand that India is a country that one can get to like if one is there long enough and not there in the role of a soldier. I know I hated it at first but that was chiefly through being with the Queen's with their ideas of life in India. I wonder how they're getting on now up at Razmak on the N.W. Frontier. Razmak is over 7,000 ft. above sea level so it must be very cold and snowy up there now. I can't say I'm sorry not to be with them. Wonder if I shall ever go back to them; when the war's over I might return to the old depot at Guildford to get demobilised, but I doubt it – more likely that I'll get demobilised in India, unless of course I choose to stay on in the I.A.C.C., where, I should imagine, with the state England's likely to be in after it's all over, my chances would be better. Still, it's a dull life really and I've no intention of stopping on longer than I have to. There's only one England, isn't there, and only one Sussex. In any case, India will probably get Dominion status after the war, which will throw a lot more people out of a job unless they make it a very gradual process [...]

As there is so little to do here in the evenings, I am thinking of buying a gramophone and starting a library of decent records and have written away to Singapore for the purpose. If I find it's too expensive a hobby, I shall probably try collecting books instead. One doesn't have to worry much during the day about what to do, as up till now there's been plenty if not too much work, and I would not have it otherwise.

I was sorry to see in your last letter, which I mentioned earlier on in this letter, that you seemed so fed up; still, it's understandable with the sort of life one must have to live in England now. Do you ever go for the old-time Sunday walks these days or is there no one to go with? What has happened to Sylvia? You said she was up in Spalding during the plum season, but that must be over now, and I was wondering whether she was carrying on in the same line. I am afraid financial affairs at home must be very sticky and I cannot see how you are managing to carry on. Tell me how it really is when you next write.

As it is Sunday, I am going for a swim shortly to a place some twenty miles away. Funny to think of swimming in January, isn't it, but the temperature on the beach during the afternoon is as near ideal as possible. I've never felt really too hot here – gets a bit sticky round about lunchtime, but there's so little variation in the temperature throughout every 24 hours that one doesn't notice it. Yes, the good old east winds will be something to face when I get back to England – probably won't like them at all.

Monday
The swim yesterday was very fine, and my back now feels rather scorched and sunburnt. However, all things come to an end, and as I want to send this off tomorrow, I will close.

Love to all from Christopher.

Headquarters, 8th Ind. Inf. Bde.
Malaya
23 March 1941

My dear Gervase,

You have been so generous with your letters lately that I feel I shall never be able to reply in kind. I notice that you often say in these letters, 'I hope I am not boring you with these lengthy meditations etc....' – well, let me reassure you; no letter is boring and yours least of all, for you often go deeper than mere facts and so I get an idea of what you are really thinking as I might were I to talk with you. Do not, therefore, make your letters any shorter or less frequent merely because you do not receive enough encouragement from me. I fear I am as bad as ever in my production of letters and you must be thinking how awful I am when four weeks or more go by without your receiving any word from me. Still, as I have repeated so often before, it is difficult writing these days when you are so far from me both in distance and time – over a year and a quarter since that December night when you and Jocelyn and Sylvia and Dickon came down to the familiar old station of Chertsey and watched me roll off to the East on the 9.57.

Well, it is Sunday evening, and I am writing this (I'm sorry, I mean typing, which I hope you'll excuse for I find it an easier medium of expression than writing these days, especially as my fountain pen happens to be broken and I have neither writing pad nor ink!) I have spent a lazy afternoon, it being a Sunday, and yet Sunday is not our official weekend here now. A couple of months ago the Brigadier decided, in spite of loud protests at first, that as the people of the neighbouring town (whose name you now apparently know – I didn't realise that the place of origin would be shown on my telegrams to you) were mostly Mohammedans and therefore observed Friday as their weekly holiday, thus causing a suspension of business on a day which we were treating as a normal working day, that we should do likewise and so now Friday is our Sunday. Although I hated the idea at first, I seem to have become quite resigned to it now and our 'Sunday' has in time acquired the real Sunday atmosphere, strange as it may sound to you.

On re-reading the above I notice a glaring anacoluthon, so obvious that you will probably deny that it is one and you will probably be right. On closing the brackets after '...ink!' I intended to say as follows: 'in the office by the light of a Petromax lamp while the shapes of the palm trees are becoming less distinct every moment in the swift-falling tropical night.' Actually, electric light should be laid on in about two weeks' time. They have been working on it for over six weeks now and most of the fittings seem to have been installed. When it is laid on, I think you will notice a distinct increase in the number of letters that I turn out, for with this light I shall be encouraged to write in my room at night; a thing which I have not so far done owing to the dimness of a hurricane lamp and the great number of mosquitoes that this dimness harbours. I have actually written out a list of all the letters I intend to write when I get started, in order of priority; this list embraces almost every conceivable person I could possibly write to and it will probably take so long to fulfil that I think I had better call it the "Five-Year Plan".

Tonight is one of our incoming mail nights and I have very good hopes of receiving a letter as I seem to have averaged nearly one per week during the last two months. It may be either from you, who are the most regular, or Mother, or (this one is highly improbable!) from Sylvia, who asked you to tell me in your last letter that she thought it was about time she wrote to me, or again from Perpetua Watkin who for some reason has been kind enough to promise to write to me every month; I have not answered her letter yet, so if she rings up to ask whether my address is still the same or something like that, you might tell her that I am in the middle of writing to her right now. I think I shall adjourn for the time being for a glass of beer or some such refreshment and then supper, and then, if I do not feel too tired, I shall come down and carry on with this, though I do not say that I shall finish it tonight.

Tuesday 25th March, 11.30 a.m.

A fine morning, and at this early stage I seem already to have finished the day's work. Sorry I didn't carry on the other night but when I got up to the Mess, I didn't feel like going down to the office again.

First, I will give you what little news there is at my end, and even that little is limited by what the censorship regulations will allow me to put... As you probably remember, about a month ago the Japanese situation in this corner of the globe seemed rather to hang in the balance and the eyes of the whole world were focussed on Thailand. Now things have apparently calmed down again, thanks largely to the arrival of the Australians, but for how long one cannot guess.

We have just finished two big training exercises. The first, which lasted for six days during the first fortnight of March, was an all-Malayan stunt and all services co-operated – we even had civil blackouts. During most of this show we were in billets and were fairly comfortable, but the last two days were more strenuous and one whole night from 6.30 p.m. until 5 a.m.

the following morning was spent on the go in our M.T.[60] or halting by the roadside with the field office in operation. I managed to get two hours' sleep, from 5 a.m. till 7 a.m., in one of our staff cars which was about the most comfortable and sheltered place I could see. Fortunately, there was a moon nearly all night which made things a lot easier, especially as our convoy was blacked out. The other exercise, a purely Brigade affair, was easier as we returned to camp each night and started off the following morning where we had left off the night before.

These stunts do make a change and are quite interesting at times, but the trouble is that when one returns to our permanent office one finds that one has got to cope with two or three days' work that has piled up during one's absence.

The weather has been steadily fine, with only occasional dull days, for what seems nearly two months now. Usually I manage to get at least one swim per week, though the sea still hasn't calmed down enough to make actual swimming pleasant. I'm always afraid to go out of my depth here because there seems to be such a strong outward pull. I have been told by one of the Volunteer Sergeants now in training with us (this particular bloke's occupation is that of schoolmaster at a Malay school some way south of here, and he has made himself rather unpopular with some people in the Mess because of his pedagogical manner of talking. He offered to conduct classes in Malay for anyone who cared to co-operate when he first arrived here – I'm sorry to say that no one did co-operate)... As I was saying, I have been told by him that in this part of Malaya one gets very little rain in the summer (actually there's no real summer here, but I mean what one calls the summer months in England), as we are on the wrong side[61] and only catch the S.W. monsoon when it's got rid of all its moisture. At the present time the N.E. is still blowing but I expect it to change now any day.

Yes, the weather is steadily fine, but it does have the merit of not being monotonously fine as in India. Work, too, goes on pretty steadily and on the whole, I should say life is static. I have been wondering and thinking of ways and means of getting a move or a transfer. On the other hand, would such a move be worthwhile?

---

60   Motor transport.
61   Christopher means, being based on the northeast coast of Malaya, in Kota Bharu – which he cannot divulge due to censorship – they are on the "wrong side" of the peninsula to catch the southwest monsoon rains.

You may be interested to hear that I am learning to drive, both motor-cycle and truck (we call a 15-cwt army lorry a 'truck' and a 30-cwt a 'lorry'). I had three lessons with the truck a month or so ago and on the third one managed to drive it six miles down the road to our nearest town (whose name you know) with a chap sitting beside me to take over control at the difficult spots, e.g. where the road was under repair or over a narrow bridge. Since then, I have had no further lessons in the truck, but last weekend after a few short preliminary trials in the morning I took a motor-bike out in the afternoon with two other blokes, one a mere beginner like me, the other an experienced veteran, to a place on the coast some 30 miles from here. I thought it was a magnificent effort myself! I got all the way there with only one mishap.

This mishap was only a minor affair: I was some way ahead of the other two and, not being sure whether I had taken the right turning, I stopped, turned the bike round and after five minutes' strenuous effort managed to start her up again (at the moment I find starting one of the major difficulties of a motor-bike, especially when water has been mixed with the petrol, as has been the case just lately). Having got her underway, I began to 'chug' back the way I had just come, only, after I had gone a few hundred yards, to see the other two 'lads' riding along towards me. I let them pass me and then attempted to turn right round on the narrow road with the engine still running. Unfortunately I had omitted to change down from top to bottom gear, and in consequence the bike, instead of turning meekly like a lamb, merely turned 90 degrees and then ran off the road with me down into a 3-foot ditch and then up the other bank of it until it eventually came to rest (after having thrown me off, fortunately without injury, into the ditch) on its side with the rear wheel still half in the ditch and the front wheel hanging over a 'paddy' field.[62] I doubt if I should have been able to extricate the vehicle on my own, but luckily one of the others noticed that I was not following and came back and together we got her out.

7 p.m., Tuesday 25th March

This evening I have brought several of your more recent letters which I hope will assist me in writing this letter of mine. I pick up one here dated on the envelope 2 Dec., and on the letter itself 28 Nov. – a lot quicker than I usually

---

62   Rice field.

am. It contains a photograph of you and another fellow walking along a road in Thames Ditton and snapped unawares; I wonder who took the snap.

You call my memory back to that fortnight's leave I spent in December before I left for India; yes, there were certainly some pleasant days during that all-too-short spell, not least among them, as you say, that Sunday when I celebrated my 21st birthday. Those were the days when we thought of the war in terms of Maginot and Siegfried Lines and stalemates, weren't they? Little did we visualise our army fighting its way through Libya and Abyssinia and Eritrea and Italian Somaliland, recapturing British Somaliland (then never touched) and landing in Greece, not to mention sending small parties in barges or by parachute into France and Norway and Italy. Nor did we think we should ever become so hardened enough to bomb Berlin, still less the channel ports of France. I passed through Cherbourg 15 months ago on my way out East. It was a cold and gloomy day and yet I rather liked the quaint town; it was far smaller than I had thought a port for ocean-going liners would be, but homely and blackout thought little of there. I remember while some of us – that's when I was in the Queen's – were consuming coffee and rolls there was an air-raid alarm and yet none of the populace appeared in the least whit disturbed; if anything, it was we soldiers who were the most agitated and wanted to leave the café and take shelter somewhere. It appeared that bombers had been trying to have a 'go' at the ships that had landed us in France, then on their way back to Southampton. And now the little town of Cherbourg is raided not by German but by British bombers. Still, that's enough of air raids, isn't it?

To return to your letter. You express the hope for a reunion party similar to that one on Dec. 3rd 1939. Alas, I'm afraid the bad news, or should I say the tragedy, presaged by your letter of 23rd Jan., in which you try to soften the blow, and confirmed by your telegram which was received by me on 13th March, has put an end to all such hopes. How can the family party be one held elsewhere than St. Ann's Lodge? As you say, it had to come, and yet although I knew matters were very bad, I always cherished the hope that at least we would manage to hang on to the old Lodge, not realising of course that its rent and upkeep were at the root of our financial difficulties. Looking back now, from a year and a half and from thousands of miles away, I see the reasons for our financial downfall with fateful clearness. The remedy was always there but no one moved. Things were just left to take care of themselves. If there is anything of the Repton family or its possessions left after this ghastly business, we must take great care that it doesn't happen again. Poor Gervase! I feel an awful brute being away from it all now that you are having such a hard time. With me here, Jocelyn at sea and Sylvia on a farm, everything devolves on you and Mother, and how you are managing to run the house on the present income, I don't know. You understand how sorry I feel about not being able to help, don't you, old boy? I will do my best to keep up a steady £5 per month and if possible increase it by cutting down my consumption of beer and gin (yes, one does drink gin in this part of the world, in reply to a query of yours, in fact it is the cheapest drink for us members of H. M. Forces, who get it duty-free of course; it is only 10 cents per small peg, which is about 2¾ d as compared with 7d in England (that's what it used to be – it may be even 9d now), so you can see the temptation, however I'm off it these days; in fact I've been 'on the tack', i.e. on the water wagon, absolutely for the last few days (only as a measure of economy)… as I was saying, by cutting down my consumption of beer and gin and gramophone records and one or two other luxuries, precious few obtainable here actually, I may be able to increase my monthly remittance to you. Of course, sending it by telegraph costs me an extra six dollars or so, but if I sent it by post this month it would cause a gap of two months or more, during which you would receive nothing at all from me.

It's now nearly 8 p.m. so I must retire to the Mess for supper. I don't suppose then that I shall carry on with this till tomorrow, so until then, goodnight and, to put it vulgarly, 'keep your chin up', old man…

Sunday April 6th

Please excuse the 12-day gap – still, this wouldn't be a letter of mine if it hadn't a large gap, would it? Since I broke off I've been in hospital for 3 days (actually the first time I've been in hospital since April of last year when I spent two days in the place at Allahabad Fort, and that was the first time I had been in since joining up) with a severe rash of sorts – I thought at first it was 'prickly heat', one of the numerous banes of tropical countries, but the M.O.[63] put it down as dermatitis; anyhow, it's O.K. now. I have received three letters in the last week; two from you arrived on the same day, one dated Feb. 7th (received on April 1st – quite good), the other dated 17th November! Today

---

63   Medical officer.

another letter from Perpetua Watkin reached me and I haven't answered her first one yet, so I repeat, please tell her my reply is on the way. She said something about going down to see you when the weather got finer; does she know that you've left the Lodge? It would be rather difficult to have her over if you're still staying with Reg and Nell, I suppose.

Your letter of 7th Feb. contained more reassuring news viz. the piece about Mr. May, and I conclude it helped things a lot, especially the move from the Lodge. Did you have a lot of things such as books, furniture etc. to leave behind or get rid of? I hope not too many. You speak of taking a house at Leatherhead or Wimbledon, but the question is how are we going to start a new home and then keep it going week by week with no capital and precious little income, and even that likely to decrease still further when you shortly have to join the army? I still hope, like you, that something will turn up, but that does not solve the immediate problem. It is very good of Reg and Nell to have helped us as they have, and I must write soon; in the meantime, you might tell Reg how I feel about it. I sent off the monthly M.O.[64] two days ago but was rather in difficulties about the address; in the end I made it out to Dad at St. Bernard's Hospital, Southall, Middlesex[65] and now hope for the best.

Today was another fateful and important day. An hour ago, we heard from Daventry that Germany had pulled off yet another of her invasion acts on the now-so-familiar lines, 'German troops entered Yugoslavia today to restore order and to thwart the evil designs of the British' – well! What do you think of it? Are Yugoslavia and Greece to be another Norway, or is this the turning point? Has Hitler at last stretched his hand too far Eastward and given us the chance to hack it off? Will Russia seize the opportunity and pounce, and what is Turkey's attitude? By the time this reaches you all those questions should be answered one way or the other and, if the right way, perhaps the chances of the war ending this year will be increased a hundredfold. What date did I say? June this year, wasn't it? Small chance there seems of that now. What do you think about the withdrawal from Benghazi? Don't like it over-much myself. However, elsewhere in Africa things are going spankingly, aren't they, and it looks as if Haile Selassie will soon be sitting on his throne again.

---

64   Money order.
65   His Uncle Reg worked as a doctor at this hospital. Christopher did not know the family's new address; they had moved from St. Ann's Lodge.

On completing this page, I will change over to pen and blue paper... as I was saying – I will change over to pen and blue writing paper as we have run out of stationery in Malaya, and for official correspondence we are now using not the white paper I have just been typing on, but some flimsy stuff of a sickly yellow hue, and though it may do for official letters I hesitated to write home on it.

Well, G., this letter to you is the first on my great list and I have been two weeks writing it so far, so if I am ever to complete my great letter-writing plan I must cut this short before it grows too unwieldy. There are tons and tons of things I should like to say in order to make even an inadequate reply to your numerous letters to me, but I cannot say them all in one letter.

I was telling you in a previous screed about my gramophone, wasn't I? Admittedly it is a luxury in these hard times and perhaps I should never have so speculated had I known quite how bad things were at home; still, it's a good luxury and does provide a mental interest in this rather stagnant corner of the globe. The gramophone is an H.M.V. and a very good one actually – reproduces orchestral and piano pieces splendidly – and now each month I add a few more records to my collection, though God knows what I'm going to do with them if trouble starts up here, or how I'm going to cart them around when we move. So far I've got 'The Emperor' ("Of course," you say, "but why not the 'Orpheus & Eurydice' concerto too?") played by Moiseiwitsch, Brahms' Fourth Symphony and Brahms' Piano Concerto No. 2. (You should remember this grand concerto. If I remember correctly it was a Sunday evening during January 1939, and after coming back from our Sunday walk through Silverlands in the rain, you and Bianca and myself turned the dining-room lights off and settled down to listen to the Sunday evening concert by the BBC Symphony Orchestra and Adrian Boult. We heard the first piece, an overture I think, through and derived a normal enjoyment from it. Then the Brahms started and at once a thrill passed through us. It's a magnificent work, and that night it was played magnificently. First Dad walked quietly in and took a chair by the dimly glinting dining table, then 'the Barrel',[66] a rare thing for him in those days, joined us! Nobody said anything when it was over; they just looked at each other and kept their thoughts to themselves. Bianca may have said, "Oh, Uncle Bernard, wasn't that simply too gorgeous?!" but if she did one would

---

66   Jocelyn's nickname.

have excused her. I then went into the kitchen and 'set to' on cold beef and a bottle of beer with a vengeance – those were the days! And now during the heavy tropic evenings, with the myriad frogs croaking in the palm-flats and the fireflies dancing outside and the mosquitoes dancing vexingly inside, I can recapture that thrill as 'bottled Backhaus' breaks the stillness of the night.) I have, too, Symphony No. 4 in G minor by Mozart (Toscanini conducting) and Beethoven's Sonata '*Appassionata*'; another lovely piece. I hope that one day in the near future I shall be able to play these records to you in England, and now, for the time being, I must say "Goodnight", firmly resolving to finish this and send it off tomorrow.

Monday 7th April

Where were we – come to a dead end, I see. Last night we stayed up late to hear over the wireless whether or not Turkey was coming into the war, but no, and still today she hasn't. Is she biding her time, do you think? We get the news from Daventry every evening at 8.20 p.m. (we're 6 hours 20 minutes ahead of you now that you've permanently got Summer Time), but the latest and spiciest news, I find, always comes from one of the American stations at either Manila in the Philippines, or Shanghai, or Treasure Island, San Francisco (the only station on the American continent that comes over well).

The old C.O. of the Queen's, while we were at Allahabad, is now a Staff Officer out here and he is coming up to visit this place tomorrow. Actually, there are two of us from the Queen's here now. A bloke who used to be in Brigade HQ at Allahabad was posted to us in late January.

I was very sorry to hear in your last letter (Feb 7th) that when you registered for service in one of the forces you put in for the Infantry – I know you'll hate it – even though you may be keen to fight for England now that the war has reached the stage it has. It is the utter subordination of the individual, the soul-destroying fatigues and parades and what seem stupid items of discipline that get one down. Perhaps the army is more democratic in England now – I doubt it, though. I should have thought that after you had heard what I had to say about the Infantry you would have thought a bit more about it and, if you had been set on joining the army in preference to the other services, put in for some branch where there is more scope, such as the Signal Corps of the Artillery or the Tank Corps or the R.A.S.C.[67] or even the Ordnance Corps, which is a fairly interesting job. A Corps is always better than the Infantry. Still, the die is cast now and I'm afraid you've got to grin and bear it. Don't get too wild with the officious Lance-Corporals and the loud-voiced Sergeant-Majors when they start giving you orders – if you look at it impersonally, you'll find they are only doing their job and giving you orders that someone else has given to them. I know that sounds rather platitudinous, but if you're anything like me, you'll undergo similar reactions to what I did in your first few weeks in the army and resent very much being told to do stupid things by 'nobodies' with one stripe on their arm. In spite of my 'fatherly' advice, too, I know you will resent things, but the only thing is it would make life easier if one didn't. Jocelyn is the luckiest of us so far. He seems to have made a well-calculated choice and now appears to be doing an interesting and exciting, not to say important, job.

It will be great after this war is all over when we meet at the Lincoln and swap yarns, won't it? There will be Humphry, a little chastened perhaps, giving us the tale of his 'English Journey', for that's what his career in the army appears to have been so far, and voicing his new and enlarged philosophy; Gareth and Dickon, quietly but persistently discussing the relative merits of Wellingtons and Vickers bombers, of Hurricanes and Spitfires, and refusing to be drawn off; Bianca arguing with H. about people and sipping cider; Jocelyn, wise and experienced, telling of grey days in Plymouth; and you talking of 'forced' marches in who knows what corner of the globe – perhaps Libya, perhaps Greece, perhaps Yugoslavia, perhaps the inevitable finale in Europe; Sylvia bursting with rude country spirits and flirting with the sardonic man in the black overcoat; and myself, a traveller home from the East and imbued with the wisdom thereof, one hopes but thinks unlikely, talking a little nostalgically perhaps of my peaceful lotus-eating days[68] in Malaya.

Yes, one hopes that such a reunion will one day take place and that it will not be marred by any casualties causing a sad gap in the ranks. The loss of St. Ann's Lodge is a bitter blow, but perhaps we can still have Sundays on the river, rowing or swimming or just lying lazily on the bank in the mild sun, and walks through England's cold, wet, but still best-in-the-world countryside, ending up this time not with buttered crumpets and '*Eine kleine Nachtmusik*'

---

67 Royal Army Service Corps.
68 *Lotus eater: A person who spends their time indulging in pleasure and luxury rather than dealing with practical concerns (Oxford English Dictionary).*

at the cosy Lodge, but with a high tea at the Wheatsheaf or some such place, *mais tout ça change*[69], as they say, and we shall have to make our own fresh delights. The sad thing about the army – at any rate, the part I'm now in – is that one can't find a single person to appreciate or to share with one the ideas that one likes. By these ideas I mean such as were expressed in our great Downland walking tours, in our winter walks, in our long Sunday evenings of tea and tennis and walks to Thorpe, in our great cycle rides etc. Probably they were just a state of mind, a dream – I know one chap who's felt the same and so do you, and he's the author of *The Flax of Dream*. (If you can spare your copy please send it out to me and I'll return you *Highways and Byways in Sussex*, which I am glad to say I have found, thus averting the 'minor tragedy'; also, please send me my diaries of 1938, which Jocelyn said he took to sea with him a short while ago. It's so long since I wrote them that they should make interesting reading now – the small, thick green books, I mean.) As I was saying, *The Flax of Dream*,[70] a wonderful book, and it was one of the things – I was reading it at the time – that made me hate the army when I first joined up.

No, I have not lost my enthusiasm for another Sussex (it must be Sussex) walking tour when this is all over, and like you I am determined that we shall have it. Think of seeing those places of one's dreams again – Midhurst and Arundel, Steyning and Poynings, Horsham and Hurstpierpoint, Lewes and Firle (I'll bet you're annoyed at the last two, not having been there) – yes, think of it!

The mosquitoes are becoming a 'bloody' nuisance, and though they don't appear to be very malarial hereabouts they're persistent little devils, so I think I'll conclude at the bottom of this page even though it is page thirteen and even though I've said precious little in all the 13 pages. So goodbye, old man, and as I said before, 'keep your chin up' and after this war we'll all work together and reconstruct.

My best love to you and to all the family.
Christopher

---

69 Christopher may be thinking of the French saying: *Plus ca change, plus c'est la meme chose*, i.e. 'the more things change, the more they stay the same'. However, he seems to have invented a new saying, *mais tout ca change*, i.e. 'but all that is changing', which reflects more accurately his frame of mind.

70 A semi-autobiographical novel by Henry Williamson, a disillusioned World War I soldier.

HQ. 8th Ind. Inf. Bde.

Malaya

26th May 1941

My dear Father and Mother and all at home,

Weeks since I last wrote and I'm very sorry, but I won't go over the old ground and tell you how hard it is to write these days; I'll leave you to understand and forgive. For that matter, it's a month since I last heard from you. Yours of the 27th Feb., Mother, and Aunt Nell's of the 28th arrived on the same day towards the end of April and that's the last time I've heard from you, bar your telegram giving me the new address.

Well, I'm glad you've managed the move alright and that it's not too near London. I always thought Esher quite a pleasant place, although the address is a bit of a come-down after the stately singularity of 'St. Ann's Lodge, Chertsey'. It's terribly sad to think that we've left the old Lodge and its glorious garden forever, but there is slight consolation in the thought that, if ever peace returns, we shall again be able to go for walks from Esher to Chobham Common and Windsor Great Park and Long Cross and Horsell and all those other, now to me, dim, dreamlike glades of the past.

My optimistic estimate that the war would end this June appears to have been ill-founded. The way things are going now makes even three years sound a hopeful prophecy. Most terrible loss is that of two days ago – H.M.S. *Hood*. It must have made England gloomy for days because a naval disaster always seems to shake us more than any other. Still, we have achieved a great deal since our nadir last June, one of the most outstanding feats being the conquest of Abyssinia in so short a space of time. The wonderful showing put up there by the Indian Army should dispel any doubts as to what they can do if anything happens out here. And yet the people they make a fuss of in this country are the Australians.

I'm not too keen on the Australians myself. They may be wonderful fighters but everywhere you hear the same thing: that they're a 'rowdy' lot and have no discipline. Our military police can't touch them so they can do what they like in Singapore and those other places. They also caused a terrific bust-up in Bombay, when passing through last year. The Mayor of Bombay wrote to the Viceroy complaining of the way they had carried on in the town, but he was shouted down by people who said that these troops were playing a great part in defending the Empire and were therefore justified in having as exciting a time as they could while they could. One may agree with this to a certain extent, but British (or should I say 'English') troops aren't allowed the same laxity. We have some 'Aussies' near here. They're not such a rough crew, but one does notice that they all seem to think that it's they alone who are supporting the Empire and what wonderful chaps they are – positively bursting with superiority complex. What does make me laugh is their national anthem, 'Waltzing Matilda'; I wonder whose idea it was…?[71]

June 10th

Another long pause, during which I've had a letter from you, Mother (the last you wrote in St. Ann's Lodge), one from Gervase (the first from 45 Manor Road), and one from Perpetua Watkin.

It made me very angry to hear from you how Dr. Buckland had behaved, especially when we always thought of him as a decent chap with an interest in the family. There was much to make one gloomy in your letter – that the piano had to go was a tragedy, but I suppose you could never have fitted it into the new house, which is very small, judging by Gervase's description of it.

Little happens here and I now seem to be settling down into a routine, more so than at any previous time during my life in the army, which will be well-nigh two years by the time you get this. Eighteen months since I last saw you all and yet I can still remember the Wednesday night I said goodbye. I left it open, I recall, saying that I should probably 'pop over' again on the Saturday, but that was because I did not want the farewell to be too final. Jocelyn was late cycling back from Guildford station, where I had parted company with him, and we became rather worried. Then he returned, and we all sat down to a late tea. After that it was just a pleasant evening spent in the same way as many another – listening over the wireless to *Eine kleine*

---

71   'Waltzing Matilda', a 19th century Australian 'bush ballad', was known as the country's unofficial anthem but has never been its actual national anthem. Despite its jolly tune, it is a tragic tale about an itinerant worker hounded to his death after stealing a sheep. 'Waltzing' means 'walking' and a 'matilda' is a 'backpack'.

Nachtmusik', which Jocelyn had with great luck managed to locate, having a small supper of an omelette and a glass of beer while chatter continued all around; those were the days when the war was still unreal, hard to believe, weren't they? When I look back on my early days of hard training in the army, interspersed with those pleasant weekends at Chertsey, they seem good days – too good to be true.

India was horrible in those first few months I spent there, not least due to the strangeness of everything. It was not until I went up to the hills that I realised it wasn't such a bad country after all. And now here I am, stuck in Malaya, stuck till the end of the war, it seems…

June 14th (and another Friday the 13th safely passed)
Your cable of the 6th arrived here on the 10th (I got it on the 12th because the local P.O. chose to hang on to it for 2 days), so in the space of but one week I have wired you and had a reply back; pretty good going, don't you think? I don't want you to send a cable every month if it's too much of an expense, but it is nice to hear that all are well on some of those months when I haven't had a letter from you for several weeks.

As things are fairly calm here now, I hope to take ten days' leave next month or the one after and am starting to save up a little for it. Actually, I've had no official leave since the two weeks in England before I left; though I'll admit that when I came out to Malaya on the advance party, I spent a fortnight in Singapore with precious little work to do.

I still get a few more gramophone records every month from Singapore and have now amassed quite a good collection, though what I'm going to do with it and the gramophone if we have to make a sudden move from here, I'm rather at a loss to say.

Some of the civilians here have got together and raised a bit of money and started a club for British troops in this area. The idea originated with us but now, as we're in a minority, the Aussies appear to have monopolised it.

June 16th
Too bad! I'm sorry! It's not because I'm too busy or because I go out every night. It's really because I have not the enthusiasm to sit down and write about nothing these days – and really there is precious little to tell you.

It's different for you because I still belong to your world and am interested in what goes on there (though at the moment living in a smaller world of my own that has little interest for you) and therefore you still have plenty to write to me about, and I do not expect your letters to flag. I do notice that there has been a falling-off in Gervase's correspondence of late, which I hope you will ask him to remedy.

Well, really, as I said before, there is very little happens here, and after nearly eight months of the place I am 'just a wee bit' fed up and am considering ways and means of effecting a change. Fortunately, there is always plenty (if sometimes too much) of work to keep one going during the day and it is only at night that one wonders what to do. Now new regulations have come out and we cannot use W.D.[72] transport for any other purpose than military duty – strictly so – which makes matters a good deal worse. In the old days, whenever three or four of us wanted to go for a swim on a Sunday afternoon or on a weekday evening after work we could always get a truck to take us down to the ferry and every night there was a sort of bus service of military vehicles to take those who wanted to go to the pictures or the club or elsewhere downtown. Now it is a case of $3 there and back for the taxi fare every time one wants to go 'sightseeing' etc.

What do you think of Russia's entry into the war? Momentous, it seemed, when the news came out two weeks ago today. However, the way things are faring at present I'm dreadfully afraid Russia may suddenly pack in, making Germany a present of the Ukraine and perhaps the rest of Poland and a few other bits of territory, as the price of her freedom to live unmolested. Still, it should all help to shorten the war.

I wonder how Gervase is liking the army – for I suppose he must be within its grasp by now. I'm glad he's going into the Signal Corps, for that's a step up on the Infantry and the pay's better if you're on the technical side. A batch of young Signalmen have just arrived up here for temporary duty and doubled the number of British troops in the area. They are fresh from England and have been through the worst of the 'Blitz' and so have a few tales to tell.

Their arrival shows up yet another of the weaknesses of our Empire. During such a period as this, when Britain is finding it all she can do to keep the home defences and the Middle East supplied with men and materials, she should not have the additional burden of Malaya. Had the right factories been built in India and Australia and a decent army been kept going during

---

72   War Department.

peace in the latter country, the two between them could have adequately defended the place and been self-supporting in every form of equipment etc., thus saving Britain a good deal of trouble. It'll be brought up after the war, I suppose.

Well, it looks as if I've come to the end of my allowance of paper and so far have written a very boring letter. Still, let's make a clean break of this one and I promise you shall have another and better in the near future – apologies and much love to all.

Your loving son,
Christopher

P.S. I enclose a few rather poor 'snaps' which I don't think I've sent you before.

HQ 8th Ind. Inf. Bde.
Malaya
19th Nov. '41

My dear Father and Mother and all at home (meaning 'in touch with home'),

Better make this a letter to all the family as it's so long since I've written and as I've just received a lovely 'variety letter' from you all – the one with 2 or 3 pages from Gervase, a short but to the point letter from Rosamund, two closely written and packed full of news sides from Jocelyn, a somewhat undecipherable page from Dickon and two small rations of Humphry and Gareth – a wonderful bill of fare indeed, the only thing missing being the 'sweet' which might have been provided by Sylvia. Many thanks to all; I'm afraid I cannot hope to reply to the whole lot as they deserve in less than six months at the least.

I feel ashamed to admit how long it is since last I wrote – over 2 months, isn't it? I cannot expect to get letters from you at the same rate as at present if that's how I'm going to carry on. The trouble is that it's so difficult to summon up any enthusiasm for writing now that I'm so out of touch with you all. I can write only about things and people that you have never seen, whereas you have at least that which is common to both of us to discourse on. However, I have resolved to turn over a new leaf for the future and to write at least once a month, even if it's only a four-page letter – that's another of my troubles: whenever I sit down to write to you or to anyone I feel that I must turn out 12 sides at the least, otherwise the letter wouldn't be worth sending away; the result, as you may guess, is often an unfinished 6 or 8 pages eventually torn up in disgust.

Very sorry I was unable to send home the usual in October. I took ten days' leave in Kuala Lumpur that month and my finances were a bit straitened thereby. Quite a pleasant 10 days but I felt a little 'out of the running' after having been away from urban affairs for so long. KL (as we term it) is the second town of Malaya (if you include Singapore) and the capital of the F.M.S.[73] It has some very fine modern buildings – though built in what is meant to be an Eastern style – and several really good air-conditioned cinemas. After the 'hot-house' climate of Malaya, stepping into one of these modern air-cooled cinemas is like going into an ice-house – very pleasant though. I meant to take some photos while I was down there to send home to you, but unfortunately at the time I left here our B.I.O.[74] had borrowed my camera for 'intelligence' purposes. I'm getting a new reel and will have some more done soon, though at present it's monsoon weather and not good for snaps. The best day of my leave was spent down at Port Dickson on the west coast, swimming.

I had your latest telegram today, in which you said you had not heard from me for some time; this letter is the result. The other remark I could not understand at all: 'All well, children evacuated' – Jocelyn, Gervase and Sylvia are not at home, so I understand, Dickon and Leila are working away and Rosamund at school, so it is difficult to see what you meant – possibly the Post Office people made a mistake with the code number; the above sentence is '68', is that what you sent?

My best congratulations to Jocelyn on getting his commission. I'll be writing to him soon but in the meantime, you might send these on. I'm glad he's done so well in the navy; suppose if he gets

---

73 Federated Malay States; a federation set up by the British colonial government in 1896, comprising the states of Selangor, Perak, Negri Sembilan and Pahang.
74 Brigade intelligence officer.

the chance he'll be staying on after the war. I don't think I can say the same of the army, at any rate at present. How is Gervase liking it? Probably better than I did during my first few months as he's got into a Corps where there's interesting work to do. I suppose Dickon will be called up soon too, which will be a bit of a blow, won't it?

Well, I've done all but a year in this place and no sign of any immediate move yet. Japan takes up more and more of the news until we begin to get quite tired of her, but still she hesitates while we go quietly on with our preparations. That's why work instead of slacking off, as you might expect if we were merely waiting for the explosion, seems to increase every day. Being on the 'Q' (provision) side of the staff, my work naturally feels the increase a great deal.

The N.E. monsoon has started again, and we get periods when it rains continuously for three or four days, followed by intermittent spells of dry weather. I like the rain, when I haven't got to be out in it too long, for the coolness and gloom reminds me of England in July (!) – not last July though, from the description of it Gervase has given me. The rain brings the mosquitoes, though, and were it not for the fan turned on my face, I should be too plagued by them to be writing this.

It's now 11 o'clock and time to turn in, so *au revoir, à demain.*

Nov. 23rd

A quiet Sunday evening after a quiet day… well, there's nothing very exciting happened during the last few months but I'll see what I can find to tell you.

A few weeks ago, I went up for a flight, with several others in the Brigade, in a Lockheed Hudson; the first time I'd been up, but those planes are so smooth that one feels no air-sickness. It seemed very queer to be able to walk up and down and from side to side in the cabin without disturbing our balance. The view, of course, was wonderful, the many-coloured paddy fields looking like crazy paving beneath us. I was surprised at the detail that could be picked out, especially when flying over our camp. Altogether we were up for about ¾ of an hour – it would have been longer, only the pilot did not like the look of a storm that was approaching from the sea and decided to land before it broke on us – I must say I thoroughly enjoyed the experience. It was funny though, how the fact that one had a parachute strapped to one gave one 50% more confidence even though we had no idea what would happen if it had to be used.

We nearly had General Wavell[75] up here a fortnight ago (you remember when the news was given out that he was on tour in Burma and Malaya). Twice the message came through to say that he was coming; twice bad weather stopped him at the last moment. A pity, for it would have been something to have seen our most successful General so far this war – at the present moment though, Gen. Auchinleck bids fair to surpass him.

From time to time we have other distinguished visitors, such as Maharajahs of Mysore, P— [illegible], etc. When the latter came up, I was asked to make out a menu in French for the dinner the Brigade Command was giving in his honour. I don't think it was very popular though, as the Brigade Command have since stated that in future only English will be printed on menus.

One day I met a war correspondent over at the Aussies' place. He told me he'd been in the Middle East and Iraq. When I mentioned my regiment, he spoke of them as having been the troops who recaptured Habbaniyah aerodrome. He may have meant the 2nd Brigade though, as they were in Palestine when I last heard of them. I don't know how the 1st Brigade is getting on – have had no news from anyone there since I left India, although I've written several times.

By the way, how's Humphry getting on these days, and what branch of the army is he in? Judging from Gervase's description, he must have spent a pretty rotten month or so in hospital. Please convey my condolences, and you might mention that he may expect a letter from me any day now ("I say, you fellows, I'm expecting a postal order…").

We were thinking (or rather 3 or 4 of us were – these matters not having been publicly broached yet) of producing a play in our Mess for Christmas. Not a long play, but a medium-length one-acter, round which other turns could be built (these 'turns' are expected to be provided by the hidden talent which we hope will be brought to light as soon as the play gets into its stride – if it ever succeeds in doing this), so as to form a sort of concert-show altogether. It was I who started the idea by buying a book of plays when I was on leave

---

75 General Archibald Wavell served in World War I and the Boer War before World War
    II. He secured significant victories over the Italians in North and East Africa between
    December 1940 and January 1941. In February, British Prime Minister Winston
    Churchill ordered him to move his troops to Greece, where the Germans and Italians
    were attacking. Against his better judgement, he did so. When this operation ended in
    failure, Churchill replaced Wavell with General Claude Auchinleck and moved Wavell
    to Auchinleck's post as Commander-in-Chief of India.

in KL. One of these, *The Importance of Being Earnest*, which you probably know very well, intrigued me so much that the idea of actually performing it came to me. Then I realised that it was too long and beyond our powers of acting, but the idea itself remained and I thought of a 'one-acter' instead. Mentioned it to two or three likely chaps and we put our heads together. Result – I sent away to Singapore for a selection of one-act plays. Response – most disappointing. A large and expensive book ($15) sent up on approval. It is called *One Hundred Non-Royalty One-Act Plays*. On looking into this book, it was discovered that none of these plays had ever been performed, that they were all written by American college students, that they were all about the wonderful American continent, that there was doubt that many would provide very successful performances, and that none lasted more than a quarter of an hour. We sent this back in disgust (having had to pay $0.50 in postage) under cover of a stiff letter and asked for a better, though not quite so numerous, selection. As yet there has been no reply to this – probably the stiff letter frightened them off. My last hope is a book called *Seven Famous One-Act Plays* which I noticed down at the local Free Library. Quite a good Free Library, though the hours are not so convenient. However, I miss the basilisk-like glare of Miss Agar when I go in to exchange books.

Swimming is not much in vogue these days. The last time I went down was with the Staff Captain a fortnight ago when he took several of us down in the staff car – 100% more easeful than a 15-cwt truck over such roads as lead to the beaches. We went to a different spot to the usual, more exposed to the open sea and consequently rougher. That swim – or rather bathe, for it was not possible to swim – was the most exhausting I've ever had. One would be standing in no more than three feet of water, searching for a calm spot to swim, when a vast and powerful breaker would rear itself up ready to strike. As one turned one's back to it, in the vain hope of getting out of its range before it reached its zenith, it would break with a roar, striking one hard on the back of the neck; at the same time its accompanying undercurrent (pulling the opposite way) would drag one's feet from under one. The result was that you found yourself absolutely out of control, spinning round under the water with the mighty breakers pounding you down. I was so surprised the first time this happened that it didn't occur to me to feel any panic. I felt a battered wreck after the experience but soon recovered. Now I shall adjourn for supper and a beer, as it's just past eight o'clock – hope to finish this letter tonight…

I've already mentioned, I believe, that work doesn't seem to get any less as time goes on. My hours are roughly 8 a.m. to 6ish six days a week and 9 till 12 on Sunday, so you see I haven't much time for sitting back and thinking. Probably a good thing, for on Sunday, the one day when it's possible to relax, I usually have a fit of gloom in the evening. Can't say I feel exactly cheerful tonight – still, just reaction, I suppose.

I have a pretty good collection of records now: a couple of Brahms symphonies, a Beethoven and a Brahms piano concerto, a Beethoven quartet and two piano sonatas, several Mozart symphonies, and a number of odd pieces, such as overtures and variations etc. Get some pretty good concerts in the evenings if I'm in the mood.

There is one rather important thing that has happened to me since I last wrote and of which I should like to speak to you – don't know whether I should mention it now or await the result, however here goes. This question of a commission. After pulling Sergeant, I'm afraid I rather lay back and said, as it were, "Well, I've got so far and can now be content to stay there awhile" – a mistake – I should have started right away to try for a commission. Instead, I've allowed myself to settle down here rather too long. However, through hints dropped in your letters, through hearing of Jocelyn's success, and then that Humphry was trying for his, I at last began to realise that it was up to me. Then came rather a severe letter from Bianca, just after she'd been selected,[76] which really made me consider trying for a commission.

Of course, you realise I can't get one in the Corps I'm in at present – promotion goes largely by seniority – so it's a question of applying for one outside it and giving up my present job. Well anyway, soon after I'd started seriously to think about the matter, a young officer – Signals – came to stay down here for a while, largely in connection with courts martial – he'd studied at the Middle Temple before joining the army and consequently they often asked him in as Defending Officer. I met him in our Mess and later had some long talks with him; he's a cut above the average army officer, less wrapped up in military affairs and capable of talking interestingly on general questions – only natural, I suppose, as he was an E.E.O. and still more of a civilian than a soldier. It was he who really persuaded me to try for an emergency commission and had it not been for his pushing I

---

76   Bianca was promoted to the rank of captain in the Auxiliary Territorial Service, the women's branch of the British Army during World War II.

should probably be still considering it. To cut a long story short – I took my application straight in to the Brigade Major about ten days ago. He interviewed me a couple of days later and told me that he and the Brig. were prepared to push my application up. Well, that's that, then – the application form's up with a pretty good recommendation by the Brigade Command and it's now merely a question of waiting to see what higher authority have to say about it. If it goes up, it'll have to go all the way back to India, I believe, as I've applied for the Indian Army. You may ask why the Indian Army. Well, there are two very good reasons to start off with: one, that I've spent over a year (i.e. more than half my service) with an Indian Brigade, and two, that the rates of pay are far better in the Indian Army than in the British. I have other reasons, of course, but I think those two are enough to get on with. Well, as I said, it's merely a question now of waiting to see what happens to my application as it goes forward. I'll let you know the result as soon as possible. If it succeeds, then I am posted to an O.C.T.U.[77] either in India or in Singapore. It might have been better if I'd waited to tell you all this when I knew the outcome; still, I thought you'd rather be told now.

This is a very uninteresting letter, I fear, especially this last part, but the great thing is that I've finished it tonight (28th) and 12 pages done at that. Yes, I'm longing, as I expect you all are, for this terrible war to be finished with and to get back to England again, though just how strange 'going back' will be I cannot foresee at present. Let me have news of all as often as possible, and please tell Sylvia and Leila that I'm expecting letters from them. I do hope that you're all keeping well and that this winter is not going to be too hard for you.

My very best love to all.

Yours,
Christopher

---

77   Officer Cadet Training Unit, where candidates were selected for training as army officers.

FIVE

It Was Touch-and-Go

1942–1945

Theresa continues her story

My eldest brother and his family were living with his brother-in-law in McNair Road, somewhere off Serangoon Road, where they were most hit by the shelling from across the Causeway. We lost my eldest brother that night in February 1942, when the Japanese landed. He was injured by a shell. My other brothers couldn't find his body the following day; so, he was never found.

It was Chinese New Year's[78] Eve when things looked very bad and we had hardly any food in the house, except for some chickens which we kept. Over the next few days my father kept all five of us girls at the back of the house, where we had an air-raid shelter, to protect us from marauding Japanese soldiers looking for young girls. It was very frightening at that time because there was no proper government yet. So, we had to stay indoors most of the time.

Then a week or so later we were asked to go to this camp somewhere in Arab Street. My father and the old servant stayed back in the shop. My brothers, sisters, mother and I were in this shop-house in Arab Street for three and a half days. On the day we were supposed to be going home, they

---

78   The 15th February 1942, the day British General Arthur Percival surrendered the island of Singapore to Japanese General Tomoyuki Yamashita.

114

took down our identities. But my eldest brother-in-law, Cheng Yong Nghee, Mary's husband[79] who was working with the police department, was there to see that we were not detained. He was with a Japanese officer at the exit point. A few of us were picked out, but my brother-in-law quickly told the officer that we were his family, so we were all let out and got home safely. Later on, we heard that those young girls who were detained were sent overseas as 'comfort girls' for the Japanese soldiers. So, it was touch-and-go for us at that time.

With hundreds of camps on the island, the Japanese military administration was able to record the identity of every inhabitant on the island. After some time, when things quietened down and there was a civilian government, I found myself a job with a paint factory, formerly Par Paint, owned by Sime Darby, but taken over by the Japanese. I was there until the end of the war, working as an assistant to an accountant. I had to take two courses in Japanese to do that job. My boss was a very well-educated Japanese civilian, and he used to trust me with signed blank cheques to pay bills. I had a very nice Japanese accountant working with me in the office.

Life was difficult, as we had food rationing – rice and sugar especially. We had to queue up monthly for our ration. My eldest brother-in-law helped quite a lot in securing bags of rice from the department where he was working. So, we were well supplied with rice and firewood, which kept us going for a long time. We used to cook with a huge wok over an indoor fireplace, as we had such a big family. Life seemed quite normal during those three and a half years. I don't remember travelling outside Singapore. There were a lot of shortages of food and other things.

We had no news of the war in Europe, as we were not allowed to listen to the radio. Anybody who was caught doing that was severely punished by the Japanese. My cousin Daisy's third uncle was imprisoned by the Japanese. He was working in a shop selling second-hand tyres, and the Japanese traced a stolen tyre back to that shop. He was taken prisoner because the owner made him the scapegoat; it wasn't his doing. He was tortured and kept in an open prison. His mother had to talk to him through the fence.

Daisy's grandfather and my father were cousins, so we were cousins twice removed. Her father was the second of three brothers. He worked as a salesman for Hume Pipes, an Australian company selling asbestos. He had

---

79   Affectionately called 'CID Man' (Criminal Investigation Department) by the family.

cancer of the lung because he was exposed to the asbestos and because he was a heavy smoker.

Daisy's grandmother adopted me as her daughter, in name only, when I was very young. Before I went to school, I used to follow her around with the market basket. She loved gambling with cards (a game called 'see sek', or 'four colours'), and when she lost money she had to skimp on the groceries. They lived in the countryside, in an 'attap' house. There were a lot of sandy beaches in those days. They had bullock carts for transportation, and a little minibus.

My two sisters, Agnes and Elizabeth, were both married on the same morning in March 1943. I remember dressing them up with their headdresses and their make-up. My sister Mary was married three years before them, and I helped her dress too on the morning of her wedding.

Life was pretty dull during the Japanese occupation. Apart from going to work and then home again, and occasional weekend visits to friends and relatives, there was nothing much to do. Life was more exciting before the war. We had big celebrations for my father's birthday, large gatherings, and lunch and dinner parties with [our] family and [other] relatives. Sometimes my whole family went to a studio and had our photograph taken. That is something I always remember from being a child. At Chinese New Year we had new clothes, new shoes, and lots of money given to us in red packets called 'ang paos'. It was the only time of year when we felt rich and had lots of food to eat.

Early in 1945, we had air-raid warnings. This time it was the British with their B-29s, coming to bomb Singapore. But they only dropped bombs near Keppel Harbour, very near the factory where I was working. We had to run out of the factory and hide in the big monsoon drain, because there was no shelter anywhere. I remember carrying my petty cash book with me, and the book-keeping books which I was looking after.

In August that year my brother-in-law came to tell us the good news. He was so very excited about the surrender of the Japanese that he celebrated the occasion with a bottle of champagne. We were still in the dark as to what was happening[80] until one day all the workers at Par Paint were given three months' full pay and food rations and told to go home. We knew then that

---

80 Theresa's brother-in-law had insider knowledge about the imminent Japanese surrender as he worked for the police, at a chaotic time when civilians were not allowed to listen to the radio.

something was happening. Soon after that, the official surrender of the Japanese in Singapore took place at Fort Canning. All the civilian prisoners of war held in Sime Road and Changi Camps were released and sent home for recuperation.

Soon after the surrender, mail came through from the UK, including our results from England. We were called back to school to find out whether we'd done all right in the Cambridge exams we'd sat in 1941 while the bombing was going on. Apparently, the papers were sent to England via India to ensure that they arrived safely. The whole class passed; six of us had Grade 1 certificates, and I was one of them. We were all so delighted that our efforts had not been in vain.

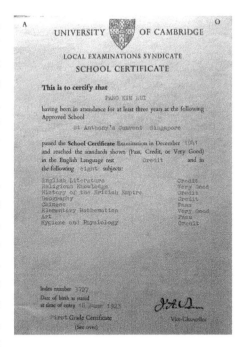

Theresa's school-leaving certificate

SIX

Rather Trying at Times

1942–1945

Singapore
2nd February

My dear family,

So sorry to have left you without news for so long – my only other effort since our war began has been an E.F.M.[81] from a place called Jerantut which I'm not sure that you've received – but since the 'fun' started at KB[82] we have been so much on the move and spent so much time in the rubber and jungle that it has been impossible to get word to you. Two days ago, on arriving in SPE[83] after having marched the last 35 miles or so intermittently on foot, I got six PCs from you in a lump (4 from G., 1 from J. and 1 from S. – incidentally, my heartiest congratulations to you, J.), for which I was very grateful. One posted on 7th Jan. took only 20 days to get here; I hope it's as good the other way. Well, I must stop here and carry on on PC No. 2.[84] I won't

---

81   Telegram.
82   Kota Bharu.
83   Singapore.
84   Christopher wrote three small postcards from Singapore in February 1942, postmarked 'Indian Section Base Office' and franked 'Passed by censor', with Malayan Straits Settlements stamps, after his brigade's retreat from Kota Bharu, days before the British surrender.

mention my unit (it's still the same), then they won't mind my giving place names.

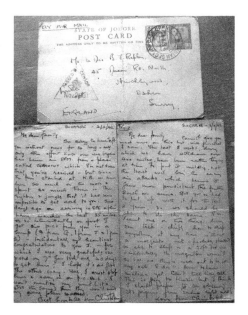

Chris' postcards after retreat from Kota Bharu

Singapore
2nd February

My dear family,

Cannot give you much news on this but will give what I can. The last 8 weeks, during which we have withdrawn over 400 miles, have been rather trying at times, to put it mildly, not the least evil being the enemy air attacks which seemed to grow more persistent the further south we came. Still, you've had to put up with it for the last 2 years, so we should be able to do the same. I've learnt one or two things during our trek – chiefly how to sleep anywhere, at any time without a mosquito net. Probably shouldn't be able to sleep on a soft bed now – incidentally, the mosquitoes weren't so bad as they're made out to be; at any rate I don't seem to have malaria yet. Can't tell how all this is going to finish but I think I should prefer to be observing its progress from India right now!

Love from Christopher

Singapore
4th February

My dear family,

I had to leave behind for the Japs my gramophone and all my wonderful collection of records, plus a lot of other stuff. Then, to crown the misfortune, all the stuff I had managed to get away in a suitcase etc. was destroyed when our office lorry was bombed at

Kuala Krai; that included my watch and camera, and those of us who had our kit in that lorry existed thereafter for a week in nothing but what we stood up in.

Christmas passed by almost without being noticed – we caught a couple of ducks and had them curried for Xmas lunch and roast for dinner! Later during our trek our Q.M.S.[85] made a wonderful haul – a large box left in some deserted rubber planter's hut, containing every sort of liqueur, wine and spirit. It lasted us over a fortnight and was very much appreciated – especially during periods of stress.[86] You probably heard on the news how our bombers bombed the 'marshalling yards' at Gemas[87] – you'd laugh if you saw G. railway station, which must be a lot smaller than Chertsey's. Remember A. P. Herbert in *Punch* on 'marshalling yards'? Must stop now.

Love,
Christopher

G. C. T. Repton
Pembury
Tunbridge Wells
Kent
TN2 4LB
28th May '97

Jack Shuttle
Staines

Dear Jack,

Someone in my family recently came to hear that I was mentioned in a book written by you, entitled *The Road to Kwai*, and my sister

---

85 Quartermaster sergeant, in charge of supplies.

86 I don't recall ever hearing Dad use the word 'stress' in the way we use it nowadays. To him this was a euphemism for an arduous retreat from Kota Bharu to Singapore, under enemy fire.

87 Gemas is still the provincial hub station where the railway splits between the East Coast 'Jungle Railway' up to Kota Bharu and the West Coast Line via Kuala Lumpur, Ipoh and Penang. The interior of the country is covered with jungle and plantations – more jungle in those days.

has borrowed the book from her local library and sent it to me, and I have been dipping into it over the last few days. Then, about 10 days ago I had a telephone call from Parvin, who lives with her husband Brian at Thorpe, near Egham (I can't remember her married name). She knows you, of course, and also mentioned your book to me. Parvin is the elder sister of Pamela, married to Gilbert Brown, and Gilbert and Pamela have been friends of mine since 1947/48.

I believe my sister has telephoned you and had a chat. She suggested that I ring you and gave me your phone no., as did Parvin too. However, after all these years – 53–54! – I feel that a phone call might not be appropriate and that a letter, at least to begin with, would be better.

Of course, I can remember many of the events, people and places mentioned in your book, including some of those who did not make it back home in 1945. You and I have to thank God that we survived those grim days and that we have been able to live normal lives since then.

Although you mention me by name in your book,[88] I am ashamed to say that I cannot actually remember you, although I do remember two of the others mentioned, namely Leo Lavender and Sgt. Holliman. Leo did come to my house for a meal in 1946, although I have not seen him since.

I left Singapore for Thailand in November 1942, a bit later than you.[89] We spent a few days in Ban Pong[90] and, like you, I had my

---

88   In his World War II memoir, Jack Shuttle describes how he met Christopher on returning to the hospital camp at Chungkai in early 1944: 'Despite the overcrowding room was found for me… alongside Leo Lavender, John Huskisson, "Holly" Hollyman and Chris Repton… who had come to Malaya with 3rd Corps HQ. He was a tall, fair lad from Chertsey in Surrey whose father was in the film industry.'

89   After being detained for several months by the Japanese Army at Changi Prison in Singapore following the British surrender, Christopher and Jack were among tens of thousands of Allied soldiers transported from South-East Asian countries occupied by the Japanese up to Burma (Myanmar) and Siam (Thailand) to build a railway. They survived a hellish train journey from Singapore over five days and nights packed into boiling hot, windowless cargo wagons without food, water or toilets. Between sixty thousand and sixty-eight thousand Allied prisoners were forced to work on the railway, of whom approximately sixteen thousand died from tropical diseases, malnutrition, beatings, work-related injuries and exhaustion.

90   Ban Pong Station is five kilometres from Nong Pladuk in northern Thailand, the southern starting point of the 250-mile railway that was built by the prisoners up to Moulmein in southern Burma through virgin jungle and across mountain gorges and wide rivers.

blanket stolen and suffered later in the cold nights at Win Lung[91]! From Win Lung we went to Wan Po and must have been there during April '43… Then we had a series of day marches up to Tarkanun, with a brief stopover at Tarsi.[92]

The cholera hit us at Tarkanun in May '43 and I was put in a hospital tent as a cholera suspect. Fortunately, it turned out to be amoebic dysentery[93] instead of cholera and, fortunately also, I received medical treatment from Dr. de Wardenn, whom you mention in your book. As far as I can recall, he treated me with emetine which eventually brought the dysentery under control. Many years later (about 1985 I think) I saw Dr. de Wardenn in a TV programme. I obtained his address from Yorkshire TV and wrote him a belated 'thank-you' letter for saving my life at that time, and I received a very friendly reply from him. I stayed in the hospital tent at Tarkanun from May until about September 1943, thus missing the worst of the 'Speedo'[94] on the railway.

Returned to Chungkai in early October, I think, and then began to develop ulcers on my feet, due to having to walk a lot round the camp in ill-fitting boots. Fortunately again, I was admitted to hospital for treatment of the ulcers before they became too serious – there were a number of amputees in that ward and some did not survive.

---

91 Christopher probably means Wun Lun, the camp on the River Kwai 6 km from Chungkai, also known as Wun Lung, Wang Lan or Wanran.

92 Those POWs who were transported by train to Thailand from Singapore disembarked at Ban Pong. From there they hiked to work camps along the railway site. Some travelled by truck, but most had to walk. 'F' Force, for example, were forced to walk three hundred kilometres over twenty days, in fifteen stages of twenty kilometres. Most marches took place at night, to avoid extreme daytime heat. Tarsi was more commonly known as Tarsau, one of the camps prisoners had to walk to from Ban Pong.

93 Both Jack and Christopher were seriously ill when they met in the hospital camp at Chungkai, suffering from amoebic dysentery. A former P OW, J.P. describes a dysentery ward in a self-published book, *The True Story of the Death Railway & the Bridge on the River Kwai*: "In this ward the ridiculously small staff worked day and night to ease the suffering of the patients who, having dysentery, laid helpless to do for themselves. An attempt had been made to separate the more serious cases from the others, who were placed in a bay together, which became known as the 'Death Bay'. I heard many hoarse-voiced men give resistance, however weak, to being moved into that awful death bay."

94 "Speedo!", which the Japanese soldiers shouted at the prisoners constantly, was coined by the latter to denote the harshest period, when hundreds of Australian and British POWs were forced to labour night and day in the so-called 'Hellfire Pass' (see the Backstory section of this book).

Due to the kindness of an officer in our group who used some of his pay to provide me with an egg every day,[95] I slowly improved and was eventually discharged to the 'amoebic hut' – that must have been early in 1944 and it was probably there that you met me, though there is also a mental picture of a ward at Nakhon Pathom[96] where we moved a bit later – around April '44 perhaps? I can remember being at Nakhon Pathom on D-Day[97] as Capt. Back came round the wards to give us the news. By a strange coincidence I met Capt. Back at a London restaurant in 1948 where I was dining with a girlfriend and we had a chat about those days.

I remember spending Christmas '44 at Nakhon Pathom but then moved to Chungkai again and was passed fit for work in January '45, I think. Went in a brief working party to Wan Po in March '45 I think, and then in April went with a party of about 200 to work at Langsuan on the Kra Isthmus.[98] It took us 2 weeks to reach there as many bridges had been destroyed by Allied air raids, in particular the big bridge at Chumphon, where we stayed some days. Spent the next 3–4 months at a small, hutted camp at Langsuan, working mainly at night, loading and unloading trains (the bridge was bombed here) and later pile-driving[99] on a wooden bridge (temporary) which the Japanese were building.

Work suddenly stopped on August 15th and you know the rest. A few days later we entrained north to Phetchaburi where there

---

95   The Allied officers, who received a higher rate of pay than the ordinary soldiers, contributed to a welfare fund to provide the sick POWs with life-saving extra rations, such as eggs. The Japanese only allotted half of the already meagre rations to those too ill to work. However, the officers shared the food out equally, with the workers accepting reduced rations to help their sick comrades.

96   Hospital camp near Bangkok for the seriously ill, to which both Christopher and Jack were moved.

97   The 6th June 1944, when US, British and Canadian troops invaded Normandy and began to attack the Nazis across occupied France, culminating in the Allies' victory in Europe in May 1945.

98   Narrowest part of the Malay peninsula, connecting it to southern Burma and Thailand, only twenty-five to thirty miles wide between Chumphon and Kra Buri.

99   The Japanese devised a primitive method of using the prisoners as a sort of human piledriver. Huge logs were cut and floated down from the forest. The POWs, working in teams, had to repeatedly pull and release in unison ropes attached to a steel ram erected high above them, while standing on the riverbed, all day long, following the shouts of a Japanese guard. Their limbs ached so badly they could barely move their arms to eat the rice gruel at the end of the day, according to a former POW. Prisoners could not survive this kind of work for long (see Backstory).

was a big P.O.W. camp and an airfield nearby. Flew out by DC-3 to Rangoon on Sept. 3rd – spent a few days in hospital and passed fit to travel. Then to a tented camp outside the city and was lucky to be chosen to travel home on the first troop ship available, the *Corfu*, which sailed from Rangoon on 15th Sept. and arrived at Southampton on 8th Oct. '45.

In those last few months at Langsuan, I was fortunate that the rations were not too bad and most of us kept reasonably fit at the camp. So by the time the war ended my health was not too bad – probably better than yours at that time [...]

Many thanks for your phone call and perhaps we shall meet one of these days.

Kindest regards,
Chris Repton

6092414
Sgt. C. REPTON

MY DEAR FATHER AND MOTHER,
I AM QUITE WELL AND IN GOOD SPIRITS SO DON'T WORRY ABOUT ME. I HOPE YOU ARE ALL WELL AT HOME.
MY LOVE AND BEST WISHES TO EVERYONE.

FROM CHRISTOPHER

Falmouth
Usual Address
15th July 1943[100]

My dear Mother and Father and all,

What glorious news! Actually, judging from our conversation on the subject one would think that it is only a confirmation of what we had thought had happened – that is, that he had been

---

100 Jocelyn wrote this from his ship moored in Cornwall, after Sylvia and her friend Paddy, both in the Women's Auxiliary Air Force (WAAF), visited him on board with the news that Christopher was alive, in a Japanese prison camp.

taken prisoner – but what a relief to our thoughts that remained unspoken, just to know that he is safe. I don't suppose that one can rely on the message being absolutely true, but in any case, he is still alive and well enough to write to us… Please let me know, as soon as you hear it, the address to which to write; if possible, by airgraph or something like that. Do you know who told me about it – not in a letter, but in person? Sylvia. She has been down here and has had dinner on board with Paddy, who organised the whole thing. That was very pleasant too, but doubly so as she was a carrier of such good news […]

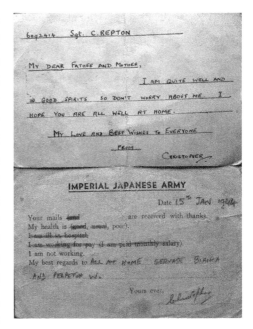

Chris' postcards from POW camps

Jocelyn

15th Jan. 1944[101]

SERVICE DES PRISONNIERS DE GUERRE

Name: Repton C.

Nationality: British

Rank: Sergeant

Camp No. 2, P.O.W. Camp, Thailand

To:-

Mr & Mrs B. F. Repton

45 Manor Road North

---

101 The last official postcard sent from the POW camp, received by Christopher's family one year later.

LOTUS EATING DAYS

Hinchley Wood
Esher, Surrey, England

IMPERIAL JAPANESE ARMY

Your mails are received with thanks.
    My health is ~~good~~ / ~~usual~~ / poor
    ~~I am ill in hospital~~
    ~~I am working for pay (I am paid monthly salary)~~
    I am not working

My best regards to ALL AT HOME, GERVASE, BIANCA AND
PERPETUA W.

Yours ever,
Christopher

SEVEN

I Am Now Free and in Safe Hands

1945

56 York Mansions
Prince of Wales Drive
Battersea S.W. 11
19th February

My dear Mrs. Repton,

I have been meaning to write to you ever since we had your letter at the beginning of January. I have just moved into a flat at the above address, and simply love it. I am sharing it with two girls I work with.

One of the girls, Elspeth Evans, is the wife of a man in the Manchester Regt. who is a P.O.W. in the same camp as Christopher. They had only been married a year when he was captured. She is extremely brave and cheerful and is always collecting things for "when Nigel gets home". I have got little news to tell you about the camp. The other day Elspeth met a man who was torpedoed, and who, though not in that particular camp himself, had been there for a day or two before he left Thailand. He had actually met Elspeth's husband and said he was extremely fit. This was last June. All the prisoners had had attacks of malaria from time to time but seem to have been reasonably well cared for. They have none of them, officers or men, had a shave or haircut since they were captured. The only clothes they have is a loincloth, but the man said that this was no hardship as if they have clothes, they find lice etc. troublesome. Apparently, this camp is one of the best, and the Japanese man in charge is reasonable. I was delighted to hear all this and hasten to pass the news on to you. They have now stopped doing the railway and are doing a bit of planting and farming. The men are not kept in their regiments but are all mixed up. I also heard one or two other things about the camp, but I shall tell you when I see you as it is better not to write too much.

I do hope poor old Christopher is better now; they certainly seem to have taken some care of him. I was very touched by his message, and I should love to write to him if you can ever spare a form for me.[102] If I hear any more news of any sort, I shall let you know at once of course. It is an extraordinary coincidence that Nigel and Christopher should be in the same camp, and I often wonder if they know each other. The most important thing I forgot to tell you – the man who escaped told Elspeth that the morale in the camp was so incredibly high that it was almost unbelievable.

The war does seem to be moving quickly at last and not only in Europe, thank God. I hear now that the P.O.W. in Japanese hands are to be sent to special recuperating camps before being repatriated when they are freed. They will need it, poor dears, after living such a primitive existence for so long. One can just imagine the joy of the first haircut, even.

I hope all the rest of your family are well and safe. Please give my love to Leila when you write; I hope she is getting on well and is happy. I do hope too that you are well, though I expect you are doing far too much as usual.

All my family are in good health. Chris is now up at Cambridge for 4 years.

With love to all and to yourself,
Perpetua

---

102 In April 1944, the British Red Cross wrote to Japanese POWs' families, telling them to limit their letters to twenty-five words. Only relatives and close friends were allowed to write, and not more than once a fortnight. 'No reference to Naval, Military, Aerial, Economic or Political matters is permitted.'

9 Park Place
St. James's Street
London S.W. 1
July 9th 1945

E. C. Repton, Esq. [sic]
45 Manor Road North
Hinchley Wood
Esher
Surrey

Dear Mr. Repton,
6092414. Sergeant G. C. T. Repton

Thank you for your letter of July 5th.

A very small batch of mail reached this country a short time ago from the Far East, but we can assure you that only a very few relatives received news from their prisoners.

We are so sorry to hear that you have not heard from your son since January last, as we fully realise how distressing this lack of information must be to bear.

As you probably know, all mail has to be sent from the camps in all areas to Japan for censoring, and the further the war in the Far East progresses the more difficult it will be for the mail to reach Japan. We would ask you, therefore, not to be unduly anxious if you do not hear from your son for some considerable time, and endeavour to place all hope in the final defeat of Japan which will hasten the return of our prisoners.

May we ask you once again to be kind enough to send the post-card you received from your son giving his address as Sanatorium, Thailand, to the Records Office of the Queen's Royal Regiment, Stanwell Road School, Ashford, Middlesex, as it is essential they should be informed of all the latest movements of prisoners-of-war in the Far East, and they will not have had Sergeant Repton's address as yet. They will return your card to you as soon as the information is recorded.

Yours sincerely,
S. G. King
For Controller

6 Sept. 45

RECOVERED PRISONERS OF WAR ON ACTIVE SERVICE

DEAR,

I AM NOW FREE AND IN SAFE HANDS.

I HOPE TO BE WITH YOU SOON.

MY ADDRESS IS:- RECOVERED POW MAIL CENTRE, BOMBAY
INDIA COMMAND,

3/9/45 C. T Repton

CABLE AND WIRELESS
LIMITED
"Via Imperial"

10.SEP.45

C. & W. LTD.

RANGOON

9 September *

REPTO   N45 MANOR RD NORTH   HINCHLEY WOOD
             ESHER   SURREY *

ARRIVED SAFELY AT INDIA *

HOPE BE HOME SOON   *WRITING *

ADDRESS LETTERS AND TELEGRAMS TO

C/O RECOVERED PW MAIL CENTRE BOMBAY INDIA COMMAND +

CHRISTOPER [sic] +

The following letters from Christopher's family addressed to Bombay were returned, as his ship had already sailed.

'Brambles'
Monday Sept. 10th

My dear Christopher,

At last, after these recent weeks of horrible anxiety your telegram came this evening. It lay on the mat for nearly two hours in the dark and might have been chewn up by the puppy. Dadda found it and brought it down to the garden to Mother and me who were picking beans. There is great joy in the home tonight, though only Mother and Dadda and I are here. Tomorrow morning I shall have a sheaf of letters and telegrams to send out, to Jocelyn at Chatham, to Sylvia in Yorkshire, to Dickon (an Ordinary Seaman) at Warrington in Lancs., to Leila in the Women's Air Force at Uxbridge, to Gareth at Halton aerodrome, to Perpetua Watkin, to Riverholme. I think that's about all except for a cable to Humphry who is somewhere in India, telling him to try and contact you. I phoned Nell and Reg, and Ina and Bianca this evening. Humphry should be home in December or January. Perhaps it is not too much to hope that Christmas will see a real full house at last.

But poor old Skinto! What kind of a hellish life have you been forced to endure these last few years? Tonight we are overjoyed and full of thanks to God that you are alive, just that you are alive. But now we wait anxiously again to hear from you, as to what sort of health you are in. These last years when things have looked very black sometimes, I've indulged obstinately in dreams wherein you have returned naturally to your old ways and enthusiasms. Now these dreams do not seem so intangible. You will be here before Christmas, for your birthday in fact.

No amount of extravagant joy nor words of thankfulness would be inappropriate on this page, but I find myself dumb and just waiting patiently for your arrival.

There must be a thousand questions you would like answered, but I shan't broach any tonight. We must hear your story first.

I'll go to bed now, feeling happier than I can remember for months and months and months. It's so good to think of you surrounded by comfort and friendly faces tonight, much more of which awaits you here.

From your loving brother,
Gervase

76 Victoria Street
Tel.: Victoria 1474 (in case you
fly home unexpected here)
11 Sept. 1945

Oh, my very dear boy,

I cannot tell you how I felt when your cable arrived last evening. We have been waiting and hoping for a message for so long, and reading of all the horrors out East, it is only the work I am still able to carry on that has kept me from going off my head.

I feel somehow that the cable – in which it is difficult at the best of times to convey much information – has a somewhat impersonal character, and I am fearing that after all you have gone through you may have had to allow the Red Cross people to make out the message.

We are all anxiously waiting for your first letter. Those miserable postcards – so infrequent and, when they did come, so uninformative – are a poor substitute for real letters. I feel this is a miserably inadequate letter.

As it happens, I was unexpectedly the first to see the cable. Your poor mother had been suffering from a carbuncle on her neck. Kept it dark as long as she could and then had to have it treated. It is nearly well, but yesterday, not reaching the house until between 6 and 7 in the evening, she was out when the cable arrived. I did not get back until about 7.30.

Mother and Gervase had gone down the garden to pick beans, and after I had had a belated tea I went to the dining room to look for the *Evening Standard* and in the dim light noticed what appeared to be a scrap of paper. When I picked it up […] and saw it was marked 'Post Office Telegram' I thought it might be from one of the others, Gervase on leave being the only one at home. Then when I saw your name, I went mad and ran madly down the garden shouting, "Cable from Christopher!"

No room for more. We sent messages all round to give the glad news.

Thank God you are safe.

Your loving Father

Bernard with Leila

THE WAR OFFICE
CURZON STREET HOUSE
CURZON STREET
LONDON W. 1
11th Sept. 1945

Sir,

I am directed to inform you with pleasure that official information has been received that your son 6092414 Sgt. G. C. T. REPTON, THE QUEEN'S ROYAL REGIMENT, previously a prisoner of war in Japanese hands, has been recovered and is now with the Allied Forces.

The repatriation of recovered prisoners of war is being given highest priority, but it will be appreciated that some time must elapse before they reach the United Kingdom. Information of a general character regarding these recovered prisoners, including their movements before they reach home, will be given from time to time on the wireless and will be published in the press.

I am, Sir,
Your obedient Servant,
[illegible signature]

BUCKINGHAM PALACE

The Queen and I bid you a very warm welcome home.

Through all the great trials and sufferings which you have undergone at the hands of the Japanese, you and your comrades have been constantly in our thoughts. We know from the accounts we have already received how heavy those sufferings have been. We know also that these have been endured by you with the highest courage.

We mourn with you the deaths of so many of your gallant comrades.

With all our hearts, we hope that your return from captivity will bring you and your families a full measure of happiness, which you may long enjoy together.

George R.I.
September 1945

45 Manor Road,
Esher
Surrey
Sept. 12th

My dear Christopher,

We are all feeling so happy since having your cable saying you were safe, and then yesterday we had your letter dated Aug. 30th with direct news from you. We are very relieved to hear that your health is not too bad but expect you need no end of rest and building up, so we are glad you will be coming by sea as that will act as a tonic.

I am afraid you have not had your mail delivered for over a year or more, because we have been sending the R.C.s[103] regularly but it was so impossible to say much on them.

I can't tell you how much we are all looking forward to seeing you again, and I am hoping to see you in your old place by the wireless listening to the Symphony Concerts.

---

103 This may refer to regulation cards relatives were permitted to send to POWs via the Red Cross.

There seems to be so much to tell you that I hardly know where to begin. Dadda has written to you so you will know he is still working (at 75 years old) but little changed from when last you saw him.

I wonder if you could possibly get in touch with Humphry, who is now, I believe, not far from Bombay. His address is S/5441854 Sgt. Repton H., 422 Platoon, 6 Supply Coy. R.A.S.C. (Light), A.P.O. No. 8490.

Gareth is still on the same job and has not been out of England, much as he has tried. We often see him, he is coming this weekend, and we also expect Jocelyn, and Gervase is at Laxton for 2 days but will be back tomorrow, and we shall all be talking and thinking of you and wishing you were with us.

Sylvia and Leila are both in the W.A.A.F.[104] but will soon be demobbed now. Rosamund is not doing anything particular; just now she has had 2 small jobs but hates office work. She has been spending most of the summer at Youth Service Camps and is now at one in Suffolk. She has become quite an independent young – what shall I call her? I expect you will find her the most changed as she was so young when you left.

I feel sure you will feel absolutely at home after five months in the house, although it is over 6 years now, and also not St. Ann's Lodge. Gervase was away for 3 years in Africa and Italy; he seemed little different from when he left.

Did you ever meet a Nigel Evans who was in the same camp as you? Strangely enough, Perpetua shared a flat with his wife during the war and she got in touch with a prisoner of war who had escaped and had spent just 3 weeks in your camp and had met Nigel Evans and was able to tell her that when he saw him, he was in good health – that was June 1943. You were in the sanatorium at that time.

I expect Reg and Nell will be writing to you and telling you all their news.

We are hoping to have another letter from you before you sail. It is all too wonderful to know and feel you are free from the hands of those uncivilised […] people. It has been a never-ending worry and anxiety to know you were working so hard and being starved by

---

104 Women's Auxiliary Air Force.

them. Thank Heaven you are now being properly cared for. Do not worry about the state of affairs in England. They are not too bad and there always seems to be enough food.

Dickon joined the Fleet Air Arm just after the European War ended. He is an Air Mechanic and is still training. He came home about 2 weeks ago in his sailor's uniform and full of beans. You have most likely had a letter from him.

We are all longing to have you back, and I believe we shall be able to get the whole family together for your return. Bianca is at home for 21 days and is then going back to Rome and later to Vienna I believe. She will probably be writing. I am sending your address to her.

Very best love, and I hope you will soon be feeling better and stronger. Your loving Mother

Home

12th September

My dear Christopher,

How wonderful to be able to write to you again and to have a proper letter from you. Since the news of the surrender we've all been expecting your telegram day by day, and as the days went on our unspoken doubts and fears became worse – but now everything is so different knowing that we can expect you home soon. I hope, as you say, that we won't seem too strange, but even if we do at first, it won't take long for us to regain 1939. Gervase came home a month ago after over three years in the Mediterranean area, North Africa, Italy etc. and he seemed strange at first but now he is the same as ever.

From what you say about your health, unless you are belittling it, I feel rather relieved, because from the cards we received from you, and the fact that you were in the sanatorium (whatever that meant in Japanese minds), I'd expected that you would be a hospital case when repatriated. I hope that, as you say, it will only be a question of a month or two of normal conditions before you are well again.

Don't worry about what you read in the papers etc. about the situation in England nowadays; you'll find it much the same as usual

– well, no! I must qualify that because of course, you saw very little of wartime England – what I mean is that the rationing system still works well, food is not plentiful but more than adequate, you can buy all you want in restaurants without coupons. Trains, buses, cinemas, theatres, etc. are normal. Everything is much more organised than it used to be, prices are higher for a lot of things… I could go on like this for ages, but you can read it all better in the papers. People are still the same. There is no real depression or inflation here as on the Continent.

Already controls initiated during the war are lifting and goods that were scarce are becoming more plentiful (in some cases though the opposite is the case, such as soap and cigarettes). Promenade concerts continue – in the Albert Hall with new conductors, as the Queen's Hall was bombed, and Henry Wood is dead. I think our new Labour government, which Dadda never ceases to curse, may do us some good.

Love from Jocelyn

'Brambles'
Saturday Sept. 15th

My dear Christopher,

We are still waiting for your first letter from India. We do hope that you are enjoying the best treatment possible which will enable you to recover quickly. I wonder how long you must wait before getting on a boat. You must tell us the name of the boat and we will try to come and meet you, to be waiting there on the quayside when you step off.

But let me give you more news of home, for you must be thirsting for that as much as we are for your news. I suppose Mother will have told you already about the job Dadda is holding down at present? But just in case she hasn't, I'll tell you of all the jobs he has held since 1942. You'll remember he was with Barton Mayhew for a time but didn't settle down there very well, so that eventually there was a conspiracy amongst the younger men to dislodge him. But now, with the ever-increasing numbers of men being called up, Dadda was finding it easier to obtain a position. His main difficulty was in tolerating the ignominy of his position and supporting the weight of work. Poor Dadda, he used to bring reams of stuff home and hardly stop during the evenings and the weekends. There followed a sticky period in which he changed jobs several times, never earning very much, never very happy or secure in his position. But as one by one we joined the forces, leaving only Rosamund and Dickon at home, Dickon who was beginning to earn quite good money at Vickers, the expense of living became less and, amid the ever-increasing sufferings of the rest of the world, one's resignation to sadness and deprivation became easier. Perhaps I'm painting a gloomier picture than that which really existed, for really, apart from you, the whole family has come through this war very fortunately.

But I must tell you how last January, when I was in Italy, I received a letter full of good news. After a silence of 12 months your voice reached us again. That was the last communication we had from you until your cable reached us the other day. It was dated June '44, and you were in the sanatorium, Thailand. That perked us up no end, so that we were able to renew our prayers with greater faith. Together with this news of you came information that Dadda had been promoted to Secretary of the company he worked for then. He still holds that post, earning £15 a week, quite sufficient for this family. Most fortunately, too, he seems to get on very well with Mr. Gardner, the boss, who keeps giving Dadda fruit and flowers from his garden. Dadda brings these tokens home with him and presents them proudly to Mother. But of course, he gets very tired and cannot work much longer. We cannot expect him to anyway.

I believe Jocelyn wrote to you the other day, so will have given you all news of himself. At one time we thought he was going to get married in America. Did he tell you that?

Sylvia is not married yet, though she's had quite a few proposals, I believe. At one time she wanted to marry a Yank.

Dickon kept the fort going all the war at home, though he was not happy at being unable to join the forces. He was called up for the navy last July. Recently he paid us a flying visit. Since I last saw him, he has grown much taller and broader, looks the picture of health and has a greater capacity than most people for enjoying life.

But Jocelyn you will find thin, and his health is not very good. One is amazed wondering how he ever earned the name of 'Barrel'.

Leila is a rather large young woman in the W.A.A.F.s; very capable. She has made up her mind to become a nurse.

Even for me, after 3½ years, Rosamund has changed beyond all recognition, so heaven only knows what you will make of her.

Look, this page is running out, but I will try and write some more tomorrow.

From your loving brother,
Gervase

'Brambles'
Sunday Sept. 16ᵗʰ

My dear Christopher,

Hope you are receiving our letters very easily now.

I'm settling down to write this to you on Sunday evening. A pleasant weekend is just ending. We saw Leila and Gareth off on the 9.05, Leila to Uxbridge and Gareth to Halton. Now we have had supper and are sitting in the drawing-room. We always have late supper nowadays. Mother and Bianca are sitting on the sofa, knitting and mending and listening to Dadda, who is reading to them from his book. Jocelyn is sitting in the armchair, looking up something in a Latin dictionary; the dog is curled up under his feet. Sylvia is ironing in the kitchen. This is a small house – you will remember, we told you – but you'll find the old Repton atmosphere in it.

Your name has cropped up a lot this weekend, you can imagine. It is as though the good news of you has unlocked a cupboard, long closed, of good memories. Also, one has heard new hopes expressed, more ambitious than before, and schemes for holidays that might please you. Gareth has been trying to revive those popular melodies, 'Blue Skies Are Around the Corner' and 'I've Locked My Heart and Thrown Away the Key'[105].

What about that walking tour? Does the thought still attract you? Or am I being a little bit premature in bringing up the subject? But the tone of your letter seemed so confident, so Christopherian,

---

[105] Gervase means 'I'm Gonna Lock My Heart (And Throw Away the Key)', which was first recorded by Billie Holiday in 1938.

as ever was, that it banished from my mind any thoughts of radical changes in your outlook and physical condition. But I must really wait until we hear from you again – tomorrow, we hope.

We went for a pleasant walk this afternoon through Claygate, across Arbrook Common, where some people were bathing in the Black Pond, until we reached the pine woods of Oxshott. At Oxshott we caught the train back to Hinchley Wood, where tea was waiting with Mother's scones. A traditional walk this has become, with a traditional ending. More tomorrow.

With love,
Gervase

'Brambles'
45 Manor Road North
Hinchley Wood
Esher
Surrey
17th September

My dear Christopher,

How wonderful to know you are safe and will be home soon. Just imagine how we must all have changed in the last six years. I expect we shall hardly know you. It was marvellous to read a letter from you again instead of those awful cards.

I was going to write to you this weekend, but the time went so quickly with everyone in the house. It is such a long time since I wrote to you it is difficult to know where to start. I wonder if you received those two letters I typed while I was working at the office. Soon after that they brought in the regulation of only 25 words per fortnight and only one letter per fortnight, and that from the nearest relatives, so Mother took that over. I do hope you didn't think we just gave up writing.

As you have probably heard, I joined the W.A.A.F. in May '44 as a Radar operator like Sylvia, and I was first stationed at two places in Pembrokeshire and then first in S. Devon and then in North Devon. Now I am what is known as a misemployed person; I am working as a clerk, pay accounts and helping with the demobilisation of the R.A.F. It is very boring after Radar, but I am stationed at Uxbridge and I get home every weekend. This is a very big station and seems queer after the tiny little places I have been used to. We have a bugle to wake us and put us to bed at 10.15 and at all odd times during the day. Our hours are 8.30 a.m. till 4.30, so we have a whole evening free to do as we like. There are three good cinemas in Uxbridge and one on camp, so you see we do very well.

You must find it very queer coming back to all this sort of life again after three and a half years of nothing. We have all been so terribly worried when we heard of all those horrible, unbelievable atrocities. Thank heavens it is all over now.

Of course, when you went to India in 1939 Rosamund and I were still at school, so you will see a terrific alteration. Rosamund's hair is almost blonde in parts and she has it in a beautiful high roll in the front and very glamorously hanging down to her shoulders. I am afraid both she and I have got rather fatter than we used to be, which only goes to show we haven't anywhere near starved in this country. In fact, there are some people who hardly knew there was a war on and others who didn't want it to end as they were profiteering well out of it. Considering what scanty rations you must have had, we have no room at all to grumble.

This last weekend when I got home on Saturday there was only Mother and Dadda and Gervase there, then Bianca arrived about teatime, Gareth at supper time, and early next morning Sylvia came in and later still Jocelyn, so you see we were quite a crowd. Gervase, Bianca and I went to 11 o'clock Mass at Claygate, and after dinner we started for the usual Sunday walk to Oxshott, taking Ros's dog Marcus; a terrier rather like Peter. Unfortunately, I had terrific blisters on my heels, so I had to come back. Gareth and I left on the 9.05 p.m. train and travelled together as far as Baker Street. I must go onto another lettercard here, so meanwhile,

Lots of love from Leila

*Bianca c.1940s, taken
in studio in Rome*

'Brambles'
19th September

My dear Christopher,

I have just received your address from Mother, so I will post these letters today. I forgot to take the address while I was home. It is after lunch now and I have about half an hour before I go back to work. We were very slack this morning, hardly anything to do, so I spent most of the morning sitting and talking to one of the girls and two Warrant Officers.

Tonight we are hoping to go to a dance in Uxbridge. Last night we wanted to see Bette Davis's new film *Mr. Skeffington*, but there was such a terrific queue that we could not get in.

I expect you will have missed hearing any decent music all this time. Jocelyn may have told you about his collection of records that he bought in America. There are some really lovely ones among them. I have got rather keen on ballet and I have seen the Sadlers Wells once, and I want to see the International which is on in London at the moment. I would have liked to have gone to a Prom, but they have become so popular during the war that it was impossible to book up. I heard the last one on the wireless and as usual everyone went almost mad at the end. Jocelyn, Bianca and Gareth went to the last but one.

Bianca finishes her leave this Sunday and if the weather is fine enough will be flying back to Italy on a Liberator bomber.

I wonder what you will think of Hinchley Wood and the house. It is a pity we could not have stayed at Chertsey, although this place has many advantages. It is nearer to the shops, which helps Mother a lot, and it is more convenient for us all coming on leave.

We still keep up the tradition of the Sunday walk, although we now go to Oxshott Common or Clandon and Newlands Corner.

Just lately when it has been very warm we decided to take a boat out instead, and one day we could only get two punts, so with Bianca, Rosamund, Jocelyn and I in one and Sylvia, Gareth and Gervase in another we started off. In the beginning it was most amusing as we went round in perfect circles in the middle of the river until Jocelyn got the hang of it! He was sitting at one end with a paddle and he seemed determined to dig up the Thames; at least that is what it looked like! We drew into the side and waited for the others to come. When they arrived, we said to them – surely they were going backwards, and then suddenly realised that we were wrong and, as Jocelyn put it, had been going 'hard astern' all the time. Another Sunday we had a double and a single skiff: Sylvia and Dickon in one and Rosamund, Gervase, Jocelyn and me in the other. That day we had two collisions and the rudder broke off the other boat. The first collision was caused by Ros, who was supposed to be steering but got panicky when she saw a Naval Cadets sailing boat coming, so we bashed into them and scraped the paint off the side. The second collision was with another skiff and it only knocked a small piece off the side of the seat!

I have not much more room here, and also it is time to go back to work. I will write again soon, but I hope you will be home very soon. It will be wonderful to see you again.

Till next time I write, very best wishes and
Lots of love from Leila

Electra House
Victoria Embankment
London W.C. 2.
22nd September 1945

Dear Sir or Madam,

It is a great pleasure to me to be able to send you the enclosed copy of a telegram from your relative who is now liberated from the Japanese.

In order to relieve your anxiety at the earliest possible moment this message has been transmitted free of charge by Cable and Wireless Ltd. from the Far East, and by the Post Office, in co-operation with the War Office.

In the same way we shall be happy to send your reply free, if you will write it – using about 12 words in addition to the address – on the enclosed form and hand it in at your local Cable and Wireless Office or any Post Office where telegrams are normally accepted.

Will you please insert on the reply-paid form the address given in the enclosed telegram and sign it with your surname.

With best wishes,
I remain,
Yours sincerely,
Sir Edward Wilshaw
Chairman

57 C CW COLOMBO 20 SEPT.
ARRIVED SAFELY AT COLOMBO HOPE BE HOME SOON
WRITING ADDRESS LETTERS AND TELEGRAMS TO C/O BOX
164 LONDON EC1 = CHRISTOPHER +

CABLE RECEIVED GREAT REJOICING ALL WELL AND AWAITING
YOUR ARRIVAL = REPTON

S.S. *Corfu*
Port Suez
28 Sept. '45

P.S. Give tel. no. if any.

My dear Mother and Father and all at home,

I don't know whether you got the airletter I sent from Thailand last month but have not written since and had not intended doing so as it seemed hardly worthwhile when, with luck, I should myself arrive shortly after the letter. As ever, as there is a chance of sending by air mail here I have changed my mind and am sending you this brief note to prepare you for my arrival (excuse the pencil – pens and ink difficult to procure).

Firstly, I was very glad to get your cable at Colombo. You will understand that I was very anxious about all of you, not having heard since before the V-bombs and the European campaign. I suppose J.

and G. are still in the services and probably abroad still. Never in my wildest dreams did I expect to be on my way home so soon after the end. Being attached to the Indian Army, I naturally expected to be kept several months in India at least.

We have been given wonderful treatment since being freed – why, I don't really know as we've been a liability for the last 3½ years. Flown out of Thailand to Rangoon by U.S. Dakotas, then an aerodrome (Phetchaburi) built by P.O.W.s for the Japanese. Everything perfectly organised at R. despite the damage to and desolation of the city and the obvious poverty there. Spent 2 days in a university turned over as a hospital and then discharged to a transit camp; tents, but very good, complete with well-stocked N.A.A.F.I. cinema etc. In fact, one was able to enjoy most of the things that one had missed for so long. The only snag was our large numbers which made long queues for everything the order of the day.

It's the same on board, but one cannot grumble at it, only think oneself lucky to have got away on the second P.O.W. ship – we are having a race with the S.S. *Monowai* (P.&O.) to be first ship home; she is a day ahead or will be, as she left here midday today, but we are a faster ship, so may do it. The voyage has been pretty good so far. Between Colombo and Aden, the seas were fairly heavy due to the end of the monsoon, but lying here at Suez it is a perfect day, cloudless Egyptian sky and brilliant sun; very familiar, I expect, to Gervase.

Spent a very enjoyable day at Colombo ashore where again the organisation was perfect. Have never before seen so many white women in the East – crowds of W.R.E.N.s[106], W.A.A.F.s, A.T.S.! Of course, they very kindly showed some of us around the place; nice but a little artificial. I had hoped to pick up a few things to bring home to you from there, but prices were exorbitantly high, so I contented myself with a little junk.

Have heard such stories of the food shortage at home that many of the blokes are buying up all the canned goods they can put in the canteen, in many cases more than a kit bag full. I suppose they expect

---

106 Women's Royal Naval Service, the women's branch of Britain's Royal Navy, first formed during World Wars I and II.

to return in the role of relieving force bringing help to a starving garrison. Unless I get an urgent cable from you, I shall not follow their example, having quite enough to carry as it is with all the new kit that's been issued. Am told that we're getting on board just about twice as much butter, sugar, bacon, tea, meat and jam as you're getting at home. If so, this is not very good training for the regime to come. However, I'm making the best of it while I can; you can understand how one has looked forward to real food again, after 3½ years of mainly rice. Fortunately for me, I soon took to rice and was able to enjoy it when hungry. It was the people who couldn't who mainly went under and died of malnutrition etc. Still, to return to the food situation at home, I suppose that being a large family one does slightly better. I presume that sugarless tea and coffee is in the fashion now. Am hoping, Mother, to find that you have been able to make some of your beautiful raspberry jam, though I don't suppose the fruit abounds as it did at St. Ann's.

Am a little worried as to whether you'll have room for me, as I understand 'The Brambles' is rather small, especially if most of the family are at home. As for inviting Bianca and H. & G. down, I suppose that's an impossibility – by the way, I hope the 'all well' in your cable included them, and Reg and Nell, Leila and Ina.

Well, this letter is dragging out longer than I anticipated, so I'll definitely finish at the bottom here.

If we sail from Suez tomorrow night (29th) we should reach Port Said by morning 30th, Gibraltar 5 days later (5th) and home by the 8th. Whether Southampton or Tilbury am not certain. Please do not any of you attempt to meet me. The army is not likely to detain us more than 48 hours after landing and then leave (in my case should be 56 + 72 days with pay etc.). I'll write you as to time of arrival at Esher station, and someone might meet me there and show me the way! If you want to give me any instructions on landing, write a cable c/o Box 166, London E.C. 1.

I must repeat again how thankful I am that you are all well (hope that you really are so). You should find me pretty fit, though expect me to have a bad cold on arrival.

Till then (less than 2 weeks with luck),
Love to all from Christopher

76 Victoria St.
1/10/45

My very dear boy,

Your letter from Port Suez arrived yesterday evening and we found in the *Evening Standard* confirmation of your belief that you should dock on Monday next.

You can imagine our excitement as we had dreaded that you might be detained in India for a time, and to have you arriving by the first boat sounded too good to be true!

We are glad that you know why relatives are not allowed to meet the boats, but I suppose it is a wise plan.

If you know the approximate time of your arrival at Waterloo, wire me:-

Repton
New Process Welders
76 Victoria Street
S.W. 1.

This is better than wiring home, as, H. Wood being only a Sub-Post Office, telegrams are often delayed. We have no telephone at home, but I can telephone to our next-door neighbour to let them know at home.

I can reach Waterloo in six minutes. If I get your telegram giving time of arrival at Waterloo, I will drop everything and go to Waterloo to meet your train. If we do not connect immediately, make Platform 5 the rendez-vous. If we do not meet at the platform at which you arrive or at Platform 5, ring me up (tel. Victoria 1474) and I will come along at once. I do not go out to lunch, and stay in the office until 6.30.

If you are very late in arrival, Esher is not the best station. You should book to Hinchley Wood (on the Cobham and Guildford Line); it is the next station after Surbiton, and it is only five minutes' walk from home.

I enclose a very rough plan in case you are very belated. This is, I am afraid, a very incoherent letter, but I am too excited to think properly.

Your loving Father

P.S. Be careful to note arrival at Surbiton, as several people coming to see us have been carried down the line. During the rush hours, Surbiton is the first stop, but during the day the trains stop at all stations.

'Brambles'
9 Nov. '45

My dear Sylvia,

Very sorry to hear you can't make it for the weekend. When are you going to have those tonsils of yours removed?

Re. your leave that you're going to apply for, I've asked Gervase to postpone his 7-day from Nov. 23rd to Dec. 3rd, as I'm due to go back to the army (only for a few days, I hope) on Nov. 20th, so there will be less chance of our missing each other then. If you could do the same with your leave, I should be very pleased, then you, Gervase and myself might all be home at once. Still, if you can only get it on Nov. 23rd, don't bother.

It's 8 p.m. and Pauline has just called to see Rosamund. Dad says, "What on earth has that appalling little female got to come round at this time of night?" The argument's getting worse now; she's like a char-woman. Rosamund's furious. I'm sure she won't play bridge with us after that.

Gareth and I took her up to London yesterday and had her buy a coat and skirt (separate) at B.&H.[107] The coat's lovely (of course it would be as G. chose it), dark blue and beautifully tailored. Rosamund's sure you'll want to pinch it as soon as you see it. The assistant told us it must be good as Mrs. Bourne of B.&H. had got herself the same one. Gareth and I have been on a shopping expedition to Kingston this afternoon and brought back all kinds of gaudy ties and scarves. Gareth's scarf is a particularly brilliant tartan with all the colours in the rainbow. I'm sure you'll want that too.

Saw *The Seventh Veil* with Jocelyn and Leila last night. J. wanted to see *The Wizard of Oz*, but we managed to persuade him otherwise and I'm glad we did.

---

107 Bourne & Hollingsworth, an Art Deco-style department store on Oxford Street.

Perpetua's not coming after all this weekend; a press conference or something. Due to Mother's continually saying things about the small house, irregular meals, no maid etc., etc., I wrote rather a silly letter to P. when I invited her, apologising for such shortcomings, and naturally she bridled at it. We're still friends, however, and I'm seeing her Monday night.

Mother was going to write to you but I'm doing this to save her. Hope you don't mind.

Why did you say, 'How funny' when they told you Johnnie was unduly informal? He's the American, isn't he – do you think David will be pleased when I tell him?

I've just been talking to Dad about the house and other things, and he says that it's time we all started saving and living less extravagantly as we'll be needing money soon, both for the family and each of us individually, as he won't be able to help us himself when we are out of the services and not yet in a job. Excuse me striking such a serious note, but I do think most of us are living on rather a high level at present and it would be as well to think of this now and again. Not you so much, except in so far as you will have to be dependent on yourself when you leave the W.A.A.F.s. I'm always making resolutions myself to cut down expenses on drink, travelling, meals outside etc., but it is hard, isn't it?

When are you going to introduce me to some of your girl-friends? Couldn't you invite one or two to come and see you during the week that you're on leave? Gervase probably won't be worried as he's having a wonderful time at present amongst thousands of A.T.S. girls. He didn't tell us this, but he told Aunt Nell.

Well, cheerio, dear, as the barmaid at the Hinchley Arms says.
Your ever-loving brother
Christopher (Sentimental Old Owl No. 2)

P.S. Dad doesn't like H.W.'s *Sun in the Sands*[108]. "The young waster's introspection is morbid and unhealthy."

---

108 *The Sun in the Sands* by Henry Williamson, published in 1945.

St Michael's
Buckingham Rd
Cambridge
16th November 1945

My dear Christopher,

I was delighted to hear from you and to know that you are safely back in England again; thank you so much for writing. I do hope we shall be able to meet soon – but I don't return to Downside until about the 10th of December or thereabouts. I have been at Cambridge one year and am now doing my second (I was ordained in July 1943) year here. I am living as a matter of fact with the Dominicans – so it is quite like old times. The superior here is Fr. Bernard Delaney, whom you will remember at school is the Provincial – but he is away a good deal. I think if you pay a visit to Laxton you ought to drop in here for a night on the way back – I am sure Henry would arrange it for you – after all it is only about 40 miles from Laxton!* I enjoyed Dickon's visit to Downside very much, though I haven't seen him since, but I believe he used to see quite a lot of Fr. Gerald Meath, who is here, when he was at Manchester.

No, I am afraid I never got any letters from you from Malaya – I think most of the mail coming from there got lost. It must be a wonderful thing for you to be back in England again after all these years, and you must so often have wondered if ever you'd get back there again. When I used to visit Chanctonbury Ring with some friends of mine who live at Shipley in Sussex, I often thought of you out there in the Far East.

I must stop now. Please write again.

Ever yours affectionately,
Christopher (Dom A. Watkin)

* In the Peterborough direction if you remember which direction that is!!

20 St. Loo Mansions
St. Loo Avenue
S.W. 3
October 28th 1945

My dear Christopher,

It was lovely to see you again, and somehow it didn't seem anything like 5 years (or is it 6?) since our last meeting.

I had hoped that I might be able to spend next weekend at Esher, but Mummy has just written to say that she wants me to go home for it as an old family friend is to be there. Could I come the following weekend, November 10th & 11th? Or if it isn't convenient, could you come to Dorking for it? I can't remember when you said you had to report to your unit – I hope it isn't that weekend?

How are you, and what have you been doing?

My love to all the family and to you,
Perpetua

18 Westmoreland Road
Barnes
London S.W. 13
Monday 29 Oct. '45

Dear Rep,

I was very sorry that you could not stay longer than you did Friday, but if it is convenient for you, we will see each other Friday next, 2 Nov. I hope you arrived home safely – it was rather good of that fellow to offer you a lift home in his car. You wouldn't have been stranded if you had of [sic] lost the last bus to Esher.

I am at present staying with two of my sisters at Ipswich. It is quite a nice place and I intend to-day to look up a P. of W. friend of mine here. Unfortunately, he was out yesterday when I arrived but his father has warned him of my coming so he will be expecting me.

I will be writing to Smudger Smith to-day and will convey your regards. He will probably be coming to London to stop at my home, if it does not interfere with his brother's leave from Germany. So you will probably be able to meet him. I will also be writing to Bill Mill. He is at present in Manchester visiting friends. I hope he is able to fix up the petrol.

This machine belongs to my brother-in-law and is of German manufacture (you can guess how he came to have it). It has one or two extras such as ü, Ä, ß. However, it does the job well.

I won't write any more as my sister is pestering me to get ready for going out somewhere. She wants to introduce to me one or two nice girls (am I lucky). Will be seeing you Friday – let me know where and when your train arrives so I will be able to meet you.

All the best.
Yours,
Hooky Walker

339 Brighton Road
Derby
27 X 45

Dear Mrs. Repton,

You may call to mind my visit a little over three years ago when I had the pleasure of meeting you and your second son. I came hoping to see Christopher, but he was serving abroad at that time. I have often wondered, since, if Christopher has been home on leave. Perhaps you will be good enough to write and let me know (when you have time to spare) how your sons are getting on. I do hope they all return home safely. I hope, some day, to see Christopher again. Although I come to London periodically, my time is mostly absorbed in business, which seldom takes me further south than the capital. I sincerely hope you are all well. Please give my kind regards to all.

Yours very sincerely,
Arthur E. Field

339 Brighton Road
Derby
3 XI 45

My dear Christopher,

Many thanks for your kind letter of Oct. 30th.

I am so glad to know you are home again and safe. After six years of army life, the greater part having been spent in a Jap prison, it must be the joy of a lifetime to find yourself at home again, and one for due thanksgiving. Liberated troops from Japan have been pouring home through several weeks. Many of them were attached to the 1/5 Sherwood Foresters (the Derby & Notts. Regiment), whose headquarters are here in Derby and they are local men. So we hear quite a lot in this neighbourhood about the terrible atrocities committed by the Japs.

When you left in 1939 your home was at Chertsey. From there I had a very nice letter from your brother (Gervais) [sic], who also gave me your address in India. I wrote you in about May '40 but never received a reply. Probably the letter was lost in transit. I sent it by air mail.

How time passed! It is nearly fifteen years since I left St. Edmund's.[109] You are quite right! I was in Douglas house, although I never intended going on for the priesthood. I loved dear St. Edmund's, though I wished I had been either in Challoner or Talbot. I was a little senior to you but was rather tall for my age. When I called at your Esher home in 1942 your brother Jocelyn told me you went later to Laxton. I know Stamford, which is quite near. It is a Dominican school. I know a little some of the Doms in Leicester and Haverstock Hill. Their church is only half built, but the one in London is great. One would imagine you would appreciate the contrast in the simple liturgy of the Dominicans after the glorious liturgical services in St. Edmund's chapel. I went to Old Hall last year for St. E.'s Day (Nov. 16th), but am not yet certain whether I shall manage it this year or not. I hope so.

My work takes me over a large area of England and Wales, and I am frequently in London. I should, if possible, so much like to see you whilst you are at home. Perhaps it might be more convenient

---

109 Junior boarding school.

to see you in town. However, will you be good enough to write me again soon? Should you prefer me to come down to Esher I would do so, else I could arrange a meeting in town. Though I am away from home a lot, letters are always forwarded. I expect to come up to town very soon. Please write as soon as you are able. Give my kind regards to your mother and any other members of the family at home.

Best wishes from yours,
Arthur E. Field

Blackfriars School

Laxton

Kettering

Nov. 1. 1945

Dear C. Repton,

Many thanks for your letter, which I was delighted to get and to hear your news and that you have come through the long ordeal as a P.O.W. and that you are well. It will be a great joy to see you here, and of course come with Dickon.

I suggest any weekend in November or December if you can let us have a card a few days in advance. I have just got Maxwell's address from Fr. Dominic – I find he has already posted you a card – at the moment I don't know Napper Young's but will let you have it when I hear it.

Yours ever,
Fr. Henry

Blackfriars School

Laxton

Kettering

Northants.

Telephone: Duddington 202

Goods by Rail:-

Wakerley and Barrowden, L.M.S.

24 XI 45

My dear Christopher,

Thanks so much for your letter; so nice to hear from you. I've been heartily ashamed of myself for a long time, for not writing to you all that time; I often and often meant to, but never succeeded; but anyway, you don't seem to harbour a grudge as you very well might, so all is well and it's very magnanimous of you!

Yes, do come along and see us as soon as you can. There's plenty more term left; we don't break up till just a few days before Xmas. Dec. 1ˢᵗ weekend I've got a chappie coming, and the next weekend I'm away, unhappily, but there's the one after that; or p'raps you could manage some days inside the week sometime if G. is on leave? Anyway, do the best you can, and as soon as you can.

Forgive this hurried scrap for the moment; much nicer to say things by word of m. than by letter, and I shall expect to see you soon, and hear all your news then.

Remember me to your people, and of course to the other bros. when you see any of them.

Yours ever,
Gerald

13 South Hill Drive
Gilstead
Bingley
Nov. 8ᵗʰ 1945

Dear Chris,

Thanks for your letter dated the 1ˢᵗ. We are now drawing to the end of our 6 weeks and no doubt you will be glad to get your demob as soon as possible and feel a bit more a 'civvy'. Things have quietened down now for me, what with Rotary dinners, P.O.W. dinners, and tonight the 4 Bingley P.O.W.s have been stung (including me) for a parade at a 'Festival of Remembrance'.

I went to Ipswich about a week ago and saw Sgt. Standring I.A.C.C., who is home from Indo-China [sic]. He looks pretty well, and I had quite a good time. Tomorrow, 9ᵗʰ, Bill Mill, the P.O. Navvy from Phetchaburi Camp, is paying me a flying visit, then proceeding to London to pick up 'Hooky' and taking him to his home in Cornwall.

Talking about raw deals, Chris, an ex-pal of mine in Suffolks who went abroad with me in 1940 has only arrived home from India about the middle of this year and he is now in Germany, and yet one hears of others never leaving England. Well, roll on the 20th and the Medical Exam.

Yours sincerely,
Ron

25 McKay Road,
Wimbledon S.W. 20
13th November 1945

Dear Repton,

I was so very glad to have your letter. I had enquired several times as to where you were, and I was told that you were in India and understood you might be taking a permanent commission in the Indian Army. What a terrible time you must have had on the Burma Road [sic]. Were you at Changi Barracks at Singapore? An old friend of mine was in Changi Gaol and I saw him last week.

How are you? If you can spare the time, do come up and have lunch with me. I should so like to see you again. Of course, I remember you very well, and I was most sorry to lose you. I note you will not be going on with accountancy, but if I can do anything for you, in way of a reference, I shall be delighted. Have you anything definite in view yet?

I am so glad that all your family have got through the war safely. We have been very fortunate here. No large damage, though we had one bomber brought down quite near, and one doodlebug which just missed the top of the house and fell about 500 yards away.

The work in town was rather hectic, especially during the Blitz. The Dutch church went up when a mine descended, and it put our telephones out of commission for 6 weeks and most of our windows went. Managed to carry on with relays of staff when I had 5 complete changes during the war. Allworth is coming back home when he gets demobilised, I hope in March.

I think you are wise to go into a commercial job, as the 5 years you have been away would have put you back so much if you had decided to go in for accountancy.

Do come and see me if you can. Should so much like to see you again and hear all your news. Your letter was most interesting. Thanks so much for writing to me.

Hoping to see you soon.

Yours sincerely,
A. W. Goodfellow[110]

45 Iscennen Road
Ammanford
Carmarthenshire
14.11.45

Dear Chris,

At long last, the freedom we have waited for is ours. You arrived home before me, but I anticipated that the medics, if fit, would be the last to go.

We had a very good trip by air, sea and train. The weather was perfect until we got to the Bay of Biscay and then we ran into the bad weather. Fortunately, I am a good sailor and did not suffer the misery of seasickness.

I called at St. Bernard's[111] during my short stay in London. It looks much the same. Those old buildings still seem to dominate the London horizon despite the bombing. Your uncle, Dr. Riches, saw me and was very nice, as usual. You seem to be giving me an unmerited good name. It was little I did for you. It was always my fervent wish that more could have been done when you sorely needed it during the times of need.

My wife is in good health, but rather thin. Needless to say, it is good to be back with her. Many marriages have ended in disaster.

---

110 Christopher noted on the envelope that he answered the letter and met his former employer, Mr Goodfellow, for lunch.

111 Hospital in Southall where Christopher's uncle, Dr Reginald Riches, was deputy medical superintendent.

Mine survived the years of separation. When you meet her, I am sure you will like her.

Well, Chris, all for the present. I will write again when I have more time and trust you will write when you feel like it. Shall be glad to hear from you.

All the best,
Dan Moriarty

Erica Villa

Rajpur

Dehra Dun District[112]

India

21 Nov. 1945

Dear Chris,

I was delighted to receive a letter from you, though I must say I'm sorry to know that England does not come up to your expectations. Actually, India is not as hot either – prices are high etc., and though not as bad as England, it is a far different India to the one we left five years ago. However, I'm glad you are deciding to come back – I think it is your best bet.

As for myself – well, I guess these last two months have been plain hell for me. I arrived home just in time to see a man (who, besides being my father-in-law, is my best friend) cashiered and sentenced to three years for a crime which I am convinced he did not commit. A couple of days before this I met my wife after five years' separation. She informed me that she no longer loved me – would not live with me and wanted a divorce. Pretty grim, eh!! 'A left to the body and a right to the jaw.' However, as you know, I can take it, although I must admit I was knocked for six.

When I return to duty, I shall supply her with grounds for divorce, then perhaps I can pick up the pieces and make a fresh start. My leave

---

112 Now known as the city of Dehradun, Dehra Dun District in United Provinces was established in the 19th century under the British Raj, and the British used it as a centre for cultivating tea. During WWII it housed a prison camp for Germans, Austrians and Italians.

ends on 29 Dec. so maybe, who knows, the New Year may mean for me a New Life. I can only pray that if fate has got any more dirty tricks up her sleeve, she'll give me a chance to get my breath before she delivers the remainder. Three and a half of the best under the Japs followed by these two is about all I can stand at the moment. Now that I have had two months to think things over in, I realise that any girl who could treat a man in the way that my wife treated me – when she knew I was down – then that girl is not worth a moment's consideration and getting free of her is a blessing in disguise. However, I mustn't bore you with my little troubles. Please don't mention anything of this to our mutual friends. If they must find out about it, let them find out for themselves. I've merely told you because it eases my mind to tell somebody and I know you can keep your mouth shut.

As regards Charles Furlong, I believe he is a Captain now at GHQ. However, if you address him c/o I.A.C.C. Depot, Ambala, it will find him. Incidentally, that address will find anybody of the Corps with whom you may wish to correspond. As regards future prospects in our Corps, I'm afraid I can't tell you a thing at the moment as I haven't bothered about it. When my leave is expired, I report to HQ Lahore District; from there I shall send you what information I can.

Cheerio for now, old chap, I hope we'll meet again soon. Give my best regards to Hooky Walker when you see him. All the very best of luck to you.

Very sincerely yours,
Don

My correct address:-
S/5441854 Sgt. Repton H.
6 Supply Coy. R.A.S.C. (Lt.)
S.E.A.C.[113]
25 Nov. '45

My dear Christopher,

I hardly know how to thank you for the spate of delightful letters

---

113 South East Asia Command, the body in charge of Allied operations in Southeast Asia during WWII.

I have received from you – not the less inasmuch as 7 of them were written, as it were, in vacuo. I'm glad you have now received my first.

Your flirtation with the possibility of seeking a job out East surprises me. Though there are certain obvious advantages, I have yet to find anything to compensate the loss of the English landscape and climate (for you especially, I should have thought, the sweet succession of Summer, Autumn, Winter and Spring), the clean, energetic English air… But these may be trifles. Think of the society in which you would have to move, the antiquated social order, the absence of the best, the dominance of the worst, that is European! But perhaps, in my superficial way, I have neglected some other, far deeper motive. Are you perhaps prompted by the suburban terror, by the fear of becoming what Gervase calls "a perfect stooge"? I can't see you ever becoming one! I am myself considering a 'civvy' job in Germany (applications to Norfolk House, London) and have asked for an application form and particulars. But rosy though one's prospects might be out here, I'm too much of a European to consider making this even a temporary home. Do let me have your views.

How, by the way, is your German? I doubt if you got much chance of studying while in captivity. Did you pick up any Japanese – that is, apart from the colourful expletives that were dotted all over Epistle No. 2? I've done a little; got as far as simple sentences such as '*Watashi ga inn in Taro no hone wo yaru*', which doubtless you know means 'I give the dog Taro's bone'; but once the need for it became neurotic, I abandoned it all for German. The grammatical complexities, however, and the totally alien quality of the syntax, are fascinating from the philological point of view.

Yes, seeing the girls after so long an absence must have been 'frightening'! Once I did not see Rosamund for over six months, and believe it or not, her metamorphosis was even then disconcerting.

I'm sorry this letter lacks fire: I'm in a curiously negative mood (I should be in mufti by early March, possibly in February) – my immediate surroundings seem impossibly remote and unreal. It's so unsatisfactory being a 'sahib' – you are only permitted a cursory glance at the surface of things. The 'natives' can be hospitable, but only by being Western themselves. The other night, walking back from Klang (I've not been to Singapore, by the way), I was enveloped in a crowd of Tamils celebrating the God(dess) of Light's feast-day. A glorious sensation, losing oneself in a crowd of almost Dionysian worshippers – drum-beatings, ecstatic yells, coconuts bashed fervently on our Macadam roads – but, above everything, the exquisite charm and fineries of rarely seen Malay women. Of course, you were right – I had not seen the Malay girls when I succumbed to the Chinese! But what's the use?

God, what fun we'll have hiking and pub-crawling – I feel an almost religious fervour at the thought of it.

All the best, old chap.
Humphry

Wood Ayven
Rylands Hey
Greasby
Wirral
Cheshire
Mon 2nd '45

Dear Chris,

Delighted to receive your letter some days ago.

Pleased to hear that you and all the family are well. I found them all at home well. Mother had aged quite a lot. I think a lot of this was due to worry, as she had had no word from me whatsoever, and I think I mentioned before that Pop was in Shanghai. We heard from him some days ago, and I'm pleased to say he's quite well. I don't think that he will be home for some time yet as they're starting up again in Shanghai, and he probably feels he's under a slight obligation to the company for his pay whilst interned.

Well, Chris, I don't know how you feel but I'm quite prepared to return to Malaya tomorrow. England's absolutely dead, and so expensive. I've bought just one pair of boots – I should say shoes – and spent over £60 on booze. Shall have to settle down a bit.

I arrived home on Oct. 16th; made a few pounds playing poker aboard, about £8. Came in handy too.

These duty calls 'brown me off', as they say in the army.

Was away for the weekend to Wales; had quite a nice time. Coming back on the Saturday night from a country pub on some mountain, fell and took the back out of a borrowed suit, but it was well worth it, until wakening Sunday.

Oh, did a little better than you regarding transit camp. Arrived in Liverpool in thick fog, got ashore about 2 p.m. and away from transit camp about 10 p.m. Still don't know if I had been through all the red tape, but came away. My sister was waiting with the car.

So pleased to hear that you had written and heard from Leo. I shall be doing a tour of the east coast [sic] of London and hope to see you all then. Pleased to hear that your sisters are pretty. I like pretty girls, and I shall have to keep you up to your promise.

Well, Chris, here are the addresses you asked for.

E. P. Powell
78 Oval Rd. South
Dagenham
Essex

R. Caward
36 Defoe Crescent
Mile End
Colchester
Essex

Must conclude at present or the pubs will be closed. Hoping to see you very soon.

Yours sincerely,
Bill

537299 SGT. CAWARD R.
BED 7
Y.M.C.A. Kingston
13-12-45

Dear Rep,

As you can see, I am still at the Y.M. but will be leaving for E. 17 on Monday.

Are you still in touch with Charlton and is he at present staying in London? Would very much like to see or get in immediate touch with him, with a very strong [illegible] to once again proceeding to Malaya. O yes! Rep, old boy. Simply cannot tolerate England any longer. Weather terribly cold. People? So frightfully narrow-minded. Each one living in his or 'her' own narrow little world. How awful this place seems after the 'freedom' of the East. People with their petty whims and so-called troubles, I find I cannot converse with and still remain friendly and civil. The girl-friend's mother told me a terrible tale of woe the other night of the "awful" bacon that they had to put up with during the war. Honestly, old man. I felt like saying, "BACON?" etc., etc., etc. Maybe I am a cynic, Rep, but all I know is that this confounded country and I do not get along so well together. Want to go abroad again.

Would very much like to hear from you or meet you in the near future (before Monday) if convenient for you. Could drop Charlie a line to his address but would like to know if he is in London first.

Feel certain that my writing is worse than yours, Rep, but hands are cold and also am in flaming hurry. So please excuse scribble.

Must close now, hoping for early response.

Your old Lang Suan Shigotoist,[114]
Ray

c/o Mrs Murrin
Dunsborough Farm
Roborough
Plymouth
Devon
19 Dec. 1945

Dear Repton,

Time slips by so quickly – it is a fortnight since I had your letter. I was up in London for one night and I told my sister-in-law to

---

114 'Shigoto' is Japanese for 'work', so he probably means 'Your fellow worker at Langsuan'.

let you know that it would be quite in order to use my name as a reference. I hope she passed the message on. I apologise for taking so long to write. I hope you get the job as I think it should suit you with your knowledge of French. Let me know if you get it. I have had no enquiries re. your application.

I hope you are feeling much better now. You didn't look too bright the last time I saw you.

My wife and I are well dug in on this farm and are going to stay here till end of Feb. at least. I weigh 12 stone now!!

Best wishes for a real merry Xmas – goodness knows we deserve one – and all luck and success in the New Year.

Yours sincerely,
G. W. Lehle

EIGHT

I Had to Make Up Words Sometimes

1945–1950

Theresa

After the Japanese left Singapore, people had loads of 'banana money',[115] which was pretty useless. Most of us, especially my family, had no British currency. Some of my brothers had to go out and work. There were a lot of army rations in the market, which were bought and sold. We managed to survive for a while with that sort of barter trade. The BMA (British Military Administration) came into being for a period before a new Governor was installed.

My third brother found me a job with the Far East Oxygen Company in Pasir Panjang, not far from where I used to work with the Japanese company. There I stayed for three and a half years. I took a course in Pitman's shorthand and typewriting in the evenings after work.

When I left Far East Oxygen, I was able to work as a private secretary. Gordon Van Hien, later at Turquand Youngs,[116] was at that time the auditor at Far East Oxygen. He was responsible for finding me a post at Turquand Youngs, where I started work as a secretary in October 1949.

---

115 Japanese wartime currency introduced to Singapore from 1942 – the $10 note depicted a banana tree. It became practically worthless by mid-1945, so people had to resort to the black market until the British Military Administration circulated new money.

116 Turquand Youngs & Co., a London-based accountancy firm dating from c. 1840, was a predecessor of Ernst & Young, known since 2013 as EY. Ernst & Whinney merged with Arthur Young in 1989 to form Ernst & Young.

I was still living with my family in Rochore Road until after 1949. Then I went to live with Agnes for a while, as the house was getting a bit too crowded.

My work at Far East Oxygen was not very interesting. I was just doing clerical work. I felt cut off from my friends in town, especially Mary Boey, who was working with Carreras – agents importing Black Cat cigarettes from Rhodesia – in the Hongkong & Shanghai Bank building. So, when I got the job with Turquand Youngs I was very pleased, and I was able to meet up with Mary at lunchtimes at G. H. Café, where a special table was reserved for us. Owned by an Armenian, G. H. Café served local dishes such as *mee Siam* and *laksa*, as well as European dishes like sausages and sauerkraut. The cook was an aunt of Mary Boey's. We used to give the waiter a twenty-cent tip, which was a lot in those days.

A few months after I joined Turquand Youngs, early in 1950, I was taken quite ill with tuberculosis. I was quickly under Dr. Thompson, who gave me a course of medication for three months. At that time, Mary Boey's friend Sim Hay Lum and his wife, who owned a bungalow in Siglap by the sea, were kind enough to let me use it to recuperate. I soon recovered, dining on fresh fish from the sea, and was looked after by a paid servant. My boss, John Phillips, refused to accept my resignation and paid me in full for those months, and asked me to return to work when I got better. Every week he sent somebody to the bungalow to deliver my wages, and he doubled my salary on my return to work. I went back to work fully recovered, and happy to work for a boss who was very kind to me.

Van Hien and my former boss, Rufus Hurley, created a new job for me straight away, a first-class job as private secretary to the senior partner, Phillips. A stenographer soon left because I got the top job. It was Hurley who had encouraged me to go to the YMCA to learn shorthand and typing. He thought I was too educated to be a telephonist.

In the beginning I used to make quite a few mistakes in my letters while taking dictation. But my boss was so tolerant, and after a while I got used to his soft voice and my work became easier. Phillips' voice was low, as he had had an operation on his tonsils. I had to make up words sometimes. If I made a mistake, he would send the letter back to me to retype, but he never complained. He appreciated my work. They told me that a lot of people who worked for him didn't last very long. I persevered. I didn't mind retyping the letters. He used to leave his *Reader's Digest* for me; every time he finished the magazine, he gave it to me.

I would get into the office before my boss arrived, and before all the messenger boys, who were called '*tambis*' in those days. They were the ones who delivered the post and made tea for the staff. It was so nice to work in town for a change, and to meet Mary in G. H. Café every day. Sometimes I had time to do a bit of shopping at Robinson's[117] or other places.

---

117 Singapore's original British department store, founded by Philip Robinson in Raffles Place in 1859. It survived World War II and burned down in 1972 but was rebuilt. The store closed in 2020 due to 'changing retail trends' and a slump in sales after COVID-19 restrictions. (Source: https://saltandlight.sg/news/robinsons-founder-leaves-legacy-in-more-ways-than-one/)

NINE

The World Has Been Forgetting

1946–1947

Wood Ayven

Rylands Hey

Greasby

Wirral

Cheshire

January 2nd '46

Dear Rep,

Many thanks for your letter of the 22nd inst.

Pleased to hear that you are still enjoying your leave. I have been demobbed ages ago; to be exact, the 8th Mon.[118] This was done through the Colonial Office, who sent all the papers and dope.[119] The only depot I had to go to was for the civvy suit; not bad either for these days. Also had the majority of pay – I think it was £438 I was credited with after advances had been deducted. It was more than I expected but most certainly the hardest-earnt money I've possessed. All that sweat and toil for a few pounds. It certainly all seems like a very bad dream now.

Yes, Rep, I have been down in London for a couple of days and

---

118 Probably Monday 8th October 1945.
119 Information, especially secret (US slang).

almost sent you a wire, but as it turned out, rather a blessing I didn't as I had sent one to the wife who is to be, to come back. Yes, Rep, I take back all I've said about marriage. There may be something in it after all. She's lovely!

By the way, a bone to pick with you: please don't get throwing out descriptions of me like you mentioned in the letter. It will be you who will be laughed at for having such an imagination.

Rep, why don't you take a job with the B.A.T.[120] or the A.P.C. Malaya? A person like you would be an asset to any company.

Fixed up nothing definite with Guthrie's as yet. No doubt shall be hearing from them in near future. They asked me when I should be fit to go back. I told them about February, but I think it will possibly be March.

Now, Rep, I'm going down to Norfolk for a few days next week. When I get back shall write to see if you can possibly gather some of the boys together for a spree. Oh, had a letter from Caward a few days ago. The sod didn't mention that he'd received my letter of November last. I enquired after his wife.

I say, what do you think of this weather? B… cold. I'm absolutely fed up with it, and longing for a spot of sun.

What kind of time had you over the holidays? Very pleasant, I hope. I managed to get a few bottles of lubricant at black-market prices, which are fairly high.

Forgot to mention what Guthrie's are doing. They say each employee has had a certain amount put to there [sic] account by the Board, mine being £720, and they propose to pay the Provident Fund for the past 4 years, but pay it in 4 yearly instalments after each year's new service. Did expect more but there [sic] a miserable lot at the best of times.

The next time I write shall tell you when I shall be down.

I take this opportunity of wishing you and all the family the very best for 1946. Must conclude for present.

Sincerely yours,
Bill (Charlie)

---

120 British American Tobacco.

St. Dominic's Priory
Southampton Road
London N.W. 5
3 Jan. '46

Dear Christopher,

Many thanks for your letter of 31 Dec. Yes, by all means quote me as a reference for your application to UNRRA.[121] You can put the above address as 'Provincial'; also, if room, S.C.F. (R.C.), Scottish Command, 1939–45. The military connection may help.

So glad you found Laxton comforting; it has the same good effect on me, after years of absence. I enclose a note from Fr. Gerald, who is here for a night or two. If I can ever be of use to you, let me know.

Ever yours,
Fr. Aelwin

Love to the brothers.

By kindness of Fr. Provincial
As from Laxton
3 I 46

My dear Christopher,

Your letter reached me here this morning – Fr. Aelwin says he's writing to you so I'll slip in this rather hurried line just to say thank you, and how glad I am you enjoyed Laxton, and that I hope you'll come again as soon as you can. I was hoping I should see you last night when I met Nash and one or two others, but the silly asses had bungled their staff work, I gathered, and failed to get hold of

---

121 The United Nations Relief and Rehabilitation Administration (UNRRA) was set up in 1943, and distributed US$4 billion worth of aid to countries affected by famine and political chaos during and after World War II. It helped refugees return to their home countries in Europe after the war. UNRRA ceased most of its operations by 1947 and the International Refugee Organisation and the World Health Organisation took over many of its functions. In 1948, it was replaced by the US Marshall Plan.

you – such a disappointment, but anyway I shall hope to see you again soon.

All best wishes to all.

Love,
Gerald

c/o South Africa House
Trafalgar Square
London
7 Jan. '46

Dear Christopher,

I expect Bianca wrote to you to say that I would try and do something for you about UNRRA and introduce you to a Col. Katzin, who was Deputy Director.

I now find that Col. Katzin has not returned from S. Africa owing to ill health. Unfortunately, I don't know anyone else. I am sorry about it, but if he should return, I will most certainly let you have a letter of introduction.

Yours sincerely,
Pat Rave

Tamuan Camp
Siam[122]
24 January 1946

[Top corner of page is missing] heat and dust.[123]

Electric light, proper reading, writing items have been installed. Canteens, picture shows regularly, and dancings, restaurants, etc.

---

122 From a Dutch ex-POW comrade. KNIL (Royal Netherlands East India Army) soldiers remained in camps in Thailand for several months after the war ended. They were then sent to the Dutch East Indies (Indonesia), which was occupied by Japan during the war, to suppress the anti-colonial revolution.

123 Parts of this fragile letter, written in pencil on crumbling paper, are missing, hence the […] passages.

Not only in camp are these improvements to be found, but all along the road to Tamuan and river road to T. Bars, restaurants and dancings are arisen like toadstools amongst bamboo bushes, banana trees, etc.

Regular leave to Bangkok is granted to us and life, for a regular soldier, is made bearable. For the militarized civilian, old buffer, the situation is a mental strangulation in slow process.

The B.A.T. is assisting their employees splendidly and we just had a London director visiting us for a few days. The main idea as far as the large business concerns is to send a number of key men to Europe or Australia for a few months' leave and have these men back, say March–April, to commence activities in Java, at the same time taking with them new materiel and machines. In the meantime the economic chaos in the [...] regions, i.e. the large harbour towns, being cleared by ex-P.O.W.s or ex-internees, who will be relieved as soon as the key men, refreshed from their short stay in a cooler climate, return.

I would stress the point, Repton, to try to get into the B.A.T. organisation, although the firm got their funny ways. They certainly back you up and help you when in a pinch.

Are you demobilised yet, and how did you find your people at home? I am very interested to hear all about it.

Did you maintain contact with any friends made during P.O.W., Rep? I am referring to Pat, the enthusiastic dancer.

In Bangkok, and as a matter of fact S'pore, Saigon, Hong Kong and Shanghai, American trade is forcing to get a firm footing. The English have put up a gallant fight in S'pore and Hong Kong to recover the lost ground, but in the other towns mentioned it will be a tough struggle. America had the advantage of being ready to trade immediately from the word 'go' [...]

Siam is clamouring for [...] business – even Universities [...] for the ex-P.O.W.s still in this country [...] however averse from granting permission, so that these jobs are taken on clandestinely. The Thai government pays for an average teacher's job at a college 1,000 ticals (£1 = 60 t.) per month. A fitter on the Bangkok electrical works gets 900 t. A bare living in a private house is possible at 500 t. a month, so that the official salaries are low. Siam is, however, a country where corruption is the main source of income, and you hear of the most ridiculous bribes – money and murder gets you anywhere in Thailand.

4,000 women and children evacuees from Java are living in Dutch villages made out of bamboo near Tamuan, Nakhon Pathom and Bangkok, and the re-uniting of families has certainly eased the tension, which was getting dangerously near to rebellion, amongst the troops. At last there is permission to land Dutch forces in Java and we are going wholesale into it.

The world has been forgetting, when backing the Indonesian republic, that they are dealing with a few intellectuals who combined form probably only 1% of the population of 40 million in Java. The remainder are savages, keen on uncontrolled murdering and looting which can easily be started off, but the only way to stop them is annihilation. This is what will have to be done to the extremist bands, which operate in groups of 500–1,000 men, armed and trained by the Japanese. And the quicker this murderous crowd is stopped the less lives of white women and children are lost. This was the reason why the troops here were getting wild. Hearing the stories of their women and children being ruthlessly slaughtered while no arms were issued to us and no troops were allowed to be sent to Java.

Business in Java will remain dangerous, but it may help to add more zest to the easy money-making in the tropics.

Repton, so long and write me soon. Kind regards to your parents and family.

Yours,
George

'Brackenside'
27th Feb. '46

Dearest Christopher,

You saved your neck well and truly with those 17 pages. I even felt a selfish grumbler when I thought of all the complaints I had made about my life at home. How could I grumble when I have such lovely letters coming from you?

But, Christopher, I do hope you are not under the impression that I am a sweet, even-tempered creature. I am ashamed to say it, but I have a vile temper. Inwardly I seethe and outwardly I present a cold, hard front. At those times I am addicted to sarcasm. Oh yes – I am of a jealous temperament. That's when I become sarcastic. Perhaps you could persuade Sylvia to tell you a little about me. She knows me as well as anyone outside the family. I would hate to disappoint you one day. Am I making you quite gloomy?

Before I finish explaining myself, I had better clear up what might have sounded rather contradictory to you. About the slight change in Maureen's and my relations with one another, I mean. We are still great friends, but, whereas once Maureen would tell me of all her fun while she was out without me, now she doesn't. You see, it involves Gavin all the time and I think she's afraid of boring me. Petty, isn't it? But still, I would like to hear all about her fun. She really is the only one of my age at home whom I can go out with and talk to at present.

I am glad to hear you are working. As you say, one can get into an awful lazy rut just staying at home doing nothing. By now you will be able to tell me whether you like working for UNRRA or not. I can imagine you walking sedately into the office wearing that hat they are all so rude about. Is it an awfully, frightfully conservative Homburg – or just a conservative Trilby? My picture would be perfectly complete if I could imagine you carrying a black leather portfolio and an umbrella! But no, you won't have quite reached that stage yet.

I have started to occupy my time by going down to the little school I mentioned in my last letter for an hour or two each day. I have been twice so far, and the time has flown. The children are perfect pets. The head of the school is an extremely pleasant man, and he is the representative for Cheshire on the Board of Teachers. A man who is worth knowing, in fact. To me he has been very kind, and I have permission to see what I like and come as often as I like.

*28*th

Good evening, darling! I have just come in from the pictures. Seen *Rebecca* for the third time. Mrs. Newton asked me to accompany her, otherwise I would have stayed at home to write screeds of letters. Mrs. Newton is the mother of an old school friend of mine – she's good fun and I enjoy her company. Ailsa is in the W.A.A.F.s and Mr. Newton died a few years ago. I'm sure Mrs. N. lives a rather lonely life.

I expect you will want to know how I enjoyed the two dances I have been to recently; one on Saturday and one on Tuesday. Allen partnered me, because, of course, it's no good going to a dance in West Kirby if you haven't got a partner – men are so scarce here. The first dance wasn't quite so snobbish as the second. In the second dance, quite the majority of people were well-known local people, all quite middle-aged. When we came into the hall we were stopped at the door and announced to Dr. & Mrs. Dickson (Dr. Dickson is the president of the Rotary Club)! Right in the middle of the dance the M.C. blew his whistle and called out, "Will the couple who became engaged at the weekend please come up here?" Of course, M. and Gavin weren't listening, so Mrs. Dickson came up and dragged them onto the floor. They received a present – "Just something for their bottom draw [sic], like!" Poor things. I wouldn't have been them for anything. Everything gets around W.K. much too quickly. I danced with Allen most of the time. Whenever there was a Paul Jones, I seemed to fall for some glorious tubby short old man who bobbed up and down, up and down, and I got rocked up and down on top of his tummy.

On Saturday I got a curious creature who suddenly, without any warning, would shoot his left leg out at right angles at his side and stand poised there while I stood stiffly in front of him, wondering what he would do next. Then, equally as suddenly, he would swing the leg to the front position and start off. I always lost my balance at this point. To cap my amusement, he said, "Such a pity – a good band, a good floor, a good tune and no room to dance in."

I answered, "Yes, such a pity" in a polite but bored tone – but only to cover my hysteria. I was dying to laugh!

How like Sylvia to mess around with her new suit. She loves to wear the things she likes all the time. And I don't mind because it proves she must like this new rig-out if she's wearing the top with her 'cords'. All the same, I think it is rather a shame to wear out her new things just around the house.

Now, before I end my letter and go to bed, I have a bargain to make with you. Here, I rub my hands together and show my teeth; an old Indian bazaar trait. No 'baksheesh' photograph for you, my lad. I want one of you in return, and I do like the one of you in the lounge, standing beside a transport. Do you think I might have a copy of it? After all, a girl has to have her gallery of horrors. Maureen has quite a goodly collection. I can't let her beat me.

So much for the present.
All my love,
Paddy

P.S. Reading the last paragraph, I found something which sounded funny. Can you picture yourself standing in the lounge beside a transport? I can, and it does look funny! I mean the photo of you in the lounge.[124]

G. S. Schultz, Lst. Sld. 251404
Camp Hong Kong Bank Lane
Bangkok
5th March 1946

Dear Rep,

I was very pleased to receive your letter of exactly a month ago relating all the experiences since we parted in Chungkai. You are now well back to civilisation, and probably by the time you receive this letter you have accepted the job in Italy.

It was great to hear that the entire family of yours got through these years in such good health, and it must have been a marvellous moment for your parents, and especially the mother, to have all the children home again. Of course, to feed all those hungry stomachs whenever they come home is in these times of rations very trying, and it is a fact that the housewife with all the servants trouble and shortage on top of that for the most difficult time. It should be generally considered that the nation should also look amongst the women that stayed at home in the kitchen for heroines and not only on the battlefield. I was jolly glad to hear that your father got a good job again, and I am sure that something will crop up for you in time, if it has not already in the meantime been fixed.

---

124 Jocelyn and Sylvia always kept on the living-room mantelpiece a framed photo of Christopher in army uniform standing beside a military lorry, taken in Bareilly, India in 1940.

At last we are getting somewhere in the Java question. Dutch troops are allowed to land and take part in the action against the Indonesians. We soon will be all out of this country and back in Java, or at least somewhere in the Netherl. East Indies. The outer Islands do not cause much trouble – here and there a little antagonism, but as a whole the population was glad to have the white men back.

It is a pity however that the relationship between the English and the Dutch, as a whole, in Java is, to say the least, poor, and as far as I can judge for myself, it is bad. It is 75% the fault of the Dutch, who to begin with do not understand the Englishmen. They all speak the lingo to a certain extent but the subtle differences in words are completely lost for the Dutch. This is only quite naturally for a foreigner speaking a language, but they should realise it, and there is where the trouble starts. The Englishman thinks that he is perfectly understood while the Dutchman is cocksure that he perfectly grasps the meaning of what is said.

The second reason for the ill feeling is that we are definitely not thankful enough for what the English have done for us. By this I do not mean that we should bear each Englishman on our shoulders, but we should certainly prove it by public courtesy. And I am afraid we are lacking very badly in politeness towards our lifesavers. We Dutch are not refined, and our actions are definitely 'boorish'. This is a national habit, let we say, and cannot be removed at the spur of the moment, but our leading men who are constantly in touch with the English, while most of them have lived several years of this war amongst the English, should have realised this and should have taken measures to prevent such a bad feeling becoming so general.

Furthermore, as the last reason I can state that the half-caste problem is still an enigma for you English. That these people can mix freely amongst the white and frequent the same haunts of pleasure and entertainment as the 'white face' is quite incomprehensible for you.

Well, well, I have let myself go again, now change to another subject. It is surprising to hear how fast business is building up in the harbour towns even on the ruins of the factories and offices. Natives are carrying in the produce which formerly was brought by the white in the country, and although the quality is poor it shows that the commercial mind is victorious to the political brain. As I have always maintained, the trouble is only caused by a few troublemakers who start riots locally, and although training centres are reported, an organised army does not exist. The Indonesian leaders are now trying to prolong discussion by postponement and tours or inspections, but it will not be long before an all-out war is ordered.

In the meantime, cigarettes, chocolates workshops, rubber factories are producing, and we are streaming back to our positions in the occupied towns. This should have been done six months ago as suggested by us, instead of evacuation to foreign countries, while the useless and sick men could have stayed here or be sent to Europe.

In writing this letter I have been interrupted numerous times, as this particular building is a homely kind of a camp. Evacuees with their children are all over the place, and although they are kept out of the office during the morning working hours, it is at night that they invade the rooms where we men try to get our home mail done. It gives you a sort of family life, but for the persons in question, this forced camp life is not so nice.

The lack of money is however the reason that men and women are still confined to camps. These are however run in a much easier style than before, but it is pitiable to see to what little space a married couple with children are detailed to live. It is in a cubicle form, so that a little privacy is obtained but it is still very primitive. Funds are still not allowed to be brought into this country except smuggled, and therefore the racketeering business is still going strong. Entire godowns are emptied in one night. And it is done in great style as the robbers drive up in motor lorries or launches, in case the warehouse is situated near the river and an actual rifle duel with machine guns and hand grenades on both sides is in full swing. It is therefore quite exciting to be on sentry duty in this country, and is in fact a good practice and moving target training for the Java sport which is awaiting us.

It is amazing to discover in the shops here stacks and stacks of pre-war material in all lines such as textiles, medicines, machinery, stationery etc. It is now being sold at enormously high prices as there is no sign of the monetary situation straightening out for the time being, and as long as the rate of exchange is not yet fixed, no foreign country will be importing any material.

As far as food is concerned, this country is not so badly off – that is to say, all Oriental ingredients, with here and there an attempt towards a Western menu. It is in any case very wholesome, and this is certainly what the evacuees needed when they arrived in this country. The children certainly look a good deal better, and also the women have improved in health considerably.

Well, Rep, I have given you something to read again and hope that you will drop me a line now and then. Cheerio, and my regards to your parents.

George

Boon & Potter
Complete Clothiers & Outfitters
86 Creek Rd.
March
Cambridgeshire
14/3/46

Dear Rep,

Having resumed 'working for pay' (sic!) I've been longer than usual answering your letter, but please excuse. Today the guv'nor is in London buying (or trying), so 'the mice play'. Since last writing I've become toothless – all out – so 'by gum', as they say in Yorkshire.

I had a very nice letter from Pat. He wasn't so lucky with his wife but all the same he seemed cheerful. Nothing have I heard from Charlton (apart from that soccer team in the semi!). Has he left England, I wonder? Our recent Cambs. Regt. Reunion was a great success, and it was great to see some old faces. How goes the love affair, old chap? Don't forget any advice 'for beginners'. I'll be only too pleased. Occupation still undecided or settled? Any news of Caward? I'd like to meet him, and in fact most of the 'Big Five' (Charlton, Pat, 'Key' Jack, and yourself, naturally). By the way, I gave your address to Geoff Williams' father at Wisbech recently so you may already have heard from him.

What of Russia's present attitude? I care not for it, do you? Well, just a few 'ex-service' news – I applied successfully for pension re. tummy[125] and am getting 10/6 per week for nearly 2 years, and at the end of that I can apply for my case to be reviewed. My gratuity is through and my leave finished so as far as cash goes, I've had it! Hence the work which I've begun. Very strenuous as you can guess…

Whenever I feel dull, I switch my thoughts to old Caward's philosophy – you know his attitude to work; that picture of him on the pontoon, watching with amazement how that heavy 'monkey' rose with so little effort – on his part!

Well, Rep, this short note is just to keep contact; sorry it's so brief but I'm wading through a whole host of backward replies. So, cheerio. Lots of luck.

Yours,
Leo

'Brackenside'
Lang Lane
West Kirby
23rd March

Dearest Christopher,

I'm sorry about the delay in my replying to your last letter, but I'm teaching all day now and I haven't had a spare evening all week to settle down to writing.

I am glad you can manage to come up and see me at Easter. Don't worry about a place to stay at. I have mentioned the fact that you wanted to come up for a few days to Mother and she says you must come and stay here. It would be much easier than arranging anything else. Be prepared to 'pig it', as we call it. (Which only means you must be prepared to be treated as one of the family!) Gavin and Maureen will be having a few days off then as well, so if the weather is good, we'll spend most of our time out of doors. Pop, I think, is

---

125 Many ex-POWs had digestion problems for years after the war, as a result of suffering from dysentery.

planning to spend a few weeks in the Isle of Man with an old army friend of his, so you may not meet him. Let me know what you think of this plan and we can enlarge on it later.

I am glad to hear Gervase's planned outing was such a success. When I told Mother about the turkey, she was very surprised. You must have done it justice after your long walk. I have been wondering during the past few weeks how you were getting on with the house problem. Do you think you will be able to find a house at such short notice?

Ha! So you think you might need shaking up. My pet, you may not like to be shaken up when the time comes! Sylvia will tell you how I used to badger her. I absolutely hate to stagnate.

By the way, I have been accepted for the teachers' training scheme. As a matter of fact, I fancy I went down well with the examiners, or whatever they call themselves. I was told that I wouldn't be able to train for at least six months, but the chief examiner advised me to apply for supply work as an uncertificated teacher to gain experience and fill in my time. I rang up our local Education Office that day, and in two days I had a job. I have been working one week at a fairly local school. My class comprises of about 25 children between the ages of 8–10 years. The girls and a few of the boys are quite good, but I have about six boys who are young devils in the flesh. I just about manage to keep myself from shaking them severely. I have seen some results of my control over them within the past week, however I fancy the teacher I am relieving has very little control over them. When the headmistress took me to my new classroom the boys had barricaded the door up and banished all the girls from the room. We had some difficulty to get in. These children are not exactly the age I want to teach. My ambition is to teach infants. One could become quite bossy after a time of teaching 10-year-olds.

Oh, I must tell you of the most glorious party I went to on Friday. A very well-known man of West Kirby was celebrating his Golden wedding anniversary. There was pots of drink: punch, sherry, gin and orange, whisky, and beer. Everyone became gloriously merry. We danced and sang to the music, and a few of the gay, ambitious young things did a few burlesques. I was exceedingly touched with the speeches. Old Mr. & Mrs. Jones are a dear old couple. It was quite pre-war-like; everyone turned out in full dress and no one would have believed that anything was rationed. At the party we younger people got together and planned a 21st birthday party. It may come off while you are here. Would you like to come? West Kirby social life would amuse you. The party will be held in a girls' indoor squash court, and we are wearing rags.

You ended up your letter rather strangely. I have a vague idea I can remember what I was thinking about when I said you didn't understand. But I confess, I don't wish to try and express myself on paper. Maybe I will tell you when we meet. In fact, I had better tell you – but only when we meet.

All my love for the present, dearest Christopher,
Paddy

Ulu Remi Estate
Loyang Loyang
Johore
Malaya
April 16th

Dear Rep,

Yes, I'm still alive – only just, though. I flew out from home on the 22nd Feb. so only had 20 days of married bliss. I must say, as yet I don't regret getting married; you should try it sometime.

I did try for a possible vacancy for the so much talked of reunion, but alas it wasn't to be. I had to go to your part of the world for 2 days. Dorking, do you know it? I know you'll fully realise how busy I was.

The Japs certainly left this place in a hell of a mess, and the labour has been spoiled what with Japs and our soldiers. We're gradually getting the rubber in again, but you realise this takes time. The food situation here is much better than home. At the moment we're being fed by the B.M.A. rather cheaply, and quantity and quality good.

Now, Rep, tell me what you're doing or intend to do. Are you coming out to Malaya? You shouldn't have any great difficulty finding a job. Singapore is full of Dutch R.A.P.M.s. Transportation is rather difficult. There are thousands of Japs about; in fact we had some guarding the factory against Communists. I have managed to give one or two a belt for old times' sake. But I'm hoping to get a couple of hundred working for me, then, oh boy. It's most annoying to see their rations – fruits, bully,[126] flour, rice. Oh, it makes my blood boil at times.

Oh, the few days I stayed in London I met young Elcone – you remember him at Nakhon Pathom? Have you heard anything from Cos. Pat Power or Les Sutton of late? Do let me know how they're all getting on.

Must conclude for present as the lights will be going off soon and I must write to the Boss (Wife).

So will say cheerio,
Charlton

> Bangkok
> 17 April 1946

Dear Rep,

Jolly to hear from you so soon, especially as this letter of yours of the 4th of April reached here in 10 days.

Hard luck on your sister to be catching this dreadful diphtheria, and it brings back memories of the old tent in Takanoon in 1943, the place where we met first. In any case, she will have much better treatment than we had and probably be in a better state of health. The semi-isolation of the family is more nasty, that is to say, if regulations are to be carried out strictly. Let us hope that on receipt of this letter she will almost [have] recovered.

I am glad to hear that you got a job; although it is only temporarily, it gives you some commercial practice, and you always meet people who may be able to get you a position later on.

Foreign countries still have attraction for you, and I wonder whether it will give you the satisfaction which you imagine you will get out of it. You will definitely lose some of your typical country habits, which I do not know whether it can be considered as an asset

---

126 Bully beef.

as you acquire at the same time some funny foreign customs. These are kept up deliberately or involuntarily, but in any case, alter your attitude towards your home country greatly. This is not to advise you against a job in a foreign country, by all means get one if one is offered to you, but I should not change the course of my career especially in order to be sent out.

The chances that we have to continue soldiering is getting worse and worse, as all the people that have been demobbed for special economic reasons and even many light sick are again called up to arms. It is apparently absolutely essential that we can show a large figure on paper of troops called up, or it is that part of the nation which is sacrificed to pacify the Dutch East Indies until they can be relieved by fresh troops that are being trained in Holland and England. These are supposed to arrive in Java in October next, so that in the meantime somebody has to do the dirty work, and as we in Siam are near, it is considered best to use us for the purpose. Thank goodness that the first shipload of really sick is leaving Bangkok the day after tomorrow, but after this ship everybody will go back to the D.E.I.

From the nation's point of view, I can see that they are right. It is only a queer feeling that you are one of the men to be sacrificed. I do not think however that it will be as bad as it is put forward, because besides actual military action, economic life has to be started up as soon as possible, or at least along with the advancing army in the interior. For that part of the semi-military job, we old-timers are necessary, as we know how to deal with the natives.

Monetary conditions are still poor in Siam as the banks are still not open to do foreign exchange business. Imports on a limited basis are commencing to dribble into the country, especially U.S.A. is doing their hardest to capture this market. They are very popular, more so than the British, but I believe the British got some hold on the Siam government so that they are not free to deal with the U.S.A. at free will. The black-market rates of exchange are fluctuating just as much as on a proper functioning financial market. At the moment pounds are low, U.S.A. dollars are steady, and the Straits dollar is very weak.

The Siam tobacco monopoly have asked the B.A.T. for assistance and the Britishers are already working for the tobacco industry of

Siam. It is a pity that these blunt army authorities will not release me as here were jobs going which I would be only too glad to accept. Another snag is that the director of the B.A.T. who has arranged this deal with the Siamese government insists on us ex-P.O.W. having at least a couple of months' change of climate in Europe. But I do think that putting us to work would cure 50% of the imaginary sick.

I am feeling as fit as anything and I am full of mischief even at my age, and that is a bad thing and could be more profitably turned into energy for creative economy. But, alas, the top notches think otherwise.

I am glad to hear that no serious love affair as yet has scarred your young life, although I still believe that a marriage at about thirty should be attempted. Even in these chaotic post-war times a sound partner can be found. Even if you should not agree, after a number of years, children or not, it can always be intelligently dissolved. I find now that I have learned a great deal during my period of real love life, although illegal, so that I can understand many situations at present between married couples which completely baffle the persons in question. Offering advice in such cases is very unpopular unless you are co-respondents.

Well, Rep, so long and write soon.
George

Batavia[127]
17th June 1946

Dear Christopher,

Fancy me getting today your letter of the 9th November 1945. That is why the 'Christopher' start above.

A lot has happened since writing you last. As you will notice from the address, I have landed in Batavia. The transfer Bangkok–Java was carried out on the instigations of B.A.T., who needed men for the reorganisation of their Batavia office. Four men were sent over by plane from Siam, but only me wanted to stay for work; queer people. Instead

---

127 Dutch colonial name for Jakarta or Djakarta, capital of the then Dutch East Indies, now Indonesia.

of being glad to be able to commence work, they 'funked' it and, under some pretence of moral tiredness or some imaginary illness, cleared out to Holland. This is the tendency of 75% of the people here, and that is the reason why everything progresses so slowly – 50% of the jobs going are being taken up by women, and some damned efficient ones at that!

Batavia as a whole is good. We are certainly crowded in the houses and the transport facilities are remote, but conditions are improving daily and natives are coming into town in daily increasing numbers selling fresh fruit and vegetables, while they are keen on getting a job as servants.

B.A.T. business is good. The N.E.I.[128] government are buying our high-class imported brands while they are stimulating the increased output of our factories within the occupied zone. Many other firms are viewing the future with optimism and only those that have as sole possession estates in the interior are still inactive.

Fighting round the main towns is still in progress, and although I am demobilised and a civilian once again, I have got a house from the re-housing organisation of Batavia on the outskirts of the safe territory, on the understanding that I am to be on guard a few hours during the night, and for that reason they've supplied me with a 'Owen' gun. It is a lovely little house, new and facing an open field. A cool breeze is blowing all afternoon and at night it is even 'cold'. The B.A.T. provides transport so that I am living as a lord.

The native servants are exceedingly timid, as the village at the back have experienced that no half measures exist – any stealing or provocations of any nature and we 'let fly'. Provided you do the job quick and thorough, i.e. before the M.P.[129] arrives on the scene, all is well and good. I still believe that as soon as sufficient troops have landed here, that is beginning next year, the whole of the Indonesian extremists will be rounded up, so that within a year we can commence penetrating the interior.

Chris, be good and let me hear soon from you.
George

---

128 Netherlands/Dutch East Indies.
129 Military police.

Batavia
11th November 1946

Dear Christopher,

Again, a long time has elapsed before taking up this piece of writing materials, but here I am, and with many thanks for your letter of the 28th of August.

I am glad to understand from that letter that you are seriously contemplating the nuptial bond. Good luck and God bless you, my lad. It is definitely the best relationship between the two sexes. An illegal attachment may have its advantages – for a man – but if you are going to set out for life, the emphasised feeling of responsibility which marriage brings in the male part of it expresses itself in the entire character of the man, and this in a young employee of a firm is to be encouraged.

As you tried to persuade me in your last letter to go on leave, is only natural. You have felt this longing for home yourself after years in the tropics and we Europeans all feel the same, but, Christopher, this is the most interesting time I have ever experienced in the East – not only from a political view, but economical. This period of reconstruction is most interesting.

Politically, the Dutch have failed in the East. The whole build-up pre-war package has been sold to the Indonesians due to the lack of a powerful head – and cheap at that! We certainly were in a very awkward position immediately after the Jap capitulation, out of which England has saved us, but with the proverbial far-sightedness of the English. They have used this situation to place us in a very difficult position against the Indonesians. We have ourselves to blame for this, as if we had had a man at the wheel who understood the English and was powerful and diplomatic enough to bring certain points to the attention of the Allied Command, the position in which we are now would never have occurred.

In a town like Batavia, at the moment cramped with ¾ of the total European population of the N.E.I. pre-war, we rely for electricity, water, rail transport, rice supply and fresh vegetable and fruit supply on the Indonesians. The result is that all the carefully set up power stations, trams and trains services, distribution system from before the war are sadly neglected during the Jap occupation and are now being thoroughly worn out due to unskilled, bad management from the natives.

The Dutch Army, under Allied Command, is not to fire a shot until they are actually shot at, and a hit, i.e. a casualty, is caused. This attitude, which in the brains of any civilised population only forces respect towards the rigid discipline that makes such manoeuvres possible, only strengthens these heathens in their belief, developed during Jap occupation by anti-European propaganda, that the white face is afraid, and does not dare to fight.

The last act of the Allied Command to allow an Indonesian Commander with fully equipped life-guards[130] to enter Batavia has caused such enthusiastic scenes amongst the natives that European women, who walked in the streets unaware of what was going on (as these things are never published until it is all over), were spat in the face and roughly handled by the natives. This did not happen to men, except if they walk alone and are met by at least 20 fully armed natives. Still our people are not being evacuated from the Indonesian internment camps; still produce and machinery from our estates and industries inland are being destroyed and burned. Still rice is being sent to Br. Indies while Java has whole regions where famine rages. Talks or conferences should never have started before these parts should have been retaken by force or otherwise.

Indonesian money, printed on non-watermarked paper, with ink that rubs off and fades when moistened, is forced to be accepted by Indonesian officials to native sellers against a fictitious currency of ten legal Dutch guilders = 1 Indonesian guilder.

You can now understand that things are interesting here, 'specially as the Investor Capital still forces the way through, notwithstanding political chaos.

Write soon once more a letter containing fresh new European ideas.

George

---

130 Bodyguards.

United Nations Relief & Rehabilitation Administration
European Regional Office
11 Portland Place
London W. 1
2nd December 1946

Dear Rep,

We were all so sorry to hear about the fever, and hope you're not feeling too much like death-warmed-up. Now for heaven's sake, stay away till you are really better and strong, else you won't be fit for Christmas. I've always heard that one sees wonderful visions with malaria, and I'm wondering what gorgeous conjuration is haunting your imagination at the moment – maybe it's lovely women, or beautiful carvings, but most likely it's just the usual run of pink elephants! Anyway, hurry up and get well, because, if for no other reason, I've no one to harass with stupid questions!

This lunchtime I spent £26 of Taylor's money on some of the most beautiful books I've ever seen, which turned me quite green with envy – well, not really because Erik really does love them so it would be churlish to begrudge them, but they did make my mouth water.

This weather is so filthy that it's no wonder you have gone under (I wanted to say sucumbed, but I can't spell it!), and you are in by far the best place. I now have lost most of my cold and have a beautiful cough which sounds like Mimi in the last act. I'm not quite sure whether my consumption is rapid or slow and lingering! I saw Wendy Hillier in *Tess of the D'Erbervilles* [sic] at the New on Saturday, and thought she gave a magnificent performance.

Now I really must do something to earn my doubtful living. I'm sure you're a model patient and drink all the medicin [sic] and foul concoctions obediently.

Cheerio, and take care of yourself.
Peggy

1947

> Lo. 5, C.C.G. Cor. Unit
> C.C.G. Ofenford
> HQ G5 C.C.G.
> Germany
> 7/1/47

Dear old Rep,

Many thanks, old boy, for your very nice card. I have called myself some stinking names for forgetting to send you greeting. I had the idea long ago that you couldn't care less, so to speak. Thus, I haven't written. Anyhow, please let me wish you all the very best for the New Year and I hope you are in good health. That is also my wish for all at home. For myself I am getting on quite well out here with a very good job that pays well in all respects. The standard of living is very good: my own car, plenty to drink and the usual. In fact, I really couldn't care less. So, a bad way to get into, but it suits me now. I shall be home on leave at the end of the month and will get in touch with you, and if you care to spend an evening on the booze, I will give you all news. Meantime, look after yourself, and again, best wishes.

Sincerely,
Pat

> c/o Neville Jones, Esq.
> P.O. Box 240
> Bulawayo
> 5th October 1947

My dear Rep, Connie, Peggy, Bill, Eric and the rest,

I hope that you won't mind a communal letter, but it would be quite impossible at this stage to write you each a separate one giving you all the news and I didn't want to wait much longer before I wrote.

How far away you all seem, and yet I can remember quite clearly the old schoolroom and the telephones going and "Tea up" and the signing-on book and those eternal stairs. By the time I have been here a couple of months I shall have forgotten what stairs are like, since practically every house here is a bungalow, and I can truthfully say I haven't gone up a single flight of stairs since I left England!

I imagine that you will have had some of the news about me from Robert. He told me he had had dinner and a drink with you, Rep, and I tortured myself a little remembering the Masons and the fun we had had there in the past. I don't think I ever managed to tell you all adequately how grateful I have been for the happy time I had had with UNRRA and for all your goodness and interest in us and in our adventure. I was terribly sorry that I didn't manage to get up to see you all on the Thursday before I left, but Robert told you, I believe, what a last-minute session I had with the Board of Trade and with my solicitors. I had an awful job getting my export licence fixed and then I had to make a will at the last minute before I left, so that involved three visits to my solicitor in one afternoon and I didn't finish till just on 6, but even had I finished before, I was so completely burnt-out by then that I couldn't have borne more goodbyes, I think.

The journey here was quite awful. I felt perfectly alright, but the children were desperately ill, sick nearly all the way, and not always into the proper receptacle, either. I got really worried at one point when they were both just lying in a sort of coma, with dead-white faces and blue all round their mouths. I was more than thankful that I had had Carol's appendix out before we started, or Heaven knows what would have happened. We certainly had a very bumpy passage – the darn plane did everything but a falling leaf, and just out from Tunis, we ran into a terrific thunderstorm. It was really awe-inspiring. The worst stretch came just before Elizabethville, when the plane behaved far worse than a ship at sea. One really couldn't stand up, and then practically every passenger succumbed and was sick. I was frightfully proud of myself because I wasn't. Just as well, since I was sitting with a sick child in either arm. I was desperately tired, though, and kept coming out in cold sweats, which I think was just sheer weakness, for I had no sleep the night before I left England and none on the plane at all.

But to cut a long story short, we finally arrived in Bulawayo on Wednesday morning, about 8, and were met by Uncle Neville, who is a perfectly charming old boy, and he whisked us into his car and off to his bungalow on the other side of Bulawayo for – oh joy! – a bath and then breakfast. Bulawayo is a perfectly lovely city. The streets are quite incredibly wide. They can take four lines of traffic and still have cars parked in the centre. The buildings are modern and all white, with green shutters and wide stoeps outside all the bungalows, and there are flowering trees everywhere. Jacarandas, which have a spire of blossom not unlike a chestnut, only a clear, bright mauve; flamboyant which are similar, only scarlet; silver oaks, which is a misnomer, since the flower is a bright orange; and everywhere bougainvillea in scarlet, purple and orange. It is quite staggeringly beautiful, against the vivid blue of the African sky.

The shops I dare not describe, since you gals would go quite crazy. Every sort of American cosmetic, nylons for the taking, DuPonts at 13/6d a pair, and the clothes! Lots of American washing frocks at comparatively cheap prices and in every fitting imaginable – even for an S.S.P., Eric! Food is plentiful, though we are rationed on butter and sugar. No books, however – one is just dished out with one's allowance for the week and there you are! Fruit, curiously enough, is expensive. Oranges are 4d each, but then here I can gather my own lemons, peaches, grapes and grapefruit off the tree in the garden, so what the!

I stayed the first week here at the Palace Hotel, a lovely modern building with a garden to dream about, surrounded by a huge stoep (quite the Colonial now, amn't I?) with tables and chairs and an army of native 'boys' who rush to serve you at the slightest sign on your part. A little different from Joe Lyons. After a week there, I got this bungalow for three months, furnished, after which I hope to get a place of my own. Housing here is quite as bad as it is in London and it is almost impossible to move about without a car, so I am learning to drive.

When I tell you about this place, you just won't believe it is I here, of course. I am 14 miles out of Bulawayo, right in the middle of the 'bundu' or bush, at a place called Khami. Perhaps Paddy Dunne will remember it. Anyway, it is near the waterworks, and this bungalow is the property of the manager of same, who has gone on leave for three months. My nearest and only neighbours are about

500 yards away and they are my only means of contact with town, since they take me in once, and sometimes twice a week to town in their car. There are no buses, no postman and no newspapers, and the wireless here is out of commission, so I am entirely cut off save for the telephone. Yet I love it and am very happy here.

The bungalow is quite a large one, with five rooms and kitchen quarters, and of course the inevitable stoep with a divan and chairs on it, and the grounds stretch over about five acres, part of which is cultivated as a vegetable garden and part as a flower garden and the rest is just rocks and scrub. The trees and flowers are wonderful and will be more so after the rains have come. October is known as suicide month here, when the heat is at its greatest before the rains. Today the temperature has been 99 degrees in the shade. And yet I don't feel it as I used to in London (you may remember I didn't like it much!!). Of course, life moves at a very easy pace and I have two 'boys', Ticky the cook boy and Johnny the house boy, who do simply everything, including the washing. Then there are three garden boys, but my neighbour copes with them. Just as well, since my kitchen Kaffir goes very little beyond "*I funa manzi*" and "Breakfast 7 *kasasa*", which being interpreted mean "I want some water" and "Breakfast at 7 tomorrow." Ticky talks quite a bit of English and when he doesn't understand what I say, he just grins broadly, nods his head and says, "Yes, *Inkoskas*." I still have to pinch myself to realise it is really I here.

The nights here are indescribably beautiful. After dinner, the boys go off to their compound and I am all alone here. Crickets chirp out in the garden, and the frogs croak, and away out in the bush, I can hear hyenas and jackals howling. Once I heard a leopard roar. There is one the other side of the river, about a mile away. It killed one of our dogs the other night, but I think it is unlikely it will come very near human habitation. Just in case, however, my neighbour is teaching me to shoot – target: a tin can hung on a tree! I can't say I am a dazzling markswoman yet, but I can load fairly fast, and I am improving and generally manage to hit the tree next to that with the tin can on!

Just now I am sitting out on the stoep, the moonlight is bathing everything with a clear silver radiance, and in a little while I shall go for a little stroll before going to bed. Once upon a time I would have been scared stiff, but somehow, I don't mind it here. However, I shan't venture too far, since I was warned the leopard might come as far as the outskirts of the grounds.

We go to bed fairly early here, unless there is a party on somewhere. Generally, about 9 or 9.30, since we rise about 6.30. It is lovely then, before the heat of the day, and I usually go for a walk with the children before breakfast at 8. At 11, tea appears and no queuing for it, either, and then I just write letters or read till lunch at 1. Then a siesta, all of us, and we sit around till teatime at 4. A walk then, since it is cooler, and then I get the children bathed before their supper at 6.30, have my sundowner before dinner at 7.30 and more letter-writing, mending or reading till bedtime. A lazy life, but I am glad of it just now, for I was pretty whacked when I arrived.

The Joneses are very nice. They have two daughters, both married, only one of whom lives in Bulawayo, and a son, John. The latter has taken me out and about quite a bit and we have been to two dances and a party already! After a dance, the thing to do here is to go to the hot dog stall for food. It is run on American lines, and the tray of food is brought to your car. The first time we went, John ordered a mixed grill, and honestly, I felt ashamed to be eating it when I thought of you all at home. A huge steak, sausage, tomatoes, chips and two eggs! The food is quite incredible. When I tell you that at the bottom of the breakfast menu at the hotel, there was a notice saying that owing to the 25% meat cut, no steak would be served at breakfast, you can imagine!

Well, my dears, please write, each and all of you, when you have time. I long for news of you all and to hear all the latest about the madhouse.

All my love,
Dee

P.S. Bill, the current hit out here is 'Give Me Five Minutes More'. The children are delighted and sing it constantly.

Highwood
Farningham
Kent
Wednesday 15th October

My dear Chris,

Thank you very much for your letter, which I have just received with my breakfast (in bed!). I am sorry not to have let you know before how I am, but I have been too sick to care about anything. Everything is still much too much trouble – you know how it is.

The Roger boomed at me on Thursday night, "Conjunctivitis", which might have been two penn'orth of liquorice for all that I know. I promptly lost the prescription he gave me and arrived home bawling my eyes out. I cried so much I had everyone scared stiff. Then I calmly turned over and went to sleep! I was so miserable.

However, after years in bed, I hope to get up for a little this afternoon. Dr. Rogers says I shall not be going back to work this week, but I think I shall be back next. The prospect is rather too grim to think about yet, though.

Poor Murielle! I expect you have driven her crazy – she has always to answer for other people's absences. Please give her my fond wishes and tell her I shall soon be back to relieve her of you.

This letter is being written resting on the venerable Benham! I wonder if I missed much at yesterday's lecture. It is time I started to read this book, I suppose. "Economics," boomed the doctor. "Huh – cause of all the trouble." By which ambiguous statement I believe he meant that it was too advanced for me and was tiring me. He is a bit dense at times, but rather a poppet really.

Mother says it has been glorious weather; I wish I had been out in it. It is not particularly good today – too cold.

I must stop now as I feel tired. Please forgive my writing which looks most peculiar somehow. Do write to me soon, Chris. I am glad you have missed me – I have missed you too, especially do I miss you now – when I would normally be seeing or phoning you for lunch or something similar. I love you.

Oh – please give my love to Dorothy and Carol and Nicky when you write. I shall write to them soon.

Bye now and lots of love,
From Connie

NB: Highwood NOT 'Highwood'!! I hate inverted commas.

Farningham
7. XI .47

My dearest Chris,

Did you manage to arrive home safely on Wednesday? I was worried first about the bus; I do hope you caught it? Then the delays on the railways due to fog made me feel terribly guilty that you had had such a time merely to see me.

How is your cold? It was wonderful to see you again, my dear; your flowers and grapes were simply lovely, you should not have bothered (but I am very pleased you did). It was such a pity you could stay only such a short time. We always suffer either from people or from lack of time, frequently both.

I shall be back next week. At the moment something very silly has happened; due to this wretched catarrh I have developed a sore throat. Mother and I had to laugh at the list of ails and woe I've presented in the short space of a month! Isn't it funny? Still, this last is the most bearable of all and will soon go.

How is everyone and everything at the office? Give my fond wishes and thanks to Lilian and to Puff, Bill Laycock, Robbie and all the others who have sent good wishes to me through you. Chris, my dear, I do hope you will take care of yourself with all these fogs and cold winds about. Please do not overwork either in the office or on your course.

I received a month's pay on Thursday, so I am feeling moderately wealthy – for a short time.

By the way, did you ask your sister about a place in Cornwall where we might stay this Christmas? Perhaps you have soured on the idea, but I still think it might be a very good scheme.

I'm sorry this is so short a letter, but I am just about to go to bed and Mother's hawk eye is watching the clock.

It was wonderful, marvellous to see you again; I love you, honey, see you very soon. Don't keep your eye on that dame so long! The green-eyed monster returns next week!

Bye now, my love, and take care of yourself.

Your own Connie

c/o Neville Jones, Esq.

P.O. Box 240

Bulawayo

S.R.

9th December 1947

My dear Christopher,

It was lovely to have your letter yesterday, and I must explain my promptitude in placing you in my debt again by the fact that tomorrow I have to go into hospital for a slight op which will keep me there for a while, and when I come out, the Christmas rush of letters, parcels, etc. will be upon me and it won't be so easy. Of course, I could write in hospital, but I always did hate writing in bed. I shall not, however, expect you to be as prompt in replying, especially as I gather from Peggy's last letter that you will be in the throes of a move to Western House soon. You poor things. I don't envy you, remembering the last to-do, and also Western House is a rather depressing place, I think, and a long way from either Tube station! Still, you will have Mrs. Taylor in the commissariat, which will be a consolation after the awful mess at Castle St.

Dear Rep! What nice things you say about me in your letter, and I was deeply touched and very happy to hear them. I like to think that you and I will always be friends. Of all the people in UNRRA, with the obvious exception of Robert, you are the one I miss most and of whom I most frequently think. I think we were a pretty good complement for each other, and I think, too, we understood each other pretty well, and that is a great deal. I have been so happy that I was to a small degree instrumental in bringing you and Connie together. I hope that one day in the not-too-distant future, I may have cause to be even happier.

What upheavals are going on in C.R. I couldn't be more sorry to hear that Bill was so mean as to tell Erik what you said in all confidence to him. But I fear that Bill is all politics and I told you once or twice before that I didn't trust him. I am so sorry both for you and for Erik, since while normally I think Erik would realise that it was nothing personal, in his present state of health, things probably loom larger than life-size to him. I do so understand how weary you must get of the work – Lormer would be quite enough to feed me up. I still remember those meetings! It would be infinitely better for you if you could pack in, but you stand to lose too much, and now, more than ever, you can't afford it.

I do wish that there were some way of easing things for you at home, Christopher. It seems so hard that at your age you should be so tied, when normally you could be hoping for a home of your own and a family. Maybe the way will open up sooner than you think – I earnestly hope so, for I think it is too great a burden for you, and not an entirely fair one.

I am so glad to hear that Connie is better. Robert told me that you had had an evening together, and I was very glad. He was very fond of you both. By the way, at the moment his movements are a bit uncertain, so I should write to his home address and put 'Please forward' on it. It is Daisybank, Stromness, Orkney. Be careful to put 'R. H. Robertson', since his father's first initial is R too.

No, I haven't heard from Linnell. I don't think I will till I write, if I write. But somehow, I don't want to, since I know I could never marry him, and I find it difficult to be natural with him in consequence. If you see him, however, say I sent my regards, will you?

Do send me the snaps of yourself and Connie. I am so glad you are to have a holiday. It will be grand for you both. I'll try and send you one or two of me when I get the camera again.

I gather from what you say about Zena that you don't know her news. She and Jack are engaged to be married and expect to be so about next June. Zena is going home on a visit in February and then will come back to England for good. I am so pleased and happy about it, and haven't hesitated to write and say, 'I told you so' to Jack – nice person that I am!

The children are well; in fact we are all much better now that the rains have broken, and it is consequently so much cooler. I was beginning to feel pretty washed out, for the past few months had been pretty trying in more than one way and I wasn't in the best of condition to face such extreme heat and the altitude.

Well, dear, I must finish here, I think, since I want to get all my correspondence off my chest before going into the hospital. My very best wishes and love to you both for Christmas – you will be in my thoughts along with the others I love at that time, and I shall imagine you in Cornwall and envy you a little your happiness.

The children both send their love to you, as I do mine, my fondest love.

As ever,
Dorothy

TEN

There's One Damn Good Chance for You

1948–1949

c/o Standard Bank of South Africa Ltd.
Lusaka
Northern Rhodesia
18th March 1948

My dear Rep,

First of all, let me apologise for my exceedingly long silence, but as you can see from my address, I have been anything but static. Life has been full and varied since I last saw you, and accordingly, I never seem to have had the time to settle to correspondence. Needless to say, however, I have given a great deal of thought to the friends I left behind.

Secondly, for various reasons which I won't go into, I am not keen on any of the others knowing where I am or why – not just at the moment anyway. No doubt you will or have already put 2 and 2 quite aptly together, so for the moment can we please leave it at that? I am satisfied that you will not divulge these details for the time being, so that if anyone enquires re. my whereabouts or well-being – I am well, fit and enjoying life but address unknown?!

Well now, these prelims over, I would have written you anyway, but I confess the letter may have been rather advanced by some talk I had this morning with one of the businessmen here – by name of

Cooper. I think I mentioned before I left that I would look out for something good out here or keep my eyes peeled for anything good. Well, something has come along.

Cooper is accountant to one of the branches of a large firm who cover most of S.A. (also have a place in London), E. W. Jarry & Co. At the same time, he carries on a business as accountant, auditor and secretary. The latter is growing, and he is anxious to relinquish his post with Jarry's. Jarry's want someone good to replace Cooper, and Cooper, who is remaining till a replacement is found, is also trying to find someone. I have had one or two chats with him, I have mentioned you, and he is very interested. I was honestly able to give you the highest recommendations, and, Rep, the job is yours if you want it.

The post is as Accountant to E. W. Jarry & Co., Lusaka. The salary to commence is as follows:-

Salary £60
Bonus every year £15
Cost of living allowance £5

_____

£65 per month
+ £15 per year
There is also a good pension scheme.

Now this salary would only be for the first 2–3 months while you worked under Cooper and while he gave you the gen and ins and outs. Thereafter, when you took over from him, which would be pretty soon, the salary would be:-

Salary for month £75
Cost of living allowance £7.10

_____

£82.10 per month
+ £20 bonus p.a.
Pension scheme still applicable.

They are a good firm to work with. Your salary (practically initially) therefore is over £1,000 p.a.

There is terrific scope out here – the country is developing fast and C.A.s are badly needed and will do well.

1. I know that you haven't yet finished your exams (or hadn't when I left and you may have remedied that), but I have checked up on the position here and you can finish here with equal facility. The exams can be taken in Bulawayo – quite a short trip by air from here. Exams are held May and Dec. and you can sit part in May and part in Dec., and you don't have to sit your finals all in one part. There is therefore no law there.

2. With regard to fare, I queried re. this and the position is no. Initially they would not pay your fare, but after a period they would possibly, if not probably, refund part if not the whole of the fare. Cooper suggests another thing, tho', but it will be done here and not directly and don't mention it if you write. If he can arrange it with his Director who is due to call here in April (early), he will suggest, and if possible fix it, that you are taken on in London, spend a month with the firm's office there, and then come out at their expense. I don't know what the position would be with regard to a wife – if you have one by that time (!) – but they sound, and I know they are, a very good firm and they might play.

However, Rep, that is the job. It is a good one; the prospects are good either with that firm or if you decide to go out on your own at a later date. Personally, I think it is a splendid opportunity and one not to be turned down lightly. I of course know how you are placed at home, but you would be able to help in just the same way from here – possibly better. I am not quite sure what the Income Tax rate is at present, but a married man with £1,000 p.a. pays something like £30 or £35 per year; at home you pay almost that per month. Living isn't any dearer – in fact, it's very much easier. The life out here is a grand one.

Now, if you are interested, I'd like you to write as soon as you can AIR MAIL to Findlay Cooper, Accountant, E. W. Jarry & Co. Ltd., P.O. Box [...], Lusaka, N. Rhodesia, giving them details of your experience. There is nothing intricate in the job and you would do it with your eyes shut. Mention your age – I guess you'll know what to give them but don't hold back. You have the experience.

The climate is good – being 4,000-odd feet up, it doesn't get too hot; in fact, I've been warned that there is wet weather ahead the next few months. There is plenty of life, fishing and shooting, and the people are nice.

Incidentally, I am remaining here. I have opened a law business. I don't intend to waste time. I'm in good company and I won't let any grass grow. There will be ample for you too. In other words, Rep, think this over very thoroughly – there is money here and a good life. I'd like you to come out and we could go places. There's one damn good chance for you, and my honest and sincere advice is to take it.

Incidentally, I mentioned that you might not be free until June. That is O.K. and would not stand in the way. Even if it were later, I think it would still be O.K., but of course, I couldn't be absolutely certain on that. All excuses and impediments removed!

What does Connie say about it? She would love it here and there would be plenty of nice friends for her. There's a good crowd here. Incidentally, most married women take jobs here and there's one for her. As all housework is done by black servants (about 30/– per month for one), the women have a very easy life and generally work.

Well, there it is, Rep! I hope you take it. Write to Cooper soon tho', as if you are interested, he would like to take up with his Director in early April the question of your being taken on in London with its paid passage out. He will try to arrange that tho', so I wouldn't mention it when you write.

I have been in Africa now for quite a while. I flew out and spent some time in S.R., mainly Bulawayo with one or two tours. Then I came up here, liked it and saw the prospects, and here I am remaining. I love this part of the world and you will too. There is a terrific future here, and N.R. and S.R. are developing fast and calling out for good young blood and men with qualifications such as ours. I made no mistake in selecting this place.

Dorothy I have seen quite a lot of, and I will be seeing her tomorrow. She and the children are well and fit, tho' they are not yet settled. She will probably come up here within the next few weeks. At the moment, tho', accommodation is rather a problem but will ease soon.

I could dwell quite a bit on this country – in fact, I could enthuse (and do) but I find it hardly fair to tell of sunshine every day (tho' with showers just now) and good and plentiful food. There is also a freedom from convention, and great open country full of game and interest. Lusaka itself, tho' the capital of N.R., is still small, is growing fast, and will grow faster. There is plenty of farming ground if one is interested in that. I am, and it won't be long till I have a farm myself. In other words, Rep, there is nothing one can't do here, and I guess I'll have a finger in a few pies ere long.

We had one or two very lovely motor trips in S.R. – petrol is unrationed and since I got the car 3 months ago we must have covered over 5,000 miles. Consequently, we have seen a lot of the country and are rapidly seeing more. I am flying down to Bulawayo tomorrow – a 600-mile trip but we think no more of that here than London to Manchester in England. In fact, less, for air services are good and cheap.

And now what of yourself? I had news of you from Dorothy and I must also thank you for your Xmas card. It was good to be remembered. I gather, and can appreciate, that life with UNRRA these days is not very exciting. What of Connie? I hope she is keeping better, and indeed that life goes well for both of you. It would indeed be a happy day in Lusaka if you decided to come out here. I have kept the personal element out of the remarks re. the job, but I don't think I need tell you how gladly you'd be received here.

I have kept very much better – in fact, Rep, I've had three damn good months of holiday: sunshine, the bush, the bathing pool; I did some gold-mining, took an interest in everything the country offered and generally enjoyed life. I have eaten hugely – put on weight – and generally I am very fit.

And so, Rep, I am now going to eat a 5-course lunch – in shirt and shorts. I will be glad to hear from you and I will await with more than interest for your reactions to the job. Whatever you do – drop Cooper a note. He'd appreciate it. Needless to say, tho', I am hopeful that you will take it.

By the way, leave is good out here and you'd probably get home at least every two years, and it may even be assisted. One can now fly to England in 2–3 days, and fares are coming down.

Regards to Connie and yourself. Cheerio then for the moment, and my warmest.

Yours aye,
Robbie (Robert H. Robertson)

Bulawayo

20/3/48[131]

I arrived here yesterday after a quick journey of 1½ hours; a very pleasant trip too – crossing the Zambezi once again with its lovely and interesting country.

Dorothy, whom I found well, let me read your letter, and as she didn't know of this job, nor of my actions, I gave her my letter to you to read. She, too, thinks it an exceptionally good opening and is writing you herself – no doubt in very persuasive terms, for she was thrilled at any possibility of yourself and Connie coming out here. This, by the way, isn't a conspiracy between us to seduce you out! I think it worth mentioning that when I left UNRRA I had a sense of relief and I am satisfied that you will feel the same. I think you are b… browned off with the place, so […]

I checked up on Income Tax for a married man with £1,000 p.a.

£500 free of tax

£250 @ 1/6 […] £18/15/–

£250 @ 2/– […] £25/–

£1,000   £43/15/–

Tho' I believe there has been some review […] since, the allowance for each dependant is £100 (as distinct from children; they have no allowance) so you'd be O.K. Admittedly, the job is attractive!

One thing I forgot – when writing Cooper, mention my name – R. H. R., Solicitor, Lusaka.

Robbie

Afraid this is a bit of a scrawl, but I've been hurried and I'm so sensitive about my handwriting that I never apologise for it.

---

131 Postscript to same letter.

c/o Neville Jones, Esq.
P.O. Box 240
Bulawayo
20th March 1948

My dear Rep,

I am replying with quite commendable promptitude to your letter, but as it is principally in order to back up Robert's suggestion, perhaps I can't claim any credit!

Well, by now the great secret is out and you can understand why I was so vague about Robert's whereabouts and why he hadn't answered your letters. He did not and does not want UNRRA to know about us, not until everything is settled, hence all the secrecy in the past. He has been out here now since November. You needn't ask, of course, if I am happy. You knew a good deal about us, or at least my side of things, and I hope you are glad for me that what I felt for Robert wasn't wasted – though I never think that loving anyone is a waste, whether it is returned or not.

Robert has given you all the details of the job and, Rep, I do add my most fervent advice to you to take it. It's an opportunity which won't come again in a hurry, and I know you could do the job. Robert would never have suggested it if he felt you weren't capable of it. You will still be able to help your family – better than before, if anything – and will also be able to start a life of your own, and you know I think it is high time you did that.

Now please, Rep, don't get one of your inferiority complex fits – I know you are liable to them of old – other people can see more than you can, and I know you would be able to do this, and also, I think you could persuade Connie to come out with you, or at least follow you. You would neither of you be strangers in a strange land – you need not ask how warm a reception you would get from us both, and it would be wonderful to have someone from home out here with us.

This is a grand chance, Rep, and I do beg you to take it. I know it means a great upheaval all round, but I think that must be faced in time in any case. Don't let it go. If you like, after you have talked to Connie about it, I will write to her and tell her a little about life out here and how much we should like you both to come. And why on earth, by the way, should you think she won't marry you? Ever tried asking? Anyway, you would be in a position to ask her with this job, and if she doesn't know by now how she feels about you, she never will. Personally, I think you stand more than a good chance. Have a go, Joe, as I used to say!

I won't natter anymore, Rep, because I want this letter to go off at once and shall await your reply eagerly. I shall be in Bulawayo for perhaps another three weeks, then I am going up to Lusaka to join Robert and act as his secretary for a while, but any mail sent to the address at the head of this letter will be forwarded to me.

Now please, Rep, this is the rest of your life you have to consider, and I think it very unlikely England will be able to offer anything as good as this for some time to come, and Rhodesia is a coming country, make no mistake.

My very best love to Connie, and of course to yourself,
Dorothy

P.S. Will you thank Geoff Hill for his letter, Rep, and tell him I will be answering soon, but in the meantime, will he send me out a brief résumé of his qualifications, experience, etc., which will be of considerable help to me, or rather to us (tho' he's not to know it's 'us' yet), in trying to find somewhere for him?

P.P.S. I'll never forgive you if you turn this down, Rep! And remember, you have a life of your own to lead. Dear Rep, please.

G. C. Repton
Twynersh
Leigh Place
Cobham
Surrey
31st March 1948

G. Findlay Cooper
Accountant
E. W. Jarry & Co. Ltd.

Dear Mr. Cooper,

I understand that you are looking out for a likely man to fill the post with Jarry's which you will shortly be relinquishing, and that in the course of a discussion which you had with R. H. Robertson, Solicitor, Lusaka, he mentioned my name to you.

As he has suggested, I am sending to you herewith a brief résumé of my previous experience and qualifications for the job. I feel sure that these particulars will satisfy you as to my capabilities, and am, myself, confident that it would not take me long to fit in as your successor.

I have thought this matter over carefully and decided that, if you are prepared to take me on, I will make arrangements for my release from my present employment as soon as possible and go ahead with the booking of my passage.

In this connection I understand from my present employers that they will be requiring me until at least June 30th 1948. However, if you decide to take me on and wish me to start before that date, I think it can be arranged.

I understand that the starting salary would be £60 per month plus £5 cost of living allowance, but that after the first two or three months this would be increased to £75 per month plus £7.10 cost of living allowance.

At the present time I am still studying for the intermediate exams of the Association of Certified & Corporate Accountants and the Chartered Institute of Secretaries, which I am taking this coming May and June. I gather it will be possible to sit for the finals in Bulawayo.

The foregoing, together with attached particulars, will, I hope, provide all the information which you require of me for the present, but should there be anything which I have not covered, or should you require additional references, I take it you will let me know.

Hoping to receive from you at an early date your favourable reply, I am,

Yours faithfully,
C. Repton

Details of previous experience etc.

AGE: 29.

SINGLE.

EDUCATION: Public School standard.

    St. Edmund's College, Ware and Wimbledon College, 1928–1937.

    Oxford & Cambridge School Certificate (with Matric. Exemption), 1936.

    Pitman's Intensive Business Course, 1937–8.

PREVIOUS EXPERIENCE:

    One year's work as auditor with firm of Chartered Accountants in City (A. W. Goodfellow & Co.), 1938–9. (Sept. 1939 until Feb. 1946: served in British and Indian Armies, mainly in India and Far East – rank Staff Sergeant.) Feb. 1946: Joined UNRRA as Accounts Clerk at salary of £400 p.a. Received several promotions during past 2 years and now holding the position of Executive Assistant to the Director of Accounts at a salary of £770 p.a.

Present work gives wide scope and requires detailed knowledge and co-ordination of the work of each section of the Accounts Branch. It also carries the responsibility for supervising a staff of some fifty persons.

c/o P.O. Box 154

Lusaka

2nd June 1948

My dear Rep,

  I hope that by now you have had Robert's letter with the news in it. I replied to your last one to me within two days of receiving it, but Robert asked me to hold it up till he wrote you himself in more detail about the job, and I've been waiting ever since then till I finally got him down to it about ten days ago. Then I looked at my own letter again and it was so out of date that I tore it up.

  I am so sorry there has been this long delay. I tried my best to get Robert to write, but to do him justice, the position just wasn't clear, since Cooper dithered about for such ages and, too, the pressure of work here is just frightful. We live in a constant state of flap, trying to keep up with the business we already have and with the new clients flowing in all the time. By the end of the day we can barely be polite to each other, and I regret to say that Robert lapses into his famous UNRRA-day silences which used to get my goat so much, though in those days they upset me more than they do now that I know how things are with us.

I read Robert's letter to you and noted that he said I would bear out all that he told you and advised, and I most certainly do, Rep. It may seem to you in the light of this disappointment, when it seemed at first so certain that you would get the job, that Lusaka, etc. will be full of similar disappointments. However, it wouldn't be so, and I do beg you to take his advice. Believe me, I wouldn't tell you that if I wasn't sure of what I was saying, and you know Robert – he would never do anything hare-brained.

I won't make this letter long, Rep, dear. It is just to back up what Robert said and make sure that you believe him.

I was so very sorry to hear about Paddy. He was always so cheerful and 'good for a laugh', and he will be missed, I know.

Give my love to Connie and tell her I hope to see her soon!

My love to you, as ever,
Dorothy

Scott & Robertson (Barrister & Solicitor)
P.O. Box 154
Lusaka
N. Rhodesia
27th July 1948

Dear Rep,

Just a brief note to let you know that I saw Green this afternoon and that he could probably find a use for you out here. Confidentially, he has requisitioned three bodies (you will recognise the term!) from London and he suggested that you contact their local office. He mentioned that he would write himself.

I might add that I have spoken to Green on one or two occasions but on these he did not think he had anything which might be suitable. Something, however, may come out of this. You may use my name in any way you wish as a reference.

Think well over the question of salary, and I would suggest that you ask for not less than £60. The contract would be for two years with free passage home at the end, or leave with return fare home paid, but no doubt they will go into all that with you.

With regard to this tying yourself down for the two years, personally I was rather in favour of your avoiding this. With present conditions here and with the ideas of which my head is full, I would like you to have been here but free for anything really good that came along. However, as they are at this stage still only ideas and must remain so for a short time, don't be influenced by that, and if Howard's offer you something good, then O.K.

If Connie comes out, I will, of course, exercise my option, though I feel satisfied that if she also contacted Howard's, there would probably be a job for her as well, and the thing you must bear in mind is that if you went to Howard's, it would be passage paid but on two years' contract.

You need not be worried about the life here. It is no 'cantonment' and the job here is to resist the gaieties of life, not to seek them. Personally, as I have told you before, I love the country and I guess you will too. When you come, however, please bring a lavatory chain – I long to pull one! At the moment, the climate is mild, and we even feel cold at times. There will, I understand, be some heat towards the end of September, but it only lasts for about 4/5 months.

We'll see you here yet. Skip Costain's, by the way.

Many thanks for your letter and your news. We often think of you, cricket, etc. Glad to hear something of the other lads but it appears that our own little circle is diminishing rapidly. I'd like Jack Lejeune's address, if you could get it, as looking back, he is one of the few who sticks.

Let me know how things are, and if anything else crops up, I shall, of course, communicate with you *toute suite* [sic].

With love to Connie,
Robbie

Hello, Rep, dear,

It's a long time since I wrote, I know, but Robert is a perfect slave-driver (warn Connie!), and what with the work during the day and hardly ever getting an evening 'in', I am a wreck. Would you believe it, the other day he asked me if I thought he was difficult to work with! I hadn't the heart to tell him plainly.

We are both pretty well, though tired, as I said, and we are longing to have someone with whom to natter over the old days and places. At least I am. Also, I need my ego bolstered up a bit and you always did it so beautifully when Robert was particularly trying!

Dorothy

Tel. No. Cobham 3253
G. C. T. Repton
Office: Langham 3010, Ext. 14
Twynersh
Leigh Place
Cobham
Surrey
30th July 1948

For the attention of Mr. Tait
Messrs. Broadcast Relay Service Ltd.[132]
Carlton House
11 Lower Regent Street
London S.W. 1.

Dear Sirs,

Messrs. Laurie & Company have advised me that you are looking for a suitable man to fill the post of Accountant at a salary of about £500 per annum.

---

132 Broadcast Relay Service, later renamed Rediffusion, was one of the first companies to relay radio programmes by wire from 1928; an improvement on the 'wireless' system. By the end of 1946, almost 750,000 homes in the UK received their radio programmes by wired systems.

I should like to apply for this post and give below the following details of my experience and qualifications.

After leaving school, where I obtained School Certificate with Matric exemption, in 1937, I took an intensive business course with Pitman's, Lancaster Gate, where I studied Book-keeping and Accounting and Commercial subjects.

From January to September 1939, I was employed by a firm of Chartered Accountants, A. W. Goodfellow & Co., 3 Great Winchester Street, E.C. 2, as an Audit Clerk where I worked on a variety of small audits to trial balance.

In September 1939 I was called up for Military Service and served in the army, mainly in India and Malaya, until my demobilisation early in 1946.

In February 1946 I joined the London Office of The United Nations Relief and Rehabilitation Administration, 11 Portland Place, W. 1 as an Accounting Clerk. During the ensuing 2½ years I have had practical experience of many aspects of UNRRA's supply accounting and have also done work in connection with the procurement and shipping of supplies.

During this period, I have steadily acquired additional responsibilities and received corresponding promotion, my present post being Assistant to the Chief Accountant, at a salary of £860 per annum, in which capacity I have also had valuable experience in the organisation of accounting systems and in office management. I realise, of course, that I should have to prove to you my ability before asking a similar salary.

Due to the imminent closure of the Administration, I expect to be released from my present job at the end of August but could probably leave earlier if required.

So far as other qualifications are concerned, I might add that I have been studying for the past 1½ years for the exams of the Chartered Institute of Secretaries and the Association of Certified & Corporate Accountants. I sat the C.I.S. Intermediate last May and passed in five out of six subjects, failing only in Mercantile Law; to complete the exam I am required to re-sit Section A only. I sat the A.C.C.A. Intermediate in June, but do not know the results yet.

In conclusion, I wish to say that I am aged 29, single and of good health; that I am a keen and ambitious worker, confident of giving you the fullest satisfaction; and that if you so wish, I can attend for an interview at any time convenient to you.

Hoping to receive your favourable reply, I am,

Yours faithfully,
G. C. T. Repton

UNRRA

This Records
The Loyal and Valued Services of
Geoffrey Christopher Repton
to the United Nations Relief and Rehabilitation
Administration in its Great Work of Relieving
the Suffering and Saving the Lives of the
Victims of War in the Liberated Countries.
Lowell P. Rooks
Director General
Washington D.C.

The Kuwait Oil Co. Ltd.
No. 1 Precinct
Ahmadi
Kuwait
Persian Gulf
8th September 1948

Dear Rep,

Just a very quick note to let you know that another 'oil-man' has been born. I have now been out here a couple of weeks and feel justified in stating that once one gets through the hot season, he is well on his way to settling down for the remainder of the year. The living accommodation is good and the food excellent. I have at my disposal a 1948 Ford Sedan [...]

The journey out was extremely comfortable and very interesting. I came via Malta – Damascus – Basra – overshot Kuwait and went on to Bahrain – the end of the run. Sandstorm had disappeared the following morning, so we set forth for Kuwait and landed in a very hot midday sun.

One soon settles down to this life, which is very easy – 600 cigarettes per month, a case of beer, a bottle of gin and whisky. Personally, I settle for the beer in a climate like this.

How are things at UNRRA? Do let me know how you are faring yourself. If you want any info on this oil business, I'll be only too pleased to supply same.

My regards to Connie. If either of you have a moment do drop me a line – mail is still a very important item in a bloke's life overseas.

Sincerely yours,
George Price

P.O. Box 275
Lusaka
28th October 1948

My dear Rep,

This will perforce be a short letter, since we are up to the hairline in work and the heat is pretty terrific – you may remember what I am like in hot weather!

First of all, my very warmest congratulations to you and to Connie on your engagement. You must know how delighted – and unsurprised – I am! My very best wishes – and Robert's – to you both. We had a drink to you when we got the news!

This is only a follow-up to the wire we are sending you today. If you haven't already answered, just go straight out to the P.O. and cable Yes at once. It is a good job, Rep, with a new and already flourishing firm out here – Doughty & Doughty, who already have offices in Pall Mall, and have another branch down in Jo'burg, S.A. I think you would do very well with them, and you would have a chance to do the odd accountancy job on the side, which would add to your income.

As for Connie, for Heaven's sake bring her out, for I have more to do here than I can possibly cope with. There are occasions when I long for the delightfully lazy life of Commodity Records, and even a Thursday morning meeting was quiet compared with this.

I won't – in fact, can't, because of work – say more now than 'Don't miss this chance, Rep. You can't go wrong, I promise you.'

R. and I are well but a little tired and feeling the strain of a good many things, but business is more than flourishing.

No more now – see you in a couple of months!

Much love to you both,
Dorothy

Monday 8/11/48

Chris, darling,

Please forgive my silence this weekend, mainly due to the dampening and gloomy effect of the weather. I felt so blue this weekend, not seeing you at all, missing you a lot, saying goodbye to Kit, and on top of all, the weather. The American influence has finally moved out (I think; maybe one or two phrases will pop up occasionally) amid a small party on Saturday: I never realised how much I could miss you until then. Everything was set for quite a good evening with an eligible guy, soft lights, good music, hooch and dancing; in fact all the ingredients for an interesting evening. The centrepiece, however, was very noticeable by its absence, and I missed you so much I had to keep imagining that Kit was you. That failed dismally, mainly because Kit wasn't playing ball on that score. We parted the best of friends, both in a rather boozy melancholia and both because of you but for entirely different reasons. He wished us every happiness (and wondered if you were worth it, but not for long) and said you must be quite a guy, and he was sorry he hadn't met you. Is it my nasty mind or is that a back-handed compliment? I haven't decided yet. Anyway, darling, there it is, and I still love you right to the ends of my eyelashes. Why the hell do you get mumps?

Having heaved that off the old bosom, how are you, Chris, honey? No complications, I trust? Why didn't you phone today? Just as well actually, as I was at a meeting all afternoon. Big stuff now, by Jove! Telling the Board of Trade where to get off! Actually (twice in one paragraph, horror) it consisted of hulking chap de Stefani and buxom C. B. meekly enquiring of weedy B of T type if it would be possible to have some figures for a statement, in due course, naturally. What a life! However, I managed to buy quite a decent mac for de Stefani (my vocation in life, I reckon – two in a fortnight and pressing you every day); it was rather twee. Have my eye on just the job for you at £11-odd.

I haven't phoned Pam, shame on me, and have not had any news from Gillie. Did you think anymore about Christmas? Mari said the Horton Grange at Maidenhead was quite fair; at 7 guineas per week it is a country club with fires in all rooms, a bridge room (!) and a cocktail bar. I wouldn't trust it myself, but maybe it would bear closer attention. I feel a nice pubby, Ye Olde Worlde atmosphere is the right idea at Christmas, which looks like Benson or something similar.

Have you heard from Robert about any of the schemes mooted at the UNRRA dance? Give him my very best when you phone. Hope to see him soon. Let me know soonest you hear from Robbie.

Would you send me the Italian books if you can spare them, darling? I am very broke.

Loved *Oliver Twist*; had lunch with one of the speaking parts in it at the Colombo a couple of days before I saw it. Coincidence.

Must stop now, darling. I'll ring you soon, until when, be good.

All my love, darlingest Chris,
From Connie
xxxxxxxxxxxxxxx ad infinitum

Dominican Priory
Woodchester
Glos.
Nov. 10th 1948

My dear Christopher,

Thank you very much for such a nice long letter; it was very good to hear from you again.

In view of the possibility of your going to Rhodesia, I've been to see Fr. Terence and asked him if it would be alright for you to come and spend a weekend down here. He says, "Yes, by all means", so you must come and bring Connie too. If you both come, I can arrange everything for you very comfortably in Woodchester. If only you can make it then you can stop at the Priory. But tell Connie I shall be most offended if she doesn't come.

Now let me congratulate you on all these offers that are being made to you. I did not realise that the Alton job was the one which you had whispered to me. But it's rather difficult for you to make a decision, I should think. I hope Rhodesia is the right one. Anyway, I see you are not committed irrevocably but can come back after a year. Everyone at home is going to miss you.

Awfully sorry that Mother's leg does not improve. I can only pray for it – which is not much of a consolation to Mother, I fear.

Isn't this an extraordinary autumn? I wish you could have seen this valley at the height of its glory. But even now, you'll love it when you come.

Oh, a car at last! How wonderful! Perhaps you'll be able to drive down here. I do look forward to your coming.

We are looking forward to a visit from Tindall, who is now by way of being a great man – secretary to the Master General in Rome. It'll be invigorating to see him again.

Look forward to news from Sylvia, Jocelyn, Leila and Rosamund. Also, from Gareth. What of Humphry? I suppose he is actually married now?

I think I'll stop here, though this is a poor effort in reply to yours. Do let me know soon if you are coming.

My love to all at home.
Gervase

216 Stockwell Road
London S.W. 9
30.IX.48

My dear Christopher,

Your letter was very welcome, and I was most pleased to hear from you again.

My first duty – and it is a pleasure – is to offer you my congratulations on your engagement. I trust you will be taking your courage in both hands and plunging into the sea of matrimony before very long – it is sometimes rather rough but with a good craft it can be an exhilarating voyage. I look forward to meeting the girl of your choice and hearing the full story of your romance. It seems we shall not meet for a while until you are more settled and have passed your exams.

You may remember from last year that this is a busy time of the year for me with our Holydays[133] beginning next Sunday evening, but at least where I am now, I have some chance of preserving my sanity – I hate to think of last year.

So UNRRA has packed up at last – anyway, you had quite a good innings and I did not think you would be batting so long.

You seem to have quite a full-time job where you are, although the journey must be tiresome – we met some people from Alton while we were at Sandown; they have a printing works there.

We were very fortunate with our summer holidays, as we had the only two fine weeks of sunshine this year and we all had a really lovely time.

My mother-in-law is sailing for the U.S.A. in a fortnight on a visit to see her daughters out there. Would you like to go out to the U.S., or do you think we are better off here in the long run? I would consider going to one of the Dominions if a good opportunity arose, but I do not particularly yearn for Rhodesia.

Poor old Hooky has been in hospital as the Pensions doctor found traces of amoebic dysentery and he had to stay in for treatment. Incidentally, Jimmy Burt was in at the same time, but it is almost a matter of routine with him.

I managed to see a bit of the Test Match at Lord's[134] – our building is right opposite, and one has an excellent view from the roof. I wanted to take Michael to the Olympic Games, but we were told there was no chance of it.

Winter appears to be creeping up on us, but the odd spots of sunshine soften the blow.

---

133 Leo was Jewish.
134 Famous cricket venue in North London, built in 1814 and owned by Marylebone Cricket Club.

There is a Burmese restaurant near St. Giles Circus – perhaps we can try their curry at our next rendez-vous.

Lily joins in sending kindest regards as well as congratulations – we trust you and your fiancée and family are very well.

Very sincerely yours,
Leo

Lynford Hall
Dec. 2nd

My dear Christopher,

I left writing to you for your birthday until today as I thought there would be a letter from you, for which thank you very much.

We have just had some instructional films, and they have finished a bit early so there is time for a short note, then I can go down to the village and post it.

Thanks for the information about evening dress. I didn't think it would be so expensive, so I think I will give up the idea of hiring it. By the way, have those dancing shoes of Reg's disappeared?

Thank heaven this fog has dispersed at last. You must all have had a very trying time travelling to work in it.

Poor old Gervase, I hope this strain hasn't had a bad effect on him, or does he seem alright from his letter?

How is your job going at Alton – has it got into its stride yet? Mother did mention that you had been offered a job in Rhodesia, and Connie as well – are you going to accept it?

Give my love to Connie.

Must finish now.
Love from Dickon

Scott & Robertson
P.O. Box 275
Lusaka
N. Rhodesia
28th December 1948

Dear Rep,

Sorry for the long delay in replying after my most urgent telegram, but since that date, this office has been most chaotic, Dorothy having to go off sick some five to six weeks, with the result that I had my work cut out to keep my head above water.

I had not forgotten you, however, but there seemed some doubt about the job. The whole position is that when a vacancy occurs here, they usually want to fill it P.D.Q.,[135] and while you could walk away with job after job if you so wished, the uncertainty of a date for your starting is a deterrent. You will see, therefore, what a spot I am in when a job crops up. There was another good one advertised this week and I know that you could walk into a number of good jobs, were you here.

I know how you feel about digging up your roots and taking a chance but believe me, laddie, the element of chance is so damned slight as to be negligible, and being quite frank, I would much rather you came out here as a free man than be tied to a firm for a year or two. There is plenty a-doing here and the chances of getting into something on your own are pretty good.

I will, of course, keep my eye open and do my utmost to find you something concrete, but as I said, don't be in the least afraid to pick up and come out. You can get £50/£60 if not more just like that and Connie is assured of £35/£40. As you know, I promised to start her at £35 and that still holds good, but I will require another shorthand typist urgently within the next month or two and would naturally be pleased if I could have Connie.

I might add that I am being forced to take on a partner and he is coming out from London within the next three months. The business has grown to such an extent that I must have more help. I might be able to use you myself at a later date, but the business could not stand a full salary for you at this stage, particularly in view of my commitments.

You can rest assured that I would not bring you out here unless I felt very satisfied indeed that you yourself would be in a position to cope with your family commitments, but emphatically you would

---

135 'Pretty damn quick!'

find it easier to meet them from here, while living in a much higher degree of comfort than in England.

Dorothy has got over the worst of her illness but apparently her tummy is still a bit 'gyppy'. I have just had two or three days in bed myself with some kind of flu. Christmas passed not too badly, and we trust both you and Connie had a happy time.

We hope to see you sometime in 1949, and that will be a step towards the good fortune which I hope it holds for you.

Kindest regards,
Robbie

1949

4/1/49

My dearest Chris,

The daffodils you gave me over three weeks ago are still alive in my room, as perky as if it were spring and reconfirming this wonderful feeling which we have for each other – at least that is how I felt when I arrived home last night and saw them.

Chris & Connie, 'one Robert took, tres bonne,
(Chris doesn't think so!)' Crowhurst, August 1949

Emily Caroline and baby Christopher,
Montreal, Canada, c.December 1918.

Christopher c.1919

Christopher (back), Gervase & Jocelyn,
Port Washington, New York, c.1922

Christopher & Jocelyn, New York

C, J (bucket on head), S or D with Aunts Ina and Leila

Sergeant Repton in Bareilly, India, 1940

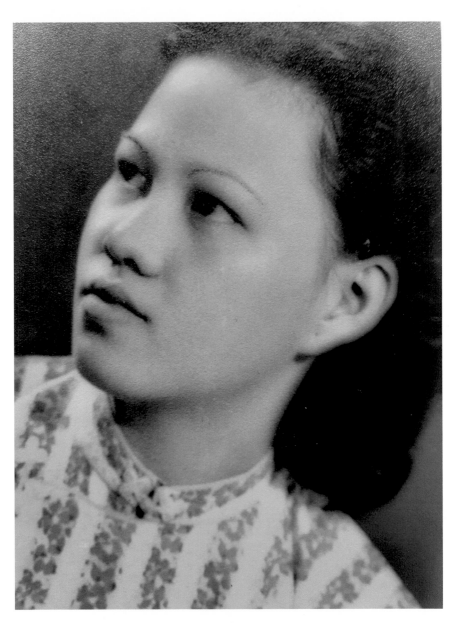

Theresa, 28th June 1947

Pang sisters 1940 or 1941

Pangs 1934 (l to r) back row: 13ᵗʰ, 12ᵗʰ, 9ᵗʰ & 5th Sisters, godsister Ji Ee, 4ᵗʰ, 6ᵗʰ, 8ᵗʰ,
10ᵗʰ & 11ᵗʰ Brothers
middle row: 3ʳᵈ, 2ⁿᵈ, 1ˢᵗ Sisters-in-law, Mother, Father, 1ˢᵗ, 2ⁿᵈ & 3ʳᵈ Brothers
front row: Pheck Choon, 15ᵗʰ Sister, Seow Guan

Theresa & Agnes, 1940s

Theresa's mother, Mary Yeo Kwee Choo

Grandfather's 70th birthday 1947. Theresa (back row 2nd left),
her 5th brother-in-law (back row, centre)

Mary Yeo Kwee Choo, 1950s

Theresa's father, John Pang How Yew, 1950s

Bernard Francis Repton, 1950s

Emily Caroline Repton, 1950s

Bianca & Alberto in Rome, 1955

Bianca & Alberto at via dei Riari 1957

Connie & Chris late 1940s

Agnes & Theresa in sarong kebayas

Roy & Stella with Chris in Java 1950

Christopher with his mother 1955

Terry & Chris at cocktail party

Terry & Chris walk down aisle

Terry signs register as 3rd Brother (out of shot), Mary Boey (Yoke Chee), Chris, Walter and Boly look on

Please forgive me for trying to stop myself loving you from motives which were purely selfish – I could not have succeeded anyway. Perhaps – no, probably – these quarrels should happen now, before we are married, so that we may both push the selfishness from our love and try to bring only the best in each to the other. When I forget myself and what I want and think of us I am quite happy and content, but lately I have done that too seldom and so have become dissatisfied, overcritical, stubborn and unreasonable. I will try harder in the future (even if you have reprimanded me for this very thing!) and try to stop this rather adolescent attitude to love and partnership. I do love you, darling, and respect you, and feel very humble when I think of the difference in you who are very wonderful, and what I really deserve.

Must stop or I will start doing something silly like crying.

Did you arrive home safely and not too late? I got in at about 8.50, having taken the taxi from Swanley. All the buses have stopped on Saturday afternoon so maybe they will do the same next week. I loved the weekend; it was grand to get away from home and London for a while. Unfortunately, my voice took on a deep, husky way-down-thar-in-de-cornfield quality today, so I have stayed home in bed. Mother has had her bottom set[136] out today and feels a wee bit queer but sends her love to you. They were both out last evening at Ted's girlfriend's home and had quite a happy time.

Please let just thou and I go away for a weekend soon; a small pub somewhere in the midst of walks – providing it doesn't snow – would be wonderful.

Must say *au revoir* now, my own. I now know why people say they could not live without the person they love.

Loving you always,
Connie

---

136 Of teeth.

11 rue de la Cité
Genève
January 10th 1949

Dear Rep,

What a horror I am not to have answered your letter long, long ago. If you knew how often I intended to, and in fact actually started to, perhaps you would forgive me. Before Xmas it was hectic shopping for parcels home etc., then Xmas itself and its attendant parties, then a week's skiing holiday in the mountains, and then of course all the 'thank-you' letters which are the worst part of Christmas. Between it all, my correspondence, usually pretty well cultivated, resembles the proverbial weed-patch.

Enough of the preamble. Firstly, please accept my warmest good wishes on your engagement, Rep. None the less warm for being overdue. Yes, I heard the news from Audrey, not that it was exactly a surprise of course! It is nice of you, dear Rep, to say such kind things about our friendship, which I always valued very much. I think that I can honestly say that friends mean more to me than anything else in life – perhaps they are the only things that mean anything, after health, and to count my blessings, I count my friends. Always, at any time, you would have my best wishes for every happiness, but especially now, and I wish you both every possible good thing, now and always. To find someone to love and be loved by must be the ultimate happiness, and you certainly deserve it, being about as nice as they come!

What you say about the mixed marriage, Rep, is hard to answer, and no one can say. All I can remark is that in a world where unhappy marriages seem to abound, the two marriages which come to my mind as amazingly happy are both mixed; one is one of my cousins, and the other is the Punches in Cobham, whom I think you know. I know we are instilled at school and at church etc. with the tragedy of mixed marriages, but we must take things as we find them, and that is my observation anyway. Neither have I ever found that similar religions ever prevented family rows, have you?! Providing that there is a good measure of toleration on both sides (which is needed above all else anyway, apart from religion, and a sense of humour), I don't think there is much to fear, Rep, and who knows, it's more than probable that Connie will be a Catholic, and pretty soon, and then you'll have to look to your laurels, because you know what converts are!

For my own news, there has been so much since I last saw you that I couldn't possibly attempt to detail it. After working with the UN during the ECOSOC Conference, which I loved, I joined the I.R.O.,[137] and now, for my pains, I'm – guess where – in the Controller's Office! You'd laugh to see the familiar names there – A. F. D. Campbell, Tom Drake, Munroe, Munkman, Bailley, Meyer Cohen etc.! All the old crew, and yesterday who should walk in but Ted Smith. It only needs you, and Bill, and dear old Dee to be just like home again. Audrey is here too, but I don't see much of her of late as we work and live miles apart, and Jimmy is Controller for I.R.O. in the British Zone of Germany. My work is mostly figures and I work very hard, surprisingly enough.

Enough about work, which is a dull subject at best. Who do you think I am living with? With Pat Worth, whom I'm sure you'll remember, and Lee Chang!! The ménage works very well and happily, and the greatest compliment paid to it was paid unwittingly by the woman upstairs, who complained that "Those girls downstairs are always laughing!" We were very lucky in finding a beautiful flat with enormous rooms, and just every mod con! We have a *femme de ménage* to do the rough work, so all in all we are extremely spoiled. Housekeeping is ease itself here with all the shops groaning with food, and I love marketing in my best French, which by the way has now regained all its old sparkling brilliance! The flat is in the Old Town, which we all love, and 'our' road is a steep, narrow, winding hill, full of curiosity shops and lovely old bookshops, all of which is my constant delight.

We had a wonderful Xmas here at home, with all the traditional things, and an 8' Xmas tree. We had 8 guests for Xmas Day dinner, and it was all a great success, and voted 'just like home'. I did all

---

137 The International Refugee Organisation was set up as a temporary United Nations agency from 1946 to 1952, and from 1947 took over the work of UNRRA to help displaced persons in Europe and Asia who could not return to their countries of origin after World War II.

the cooking, and nobody will know how scared I was until all was proved well. On Boxing Day Pat and I departed for a week's holiday in the mountains, at Saas-Fée. We stayed in a perfect chalet hotel, quite luxurious, and had the time of our lives, especially as there was such a happy, friendly crowd there. It was heavenly: deep snow, warm sunshine, and if I never see another beautiful thing, I shall always remember the sheer beauty of those dazzling white peaks against blue skies, and the green glaciers. We skied, climbed the minor mountains with the guides, and danced in the evenings at the hotel. It was all too short, as good things usually are.

Life here is very pleasant – plenty of friends and gaiety, but most of all we like to stay at home and have friends round. Yes, I still intend to go to the States, next August or September. The longer I live the more I want to go, and the more I see of other people, be they ever so nice, the more I think that Norman is the finest of them all. He writes weekly, but four years it will be since I saw him when I do arrive, and that's a mighty long time, Rep, so wish me well. I shall need it! I've taken a good few knocks in my time, and one more in this direction would about finish me. But I shall be home before then, and I hope I'll see you in Cobham. You'll find me much the same, I guess, though feeling 100% better than I used to in the London days. I don't wilt with everlasting tiredness as I used to then.

Yes, Mummy certainly is a wonderful person and I love her dearly. If ever you have a minute to spare passing to the station, they'd be so pleased to see you. Mummy is very fond of you, and they are always so pathetically pleased when any 'young folk' take the trouble to notice them. And they are pretty lonely these days.

Cheerio, Rep – and every good wish and happiness to you both once again.

Much love,
Peggy

Prinknash Abbey
Gloucester
21st February 1949
Telephone: Painswick 3224

Mr. Christopher Repton
'Twynersh'
Leigh Place
Cobham
Surrey

Dear Mr. Repton,

I understand from your brother that you would like to spend a few days of quiet and retreat at Prinknash. I shall be very pleased to welcome you and shall be glad if you will inform the Revd. Father Guestmaster as soon as you are able to arrange a date to come.

Will you give my kindest remembrances to your brother? I understand he will have left England by the time this letter reaches you. With the assurances of my prayers and good wishes,

Yours sincerely,
D. Wilfrid P.B.
Abbot

Dictated by Rt. Revd. Father Abbot and signed in his absence,
Albert Styles B.B.
Secretary

Ulu Remi Estate
Loyang Loyang
Johore
Feb. 21st '49

Dear Rep,

Many thanks for your letter of the 4th inst.... You're quite right: it is some time since you wrote, but it came as a pleasant surprise.

I have only just arrived back after six months in England and have come to the conclusion that it is better to get a belly full of lead here than exist at home. Whilst in England, stayed a couple of days with Les Sutton. Naturally made enquiries regarding Old Rep, but Les hadn't heard from you for ages.

The Banditry is going quite strong. Sleep with a couple of grenades under my pillow and a Sten[138] at the side of the bed. We have lost one European off this place whilst I was at home, but it's been fairly quiet for some time. In fact, life goes on in the usual way.

You certainly seem to be getting about a bit, and I'm pleased to hear that you are doing so well. Delighted to hear the news of the forthcoming marriage. May I take this opportunity in congratulating you. I have no regrets at taking 'the plunge', only wish I had done it a few years previous. But then I'm much older than you. Do let me know when the marriage takes place. I may have a credit at the bank at that particular time.

I say, Rep, your writing is just about the world's worst, but I suppose you consider this a very debatable point after seeing mine.

Next time I come home, 1953, I hope to pack it in and buy a small farm, but it's a long way ahead. Things may change, and one also has to take the Bandits into account.

Well, Rep, I must conclude for the present. Don't let it be so long before you write again.

Trust all your folks are well.

Yours sincerely,
Bill

Swanley
28/7/49

My dear Christopher,

I was in London on Friday evening and decided to try the Prom. It wasn't much, but I liked Honneger's Third Symphony: what a climax – nearly blew the roof off and easily the loudest I've ever heard. My neighbour remarked that it livened things up a bit. Earlier I had pointed out that it was impossible to hear the piano though we

---

138 Sub-machine gun.

could see the pianist going through the motions. He confessed that he had not been aware of the piano at all.

While I was queuing a different person – he had a monstrous swelling on one side of his nose – asked me if I had booked for any of the Vienna Philharmonic concerts (five only) in October. I hadn't, but repaired the omission at the interval. So now I have two tickets for October 4th, and here's the programme:-

'Variations on a Theme' by Haydn (St. Anthony's Chorale)
Violin Concerto in D Major, Symphony No. 1
Composer: Mr. Brahms
Soloist: Yehudi Menuhin
Conductor: Wilhelm Furtwängler

The seats are in a second-tier box, price one guinea. You can have first refusal on one of them, and it'll be time enough to let me know when I return from Germany on Sept. 19th. Note: these were the only seats left.

I hope Aunt Caroline's leg is making good progress, and that you will send me an invitation to Cobham soon after I'm back.

Love to everyone,
Gareth

THE ANGLO-DUTCH PLANTATIONS OF JAVA, LIMITED
5 & 7 EASTCHEAP
LONDON E.C. 3.
7th October 1949

G. C. T. Repton, Esq.
'Twynersh'
Leigh Place
Cobham
Surrey

Dear Sir,

We confirm the interview you had yesterday with our Java Company's Chief Accountant, Mr. J. T. Saffery, when you were offered a position in the Accountancy Department of the *N. V. Maatschappij ter Exploitatie der Pamanoekan en Tjiasemlanden*, Subang, Java, on the following terms:-

1. Basic salary f. 700.– per month.
2. Plus cost-of-living allowance, the calculation of which is:-
    On the first f. 300.– 50% = f. 150.–
    On the next f. 200.– 15% = f. 30.–
    Remaining f. 200.– 7½% = f. 15.– 195.–

    _____

    f. 895.– per month.
3. Free accommodation.
4. Free medical treatment.
5. Six months' leave on full basic salary, plus half cost-of-living allowance, after four years' service.
6. Free passage to Java and a free return passage when going on leave. (In the case of a married man, free passage for his wife corresponding to those of the staff member.)
7. Outfit allowance of £41.
8. Annual increments to be decided after three months' probationary period.
9. You will contribute to the Provident Fund as from the date of joining the Company on the basis of 7½% of basic salary and, in addition, the Company will contribute 12½% of basic salary. These are the rates of contributions at present in operation.
10. The local income tax on your salary and cost-of-living as a single man will be about 24%, but this is difficult to calculate as we have not full information on this side. (It is likely that there may be an alteration in the rates of tax for 1950; probably on the downward trend.)

We understand from Mr. Saffery that you were advised by him that while the Company prefers to have married staff, it must be clearly understood that, at the moment, the housing accommodation in Subang is somewhat limited because many of the houses are occupied by the Military. However, it is thought that as they will be leaving the property shortly, accommodation will become available. Therefore, in your special circumstances, we will arrange accommodation for you as soon as possible, and as far as we can see at the moment, the longest you would have to wait may extend to a period of one year.

We have taken note that you are able to leave your present position upon giving two weeks' notice, but we think it better, before you take any steps in this direction, to submit yourself for a medical examination by the Company's Doctor, as this appointment will be conditional upon the Doctor certifying you fit for work and residence in the tropics. Therefore, kindly let us know as soon as possible so that we can arrange an appointment for you with Doctor Bernard Day, M.D., M.R.C.P., 39 Hans Place, London S.W. 1., telephone number Kensington 2400.

Upon hearing from you of your acceptance of this offer, we will then advise you what steps are necessary in relation to your departure for Java.

Yours faithfully,
Per pro FRANCIS PEEK & CO., LIMITED
F. W. Locke
Secretaries

Newlands
Marine Drive West
Barton-on-Sea
Friday

My dear Christopher,

I'm afraid you had such a rush on Tuesday – I wish we had gone to Riverholme, but it might have upset them, and Cynthia and all of the family here wanted to see you. They really want you and Connie to come and stay when you can. I hope Dickon will be able to get home for the weekend.

Reg says you must be careful with your diet, not too much green food or uncooked fruit. Reg and I have just been to New Milton to do some shopping, and I found these handkerchiefs for you. They went off to the I.O.W.[139] this morning and are returning next Thursday. We hope you have your birth certificate by now. As it is just teatime, I will post the handkerchiefs tomorrow.

---

139 Isle of Wight.

Nov. 5

What a pity it is such a wet day. I wish we could be with you all. We shall think of you on Tuesday and hope it will be fine. I have put in a few of the old pills for your voyage.

Take care of yourself, and don't stay if the climate doesn't suit you. I will either give Mother that £1 or invest it for her when a good opportunity arrives.

Lots of love from Reg & Aunt Nell

Hankys [sic] don't need washing before using.

> 69 Peartree Avenue
> Bitterne
> Southampton
> 7.11.49

My dear Christopher,

How very quickly the time of departure has come round. We all feel very sad to think you are going so far away, and it will be a great miss to your mother and father.

However, it is good to know you have got a nice post, and we all hope you are going to be very happy and successful, and trust there will be some nice companions for you so that you will not be too lonely.

We got the bottle of whisky, only it is Red Seal and not Haig's or White Horse. Someone will bring it along one day.

Well, my dear Christopher, here is wishing you the very best of all that is going and hope you will find it all that is desirable and get settled in comfortably.

Do hope you are feeling better.

With much love from all,
Yours,
Belle

Train
Tuesday 15/11/49

My very dearest Chris,

I was so very pleased to receive your card and letter last evening when I arrived home, and to know that you are safe and well. I can't begin to tell you how much I've missed you and how often I've thought of my poor old poppet making that long journey all on his own, or how much I've hoped and prayed that you've been well and having a good trip.

It's enough to say that I can't wait to come out to you, to see you, hear your voice and be with you again. The news of troops withdrawing in Java fills me with hope that it will not be a whole year before we are together again. I'm a bit scared about your safety out there and want to share every possible danger as soon as I can. We must pray hard that the time will soon pass and that we shall soon be married and start our life together. I look forward to it all so much; however difficult conditions may be, nothing could be worse than not sharing life with you and so making conditions a secondary consideration.

However, as Fr. Gorman said tonight, maybe the separation will give me time to think about important things less emotionally, and so good will come of this bit of life. I hope so, anyway. Lots of clichés, but not, not, not meant as such; it is so difficult to express what is truly in one's mind without seeming to be hackneyed. The curse of words, I s'pose.

Glorious, yellow, heavy-all-day London FOG! Ugh! It gets in head and throat and eyes and mind, dampening, clogging, soiling everything. Still, it's lovely when it suddenly lifts, as it did (comparatively) at 4.30 p.m.ish today. You can see the window-ledge, the lights in the road, the road itself, a car and, well I never, now I can see across the road. The dullest old buildings across the road take on the welcome appearance of an old friend suddenly met again after an absence. The buildings opposite are mostly duller than uninteresting, but one intrigues me – a sometime church, with improvised big windows, all dilapidated and bomb-damaged and deserted. I sit and wonder whether it was a church, or whether someone had a liking for that kind of architecture and finished the job by popping a stone crucifix on top. And why was it turned into a warehouse (apparently)? I doubt I shall ever trouble to find out – probably a very ordinary reason, and that would spoil the whole situation.

Phoned Gillie today and he had just received your card of Saturday. Sorry you had a rough crossing, darling; were you ill? It did look a bit choppy. I hated that parting and yet was glad it was quick as otherwise might have got tongue-tied, not knowing how to say things, and then eventually cried. But it all seemed so unreal somehow, *n'est-ce pas*? I do love you.

Also phoned Jocelyn today and he told me he had heard from you and gave me some rather disturbing news – no doubt he has told you. But anyway, things are not too bad, it seems. (In case he didn't, your mother fell down the stairs on Saturday and fractured a femur on her bad leg, but it is quite straightforward, no complications and she will be perfectly alright and home, it's hoped, by Christmas. Will write to her soonest and see her, I hope, very soon.)

Have been hectically busy all day and frantically rushing around doing odd things. Now I'm just a wee bit tired.

Reading lots of things – *Confessions of St. Augustine* particularly, which is excellent.

Must stop now as train is dragging itself by many stops into Dartford. Fog Service!!!

Phoned Escombe, McGrath today, who told me that censorship at Port Said and Port Sudan takes seven days!! Will, therefore, post this c/o Halal in Aden and hope for the best. Let me know sooner than quickly how you are and what is happening.

All my love to you, my darling; take great care of yourself. I love you, Chris.

Your own Connie

69 Peartree Avenue
Bitterne
Southampton
17.12.49

My dear Christopher,

A very happy Christmas with pleasant company to help you enjoy the holiday amongst your tropical surroundings; and may the New Year be one of the best you have ever had.

I expect you have been missing all your friends, especially Connie, and your home life. Everything must be very strange and unreal to you, but I hope this part will soon give way to more friendly relations with your immediate neighbours. Colonial life – or, I should have said, life in the Far East – is much more sociable, and one makes friends so quickly.

I do hope you like your work and find the people with whom you work all that you would wish. Have you been provided with good living quarters? Are you in a town or out in the country, and what are the Javanese like as a whole? Friendly, I hope. There are lots of things we shall be interested to hear. Write a letter which can be passed around, and that will be satisfying to all, and you will not have so many to think about. We are all interested in how you are getting on and what you are doing, and of course you have lots to keep you busy.

You had a long time in Genoa; thanks for the card. It is a fine city, but the poorer parts are very squalid. Did you feel rested after your voyage? It was a pity there were not more passengers. However, I hope you met that friend in Singapore. What were your feelings when you went ashore there?

You heard, of course, of your mother's accident. It is a great pity that it should have happened again, but these things happen just when one least expects it. Anyway, she is back in hospital and every care is being taken of her. I think this time she will not rush the treatment but will stay until the Dr. pronounces her fit to leave. It must be a worry to you; however, it does not help anyone, so try not to think too much about it.

I took the bottle of whisky up to Cobham, and your father found it very comforting. I expect you have heard from him. You know we did not want you to pay for it, so sent your cheque to your mother. Back it came […] when Nellie and Reg returned from a week's stay with the family. Thank you – the whisky cost 33/4, so we are 1/8 to the good!

We shall all be glad when the festive season is past. We older people like our armchairs by the fire. Unfortunately, Mother has a bad bronchial cold. It is improving and she has just said, "Give Christopher my love." It was very nice to see you for that short time, and thoughtful of you to spare the time, considering how much you had to do in the little spare given you to get ready. Am glad you had recovered from your indisposition by the time you left home. Take care of yourself, my dear, and I hope you are settling down and finding life pleasant and the natives friendly.

I will write again and shall always be interested in what you are doing. In the meantime, best love from us all.

From Aunt Mary

Home
Saturday 19/11/49

My very dearest Chris,

How are you, darling? I'm longing to see you again; somehow the time, especially at weekends, seems to drag along, the only consolation being that I'm getting nearer to you each day that passes. Think of you almost all the time and bore everyone by telling them how you are, what you are like, and showing them photographs, and talking about you nearly all the time. When your letters come, of course, I get very excited, and everything stops whilst I read them. Your letter and card from last Saturday at Genoa reached me on Thursday night and I was so glad you have at last boarded the *Trafalgar* and started your voyage. By the time you read this, you will be at Singapore and the best bit of the journey will be over. So I'll wish you good luck for the next bit and hope you arrive safe and well at Subang (or do they still spell it Dutch style, Soebang?). Also, many, many happy returns of the 3rd, your birthday. Hope the dressing gown is proving useful! Let's hope we can celebrate the next one in our own bungalow in proper style, darling.

Went out with Pam and Gillie last night for a quiet drink and a meal at Verrey's; it was grand seeing them again. Reimbursed Gillie £2 to cover his journey to Dover and the meal we had etc., but didn't give him a cheque, as he preferred to have cash! He and Pam are writing to you this weekend, I believe, and will no doubt give you all their news. Pam is much fitter, I'm glad to say. I left them at 9.30 at Charing Cross, but as there was a terrible fog, I had lost my last bus by the time I got to Dartford and had to get a taxi home! Almost completely broke me, as it costs 10/–!! Worth it though, instead of walking.

Wrote to your mother this afternoon and sent her a get-well card. Hope to see her and all at Twynersh soon.

You are a beautiful poppet to think about the nylons. (In case you send me anymore ever, my size is 10, or 7 for shoes.) It was really terribly sweet of you, darling, and I'm very appreciative. At least 2 big kisses, popsy!

Have been trying to shake Mother out of a grand depression, but I'm afraid she won't budge. Took her out to Dartford today to look for a dressing gown and she brightened up considerably whilst we were out, but as soon as we started to come home, it was back again, as bad as ever. It is terribly trying, but I manage not to lose patience somehow, I hope! I've written to a hotel in Shanklin to ask about Christmas accommodation; Father was quite enthusiastic, but Mother didn't say anything much and said she couldn't get interested in anything or anyone. I fumed inwardly but will wait to see what she feels like next week before I scotch the idea. It would be a good idea, I think, as we shall have the holiday together without Maman having to worry about cooking and so on. Also, she and I can pop into Newport and Carisbrooke to see my aunt and grandad. *Ma*,[140] maybe nothing will come of it, so it's best not to worry about it too much, I guess.

Have been awfully busy at work this week. A new chap, Thomas, came; he seems quite pleasant, and I've lunched with

---

140 But (Italian).

him and Richard Hotoph once or twice this week. The whole time was spent in raucous laughter at one thing and another. Tuesday I had to go to the Business Efficiency Exhibition at Olympia to look at desks and so on; Wednesday I went to a Copper Mining and Ore Refining film show, held by Rhokana (one of the monopolies in copper) and the other five companies at Wardour Street GB cinema. Very interesting, and the cocktail party afterwards (only three women present, including me!) was grand. In between, we have had tons of work, mostly dictation in Italian, poor me! Still, it is an excellent way of learning *la lingua*, even if it's the most painful.

Doc continues to spoil me with remarks about '*gli occhi belli*' – "*Carina, come sei bella?*" – which I've no doubt you appreciate (worthy of Jocelyn? Not quite), so I will not bother to translate.

The job is very interesting, apart from all that, and I don't mind the terrific hard work somehow.

Father Gorman, whom I saw last Tuesday after three weeks' absence, said he had arranged for someone to meet you at Singapore, so I hope you did, in fact, have someone there to welcome you. I'm wondering whether he meant Java, though, as I don't think he knew the ship on which you were travelling, unless you told him, and I should think Java would be more sensible, anyway. The person would no doubt give you some clues about the church etc., I guess. I will try to clear with him and inform you in a further letter.

Letters I and II, by the way, went to Port Said; I hope you received them, together with all the copy letters which I typed for you. If not, I have copies and will send on to you. III went to Aden, and this is, of course, IV. Delays in arrival at both places were expected owing to fog and censorship, so I hope you did get all three, in spite of that. We just couldn't find out when you were due at both, so maybe I posted too late anyway. (Talking in the past tense when the actions are happening now or in the future is awfully queer. Good job I'm not too superstitious!)

Haven't had your photo-enlargement made yet, or had my own portrait snapped. Will send a copy of each as soon as they are ready, and thought for Christmas your mother might like one of each in a leather frame? All very tentative!

Got my Income Tax Code No. for 1950–51 – Code 21!! Only hope I fly the country before they manage to collect it all! Have forgotten to tell them that £25 or £30 of last year's money represented one month's pay in lieu of notice which is, therefore, not taxable. Hope it's not too late now.

The countryside is beginning to take on that openly bald winter appearance very rapidly. The most noticeable sign is the ability to see cattle grazing in a meadow right on the other end of the valley. Lines are much longer and only hedges stop the gaze from running on for miles. Trees do shorten one's visibility, but how pleasantly and softly! The valley looks as crestfallen as a newly shorn poodle! The sun has been streaming in bucketsful into my room every morning, except one day last week when we had hard frost and quite thick fog. Chaos reigned on the Southern Region railway of course! But last night was the epic!

Have taken up smoking again, I'm afraid. Gillie and Pam were very pleased that the pipe was proving a success. Bet you've been plugging away at it, with tobacco how much an ounce? Hope the same doesn't apply to drink, to the same extent at least? Your remarks about the Poona type and rum, and the drinking lunch to Paris and your bill at the Colombia all make me wonder!! (It's only envy.)

Don't forget to let me know how things are out there, especially in regard to household goods, and clothes generally. Shan't start buying too much until I hear from you, so would like to know, particularly, regarding 1) sheets and bed linen; 2) towels and tea cloths etc.; 3) table linen; 4) cutlery, as all these are going up in price next year and I want to buy at as good a price as possible. Prices, if existing, would be invaluable. I can convert Guilder prices, but not local currency, if purely Javanese. (Don't think so, but just in case.)

Must stop now, poppet, but will write soon. Play on the wireless now, about Christopher Columbus – not nearly such a nice Christopher as you, my darling. Gosh, I do miss you!

All my prayers for you – almost – and my thoughts too. I love you so much, Chris.

Your own Connie

Office
Tuesday 29th November 1949

My very dearest Chris,

After my sleepy notes of last evening, I'd better buck up and write to you a more lively letter, *n'est-ce pas*?

Phoned Jocelyn and gave him your message about your mother; he was a bit worried that I had told you. I am very sorry, darling, hope it doesn't worry you and spoil your voyage, 'cause she is really very fit and looking well, only annoyed about the whole thing, and back to exercises and that wretched bed again.

Your Accountancy books arrived, and I have just been trying to sort out the arrangements to be made [...] I am trying to send out the books to you via the *Bali*, which leaves London on December 14th [...]

Keep wondering which of our Anniversaries we shall be able to celebrate together next year. June 30th? September 15th? December 3rd? Have cancelled February 20th of course, as I cannot imagine being lucky enough to be anywhere near you by then. They are rather nicely spaced out, aren't they; hadn't noticed that before. 2½, 3, 4 and 2½ months between each.

Am getting a wonderful collection of stamps and am, of course, saving every one. Maybe our son will appreciate them some day; anyway, I appreciate them a lot in the meantime. They trace a picture of your voyage most effectively. Rushing aeroplanes from Genoa; fat, horrible old Farouk from Port Said (their wretched censorship); dashing man on fleeing camel from Port Sudan; the King and antique temple; also a lovely Universal Postal Union stamp from Aden. Wonder what it will be from India? And Malaya? And most of all, Subang?

You promised to tell me of some of the amusing incidents on board, and also of the antics of Mrs. Scriven. Would love to hear all about it, and any other information about the passengers, especially John, whom you speak about quite often, without telling me much about him. Is he the only constant companion you have, or do you not have much in common? Give, brother, give.

In case you are wondering about these letters, by the way, will give you a brief history: I and II – Port Said; III – you received at Aden; IV & V – sent to the Ship's Agents in Singapore, Messrs. Harrison

& Crossfield, Hongkong Banking Chambers, Singapore; VI & this, VII, Francis Peek at Singapore […] I am expecting you to have to stay at least two or three days waiting for transport to Batavia from Singapore, so hope you will receive all of the letters. After this I will send to Subang. Think I will revert to Arabic too; all these Roman figures get a bit confusing when you reach the 'L' stage. (What a thought!! Makes it seem YEARS before I shall be saying, not writing.)

Wednesday evening in the train, 8 p.m.

Had to break off for some reason there and had no opportunity last evening or today to finish, so will try to complete this tonight and post tomorrow at the latest. Miss you awfully.

Went to Cheam last night to see Jackie and Bill and Lesley, the latter being nine months now and quite pleasant. Just getting second two teeth and consequently is hating life rather a lot. She is very bonny though. All three are very happy, and Bill is as perfect a father as he is a husband. They are both still terribly in love and make me feel quite sentimental when I go there. Bill washing nappies was perfect; they both do it together, actually, and get a nauseating job done in about two seconds between them. (Hope you are reading this very carefully.) They hope to have another but plan to have it when Lesley can take care of herself a bit more. Jackie finds it a full-time job and looks rather tired, I'm afraid. Still, they both seem to love life a tremendous lot. We had a good time and spent most of the evening discussing religion. Bill is, of course, a strong C of E,[141] and Jackie is too but with Non-Conformist leanings. Bill is a very good discusser and I wished that you had been there to iron out some of the points he brought up, with which I often found myself in agreement, I'm afraid. The point he raised which I had Sunday night raised with Jocelyn, for example – the unequal distribution of wealth in the Catholic Church. *Ma*, mustn't start on themes like that or I shall infuriate you, I s'pose. Trying to support the Catholic idea is rather an odd line for me!

Am home in bed now, pink and rosy from my bath and smelling of Yardley's talc and toothpaste! *Maman* is furious 'cause Papa is out and has been all day. Life with them is somewhat trying at times. No doubt, they've said exactly the same of me though, and with justice, 'specially when I was a babe. This is a 'baby' letter – went to the Mothercraft exhibition this evening which no doubt

---

141 Church of England.

explains it. Quite interesting but nothing awfully helpful – I probably don't know what to look for. Bought a booklet on the care of babies and children in the tropics which states a few obvious things but is quite helpful.

Doctor Damiano told me to take myself off to the theatre, and also almost refused to tell me how much he was debited for you. Managed to get it out of him at last, however, though haven't worked out how much sterling 11,000 lire at 1,800 to the £ is. He said £5 or £6. Shall I pay or take it out of the £25? because I've drawn two cheques totalling £8–16–2 so far, one for £6–8–6 covering my season, as you told me, in repayment of the £6 you borrowed before you left (2 lots of £3 from my P.O.) and £2 in payment to Gillie. This last item was actually paid in cash. I bought some tablecloths for our bottom drawer yesterday, though, and paid Peter Robinson's by cheque. So, I owe you 16s 2d less 4/– for cheque book paid by me in cash. Hope you agree with the above; if not tell me and I will alter accordingly. The tablecloths are linen with coloured borders; rather pretty, and of course extremely necessary. I hope to fiddle some utility sheets from Miss Hodge this week too, which I may pay for by cheque and reimburse the account by cash. I will endeavour to buy all the linens we shall need and leave you to think about paying for (or splitting, perhaps) the cutlery and crockery if needed.

Must stop now and sleep. What a dull letter this must seem! Sorry, darling, but it's difficult to find much of particular interest. This pen is driving me silly.

I love you very much, my dear Chris, and long to hear from you soon.

All my love,
Your Connie
xxxx

'Ridwan'
45 Alexandra Grove
Finchley N. 12
December 13th 1949

Dear Christopher,

Just a little over a month has elapsed since Connie and I waved you farewell from Dover, and all this time you have been increasing the distance between us, and in so doing increasing our desire to just have another look at you. Connie has kept us well posted as to your whereabouts and both Pamela and I feel that we too are really sharing your episode into fresh fields – perhaps with the exception of the 'ducking'.

The formalities dealing with the car are neatly tied up thanks to Connie's admirable staff work, and am having 'Susannah' transported to Finchley in the early part of next year, but I have yet to obtain a licence! Pamela and I must really thank you for the grand gesture you made and all the trouble of simplifying the innumerable small items in this connection.

I decided my cricket was so dreadful that it warranted some close season attention, and have been attending a Cricket School in Chiswick. Last week Sharp of Middlesex C.C. passed his verdict on my interpretation of the noble art – sorry, not for publication!! At the time of going to press no mention has been forthcoming regarding UNRRA's future activities. I feel Robert might be given a rude awakening very soon but can ill afford a hectic session so near the festive season to thrash out matters – just something more to be shelved until the New Year.

The Anglo-Iranian Oil Co.[142] is still the cornerstone on which I am resting and further developments with the third party mentioned on the *Golden Arrow* are awaited, although these are not expected to materialise for possibly some months – will keep you posted on this score.

Pamela, I feel, sitting beside me, has knitted enough and is just longing to put pen to paper, so here we have the change from scribble to copperplate – over to Pamela.

Gillie having now taken over the knitting (I don't know why he grumbles because it is a cardigan for him), I am at last writing these few lines to you, which is something I have intended doing ever since you left. I was certainly very sorry not to have been able to see you depart from Dover, which seems to both Gillie and I very much over a month ago, and through Connie have been following your journey to what appears to me to be the other side of the world.

142 Pamela's father was Iranian. Gillie was working for the Anglo-Iranian Oil Company (AIOC). In the 1940s the AIOC was controlled by Britain.

The three of us spent a very pleasant evening in Verrey's a week or so ago, and do not need to tell you how we felt about the vacant chair. I know Gillie missed your reliable support more than a little. Connie certainly looked extremely well and is, I believe, working hard, which is probably a good thing. I ring her, or vice versa, most days to have a chat, and tomorrow we are having another 'threesome'; fortunately she is staying with me at Finchley so need not have to dash away quite so soon.

We are both very much looking forward to hearing of your new surroundings, and I expect that by now you will be glad to have arrived and getting on with the job. You may be sure that we shall be thinking of you and missing you, especially at Christmas.

Owing to the 'post early for Xmas' – and Gillie's last train – must sign off. Look after yourself, Chris, dear.

With love,
Pamela & Gillie

P.S. Both my mother and father and the rest of the family send their very best wishes and regards.

P.P.S. Thanks for the card from Genoa – my address, incidentally, is:-

136 Chesterton Road
Kensington
London W. 10

Cheers!
G.

Sunday at home
18/12/49

My very dearest Chris,

How wonderful to get three letters from you at the beginning of last week! The one from Singapore and the second one from the S.S. *Jan Riekan* came together; the first from the latter ship (and the one from Singapore) got sent to Farnborough before they were sent to me. The Christmas P.O. helpers, I s'pose! Sorry I haven't replied or written before today, but Doc has been rushing me off my feet at work and Christmas preparations at home have left no time for anything! Have left work at 6 or thereabouts most evenings; got home and packed and cooked and sent cards till 12! Still, it makes a change, I guess! Doc finally left yesterday with, I hope, all the papers he required! He goes to Milan, then to Basle and then on holiday to the Dolomites.

Am very glad to hear that your cold has got better and also your depression – a much worse complaint. The money situation sounds grim. We (Pirelli) are very interested in the currency situation, of course, and I read the bits out to Doc, who was most appreciative but rather worried, both for us (you and I) and for Boenisari Lendra, our company in Bandung. Suggested that Pirelli should pay you a commission for such information, but it didn't catch on, I'm afraid, honey! Doc may be going to Singapore after all, next year.

I've been frantically cooking for Christmas today and am thrilled to bits; expect you will laugh but an epic day is this for me! I cooked my first big cake – my first Christmas cake – and it is extremely successful! At least, it looks very professional: dark, flat-topped (for icing, of course) and risen b-e-a-u-tifully! Gosh! I also baked biscuits and made mincemeat – all very successfully. I hope to send you a piece of the cake when I've marzipan-&-royal-iced it, so if you don't receive it, you'll know it wasn't worth eating!!

Talking of sending parcels – your books are, so I suppose, still at home as I left it with Jocelyn to send them to me at work when I should arrange for the shipment, clearance forms, etc. So far nothing has arrived, and I have been so busy that I have been unable to phone Jocelyn to ask him what the score is. Will try to do so next week though and send them to you on a boat in early January, if possible. Will write to you again on the subject next week, when I hope to have everything tied up.

I have piles of work to do at the office, though. Doc left a number of odd things for me to clear up and my desk looks like a mountain! Among them is that of sending an odd 70–100 cards off to his various friends, relations and business connections, all the cards bearing different sorts of his signature according to who the addressee is, though the cards are all similar with his printed address! A ghastly job! The worst part is finding out where they all live, since he has forgotten and I don't know, having no record whatsoever!! My hair is fast greying! Still, I am a confidential secretary, and as the definition went at college (not officially, of course, only among the girls), that covers any and every sort of job that no one else will touch, usually at a salary that no one else would consider! – except for love. I love the work (not the boss, of course, though I must say he's quite a poppet usually. Last week he was almost bad-tempered, worrying about all his travel – papers etc., etc.). I've been working late in the evenings and every Saturday for what seems years! Coming home, I've stayed up late to do all the odd jobs and have been late to bed too, so have been feeling quite tired. Consequently, I decided to lay in bed longer today and thus missed church – always rather disappointing.

Fr. Gorman, by the way, was interested to hear you had got to Singapore and hopes you got on quite well, in spite of not calling on Douglas's help. He was emphatic last Tuesday that I must stop drifting and make up my mind one way or the other about Catholicism; until I do, he said it would be of very little use my going to see him again. I feel a bit worried about it all, and I suppose it's the best thing as otherwise I shall drift on. On the other hand, I don't feel completely convinced about it – I know most of my worries are based on what must seem to be side issues, but I just don't see how I can say, "Yes, I believe all that the Church says must be correct, logical, reasonable and to the greater glory of God" when some of the things she says seem to me to be very arbitrary and, if I use my own reasoning as I believe I must do, wrong. If I say that I cannot see that she is right and that in my opinion it (whatever 'it' is, and there are lots of apparently insignificant things) is quite stupid or wrong when she has said it is right, but that I accept it as being right because she is the Church, I think that I am being hypocritical, but I'm not sure.

I expect you think I'm hedging, but I don't honestly think it is all an attempt to put off the decision. From my point of view, life with you would be much simpler if I were to become a Catholic, but for that very reason I am trebly anxious not to be too eager to agree –

stifle the odd incompatible worries that arise. I want to love, know and serve my Maker but I don't want to do so only with my heart, my soul, my life etc. but with my mind. How much of this desire is really selfishness and how much sincere, though, I'm at a loss to decide. More than I admit, I suppose. Oh dear, Chris, my love, it is so difficult to keep on fighting it – my pride has a lot to say in the battle, I'm much afeared. Please forgive me for writing so much about it. I know it is my decision – only mine, God help me.

So many things seem to have been happening this week. Wednesday I went out with Pam and Gillie and we all returned to Finchley for a meal, and I stayed there the night. Mrs. A.[143] wished me to send you her sincerest good wishes, especially for Christmas and the New Year. We've had ghastly weather – galing rain and wind – and poor old Gillie wandered out into the night (he couldn't stay as well as I, and in any case wanted to get home to see his mother) fearing a long, delayed journey due to the power workers' strike at Barking (also at Dartford), but he got home quite safely. Both send their love, of course, and we all roared over the bit in your letter about fatherly advice on the Evils of Drink by G. C. T. (Soaker) Repton!! Incidentally, I usually only read bits out to people and only left those two with your mother minus the end sheet of one, and rather contained any dubious-about-it-all phrases. Naturally, I should not tell her or anyone else much about that.

I do hope I haven't frightened you off by my somewhat virulent remarks on your doubts – it is a way I have of being more emphatic than Queen Victoria, especially if I feel a tiny bit doubtful myself. It is only natural that we should both feel wondering and doubtful, but not, I hope, because of faint-heartedness, only because of the nature of the move; it involves a revolution in our lives. Most worthwhile things do, of course; the only thing is that they should be bloodless revolutions!

I look forward to hearing from you direct from Java. Hope you will like the Christmas card – thought you would like a reminder of the English countryside, though it is probably cruel of me and will make you even more homesick, my love! I hope not. Maman also

---

143 Pam's mother.

puts in her card, though she says it looks a bit mean – as I told her, at 1/– a half-ounce she can afford to look mean! She and Pop send fondest love. They love hearing all the news I read out to them from your letters. Hope this gets to you in time for Christmas.

We always drink to absent friends at 3 p.m. on Christmas Day – 11 p.m. your time – so if you are up and about, have a drink then and join us in thought – though I shall be thinking of you all the time of course, and hoping that the time will soon pass to the day, hour and minute we hug the breath out of each other again.

I always say goodnight to you last (very last) thing at night and imagine you fast asleep on the other side of the earth – at about 10–11 our time, 6–7 your time. Oh well, I suppose you would be just about waking up then, so I'll have to change the picture. Bother! Seriously though, I do miss you and am longing to tell you how silly I was to say that perhaps being parted from you would prove to us both that we did not really love each other. It's such a silly way of proving I was wrong, though!

Write soon and often, darling, darling Chris. Happy Christmas, poppet; I do love you so much.

Your own Connie

xxxx

P.S. Your letters are wonderful – stop apologising for them, 'cause I think they are excellent.

Ladang Geddes Estate
Bahau
Negri Sembilan
Malaya
19th Dec. 1949

Dear Chris,

Many thanks for your most welcome letter, which arrived a couple of days ago from Malacca, letting me know how things are going with you.

Before I let you know what this place is like I'll go back a bit, to when we left the *Trafalgar* – it was a pity that we did not have a chance for a farewell drink; you must have had one hell of a rush. I stayed in what one might call a luxurious suite at the Raffles on Monday, Tuesday and left for Tampin by train on the Wednesday morning. I went back to the ship on both Monday and Tuesday evenings – saw the two Sisters on Monday evening and they were quite upset at not having had a chance to say cheerio but were quite pleased to have a chance to say it to me and get me to pass it on to you. Talking of them, I wonder how Sister Johanna is liking Manila. I saw the Scrivens also on the Monday; luckily, fairly early on, as I found a nice session going on with the Steward, Chief Officer, Blondie and Randi – and must confess I was rather tight by the time I left the ship at 10.30 p.m. I took Randi on shore on both Monday and Tuesday evenings, and we had a very pleasant time at the Raffles, Airport and New World!!! (Altogether I got through $200 before I crawled away from Singapore.)

So much for the past – now for the present. As you will have seen by the address, I am at Ladang Geddes, about 6 miles from Bahau (Frank Morgan's estate), 55 from Seremban (the nearest town), and 105 miles from Kuala Lumpur. Singapore is about 200 miles away. This estate is one of Dunlop's biggest – 13,000 acres – and consequently is rather too well organised and overpopulated: we have approx. 10 Europeans, three of them 'Big Shots'. I have got an area of 2,250 acres to look after with 200-odd coolies and find it quite interesting (as yet, anyway). The language is coming quite easily; it's very simple. I have not managed to get an A40 after all, but I've got something which pleases me just as much: a Morris Minor Shp. Tourer – you know the type of thing; well sprung, spacious body that can be driven open or closed (and it only cost me $3,200 as opposed to the $4,000 that an A40 costs). I am still running it in at the moment, but I went to Kuala Pilah, Seremban and Kuala Lumpur during this last weekend, on a rather glorified, and decidedly expensive binge – and she is doing fine. The crowd and chaps here are not bad at all, mostly ex-service, and I am sharing a bungalow like a barn with a rather good chap called Gahern, ex-Indian Army Captain, and we get on quite well. I have joined the Auxiliary Police here and that takes quite a bit of spare time, and I feel quite war-like toting a pistol around in my belt and a loaded Sten in my car; as a matter of fact, the bandits are quite playful in this area and one or two nasty things have happened recently, including the police truck business of a few days ago; 16 killed, it was about 10 miles from here. So, we all look after ourselves. There are facilities here for squash, badminton and tennis and quite a lot of rugger is played – I had a game last week as a matter of fact (and it d*** killed me – Norwegian food and 'Export'!!).

Well, old chap, I think that's about all the news for now – I'll close, wish you a very merry Xmas and the best for the New Year, and hoping that your new job and surroundings are going down quite well; at least, no worse than mine.

Cheerio for now, and all the very best.
John

P.S. Drop another line when you have time.

P.P.S. The price of rubber is going up!

ELEVEN

There is Something About Asia

1950–1952

My dearest Chris,

Hello again, honey! How are things? Thanks for your No. 9 of 14th January; sorry you haven't received my mail regularly again – I hope it will catch up on itself in future.

Well, what was I saying last night? Sorry if my 19 was scrappy, but I felt so tired and cold last night – we've had a bit of snow here already, but not much, as the temperature has dropped rapidly since; it's really wintry, but thank goodness, the sun manages to shine during the day at intervals. Life is pretty good at work these days and have had lots of dates and odd things to do outside work, so had to spend this weekend hibernating to make up on my sleep! So you hope I'll hide nothing from you, huh? Well, not much! I tell you most of the things I do and leave it to your imagination what is said! I told you I'd been to (a) a party on Monday, (b) dancing Tuesday, (c) out with Woolmer Wednesday, (d) home Thursday (couldn't face evening classes), (e) out pubbing Friday, (f) Rugger match Saturday, (g) recuperating Sunday! Phew! Needless to say, it isn't usually like that – I'm usually out Thursday too! Seriously though, it was an unusually hectic week. Enjoyed it though, I must say [...]

Jocelyn phoned today and invited me to Cobham next weekend; shall be very pleased to see them all again, especially your mother, who, I was shocked to hear, is still in hospital but making a good recovery, Jocelyn said. He was apologetic for not having phoned before, but it was pretty mutual, I guess; anyway, it was good to hear from him again.

General election, huh? Well, I know which way I'll vote! And I bet I know which party gets in again! Shall try to find out how you can get a vote but am somewhat doubtful about the whole thing – still, it's worthwhile trying. Which way, Chris?

Mike, Richard and I all agree on politics and Tommy is non-committal; probably Tory, or right-wing Liberal perhaps, since he comes from Wales originally – though you wouldn't guess it. So lunch-hour seldom revolves round heated arguments; mostly raucous laughter! Very good too. They are grand types. Doc keeps saying, "Must get you to Italy when Richard's there. He can escort you – excellent!" Sure he thinks we'd make a match! Jealous, honey? Shouldn't worry too much! Though of course, you never can tell!!

Your letters are very full of description, Chris; certainly help to give me a good picture of the place. I can't get frightfully thrilled about it though, I'm afraid, especially with all this prophecy going on about Communism spreading in Asia. Vernon Bartlett wrote a very good article in the *Chronicle* today on the subject, but no one is very cheerful about future prospects. Asia's the last place I should want to be if it did come to war – how about you? Guess all this pessimism lately has got into my system, but every day seems to bring reasons why leaving England for S.W. [sic] Asia seems crazy. The 9 p.m. news has just started and there's something about a rebel force leaving Bandung – must stop to listen. Westerling![144] Sounds ghastly. Oh

---

144   Raymond Westerling was a Dutch Army captain who crushed the Indonesian insurgency against Dutch colonial rule in Sulawesi in 1946–7, with thousands killed. After leaving the army in 1948, he formed an armed militia in western Java. On the 22nd January 1950 he staged an attempted coup against the newly independent Indonesian government, leaving many dead. His men captured Bandung but not the capital, so the coup failed. The Dutch government smuggled him out of the country, and Indonesia accused him of war crimes.

dear, Chris! It's as if the coincidence between that announcement and my writing were too pointed! Shall worry so much until eight to ten days' time and from then on – I know how you are. Please take care, darling; news like this makes me feel sick inside. *Ma*, mustn't start on that tack, or shall depress you terribly. Sorry, darling, it's just that going out there when the area seems about to erupt and blow everything in it to smithereens seems mad.

What do you think of Australia all out for 75? Gillie's eyes popped out on Saturday as he read it out. Good old South Africa! What a shock for the Aussies! S.A. didn't enforce the follow-on and after being 75 for 2 at lunch today were all out for 99. Australia need 350-odd, I believe. Do you long to start cricket when you see the sun and feel the heat? Especially when you play tennis already – cricket and tennis seem to go too much together, no?

Haven't kept pace with reading or the last of the Proms lately. Still wading through Huxley's *Those Barren Leaves* and enjoying it immensely. I'm always amused by him, frequently in agreement with him, interestingly enough in contradiction to him, and always amazed at him. One of the best contemporary – no, really the '30s were his era; anyway, one of the best first-half-century writers. Mike Hurford was saying someone else – can't think who now, bother. Anyway, I would certainly include the earlier Huxley, Robert Graves (except for his last effort, the Crete story – *Seven Days in New Crete*), of course Somerset Maugham, though he's astride the very last bit of last century I believe, Shaw of course, early Linklater… oh, mustn't go on or shall include the lot – anyway, there should be runners-up for the honour! What do you say? Do you get enough books out there? Couldn't live without them! In fact, when I start realising all the advantages of England, especially if one has enough money, can't think why I didn't realise them before. I can't imagine life sans work, sans theatre, sports, music, London, countryside, large and airy libraries, balanced diet, trips to the Continent, and a pleasant family life with a couple of kids at home at least for the holidays! *Ma*, silly to start getting sentimental about these things, I guess. After all, so long as you can laugh and make the best of it (sounds rather like an overworked cliché, though, *n'est-ce pas*?). What a gloom-pot I am! Sorry, popsy!

Am hoping to get weaving on arrangements for my *Grand Tour de l'Europe*, or at least *d'Italie, cette année, juin, j'espère*. Get quite excited at the prospect, but wish you were coming, though perhaps you would say, "Can't afford it!", mm? S'pose I can't really, but hell, I haven't ever been before and simply must take this opportunity or I feel I never shall go.

It was very sweet of you to tell me to go and buy a present for myself for Christmas. Thank you, poppet – what shall I choose? (And how much may I spend?!?) Shall wait until I see something I really feel I must buy and then tell you what it is. Shall you mind if it costs more than you say, and I contribute the rest; or, as you say, maybe it could then be a combined birthday and Xmas? Anyway, haven't seen what it's to be yet, so mush! And thanks a million, honey-chile, you shure is a super-baby! Sorry I wrote such a list though! Too much like a direct hint! Ghastly show! Only did it in excitement, I think, to tell you all about our Christmas. I'm a shocker, aren't I? Still, seems to have produced results! I feel, in view of the fact that letters so often convey the wrong impression, that I should epilogue all these supposedly funny or semi-humorous remarks with '(funny-ha-ha)' or '(laugh here)' or even '(forced laugh through teeth hissing under breath)' – one too many! But as paper mounts up, guess I'll have to leave it to your imagination and common-sense (query)!! (Funny laugh.) Ah, lack-a-day! […]

Well, must stop now. Write soon, luv, and tell me how life is with you. Don't work too hard or worry too much. Let me know whether you still think Java is worthwhile (a) for you solo, (b) for both of us. Will try to send you that parcel soon and will write again soon as possible. Meanwhile, all my love, Chris, and for Pete's sake take care of yourself.

Much love from Connie
xx

Saturday night, 11/2/50

My dear Chris,

I've written this letter to you so many times in the past and now it seems funny that I shall at last post it to you. I wish I could give it to you instead and maybe make the job easier.

The last few weeks have been full of doubts and worries about us, as indeed has happened before, but then we've always managed to patch the situation up and fool ourselves into believing it would all work out right, though quite how we never dared to think. Now I feel certain as I have never done before that we must break off our engagement. Knowing how bad you're going to feel about it makes it difficult for me to write to you, but it has to be said for all that.

I have decided to enter into the Protestant Church, if I can be accepted, and I think I shall, and have, I think finally, dispelled all worries about Catholicism being the only answer – there is so much in it that I shall never be able to accept and which is to me so totally unnecessary, that I can only wonder how I managed to think I could ever knuckle under to it and believe in it. As you say in your letter, the main difficulty was always in regard to the Sacrament, but though you always tried to convince me that, this hurdle once past, the rest would be completely acceptable, I cannot believe it ever would have been.

To me it now seems impossible that I should believe in Catholicism, and I cannot, therefore, agree that we can still get married. We both realise what an important part it plays in life, especially in yours – to the exclusion of many other, to me, equally important facts. I should always feel a great gap between us, a gulf which nothing except my acceptance of dogma quite unacceptable to me could bridge. There are so many differences between us apart from this which we have always admitted but which we thought might work themselves out provided the other factor were there; as it cannot be, I don't think we should find life together very constructive or objective. The mutual criticisms would gain impetus from the main difference on fundamental outlook and, added to our differences of temperament and objectives, make life extremely difficult.

All this you know, my dear Chris, and yet you may think it possible to work the thing out in spite of it all. I would like to think so, but I have tried to be detached in viewing it and I cannot think that it ever could work out. It would always be a question with us of 'Who gives way?', and you, I know, could not compromise with your Faith as I could not betray my reason. It would crop up over every stage of life together, children especially. How could I see them learning a religion which seems to me to be so out of touch with reason? Before that, too, the difficulties we have never solved of birth control and a planned family would frustrate our attempts at making our marriage work out. To imagine a life together without this mutual tie of religion is to delude ourselves.

I wrote to you this week at a high pitch of emotional chaos, beseeching you to say we could get married. Part of me still cries out to you for this, but I know that it is not the reasoned side of me. True, we could still get married on the basis of your remaining Catholic and my becoming Protestant, but I cannot think we could arrive at a perfect compromise. I know that to you, compromise on Catholic dogma is damnation, and for that I respect you and your Faith, though I cannot, of course, agree. But the difference between our religions is also a mark of the difference between our outlook, for the one is naturally subjected to the other. We don't look at things in the same way because we are very different in temperament, but add to that a more fundamental difference in religion and I cannot see how we could expect our future life together to be happy. Perhaps you don't expect that anyway, but I cannot get married unless I'm sure of it.

Chris, please don't hate me for this; God knows, I would have had it otherwise, but it can't be. To write this to you is awful, and if I were not sure, completely certain, that we must break it off or end up making each other miserable by our fundamental difference, I could not write it. I think it is harder to do than anything and I wish I had not to do it. I still love you so much, though I suppose not enough – I don't know, except that I cannot think about the future now just yet, for without you there it seems so terribly empty. We have had so much, and should have, it seemed, so much in the future. But it is not possible anymore.

My dear, I can't bear to think how much this will hurt you – try to believe, if only because of what we have had together in the past, that I couldn't do this for any other reason than because I know it will not work out. To read you think I could 'dally with another' or anything similar hurts me deeply, but I know you wrote under great emotional strain and would not have otherwise thought so badly of us. You must know that only religion could come between us; in comparison, talk of others or of fears of our future in Java is pointless.

Oh God, I wish you were here so that I could tell you all this; I feel so awful writing it to you, alone and miserable so far away. Please, please forgive me, Chris, for having to say it and know it could not be otherwise. You could never betray your Faith without betraying yourself – it is I who have failed you, I who stand condemned for my failure, but try to believe I tried, as I have never tried for anything else and never shall, I think. I cannot change myself and cannot be what I am not. Can you forgive me? Can you understand?

I can think of nothing clearly now and can write no more but that I do still love you, though I don't expect you will understand that I do.

Connie

136 Chesterton Road
Kensington
London W. 10
17th July 1950

My dear Christopher,

For the same reasons put forward by you I too have indeed found letter-writing extremely difficult. To have the quartet unbalanced by your departure was truly hard to see and feel a rift of a nature so completely beyond my humble powers produced a certain numbness within. Having realised from the very beginning interference in such a domestic affair could not help one scrap, both Pam and I felt our attitude had best be one of example – to try and accentuate the fact that when the quartet was gathered together how wonderfully happy we could be. Since your departure the 'trio' has met quite often, and I feel that weekends at Farningham and Finchley and one at Peper Harow[145] have more than ever shown up that vital missing personality, and nobody has realised this factor

---

145 Cricket ground near Godalming, Surrey where the UNRRA team played.

more than Connie. During the past months, having had time to chew over the full consequences involved, I personally feel the gulf is considerably narrowed and much, if not all, might well be solved in a meeting. The foregoing may be a very sketchy summing-up of my feelings, but I think perhaps you realise my implications.

'Susannah' made a very graceful departure from Cobham and duly arrived at her new home in Finchley. Her battery immediately began to play tricks and I managed to purchase one through the A.I.O.C. for about half normal price. Events went swimmingly, I applied for a test and much to my sorrow 'Susannah' developed clutch trouble and I failed to pass. At present, she is lying idle awaiting a friend casting a mechanical eye over her to diagnose the root of her complaint. This may sound a tale of woe; in actual fact we have had a lot of good fun from the old bus and I am determined to have her fit and well just in case you appear back on the scene quite soon.

The UNRRA Cricket Club, complete with a constitution, is finished as such; occasionally a 'Mr. Robert Himmels' XI' takes the field and a certain amount of the old fire and 'spirit' is brought back into play. On the 13th August we return to Peper Harow to do battle once more, having been well beaten earlier in the season by the same crowd. Fielding in the slips to someone like Bill Bates is quite uninteresting after looking up and seeing you bound up to the crease. Whether when you sailed for Java you took along with you some of my limited cricketing ability I don't know – but it is strange that since you have gone, I seem to be epitomising that 'duck' which used to sometimes appear at Sittingbourne or Peper Harow.

Having read quickly through the foregoing I think perhaps Pamela should have come before 'Susannah' and cricket – however I believe in saving the choicest morsel until the end. Apart from facing frustration after frustration in the direction of either hoping to build a house or buying something reasonable at a fair price, Pamela is bearing up very well. The present bureaucracy and its effect on the young generation's struggle for the basic necessities in life is a little short of bewildering.

There is much that has been left unsaid, but I feel that if once you have forgiven my inexcusable tardiness and both of us can get into our stride, the writing of letters will not be quite so infrequent.

Stella, Chris and a friend with local children in Java, 1950

Well! Christopher, it's grand to have had this one-sided chat. Please write soon. I promise to reply very quickly.

Cheers! for now.
Love from Pam and Gillie

Pamanoekan & Tjiasemlanden
Soebang
Java
23rd September 1950

G. Ch. T. Repton, Esq.
SUBANG

Dear Sir,

In connection with your resignation, we confirm having made the following arrangements:

1. You will be granted salary to the end of October with the same allowances as in September.

2. The Company is arranging a passage for you to Singapore, and from there an onward second-class passage to England may be booked

with the assistance of Messrs. Francis Peek & Co. The cost of the passage will be borne by the Company.

3. We have authorised Messrs. Francis Peek to advance you Str. $100.–, which amount you have agreed to repay to them as quickly as possible in sterling. All expenses in Singapore are for your own account.

4. You will authorise the Secretary of the Provident Fund to pay the amount due to you to the Company for the credit of your account.

5. After your account has been closed, a statement will be sent and any amount due to you will be paid to a 'Gurni' account with the Hongkong & Shanghai Bank, Djakarta. Should your account show a debit balance, you will arrange to settle this by payment to Anglo-Dutch in London.

We shall be glad if you will sign a copy of this letter for agreement.

Yours faithfully,
John Saffery
Chief Accountant

> c/o Hotel de l'Europe
> Oxley Rise
> Singapore
> October 22nd

Dear Chris,

First of all, thanks for your Colombo letter; we didn't drop you a line back until now, because we weren't sure of your old scow's antics. Your luggage has been put on the *Orange*, we think; at all events I do know that Donald Thompson has written to you direct, with all the correct 'gen', so let's hope that you'll get it all safely, quite soon. Ours was due to arrive today; let's hope it did.

You'll be wondering about me and jobs, of course – well, I've accepted an offer from Anglo/Thai. I'm to be taken on at local terms until December, when the Managing Director comes back off leave, when I shall be placed on 'home' terms, which, apart from leave etc. paid, will mean that I'll get an increase in salary, bonus etc., etc. My starting salary is $1,100, so I feel I can't really complain. The idea is that when I've got the M.D.'s O.K., I shall go up to Kuala Lumpur to manage the firm's branch there, and there will be a house and car provided! All in all, I think you'll agree that I've been quite lucky. It's certainly bucked Stella up no end. She's managed to get herself a job with Qantas on the secretarial side, and at quite a fair salary, and transport to and fro. We've moved into your old room, or rather will do tomorrow, and won't trouble to try and find alternative accommodation just for the three months.

Well, this is a very short note indeed. I'll settle down and give you a decent letter later on, just to give you all the news. I'm playing a spot of Rugger. Ross, as you may know, has a job. Peter McWilliam has left P. & T.[146] and is passing through here on the 2nd, and Stella sends you all her best regards, in fact love and kisses, as I do. Regards, too, from Ross.

Cheers,
Roy

94 Poundbury Camp
Dorchester
Dorset
Nov. 6th 1950

Dear Christopher,

Thank you so much for bringing over and sending on to me the parcel from Stella; also for your letter. I was very relieved to hear the good news of Stella & Roy, and also that they had left Java.

I had heard from Stella that you might come to Dorchester on your way home but shall look forward to meeting you 'one of these days'; have heard so much about you!!

Once again, many thanks.

Yours sincerely,
B. R. Wilkes[147]

---

146 Christopher met Roy while they were working for Anglo-Dutch company P&T Lands in Subang, Java which had plantations growing cash crops such as tea, rubber, sisal, teak and other hardwoods. By late 1950 they and many of their colleagues had resigned and left Indonesia because of ongoing killings of Europeans by anti-colonial guerrillas. Indonesia was still unstable, having recently gained independence from the Netherlands.
147 Stella's mother.

Gleneagles
5 Napier Road
Singapore
15/11/50

Dear Chris,

At last, a letter from you; we were beginning to be a trifle worried, not hearing from you for so long, but we can easily imagine that you've had plenty to do. We've heard from Stella's mama re. the parcel, which she safely received – many thanks.

How did the remainder of your trip go? We really did think of you many times, and said, "Poor old Chris, how on earth will he put up with that awful boat?"

Firstly, in case you haven't heard, when Jimmie Lyons passed through, we wined and dined him, and he told us that another Dutchman was murdered at Tjilumpan Estate – just as Dawkes arrived!! I picked up the paper yesterday and was horrified to read that they've also murdered poor old Adriani at Manjingsal Estate. Isn't it terrible; after the lousy time he had during the war, and then losing all his money? I feel so sorry for his wife and children in Holland. Our friend Van der Molen, who apparently had an engagement party (to Junie, of course) in the club at Subang, was apparently threatened by the T. & I., and left on the first plane. To June's parents' home, I presume!!

We're very pleased to hear that there's a strong chance of your being with us again sometime in the New Year. The actual 'gen' on my position is this. A/T have taken me on at local rates ($1,100 a month +) until their managing director pays his annual visit in December (early). If he agrees that I'm O.K. (staff can only be taken on at home normally) I shall be placed on home engagement terms – increased salary etc. – and sent up to KL to replace the manager who is going on leave. This is quite good, as it means an entertainment allowance, free house and free car. What will happen when the manager returns, I don't know yet – he, or I, may return to Singapore. At all events, we're a darned sight better off than we were in Java, n'est-ce pas?

Souter has vanished from the scene, breathing threats. As you know, he was fired, and has now sued them (Peek's) for his passage home.

Baggage: Peek's were rather clueless about it, although ours did eventually turn up. All my clothes were full of bugs – I hope yours will be O.K.

Cricket bat: Send it out, collect any time you feel like it – I shan't be needing it for a bit.

You haven't mentioned Connie – we do hope that everything is as you want it to be.

Ross has been doing well, I'm glad to say, although from time to time he says (!) he's going to leave unless they raise his salary. We see him quite often, but not Bep. Having heard from him all this nonsense about her leaving Ross, if the other type wanted her, etc., etc., Stella was so disgusted that she has flatly refused to say, "*Jambo*"[148] – so it's a bit tricky.

Stella is a little better, although we've both been in bed with bad colds; the weather here is very changeable, but she'll be very much better when we move into our own place. As you'll have seen by the address, we moved out of the Cockpit[149] (after 5 weeks) and are now in a very nice boarding house, sprinkled with Brigadiers and other genteel types!! However, food's good, and service better. No complaints.

Rugger: I play occasionally; not with the fervour of before, I regret to say, and very occasionally score a try. I'm afraid I'm getting (!) too old and too fat – yes, we still have big arguments about my age!

Finance: I wrote to Fletcher after you left and said, 'Try hard', and he sent me back $1,200. Not bad when you consider that they'd already paid a) my passage (and Stella's) by air, b) baggage, c) $200. Someone there must feel guilty about something.

Well, all the gossip for now. We expect to have a respectably long letter back in due course.

All the very best from Roy & Stella

P.S. Singapore has had big 'Our Lady of Fatima' celebrations, which I duly attended on my and your behalf.

---

148 *"Jambo Bwana!"* meaning "Hello Mister!" in Swahili, was an old colonial greeting used in East Africa.
149 A mid-range hotel in Singapore.

P. & T. Lands
Subang
Java
22nd November '50

Dear Chris,

Very many thanks indeed for your letter just received.

I was certainly surprised, and also very glad to read that you have got into Turquand Youngs. I have always understood that they are an excellent firm, although I have never had any actual dealings with them. Here's wishing you every success!

I myself am retiring from here at the end of the year. I am flying home for Christmas.

I am sorry to say conditions on the Lands are extremely bad. Since you left, a young assistant, van Haastert, was murdered on Jalupang and then, ten days ago, poor old Adriani was murdered on Manjingsal. In addition to this, Indonesians – employees and otherwise – are constantly getting bumped off and wholesale thefts of produce and stores take place every day on almost all estates. There are signs, however, that the government is now starting to take very serious action to stop it. Meanwhile, many of the estates have no Europeans on them at night-time as it is too unsafe.

I will show your letter to Fletcher. He has been very ill and is still in hospital but goes off on leave on 7th December. He is flying to London.

I will give you a ring on the 'phone sometime after Christmas. Meanwhile, all the best.

Yours,
John Saffery

'Gleneagles'
Singapore
3.12.50

Dear Chris,

Many thanks for your 10-page epistle. First of all, I must tell you, Stella is to present me with a son-and-heir in May, so you'd better hurry back and be its godfather!! Naturally, we're both terribly excited, and Stella, who was with Qantas, has now left and spends all day drinking milk.

Before I forget, herewith one snap of the pool in Java. Stella is having other copies of the reel printed, and they'll be forwarded to you later on.

I'm still playing Rugger here, believe it or not, and had quite a good game on Wednesday in the annual Scotland v. the Rest match. I served a couple of quite good tries and had a decent write-up in the *Straits Times*. There's just a little energy left but won't be able to turn out much longer.

Paddy Knights came through on Thursday, and I duly contacted him, and in fact had lunch with him, Thompson and Ross Smith and Stella. He looked very brown, but obviously very worried about the Java situation. He told me that he'd been making enquiries in S'pore and had in fact spoken to Turquand Youngs about the possibility of getting a job in S'pore. He certainly made it quite clear that if he was offered anything decent, he would be off like a shot! I saw him again in the evening, as Stella and I visited the *Ruys* to see a friend of ours off to Java. He mentioned something about your wanting food parcels. Is that so? If so, write and give me details forthwith. There were two other people from P. & T. on the boat – Gough's wife, and a new youngster – pity!

Very pleased that Ernest Hedley has managed to get fixed up satisfactorily; he was certainly lucky. As I write, the local rags are full of news about the Bandung revolt, and the fact that the whole of Java is completely out of control, the country swarming with guerrillas, bandits, etc.

The Managing Director of my firm is out here, but haven't had my interview with him yet, but imagine that I will do so sometime this week.

Sorry to hear that you'd such a lot of nonsense with your *barang*.[150]

I'm terribly sorry to get your news about Connie and feel that it's completely inadequate to try and console you but do hope that you

---

150 *Barang barang* is Malay for 'belongings'.

won't let it depress you too much. Get down to your exams, Chris, as Stella and I are both looking forward to seeing you again soon.

Well, must close now, old son, as I have to write my mama the news about Stella […]

All the very best from Roy & Stella

P.S. We've just heard that Norman Winning has been murdered. It happened on Saturday.

'Gleneagles'
Singapore
31.12.50

Dear Chris,

At long last, a letter from you. Just in time too, as the New Year is hot on your heels!

Many odd things have happened since you last wrote, including, of course, the riots. As you'd like a brief report, here goes.

Oddly enough, I was on the spot when it started. We were passing the Cricket Club (which, as you know, faces the Supreme Court) when a mob dashed along and attacked the car in front of us. It was a small open Fiat, and the occupants couldn't move a muscle. Whilst all this was going on, incidentally, the pavement was lined with Malay Police, who just stood there, and made absolutely no attempt to intervene. That incident was repeated time without number all through the riots. As you've no doubt read, many Europeans were murdered in cold blood, again with the Police just looking on. Without any doubt, the whole thing started as a religious rumpus, which could have been put down by a dozen policemen, but they funked it and then the whole hooligan element in town took over. We were under a curfew for quite a time, and still the atmosphere is anything but pleasant. People just don't walk around the side streets anymore. The judge who tried the case is still receiving threatening letters. The least they promise to do is to murder him. It's difficult to visualise the extent to which these rioters went. For example, they broke into a cinema, dragged Europeans out and attacked them with axes!

Still, enough of that. I enclose the balance of the snaps we owe you. Stella apologises for not writing, incidentally, but says that she feels sure that you'll understand, things being as they are at the moment.

Ross is still going strong, and I had a letter from Paddy yesterday saying that a) he had resigned, b) Joan Churchward and Isobel Cammell had flown to Australia, and c) life over there is just falling apart. I believe he has written to you.

I'm still playing Rugger and getting the odd write-up. This is going to be a short letter, Chris, as I want to get it off to you, but I will write again in the very near future. So in the meantime, all the very best from us both.

Stella & Roy

1951

'Gleneagles'
S'pore
31.1.51

Dear Chris,

I really must apologise for not having written before, but quite frankly I've had so much to do that letter-writing has had to take second place for the time being.

Your letter was really very chatty and informative, and you certainly seem to have had quite a reasonable time at Xmas.

Nothing very exciting from Singapore for the moment. The Rugger Season, with the exception of the 7-a-sides, is over, and thank goodness for it. Stella is looking very well indeed – in fact I've never seen her looking fitter. She has had no trouble at all, and the quack is quite pleased with her.

I'm due to go up to Bangkok in a week or so for the firm, as soon as my visa comes through, and if I like it up there, I may be posted there. Actually, not to Bangkok itself, although I think that I'll go there first, but to a small place called Singora. That will be my HQ and presumably I'll circulate around.

I had almost forgotten, I had a letter from Paddy Knights the other day (he hates you – says you haven't written); apparently Jackson is now at Subang in Dawkes' place, and Paddy has now agreed to stay on. He admits that he's nuts but says that they have now agreed to give him the terms he originally asked for, and also that he really couldn't afford to leave anyway – passage etc.

There is one thing, Chris: the *tuan besar*[151] of this outfit is a gentleman called Miller, who will be back in England when you get this. Now, when I last had a conversation with him, he did say that the firm needed an accountant type rather badly, for the S'pore office. He was thinking in terms of a youngish type, not qualified necessarily, but working that way, who would take over from the type now enthroned. I can't give you any further information, but if you are interested, do your stuff, without mentioning my name, of course.

Nothing much else for now, old son. As you can imagine, I'm typing this in the office, and haven't your letter by me, so I imagine that I've left out all the things that I wanted to write. Stella sends her love, and we're both waiting for your next letter.

All the very best,
Roy

'Ridwan'
45 Alexandra Grove
London N. 12
13th April 1951

Dear Christopher,

I should first of all like to tell you how very pleased I was to know that you would be Gillie's 'Best Man'. It will, I assure you, mean a great deal to both of us.

I hope you will excuse my slight incoherence on the telephone on Tuesday, but we had been having quite an evening with Robert which came as a very pleasant surprise – although I felt sure he would give

---

151 'Big boss' (Malay).

us a call eventually. He was looking extremely fit and is interested in getting back into harness again regarding cricket – to quote, "I am going to take it seriously this year!" It was good to see him again.

Gil rang me this evening and said he had spoken to you on the telephone – you must have been very shocked to hear the news of Eric Taylor.

As you will see, I am returning to you your scarf, Chris. Please forgive me for not doing so before.

I hope you and the rest of your family are all well, and look forward to seeing you very soon.

Affectionately yours,
Pamela

c/o Hongkong & Shanghai Bank
Collyer Quay
S'pore
May 30th

My dear Chris,

Firstly, many thanks for your cable – it was very good of you, and Stella appreciated it a lot.

You'll be pleased to hear that Stella had a very easy time, and was and is, together with the babe, in the very best of health. You shall have a snap or two of your godson as soon as possible. I am informed that he looks exactly like me (!!) but he still (after 8 days) has Stella's blue eyes.

You'll be interested to learn that I may be going up to Penang. Nothing has or will be settled for another week or so, but if it turns out as I expect, it'll probably mean my going up there in the very near future. Long, involved story, again, but will tell you all one day. One thing is quite clear: it's certainly less expensive there than here. Things cost outrageous sums here; I really don't know how people can afford to live. I think, too, that the climate up in P. will be better for my family. (I can't get over that word applying to me!)

Anyway, the moment everything works itself out, I will give you fullest details. I quite understand and agree with all you say about T.Y. etc., but I'm awfully afraid that you'll (as the most recently joined accountant) be pushed upcountry to vet the estates. If we are still here when you arrive, we'll be more than overjoyed; as it is, we are reckoning on your being here about August. Try therefore to get on a boat that calls in at Penang, just in case we do go up there!

Today is a big day in Christopher's life – we bought him a pram; a very ingenious contraption. It folds into the size of a pocket handkerchief, on the slightest provocation. Complete with tasselled whatnots!

Well, I'm awaiting the Persian oil news with great interest; today is the deadline. I think to let go there will be just about the end. Still – there's always Shinwell!!![152]

I was very interested to hear that Connie had broken off her engagement.[153] Is it too much to anticipate?

I don't know how much Indonesian news seeps through to England – very little, I imagine. The old killing of Europeans has broken out again on the estates, and the I. Govt. has announced that it's going to nationalise all 'foreign' estates. So much for P. & T.; they have now had it!

Glad that you've at least played ONE game of cricket. You'll be in great demand when you get to S'pore. The cricket team here could do with a bit of bucking up. I must say that I rather jibbed at the idea of playing – can't take it anymore. I've had one or two characters after me to captain the Club at Rugger this coming season, but I had

---

152 Manny Shinwell was British Defence Minister in the Labour government in 1951. That summer, when Iranian Prime Minister Mohammad Mosaddegh nationalised the Anglo-Iranian Oil Company, Shinwell wanted to send British troops to the Persian Gulf but was prevented from doing so by the Cabinet. In the 1940s and '50s the British government believed that it owned Iranian oil, since Britain had developed and exploited it. In August 1951 Britain imposed sanctions against Iran and withdrew its oil workers from the country. Most Western countries followed suit, except Italy. Two years later, the CIA and MI6 organised a secret coup, ousting the democratically elected Mosaddegh and his government, returned Shah Mohammad Reza Pahlavi to power and installed a new Prime Minister. In August 1954, a Western-led consortium took over the AIOC, splitting it between US oil majors, British Petroleum, Royal Dutch Shell and France's CPF, allotting Iran just 25% of profits, while Saudi Arabia and other Gulf countries received up to 50%. This situation continued until 1980, when the AIOC was nationalised by the Islamist government which took power after the 1979 Iranian Revolution.

153 Connie appears to have got engaged to someone else after breaking off her engagement to Christopher.

to respectfully decline. The time has come at long last to hang up my boots. I still manage to waddle round a squash court occasionally.

Well, all for now, Chris. We're looking forward to hearing from you very soon and will be thinking of you during your exams.

All the very best from us both.
Stella & Roy

P.S. Stella's letter enclosed.

The E. & O. Hotel
Penang
Sunday July 15th

Dear Chris,

What an old so-and-so you are – it's months since you've written to us. Did you get the telegram we sent?

We've been up in Penang about 3 weeks now and expect to be here some little while. I'm up here on business, incidentally, not pleasure.

What news of the exams? Did you manage to cope, in spite of the short time you had? Do let us know.

Christopher is very well and getting healthier all the time. I enclose a snap of him taken when he was a month old. See any resemblance?

This isn't going to be a long letter, you don't deserve it, but will give you a long account of my activities when I get your letter.

Stella is very busy with C. and rather tired, but sends all (!) her love to you, and also wants to know why you haven't written.

For your information, several other people have been bumped off in P. & T. We had Fletcher to dinner with us recently, when on the way back to Java from the West Indies. We had the usual experience – he got drunk of course, and amazed our other guest, a young American Air Attaché. However – c'est la vie!

All for now and let us know all the news.
Ever yours,
Stella, Roy & Christopher

E. & O. Hotel
Penang
2.8.51

Dear Chris,

Many thanks for your letter – at long last. We were getting quite worried about you; thought you'd volunteered for Korea, at least.

Sorry to hear about your discs[154] – and hope that it won't have any lasting effects. We're all awaiting your mid-August results with crossed fingers and hope that you managed to get through O.K. Please let us know as soon as you can.

Keep writing to Penang, as I have taken a job up here with a firm of importers and expect to be here some time. We haven't managed to get hold of a house yet but hope to have done so by the time you come out, so that you can spend some time with us. It's very nice up here, and just the place to recuperate from disc trouble.

Christopher is blooming, and as soon as my baptismal certificate arrives, we're having him christened. He will be Christopher Royden, and you are godfather, and Stella's sister and my sister joint godmother, O.K.? He is now getting quite interested in things; and looking forward to seeing you.

You make very little mention of Connie; we were hoping…

Your idea of a trip to France is one that I really envy but will have to wait a bit.

Have you any idea where you'll be stationed, if and when you come out? It would be really wonderful if you managed to get up here. There seems to be plenty of tennis and cricket here, and the All-Malayan Championships are being held in a few days' time – and then the Rugger season starts all over again. I think I sent you a snap of the offspring, or didn't I? Let me know. Also, if there's anything we can get you, just mention it.

Must rush now; am extremely busy working these days, believe it or not, and have very little time for pleasure!!!

All the very best from the C-G family,
Stella, Roy & Christopher

---

154 It sounds as if Christopher had slipped a disc in his back.

The E. & O. Hotel
Penang
Tuesday 18th Sept.

Dear Chris,

Many thanks for your letter. I've seen Murphy, and it's quite O.K. to stay over for the christening, which is being held on 14th October. He tells me that you're going to KL and not to S'pore, which may or may not be a good thing – Clarke, the partner there, is apparently a very nice fellow.

The *Selandia* may be a bit late, but we'll have a room lined up for you somewhere, whenever it does get here.

Pardon the scrawl and haste, but must get this off, else I may miss you. Have an enjoyable time en route; we're all looking forward to seeing you soon.

All the very best.

Yours,
Roy

Florence
25.9.51

Darling Chris,

This is my first letter to you, and it makes me wonder a little how many there will be… Hundreds, thousands? Depends on when we will be together again.

You left on Thursday the 10th… and I watched that train pull out of the station and it was like dying a little death. No more Chris to see, to talk to […] it just could not be as bad as it felt, but it was, all of it. The going back to work, the working, the talking – and I felt all frozen inside. I don't know how I got through that day and that night – just for once I got the feeling I was dead beat. Friday was a nightmare at the office and then just when I was ready to cry, Sylvia rang me. I saw her for coffee in the afternoon and she gave me your present. Dearest heart, so very many thanks; that little cross round my neck means more to me than the Crown Jewels – and it will bring luck to us, I am sure.

Saturday I had my first really big fright for a long time. When I had finished rushing around and got ready to pack in the afternoon I suddenly had to sit down – I felt too weak to stand up, too weak to lift an arm, so weak I could have died there and then. I thought, *Old girl, with your thinking you can do anything. You have expended your last ounce of willpower, energy and strength – God help you.* He did – I got over it, crawled round and packed, rang my friends to say goodbye and then went to bed, and at 10 a.m. Sunday I set off for Italy.

But before I begin that saga, there are a few very important things to say…

I love you; I will keep on loving you and all I want is that you love me back. I am with you all the time, remember, and nothing can happen to you; you are safe, dearest.

Also, I must tell you about Sylvia. I think we will get on together. She has plenty of trouble of her own and I only hope I will be able to help her a bit.

So, the boat-train pulled out with me sitting decorously in a non-smoking compartment with 3 other females – me reading the *Sunday Times*, thinking that from now on I won't have anybody to talk to. I didn't – for 10 minutes. Then a waiter brought coffee and that broke the ice (if there was any). My fellow travellers were two American tourists and a girl whose nationality I could not place for a while. Within ¼ of an hour we were having the time of our lives. We crossed over together on the boat (such a calm, uninteresting journey; nobody was sick), and it turned out that the one American girl was a journalist, the other a secretary – both from the South. So they taught me 'Dixie Land' and I taught them limericks. The third one – a pretty young thing – was from Riga (Baltic, you know; now Russia). The poor devil had been through hell – the war in Germany, Russian occupation, flight through the night, starvation in camps. Her mother got to England and works there as a dentist, and when it became apparent that the girl had got TB, managed to send her to a sanatorium in Switzerland.

Amongst our fellow travellers were also the people you always meet: the 'disgusted lady', beautifully turned out and too blasé to even bother to look at anything; the disagreeable woman who 'keeps herself to herself' and disapproves of everything (on principle); the hearty buffoon who must (at all cost) make everybody laugh and never does. They were all there, the whole damned zoo – and I love them all; they are humanity.

I had time at Ostend and so had the girl from Riga, and I took her out on a spree to cheer her up. When at last I got into my sleeper at 6 p.m. I was poorer in pounds and richer in experience and had three more people to look up if I ever come their way again.

(Most important notice: I LOVE YOU.)

I like travelling in a sleeper. As soon as the train started it began to pour with rain, and there I sat, snug in my little cell, watching the Belgian countryside flash by, dripping wet. At Brussels an elderly Belgian lady got in with me (she had the upper berth), and so (as you can guess) I started talking again (but honestly, darling, it would not be me if I did not). Then I went to have dinner and sat opposite a nice young man, a Swiss, and so I could talk in German. He practically told me his life story, and when I looked at my watch it was 11 p.m.! Oh, by the way – I heroically stuck to my promise and had mineral waters all the time. How is that for 'character'? Full marks, I guess.

I slept like a log – a nice log of course – until a voice (which I first thought must be that of the recording angel) shouted in my ear. I was wrong – it was only the Swiss customs officer at Basle – at 6 a.m. I cursed him in 3 languages to make sure he understood and then got ready to sleep again. But oh no!! At Basle the train dithers… it is shunted backwards and forwards, again and again for ½ hour; I lost count how many times. When it finally does pull out it is entirely reorganised – the Swiss in their thoroughness have taken it to pieces, shaken out, dusted, brushed, blown its nose, etc., and all at the expense of our sleep. Blast them.

When I woke up again, we were in Lucerne. It was cold and the air smelt pure and strong, and oh, Chris, it was wonderful – for hours I watched the mountains, grim, forbidding, the dark silent forest, the mountain stream, the lakes, colours black and dark green, and frothy grey waters. I had not seen these since I left home – and I felt their pull, their call stronger every minute. They seemed to say, *Come out, come up! Here is quiet, here is peace, here is strength! Your strength, that we gave you at birth, the strength of me, the black rock, battered and polished by the seasons and forever the same. The strength of me, the dark forest tossed and bent by the winds, and still the same. Come out, come up. You are our child; come back home.* Oh, how I longed to get out, to walk on the carpet of pine and fir needles with my feet bare, walk up and up into the great silence, to dance in the sun between trees, to hug the rocks, to shed all fear – for where no human beings tread there is no fear, other than death and death is nature, just like life. I felt – for the first time in my life since I left home – homesickness.

We passed the mountains, descended over the Gotthard into Italy. Slowly the scene changed from frightening grandeur into peaceful loveliness. Vines began to appear, and the steep-roofed stone houses changed to coloured ones with flatter roofs. Into Italy, into Italy – the language on the train changed. I understood less and less, and after Milan – where I had to go into an ordinary compartment – I was left alone in a wilderness of people whose language I did not speak. On and on – into the fruitful plains of Tuscany, vines and fruit trees and a blazing sun. So, I thought, *What ho – I'll speak Italian too.* I know about 100 words and strung them together like a child does, and lo and behold, within a few minutes the whole compartment insisted to teach me Italian. I have a good ear and can imitate well, and soon I could say lots of things with a northern and southern accent. At Bologna I bought fruit and cursed the man (in Italian) for charging me too much, amongst the cheers of the whole compartment. Then I wanted to go to the lavatory and could not get the door open, and (in Italian) got two railway policemen to help me (to their great delight), and as the door would not lock, they stood guard.

It got quite dark and finally we pulled into Florence – first stop on the journey. It is so exciting to meet a new city – you look at it, you smell it and I thought, *Hello, we are going to like each other!* And we do.

I have now been writing for hours and must stop and go to bed. As they say… The next instalment follows tomorrow. Dearest, I love you so much. There is a little burning pain in my heart – and it is so wonderful to love and to give. Oh please, love me back! I am all I have – but I am all yours, such as I am. Why is this language so clumsy? *Je vous aime, je vous adore, je suis folle de vous. Je vous aime plus que hier et moins que demain.*

Goodnight.
M.

Ladang Geddes Estate
Bahau
Negri Sembilan
21st Oct.

Dear Chris,

Very many thanks for your letter of 28th which I got yesterday. You are quite right when you say that it is ages since you heard from me, and it is quite likely that I did not reply to your last letter – as a matter of fact I don't think I have written or received one letter in the last year with the possible exception of yours.

It was with some surprise that I read that you were in Malaya – because, although you mentioned that you might be coming out to Singapore, I thought that after your experience in Java you might have changed your mind. Also, you did not mention if you were married or not – is the path of love still running smoothly?

As you will see by my address, I am still at Ladang Geddes and I think I shall be here for another two years (i.e. until the end of the contract). At the moment life is very easy here as the whole of the Bahau area is on strike due to the bandits' threats – they have promised to shoot any tapper who works at all, and have backed this up by shooting 4 people to date. Consequently, the day consists of getting out about 6 a.m. and going out to see what is happening with the labour force and then returning to the bungalow and drinking one's way quietly through the day – just the kind of life I like.

I do not visit KL very often, due mainly to the distance (105 miles), but I will probably be up there for 2 or 3 days in November or December so I will call you up and we can do a spot of quiet soaking and chat about old times.

Cheerio for the time being.

Yours sincerely,
John A. Millward

Det Østasiatiske Kompagni
Singapore
24th October 1951

My dear Christopher,[155]

Since we have never had the chance to speak French together, let's converse in this language this evening. It will be less tiring for you as you won't have to correct all my mistakes, and it will be nicer for me to imagine you nearby.

Your letter was a delicious surprise, the first that I took out of a big pile which was waiting for me, and I leapt on the small, decisive handwriting which is one of the intriguing elements of your personality. Thank you, Christopher, for once again opening your heart to me, and thank you also for the frank and natural tone of your message.

That Friday was a dream, a sort of brief pause in the course of normal life. We lived for a few hours at the same pace, happy to be together, so in tune with each other that it was as if we'd already spent a lifetime together. That reinforced my idea that it had been much wiser for us to keep our distance during the voyage. And believe me, it was horribly hard, but you have your whole life ahead of you; it is up to you to choose.

There is so much uncertainty around you and inside you at the moment and I am strangely worried, tormented. I almost telephoned you on Saturday morning, but that would only have made things more difficult. I spent a long time praying for you; I get a feeling of danger and fear. Chris, I beg you, try to see clearly inside yourself. At this moment, the only question that is important is – KL or Singapore? But one could live happily anywhere, and if the work is interesting on a professional level, why change?

Life on board ship continues uneventfully. Mrs. Kabell bravely disembarked at Port Swettenham. She had tears in her eyes when she said goodbye to me, and so did I. Her life will be very hard. Her

---

155 Translated from French, this letter was written by an anonymous Frenchwoman Christopher met on board ship en route from England to start his new job at Turquand Youngs in Kuala Lumpur.

husband is a child, who is unaware of the danger he is exposing her to. Mr. Joseph joined his brother and his seven dogs today. He is a very good man, with a soft heart under a tough exterior. The Hainsworths disappeared, and with them the noise and the chaos. No more shouting or scenes. Twelve passengers embarked in Singapore, and a melancholy-looking woman joined us in Penang. I wonder what you would have said about her; perhaps you would have found her pretty, men are strange. Mr. Hunt, after having made the most shocking proposals to me, disappeared at Port Swettenham. If I write a novel one day, I will base a character on this strange chap. He is the one who does certain things in the story and is rightfully punished. But I probably won't write a novel!

Bridge – after all, Chris, your favourite pastime! – continues 100%. Two tables are fighting it out and it seems like a serious battle. The Captain is telling stories – which I don't understand – and I am dreaming that you are still there, and I feel like telling you something jolly. Martin is feeling better and speaks of his day in Penang with delight. I am so grateful to you for that. It is my greatest joy to see him happy, and that's why I don't have the right to throw away my life.

Dear, I am happy to have met you. Let us remain friends. You know well, without my telling you, that I am affectionately your

Z.

Twynersh
4th November 1951

My dear Christopher,

I am sorry there has been such a long delay with this letter, but every weekend I have made up my mind to write to you and somehow or other I have not done it.

The house is very quiet this weekend. Sylvia is on watch all the time and did not even come home today from 3–6 as she was going to tea with someone. Jocelyn has gone to Oxford to meet Evelyn in hospital. Gervase was going out walking with Russ, but as it has been pouring with rain all day he came back after lunch. Marcus has just jumped up and put his paws right on this letter. He is feeling rather bored as no one has been able to take him out today. It has been the worst day for some time – steady rain and very damp and cold. Last night I went to London to meet Ruder[156] as I was deprived of my Friday night out, as Mr. and Mrs. Lever wanted to discuss business with him. I managed to miss the 11.12 by one minute, so came home by Tolworth, as you did once. I caught the Green Line easily, so all was well.

Mr. Lever and his wife got back two weeks ago, and on their return, they stopped at Singapore for a night and day. Quite on the spur of the moment they went to the biggest store there (so they said), Robinson's, and they recommended an agent, and the final result was that they took five orders and discovered that it is a very good market for our goods, as they use prints all the year round in Singapore. So we have opened up trade with the Far East. Work has been absolutely hectic in the last few weeks, but I think we are slowly getting over our financial crisis. Money is going to be rather tight for a while, but I think it will pay off in the end.

What do you think of Gervase going to New Zealand? The family does seem to be splitting up gradually, but it is probably a good thing for us all.

It seems ages since we saw you off at Victoria that day. What a gathering it was! Major Shelley was quite different to what I expected, but nevertheless a very pleasant person. The same applies to Maria. When I got back to the office, I felt half drunk and nearly fell asleep over my typewriter. Whether the rum was responsible or not I don't know, but that afternoon my knee, which I had grazed about two weeks before, suddenly became very swollen and painful and I had to go to the Middlesex Hospital and have it treated. Then I went on and off for ten days to have it done [...]

Love from us all,
Leila

---

156 Bill Ruder, Leila's future husband.

c/o District Office
Bentong
Pahang
November 5th

Dear Chris,

Thank you so much for your letter – it was awfully nice of you to write. Please don't worry anymore about that nonsense with the ship's Captain. No one was to blame but he himself, and I think an extra drink or two on his own part accounted for a lot of it. Sven wrote him off at once as a pompous old ass. It's just that I'm not very good at being bullied, which is my own fault anyhow. And if it comes to apologies, I blamed myself that you wouldn't have broken your glasses if I hadn't been so damned slow on the uptake about jumping off the hold that afternoon. So that's alright.

I'm sorry you got stuck in KL, which I should imagine is a bit deadly. I don't think any tropical towns are much fun. I hope you'll soon get the change you want, but it would be very nice to meet again before you leave the district. If we ever come to KL, we'll certainly try to see you, or we should be very glad to put you up here. The difficulty is, of course, that the roads in this area aren't too healthy. We came in the D.O.'s[157] armoured car, and we have a nice little Fiat for running about in Bentong, but don't go further afield as a rule. I think they are starting an air service next month though, so if you could manage a weekend, do let me know. We've got a nice house with a spare room, but are getting our meals at the Rest House,[158] which is conveniently halfway between our house and the D.O.'s office, where I am working part-time. I don't speak enough Malay yet to run the housekeeping very well, and also servants are hard to get, Bentong being an unfamiliar place. We are lucky to have a very good amah for laundry and cleaning. There is a very pleasant crowd of people here – luckily, as the circle is rather small. Yesterday we were at a Malay wedding, which was most interesting and entertaining.

---

157 District Officer's.
158 Rest houses in Malaysia, dating from colonial times, are reasonably priced government-run motels with restaurants.

281

The poor Cochranes chose an unfortunate moment for settling in Egypt, didn't they?

I do hope that you are feeling pretty fit, and that you have good news from home.

With all good wishes,

Yours sincerely,
Margaret Kabell

Penang
13th November 1951

Dear Chris,

Many thanks for your letter, and a very nice long one it was too. Firstly, Christmas is O.K. and begins the time you arrive, whether it is a week or a month before the allotted date. You surely didn't need to ask that one.

As far as Turquand Youngs are concerned, I had a chat today with Mr. Fred Weatherly, who remembers you, and he has agreed to do all he can in the required direction. If I might offer a word of counsel, you would perhaps be wiser to consider the commercial rather than the professional side, as you have no doubt already decided. As a point of interest, an insertion in the leading Singapore 'Rag' would probably achieve some amazing results, and I believe it is more worth considering.

I was very interested to hear that you have gone to Frank Warren the other day, and I am glad to learn that he is still in one piece.

I was on to Singapore today to a certain Capt. Kirk Myers about your accommodation. Unfortunately, this type, who is a friend of mine, has just moved out from his house to the 'Cockpit', but will, he hopes, be moving into another house in the near future. If he manages to achieve this, he will be delighted to put you up from the 6th to the 8th. He is the Assistant Air Attaché at the American Consulate in Singapore, and should you run into any difficulty whilst down there, he is the man to see, as part of his job is accommodating various V.I.P.s when they pass through. He says he would do his best for you either way and you should contact him when you can.

Everything seems to be going rather well, Stella and Christopher send their love to you, and we hope to see you very soon now.

All the very best.

Yours,
Roy

Mr. G. C. T. Repton
c/o Messrs. Turquand, Youngs, McAuliffe & Co.
Anglo-Oriental Building
Kuala Lumpur

Sorry this is a bit stuffy but had to dictate it – no time.

November 19th 1951

Dearest Chris,

I have heard from Pam that you finally arrived in Malaya and that they have had the nerve to push you upcountry to Kuala Lumpur. How are you? Remember me? Do send a line sometime to let me (and Mother too, she sends you her love) know how you are getting on in that ghastly country, and whether things are as bad as they say in the papers. We hear continually of murders and ambushes and I get very worried about you, wondering how you are keeping out there.

We have nearly been flooded out here; it has been raining incessantly for weeks. Apart from that, the news in the papers every day about the Far– and Middle East situations is hardly encouraging. Also, the new Government's austerity is rather gloomy, but I've no doubt it is all very necessary. I do wonder whether we shall ever be normal, in the sense our parents knew; life seems to be one continual struggle against artificially enormous odds, instead of a struggle against the problems of overpopulation and under-development and insufficient food supplies which could be solved if everyone were at peace.

Do you see a lot of Communism? How does life compare with Java? I cannot remember whether or not you said that your friend and his wife and young baby (her name was Stella, but can't remember his – Roy, wasn't it?) went to Australia or not; have you seen anything of them? Do you want anything sent out to you? Magazines or books? Do let me know.

Mother has just recovered from flu and I have recently had a cold, so I haven't been out a lot recently. I did go to see Orson Welles in *Othello*, which I thought was quite good. I haven't seen it done before, so I cannot compare, but I liked the production in the main. Most of my entertainment has been reading and through the wireless and TV. Awful! But I haven't had much time or energy to get out, and the weather has been so beastly, too.

I was to have gone for the night to Pam and Gillie's new flat on Friday of last week, but Mother was too coldy for me to be able to. However, I hope to see something of them this week or next and hear all their news [...]

What have you been reading recently? I have just finished the first volume of Somerset Maugham's short stories and was lucky enough to have it autographed by him, when he visited Casa Prada one evening for dinner. The stories are so well written and so interesting; a lot, of course, dealt with life in Malaya and in the Far East, and I particularly enjoyed them, and thought of you in somewhat similar surroundings to those he describes so vividly. I am now reading a somewhat lurid, but for the most part enthralling, story of corvettes in wartime, written by Monsarrat. He rather tends to dwell on the seamy side of sailors' lives, but apart from that I am enjoying it immensely; title – *The Cruel Sea*. Oh, I must tell you – the other day I was looking around the local market and picked up a beautiful edition of *Idylls of the King*, hand-stitched in full red morocco for... guess how much? One shilling! Isn't it amazing? Everyone thought it cost anything from 25/- (my brother's estimate) to £2 (Wyn's estimate). I was pleased [...] I have the feminine love of bargains, I suppose.

Incidentally, both Teddy and Wyn send their best wishes to you and would like to know how you are. They came up for tea and dinner a week or so ago.

I had a letter from Colette, my girlfriend in Chicago, the other day. She recently got married to her George, and the last letter was full of anticipation about an addition to the family! She is quite a gal.

I have just had this typewriter; it's new and quite good, but takes some getting used to. Any excuse!! I must go and eat now, or I shall die of hunger, but don't forget to write soon, or I shall be very upset. I have heard nothing since those two welcome cards from Italy, so please do write, darling. Forgive me typing this, won't you?

Lots of love from Connie

xxx

P.S. Would you like this snap? It's not awfully good.

23rd Nov. 1951

Dear Chris,

I got your letters of the 12th and 14th Nov. They both arrived together last Tuesday, and I am sorry I have not been able to write before; but as I once told you, I must be alone to write to you and the blessing of solitude is not very often granted to me.

Your letter of the 12th was the reply to my letter of 1st Nov. I apologise, Dear, if I hurt or annoyed you with that letter, and also if I have been rude. I thought it was a mild one (for me at least) compared to the stinkers I can write when I really let go. I neither intended to 'lay down the law' nor 'to lecture you' – I just said what I felt and thought (this probably makes it worse).

But let us not dwell too much on it, but draw the ensuing conclusion: our future is to be a partnership; right?! (You are probably quite right in judging my character there; I am just not cut out for the clinging ivy stuff, but like everybody always wish for the impossible; you know, like the girl with straight hair who wants it curly, and vice versa.) I shall try never to sound as if I wanted to lecture you again, nor lay down the law. As to your saying you don't remember having promised to go to Singapore only, did you think I made that up?? I am not in the habit of doing that. You say, 'It is not very wise or kind of you to hold such promises up against me.' Sorry, but here we differ emphatically: I see nothing wrong in reminding somebody of a promise – but I shall not do it again unless it is absolutely essential.

'There is something about Asia which has an attraction for me despite all more sober judgement,' you say. I quite believe that; I have felt the same about many places; unfortunately for the last 12 years of my life I could not indulge in the luxury of being fascinated, I had too many responsibilities to carry on my shoulders to be able to go against sober judgement.

The most sensible thing I can say about the whole controversy which has so unfortunately arisen is that it is much too early for both parties to say anything. You have not formed a very clear picture yet; there are lots of informations [sic] re. money, costs, housing you want to find out about and write me and had no chance to do it. You are rather harassed what with having to swot, etc. Also, just our luck, the situation over there is getting worse and I am naturally rather perturbed about that because your safety is very precious to me. So, let us bury the subject for a few months and see how things go. Oh, just one last word – if I seem not very much in favour of coming out there, and am reluctant and worry about this, that and the other, the main reason, or one of the main ones, is that (as I am used to do) I am thinking further into the future (the long-term policy) and am considering children which (I hope) you also want.

So please, let me apologise again for having hurt you. Please don't worry about writing only short letters; I quite understand and my main concern at the moment, as is yours, is that you pass your exam. If you want to do me a favour, please don't talk to anybody about me; Father Odette may be alright, but I fail to see why we have to have his help to get married.

I met your brother Jocelyn for a drink on Monday night – the drink stretched over the whole evening, we got quite merry and had a good time together. He is nice, and one can have lots of fun with him; I like him tremendously. By the way, he told me that you had written home hinting at some big surprise or other, and he asked me if I knew what it was. I said I had no idea, but perhaps you had married Connie on the sly, or even a Malayan girl, and were trying to break it to them gently. That finished that subject. His sidelights on the family are very illuminating – he is so very normal and has common sense. Am looking forward to seeing him again.

On Tuesday I took Sylvia out to dinner; she very kindly brought me a nice snapshot of yours, an old one taken in Torquay, which is so very much like you that I love it. She is a queer girl, rather shy, and it is difficult to get talking to her about a subject. Got a bit of a messed-up life and needs millions of knots untying inside. But she is very kind, I think, and also discreet and will keep her mouth shut; I think personally if she could get away from home and had a nice husband she would unfold like a blossom [...]

Jocelyn c.1951.

With a very loving kiss, and ever yours,
M.

Nov. 29/51

Dear Christopher,

I am afraid that I compare very unfavourably with the other members of the family in the matter of letter-writing, but as you know it is difficult to settle down to this job what with shopping and taking Marcus for walks.

I have been worrying a good deal about the conditions in Malaya, and think you have 'been sold a pup' about Singapore and Kuala Lumpur as a base. The London partner who agreed to your staying for six months in Singapore was well aware of the Branch's dislike of dictation from the Head Office and washed his hands over the overruling of his agreement.

In addition to my duties referred to above, I spend some time on 'Pools'[159] in the hope of a windfall which would enable me to have you back in England even if it meant refunding the expenses paid by

---

159 Football pools lottery.

the firm. It is a pipe dream, but it is a harmless one, and it does give a little excitement at the weekend.

I am hoping that this epistle may reach you on your birthday and I wish you many happy returns – should be in capitals.

The family will have given you all the news. Rosamund has not come home yet. She wrote last week saying that she might be coming on last Saturday but might go for another week to a camp near Nottingham, but as she did not turn up here, we assume that she adopted the alternative.

I do hope that Lyttleton's visit[160] may produce some organised plan to get rid of the appalling conditions in Malaya. It is very worrying to think of you in the midst of all the unrest.

The cricket season, alas, being over, the only people connected with it that I see now are old Taylor and his son; the others seem to go underground in the winter.

Many Happy Returns again. I am rather hoping that you may get fed up with this repetition of the conditions in Java which brought you back last year.

Your loving father

5th December 1951

Darling Chris,

No letter from you this Monday, which is quite unusual. It is Wednesday now, and I hope to God you are alright. Am enclosing a few more clippings to show you the reports you get. Can you wonder that I am alarmed when I hear you are buzzing about in your car all over the place, and don't even just stay in KL, which is bad enough? I live in a constant state of terror that the phone may ring, and your sister may tell me that they have been notified that something has happened to you.

I had such an odd day today, Darling, that I simply must talk about it now or bust; and of course, I must talk to you. First of all, I got myself nearly arrested; at about one o'clock I decided to go

---

160 Oliver Lyttleton was British Secretary of State for the Colonies from 1951 to 1954.

to lunch in my little Fleet Street caffee [sic], and as usual walked along in thought. All over sudden [sic], I looked up and saw, coming towards me on the pavement, two tall men, fully dressed in Nazi Party Uniform, with the traditional armbands displaying the swastika! I saw just that, and then the most extraordinary thing happened to me. My brain just stopped to function rationally; I just saw those two men – and I saw red. By that time, they were quite near, only a foot or so away, and without thinking I took one terrific leap towards them with my right arm raised, backhand fashion, to hit them both in the face. A minute fraction of a second before I actually hit, I saw over their shoulders a man holding a large placard with the letters 'No weapons for Nazis.' So, I just stood stock-still, like Lot's wife, with my arm raised, and they stood staring at me, thinking I was quite demented. Only then did I realise that there was a large crowd assembled round us and that next to me was a policeman. He seemed to enjoy our playing statues and asked what it was all about. I apologised and explained that I had thought for one minute that the two chaps were the genuine article and that I was getting ready to hit them good and hard. It seemed to amuse the policeman no end because the men were each about 6 ft. 2" tall – the whole thing was like a Pekinese attacking two bulldogs. Anyway, he said he was glad I had not done it, because he would have had to ask me all sorts of questions, but he booked the two chaps. Apparently the whole thing was a Communist demonstration against rearming of Germany. Still – it upset me no end; I did not know that I still, after all those years, had that blinding, furious hatred in me against anything that smacked of Nazis, and believe me, if I had had a weapon I would have killed. As it was, nothing had happened, but I just went away, white as a sheet and shaking like a leaf.

The second thing was much more amusing: you probably don't know my passion for tidiness, clearing up, and throwing things out. It is very well developed, I assure you. For years now I have been doing the football pools, and on Sunday I usually check whether I have won anything. I never do. Last Sunday I checked again (I do the pool where you have to guess 8 draws) and found the first one correct, the next two wrong, and threw the copy of the results out. Tonight, when I came home, I found an envelope from Liverpool, and when I opened it found about £3 in it: I had won a 4ᵗʰ Dividend and never knew because I had not checked any further. I certainly was surprised!

By the by, I met Jocelyn last night, and we had a little pub-crawl together. We do get on well, you know, and have great fun in each other's company and think we will become real friends. I find much more contact with him than with Sylvia, by the way, though she is a woman, and you told her.

At the moment, I have a blinding headache – so please forgive me if I end rather suddenly and continue the letter tomorrow. Since yesterday I have the Auditors in, which rather increases my work, and also, I have some beastly estimates, costings etc. to do – all figures, and the light on my desk is so bad that if you put it too near it blinds, and if you push it back a bit you sit in a semi-gloom. Hence the headache. Anyway, the bunch of Auditors I got this year (or rather the one and his assistant) are pure paradise compared to what I had last year. That chap (let's call him Mr. F.) nearly drove me to suicide. Some of the gems of his auditing only came to light now, and as he has left the firm, I cannot even blow him up. I simply must tell you some of his neatest tricks (you of all people will be able to appreciate it). He simply insisted on transferring some stuff bought from 'works petty cash' to 'plant'; and by the time he got round to that I was so exhausted arguing that I simply did not pay any attention. Now when I had more time I fished out the vouchers he had referred to and to my great delight found the following: one voucher for £6.1.– contained about 10 items or more, one of which (the biggest) was £1.3.– for some radio spares (our 'music while you work' radio at the factory), but it also contained items like 10d for screws, 3/– for a plastic soap-dish and, to crown it all, 4/6d for a holder of toilet paper. All that is now in 'plant'!! Also, he put the concrete base for a machine into 'furniture', together with 6 cups and saucers, and lamp-bulbs. God bless his socks, he certainly was in the wrong profession and I always knew he was an ass, but he has now gone over to commercial and there, unless he pulls up his socks, I can promise him some shocks. Anyways, the chaps this year are a pleasure to work with. And it is not as if my books were difficult to audit; they are kept scrupulously correct – no fiddles, obvious or otherwise – and when the Auditors come in I provide them with trial balance, complete balance sheet, list of reserves, provisions etc. and a complete list of snags peculiar to our business. The chap today said he wished all his audits were made as easy and as pleasant as mine.

My head is so bad now, darling, I must finish. So, *au revoir* until tomorrow, and I love you so very much, dearest, and I am so worried.

M.

29th Dec. 1951

Darling Chris,

Such a lovely surprise: Felice brought me three letters last night, dated 18th, 20th and 21st inst. Of course, Christmastime the mail usually goes haywire, and especially in London they seem to be unable to cope.

Saturday afternoon:– tonight I am going to see a play, *The Love of Four Colonels*. Felice bought me a ticket as an Xmas present, and I am very much looking forward to it. Did I tell you what she bought me as a main present? A magnificent book about Fra Angelico (Early Ital. Ren. Painter) with whom I fell in love in Florence; it is beautifully illustrated, the reproductions being both good and tastefully coloured. I go to bed with that book every night. Now you want to know about Xmas. When I last wrote to you, I was just about to go out to Ch.'s. I got there about 7 p.m., we had a meal, we sat and watched television, and then we went to bed: anything more unlike Xmas Eve I could not imagine, especially as they were both in a bad mood. I took my sleeping pills and slept like the dead. That was the worst of Xmas over; in the morning on the 25th we came down and got our presents. It was a truly magnificent array of articles that we all gave each other; we could have opened a store with the stuff. I got a marvellous H.M.V. radiogram from Ch. and Peg; I always wanted one, but they cost about £60 – some present, *hein*? So, don't you buy one. And then – Darling, I don't think I have ever been as bored in all my life as I was those two days. I don't know why but it was almost unbearable – the same things being told me again and again, stale, bare and unprofitable (or am I quoting wrong?). I don't want to be beastly, and they are so nice and generous, but all I wished for was at least to be alone and have peace.

Well, time dragged on and on the 26th at about 5 p.m. I said I must get home pronto – and did. Oh, what a haven my quiet flat was; I simply wallowed in the pleasure of being alone and not to have to talk or listen. Which makes me wonder if I am not getting a bit peculiar and am still 'fit for human consumption', meaning for a married life together. I wonder if you have ever considered that side of marriage:– even if there is utmost harmony, it is fatal to try and make either of the partners submerge his personality and become a mere echo or foil. It is equally disastrous to abandon one's privacy completely and not to grant each other the privilege of being alone when they feel like it. All this belongs to the chapter that deals with the subject 'How never to get bored with the other partner, and how to retain one's news-value.' (Separate bedrooms belong to that chapter.) It is amazing how very few people regard marriage as an art, something to be studied, worked out etc. When you think of the care that is taken in drawing up articles of association, partnership documents, the thought and study that one devotes to friendships, illicit relationships etc. Yet marriage, the most tricky combine of them all, because it lasts a lifetime (one hopes), is accomplished by having a little set of rules babbled at one: "Have and hold, love and cherish, etc." It just is not good enough. A woman (no, not I, Dearest) will take hours of trouble, pain and thought to concoct a good meal, but she will not devote much time and thought on how to make her marriage a real go – they are legally bound, there is no escape, and somehow it will go on. (You will now say I should not preach water and drink wine, but that is not so. Believe me, I have thought about it a lot, and my failure is not due to not taking care, but simply to general incompatibility and not being suited.) Have you ever watched a man at any game? He will take no end of trouble to become good at it; the same has to be done with married life. Love and mutual trust and respect are the basis – then it is up to the two people to build the superstructure that makes for a happy relationship; and believe me, it takes more tact, patience, forethought and adaptability than any other thing in the world. That's why there are so very few 'happy marriages'. People would always rather bother about being good at their professions, games, appearance etc. than at 'marriage'.

Now I do run on about that subject. But since I have known you it has become very important to me; and I am thinking about it seriously because carelessness may make or break two lives: yours and mine. Now I shall stop sermonising, and for a change tell you how very much I love you, Dearest, mucher and mucher.

Now to your letters:– Thanks for the financial statement. One thing is clear – salaries are much higher than here, but so is the cost of living, if not higher, and the question of whether one can save anything is very debatable. I personally should say no! Not if one wants to live somewhat comfortably; income tax is not as bad as here, that's one thing. Unless one can cut oneself in on a good thing out there, I should say it's not much of a financial boon. You yourself say you have lived fairly economically, and I think you have, but you can hardly make ends meet. (See what a good thing it is that we did not throw caution to the winds and I did not come out. By now we would be both thoroughly miserable; you because you cannot give me what I could provide for myself, or more, and I because I should just hate having to count the pennies after all those years of independence.) Am awaiting further data from Singapore, esp. re. housing, servants, prospects etc.

Re the 'Nazi incident'. You ask what would have happened if they had been genuine. I should probably have got killed – but so what? If your convictions are not worthwhile fighting and dying for, what is?

Oh, and a funny thing happened: I won the Pools for the second time in two weeks. Again 4th Division; this time it was £2. God, if I only could win first, it would solve all our problems.

Now, don't be jealous of Jocelyn. He is not at all like you, except for the general family traits that one always finds, certain turns of phrase etc. He is much more independent and practical than you are, much lighter and less burdened with problems, livelier, and definitely has no religious bug. We get on marvellously – but I think that although we click as good friends, as a couple we would be no good: too similar. Yes, he told me about his 'Oxford Pilgrimages'. Re.

Sylvia, she told me about that bloke John; what she needs is a pep-injection.

I like your telling me about what you do with yourself in your spare time, and about your various friends and acquaintances; seems like a rather mixed but interesting crowd. Re. your being safe out there: well, I hope sincerely that it is as you say. I would much prefer you to be safe and me to have to face troubles – I think I could meet them more ruthlessly than you could. As to raising Cain if anything happened to you – in spite of the awful lot of jungle and the few bandits I should manage to create merry hell. (Thanks for telling me about that book; I shall try to get it.)

Dearest, I am sorry if I worried you with my unhappy letter. But I did warn you that there were a lot of personalities in my make-up and that is just one of them. Of course, I can be influenced by my surroundings, nature and people, everybody can; there are only the very rare few who manage to rise above that – usually philosophers and saints: I am neither. Don't bother about my being psychic – I don't do it every day, and in all my life I have been like that about 10 times, but when it hits me it's bad because it's usually true. So, you are going to be the morose and difficult partner? You could not be more mistaken – I shall have my share of it too. Hope you get back alive from the Penang flight, but I still cannot get rid of that foreboding of something bad to come – sorry, darling.

Thank you so much, Dearest, for saying you will think of me all through Xmas and the New Year's Eve. I shall too. Ch. is having a Huge N.Y. party – evening dress, orchestra and all the trimmings. No doubt I shall look very gorgeous in my evening dress and be bored stiff. Still, there is hoping that something might amuse me yet, although it is a faint hope. Darling, I shall not mind if you beat me, or commit adultery, but if you bore me, I shall certainly run away; I shall run like a rabbit, married or no.

At the moment I have another bit of trouble to contend with: for weeks now, my eyes have been hurting; a sort of burning sensation. I hope it is only an inflammation and nothing else. I simply have not had time to go to a doctor. I wear dark glasses and try not to read too much but in my profession that is rather difficult. No doubt the trouble is caused by the lousy light I have on my desk; it is a desk lamp giving a strong, concentrated pool of light which is bad for figures, and if I type I am in a sort of half-glare, half-gloom. All in all, it is most unpleasant, and also it hurts. I know you are going to say that I am too careless of my health etc., etc. But the day has only got 24 hours, and I have only one pair of hands, and one pair of feet, and with all the things I have to do and manage, it is just not enough equipment. (Before I forget, please, Darling, tell me when to start writing to Singapore instead of to KL, and is it to the old address: Hongkong Bank Chambers?)

You and I agreed that we should always tell each other everything, good or bad. May I? Darling, the thing that is worrying me most, more than anything else and almost constantly, is that we don't know each other at all. And (forgive me for saying so) I always have the feeling (I wish to God I could rid myself of it) that I am the 'Senior Partner' in this combine; the one who looks at things soberly and seriously, weighs the consequences, judges the risks and has taken it upon his shoulders to steer a safe course for all. And, again and again, the worrying thought comes into my head and causes me sleepless nights: we don't know each other at all, we just are madly in love (I am; hope you are). I try to classify my feelings and there is for you love, I respect your integrity, I know you are honest, I know I can trust you. Integrity, honesty, trustworthiness: there are your sterling qualities, and I know you have them. But I still don't know you at all: these qualities may constitute the basic colours in the kaleidoscope of your make-up, but there are millions of others that I am not aware of. Are you moody, or even-tempered? Are you sanguinic, choleric, pessimistic, optimistic, or all of it, or part of it? How you react to things I don't know; all I do know is that you are stubborn, otherwise you would not have gone out East and made things more difficult than they are already. Are you capable of dealing with life, are you sure or unsure, can you handle difficult situations when they arise? I could go on like this for the next 1,000 pages. Do you understand what I mean? And all that I have written above relating to you goes for me too. You know damn-all about me, to put it bluntly. You know my most striking qualities, and certain incidents from my life that I told you may give you a vague indication of my character, but that is all.

Are you very cross with me for writing the above para.? I sincerely hope not, I could not bear it if you were, because I am relating to you my worries in utmost sincerity so that we can talk them over, and thereby, I hope, dispel them. Darling, I want life with you more than anything in the world, but I know that if I made a mistake, I would cut my throat with the greatest of ease – I don't know whether you have noticed it, but I set little value on my life; I know I have touched on this subject in many of my letters, but you have never discussed it in yours. It would all be so easy if you were here, and we could get to know each other; because those mad two weeks, crammed full of emotions and having a rather dreamlike quality, gave neither of us an inkling of what we would be like in ordinary everyday life. They showed us both at our best and at our worst. As I believe I said before in one letter – if you were here, I should ask you to live with me for 3 months, to find out how we fitted in with each other (and I am leaving all sexual relationships out of this trial period, so don't be shocked). Are you tidy, or the reverse? Are you fastidious or easy-going; have you got a strong aesthetical sense or not; are you practical or the opposite? I just don't know. Please tell me more about yourself and ask any questions you wish to ask me, and I promise I shall reply honestly. (*Parbleu*, I am writing as if I were a middle-aged sensible man contemplating marriage with a *jeune fille* and being sensible about it. I wish I could be sure that our positions are the reverse.) Don't be cross, please, please. But I do so want our love to be one with our eyes open, adult and enduring.

Give you one instance: you say you will pray to God for our happiness. I say: I shall do my damnedest to make it work, go to no end of trouble, and whilst I am slogging away, take time out to wipe the sweat off my face and on that occasion say, "Dear God, I am sweating my guts out to achieve something; please do your darndest to help when you see how I do my bit."

Or another one: you keep on writing what fun we could have out there together, and I could not agree more. I keep on thinking, *A few years of fun, but where is the solid basis for the future and the children?* I love fun as much as you do but, having carried the burden of responsibility for others for a long time, I do not seem to be able to dismiss it from my thoughts. (I wish I could.)

There is one good thing about it:– we are so diametrically different that once we have got together on a solid basis, we shall be a formidable team. One fear I have (apart from my phobia about your drinking) is that I shall supply all the drive and strength in the team – which has already proved fatal once in my married life. I don't know whether I told you much about it, but here you have a classical example of a man with good qualities, passive rather than active, enduring rather than doing, and the woman slowly supplying all the strength, stability, drive and practical initiative. The result – a feeling of pity, mixed with impatience, from the stronger partner; a recognition of the good qualities of the other, tinged with contempt. True, as you once said, I am just not cut out for the clinging ivy stuff, but the partner can be equal. (For God's sake, do I sound as hard and as vain about my achievements and qualities as I think I do? That would be dreadful – if ever I do, just remind me that my bad qualities far outweigh my good ones. The reverse is true of you, I am sure. Let's swap, shall we?)

Darling, I ought to be shot. I go on and on about things and if I am not careful, I shall bore you, and that would be the end. I love you so, and I do need your reassurances in so many things, and I cannot have them here and now. Please, Darling, wish for a magic carpet and be here suddenly, and within 4 weeks all the loads that weigh so heavily on me will be taken off my shoulders. You see, one thing I cannot do is pray and shift them onto God's shoulders and let him get on with them; I have to work out my own salvation for better or worse. (And knowing myself, if I did not have any loads on my shoulders I should go out and look for some.)

Darling Chris, I must finish now; I have been writing for hours. And there is one thing I dread more than anything else; that is, your being cross with me – and yet something in me forbids me to destroy this letter and write another one in its place. Please don't be cross, but try to understand and help. I am not unhappy, Darling, only sometimes, *et ça passe*, and I know you love me and that makes me happy.

Am not alone anymore and must close. I love you.

Ever yours,
M.

1952

Theresa

As confidential secretary to the senior partner, I had access to the details of all the assistants recruited in the London office. One person who came to my knowledge was Geoffrey Christopher Tyrwhitt Repton, who was taking his finals as a certified accountant. London recruited him for six months and then sent him out to Singapore to work, as the Singapore office was very short of assistants. Christopher had to do his final exams in Singapore, and he also took his chartered secretary examination. So, he had two qualifications – chartered secretary and certified accountant.

Christopher finally arrived at the Singapore office at the end of 1950, but as the Kuala Lumpur office needed somebody urgently, he was sent there for a few months. But he did not like it there, and asked to be stationed in Singapore, according to the terms of his contract. And so he was. He came to the Singapore office at the beginning of 1952, when I first met him. In the early years of our working life, we didn't see each other socially, but my boss allowed him to give me some secretarial work. That was quite a privilege for him because the other partners were not allowed to give me any work.

Mary and I used to notice him having lunch all on his own in G. H. Café. Christopher always sat at the same table, under the clock, having a sandwich. One day we invited him to join us, but he declined.

20th January 1952

Darling Chris,

Quite unusual – there was not a single letter from you this week. That has never happened before. You must either be terribly busy (even in the evenings), or ill, or the mail has gone haywire. Do you realise, I have not had a nice, substantial letter from you since before Xmas? Then it was your trip to Penang, then your return, then your impending departure etc., etc. I really wish you would write; that is our only way of keeping in touch, you know, and is rather important. Letters are like echoes in a way; unless they are descriptive, like mine from Italy, or yours from your journey, they tend to become monologues, and as such begin to seem futile. For a while, one can talk without getting that answering echo, but then one begins to feel so foolish somehow. I mean the type of letters we have been writing to each other: of thoughts, reflections, ideas, feelings, problems. Straightforward descriptive ones, of course, one can write into the void ad lib.

There is just nothing to tell about my everyday life. Seen the latest Noël Coward show; great fun, not very deep, but very, very amusing. A typical N. Coward. Am now planning to go and see John Mills in *Figure of Fun*, and some of the classics at the Old Vic. I have not seen many of Shakespeare's plays, which is a sad lack in education. (I agree, many English people are not well up in the German and French classics, but that is no reason why I should be as ignorant as they are.) Apart from going to shows, I eat, I sleep (not too well) and I work.

At present it is beastly cold in England, but, of course, no snow. All the inconveniences of winter with none of its amenities and joys. Thank God, I have a centrally heated flat; I would not miss that for the world. When I don't eat, sleep or work, I sometimes wonder where our magic has gone; it seems to retreat further and further. Felice has been ill again, and I spent the afternoon and evening with her yesterday. When the postman came at 4 p.m. (last delivery) and there was no letter for me, I got such a funny empty feeling, as if a door closes, and you are alone in an empty room. Don't forget, you have changed your surroundings by going away; I have stayed behind, I move in the same surroundings as I did before our magic ten days, the same for the past eight years, and it sometimes begins to feel as if I had dreamt the whole thing, especially if there is no letter from you to reassure me. Oh, enough of that. You will write when you feel like it, and if you don't – well, there is nothing I can do by talking about that.

Things seem to have quietened down in Malaya just now; wonder if they will flare up again when the new chap goes there as Governor or whatnot. So that things don't seem too rosy, Egypt is getting into a frightful mess. Oh well, there is no limit to human stupidity and the sooner they blow this earth up for good the better. History is constantly repeating itself, and it is getting very boring for the bystander.

What do you do with yourself in your free time these days? Since you have gone to Singapore I know less than ever about your surroundings, life, friends, lodgings, work, recreation etc. and you are becoming like a shadow moving in even shadowier (is there such a word?) realms.

Of course I love you, darling, and you don't know how my heart aches to recapture what there was, oh, so long ago. I remember some things so very clearly: your worried frown, your slow smile, your hands, the way you held me sometimes; your voice saying, "Don't go away." 8,000 miles are very far, aren't they? How different it would all have been had you been here. (Did you see the film *La Ronde*? That melody has been haunting me for days; the going round and round and round in circles, just not knowing, being at the mercy of the postal system.)

I must finish now, Darling, and go to Felice, who is still ill in bed. Perhaps there will be a letter from you tomorrow, and I will then make a supreme effort to write you on Monday or Tuesday. I just want to post this so that you know I have not cut my throat yet, although I must say sometimes the idea seems appealing.

I love you so much, Dearest, too much. Goodnight, Chris, my one and only.

M.

10th Feb. 52

Darling Chris,

Thank you for your letter of the 31st Jan. In it you refer to your 'last letter'; please let me know if that is the one written on the 4th Jan. describing your trip to Singapore. That was the last one I got from you. If you refer to a later one, it must have got lost in the post. This is my first letter since the one posted 3 weeks ago; I simply did not dare to write as, for all I knew, you might have been dead. Fortunately, you are not.

Of course, I forgive you for not writing; I can forgive anything, we all can. But I do not understand – in terms of psychology I can comprehend your silence, but I cannot understand it with my heart. But – as I said again and again – I do not know you at all. I do not know what your reactions might be to any given circumstances. I am sorry you feel unhappy and uncertain – there is very little I can do for you at the moment. I am carrying the same load as you do – with quite a bit added; but that is irrelevant. There is one thing I can say to make things easier for you – if at any time you feel it was all a mistake, if your feelings change, or if you think it is too much for you to stand, all the obstacles, difficulties etc., please tell me so quite frankly. I could stand it – better than being in doubt and uncertainty all the time. I can look the devil in the face if necessary – but I cannot bear uncertainty.

I won't write much today, my dear; this is just a sign of life, and to say I am not cross; who am I to condemn any human weakness, when I have so many myself? Your letter has made me realise how old I am – older than my years by far. It also made me feel a bit lonely. But don't worry about me – I have the unfailing remedy of work which always sees me through any crisis; 24 hours of it, if necessary; bodily and mental work to tire me out until I drop: it never fails.

Without wishing to sound sententious in any way – here is another bit of advice that might help you. When you are really down in spirit, when even work won't help you, look around you and concentrate on other people's troubles – soon your own will appear mere molehills compared with the mountains others have to bear. After all, if you are only troubled about our future – that is a worry time will help to clarify. There is only one finality – that is death. There is no appeal against that. I don't think you can be in as bad a state as I was when Mummy died and my whole world seemed to collapse. Then my remedies were work, as I said before, and going round looking at other people's troubles and trying to help them. I went to homes where lonely old people lived, brought them some little things, read to them, listened to them: and like a miracle, out of my own misery I created happiness. And out of the knowledge that I could still give, my misery decreased. You probably pray for help. I could never do that properly, but I kept remembering that something like 'Give and it shall be returned to you' or something amounting to that had been said, and by doing so, found out it worked. One can run round and round in one's unhappy thoughts like a squirrel in a cage, and not see a way out. Then when one has got outside oneself, and worried awhile about others, it often happens that a solution presents itself. When I am happy, I am rather inclined to draw that cloak of happiness around myself and hug myself in it and forget about others. When I am unhappy, as I was with your prolonged silence, I open my eyes and see what trouble there is in other lives, and then try to do something about it. See, your silence has done other people a lot of good:– I found living accommodation for a girl I know, got another one a job, sent a lot of stuff to people on the Continent who have no clothes and nothing to eat – and the reward comes back in the shape of a letter saying that you are neither ill nor dead, nor has anything dreadful happened to you.

No doubt all I have been saying is dreadfully commonplace, but that does not make it less true.

I am very much looking forward to your next letter and hope you will feel better by the time this reaches you. Please don't send any more cables to the office as Ch. is returning from U.S.A. and opens everything that comes, irrespective for whom.

At the moment don't worry about me, my Dear; I shall manage as I have always done; one can, if one has to. Bless you, my darling, I wish I could help you more. I am not cross, I love you, and I shall always try to understand you.

Much love,
Your M.

4th May 1952

Darling Chris,

I presume that when I write this letter, you will already be in possession of the one I wrote last week; and as I promised to write every week, I thought I'd drop you a line today.

This is one of the dreary weekends this climate is capable of: grey skies, heavy, moist air, and a continuous drizzle that maybe does the soil and plants a lot of good – but I am no plant. I had arranged to play tennis today and also yesterday, and that's off. Actually, I don't mind so much; I can always find something to do – a book to read, radio to listen to, things to sew… any amount of housework to do. For instance – I like doing things with my hands, so I tried them on a bit of carpentry today, such as putting new hinges on doors, fixing a Yale lock etc. I find manual work is very soothing, although it is playing havoc with my fingernails and hands. By the way, for the last week, ever since I wrote to you, as a matter of fact, I have felt much, much better. Whether it was the fact that I wrote again as I used to, or that I have the feeling things are straightening out for us, and the worst is over, I don't know – but for the last two nights I managed to sleep without pills – not much, but nevertheless I did. Only somebody who has been through the sleeping-pill mill himself knows what a victory that is – equal to D-Day at least. I don't know how long it will last, I don't know how long it will last, but at the moment I am thankful for small mercies.

And how are you, my Dear? Stewing in the heat? I still remember how I used to like our hot summers at home – but then they were dry and hot and pleasant; nothing like the killing steam heat that I experienced in Washington in summer, and that made me feel like a piece of laundry being put through the boiler. No wonder that it ruins all women's complexions in no time flat; whatever I have against this climate here, at least it is good for the skin – mine is still like a baby's, in spite of all my drinking (in the past) and the late nights. Talking of late nights, there is going to be a big christening party next Saturday – sort of dinner dance and a grand affair; I had a wonderful dress made and wish you could see it. It's in champagne-coloured silk-chiffon, slim and long with a little train, very flowing, and a low front, but not too low, and makes me look like a million dollars (wish I had them). You would be terrible proud of me, or so I hope (vanity of women, *hein*?).

I am so much looking forward to your letter in reply to mine last week. Hope it comes next week; it should with the mail taking about 5 days, that is, if you have replied immediately as I asked you to. I do so hope you will.

I have just finished having our offices redecorated, and they look wonderful; makes one work much better. Also, as my eyes still trouble me, I won the battle for better lighting, and hope that will help. And I am duly thankful that I finished our half-year balance sheet – that is usually a nightmare. Not because it is difficult, it's just that I never get any peace to work on it, and I cannot do figures with bedlam going on all around me. One of the nicest French remarks is '*Ça passe*', and it honestly covers about everything; when I get thoroughly fed up, I say it, and it usually proves to be right.

How is the old cricket going? And do you know, I was firmly convinced I told you how pleased I was about your passing the old exam, and if I just thought I had told you and did not put that thought on paper, forgive me – just one of those silly lapses; I really was glad, after all, if you have to be in that lousy profession, you might as well have a few letters after your name. Are you going in for anything else now?

I don't think, somehow, I shall be alone much longer to write in peace. So here is all my love, dearest, and even if the letters are not all very long, at least we are writing again regularly, or at least I am, and thinking about you quite a lot, my Darling, believe me. So here is so much love.

As ever,
M.

26th May 1952

Darling Chris,

This was a wonderful week for me: two letters from you, dated 12th and 20th May; the one of the 12th came delayed, I think. Yesterday was really my day for writing to you, but for once I took your advice and spent the day in the fresh air, instead of sitting at home, and therefore I have to write from the office today – which is alright, because at the moment everybody is out.

Please, Darling, don't worry; I honestly and truly feel so much better now, that the bad spell I had seems like a dream, and unless something happens to upset me very much, I don't think I will have to go through that again. I am trying to be out as much as possible, don't take sleeping pills, and have stopped drinking altogether. Not that I drank much, but I even cancelled the odd beer and cocktail.

Saturday, I spent 3 hours gardening – at Mother's grave. Funny how even a little plot like that, 3' x 6', can take up time; there is weeding to be done, old flowers to be tied up, new ones planted... it was a glorious hot day, and there I slogged away amongst the stillness of hundreds of graves, feeling very peaceful, and hearing nothing but the railways going by, and surprisingly, a cuckoo calling loud and clear. Then yesterday I spent the whole day with Peggy, Charles & the baby. He is a Darling, my little Peter; not quite 2 months old and looks as if he were 6 months at least. 5 p.m. to 6 p.m. is his playtime, and I had him all to myself yesterday – of course, he cannot understand a word one says but he makes funny crowing noises, until he gets hungry and then he yells.

Life should be a bit easier now; the 'invasion' of American visitors has stopped, and we are more or less back to normal, much to everyone's relief. That continuous entertaining gets me down: I find it a real strain to have to be amusing, polite, entertaining and clever all the time, without a break, and although not drinking makes the morning after less ghastly, the lack of sleep is not too good.

Thank you for telling me about your 'inmates'. At least I can imagine a bit the people you spend part of your time with; the one who plays the piano sounds nice, according to your description. Chris, Dearest, I don't get that bit you write about difficulties re. getting your admission as A.C.I.S.[161] Once you pass the exams, I thought that this was automatic. Now you say that you have to get signatures and what have you – do explain. Also, if and when you feel like it, tell me about the work you do – I presume it is not too hush-hush, and I am genuinely interested, first of all because it concerns you, and secondly it is a bit in my line now, I presume. Also, what do you do in your spare time? Cricket, squash (I never played that game, too energetic for my liking), drinking – what else? Are there dances, do you play cards, take rides in the car (how is it running, by the way?)? I want to be able to visualise your life as far as possible from that distance.

The last few weeks have been glorious here – sunshine and soft winds – England at its best in May. How I long for a car to get out in the country early in the morning, laze about meadows, let the sun shine all over my body, and bathe. But even if I had a car it would not do me much good, as I am scared to drive it, as you know. The one thing I hate about London is the air – it stinks, to put it politely. Whereas just now the grass smells beautiful, and so do the trees. I

---

161 Associate of the Institute of Chartered Secretaries & Administrators.

don't feel much like working either just now, with the sun pouring in through the window, but this is the end of the month, and not a hope in hell to get out earlier. (Sorry, Darling, I am swearing again – yes, I am. All my good intentions have gone by the board; also, I have not been to church since I came back from Italy; I just don't feel like it. Very naughty – but you do it for the two of us, I hope.)

By the way, did I tell you in one of my last letters that I had been assaulted with felonious or immoral intent – I never asked which? If I have not, let me know; it was rather funny, only not at the time, then I was just plain mad. When you read the newspapers nowadays, London is beginning to run a very close second to Chicago: what with mail robberies, murders, thefts big and small, burglaries, shootings, etc. I think I shall have to get myself a gun for self-protection – as this is not so simple to come by, I will settle for a knuckleduster.

Darling, I miss you so much – as much as you miss me, I hope. And I do love you, Dearest, and now that we are writing again, this makes me feel happy and confident. Do keep on loving me, please, as I do [you]. I shall have to get back to work now, but after talking to you for two pages, life seems much brighter.

Bless you, Dear Heart, I love you as ever.

Yours,
M.

50 Peel Avenue

Penang

18th June 1952

My dear Chris,

Many, many thanks for your letter and offer to come up here – it is very sweet of you, but there really is little anyone can do except pray that everything will be alright in the end. As you can imagine, it has been a terribly worrying time for us both, and under the circumstances I feel sure you will forgive me for not having written before in reply to your very kind letter. We both appreciated it no end and have always known that in you we have a real friend who we can trust and rely on in the most difficult circumstances.

As you may have heard from Pim,[162] Christopher and I are flying home, leaving Singapore on Saturday 21st at 9. As far as I know, I'm coming down to Singapore on the 4.15 plane on Friday. I'm still trying to get the morning plane – but so far have had no luck. At all events, I hope to see you then. I shall be spending the night at Raffles. Would you like to be an angel and make sure they have a cot organised for Christopher – I'd be awfully grateful. I feel very mean leaving Roy just at this time, but I do think there is little or nothing I can do, and he assures me he will be much happier knowing that I am at home with my family.

Will tell you all the news when I see you on Friday. I am so unhappy leaving Roy, but I know it's the only sensible thing to do. Do drop him a line c/o H. & S. Bank, Penang – he'd love to hear from you, I know. He's had a very dirty deal from his firm[163] but I am sure they will pay doubly for their twisting and crookedness – they can, unfortunately, never repay us for the damage they have done to us personally and as a family. But when it is all over, we shall try to forget.

Thanks again for your kindness and thoughtfulness so much appreciated at this time.

Our love,
Stella

Harper, Gilfillan & Co. Ltd.
Hongkong Bank Chambers
Penang
25th June 1952

C. Repton, Esq.
c/o Turquand Youngs & Co.
P.O. Box 384
Singapore

---

162 Pim Drooglever, a mutual friend of Chris and the Coulson-Gilmers.
163 According to press reports, Roy was accused of committing breach of trust amid allegations of goods being smuggled into Siam while he was manager of the Penang branch of his company. He denied all charges.

Dear Mr. Repton,

Many thanks for your letter of 15th June, which arrived in Penang on Saturday 21st June, the day after Stella left for Singapore. I am returning your note to her as well as the envelope, from which you will see that, although your letter is dated 15th June, it bears the post-mark of the 20th June in Singapore, and it would, therefore, seem that possibly your office *tambi* or post clerk mislaid the letter and posted it later. Perhaps Pim Drooglever told you that Stella was in Singapore on Friday night, and therefore, I hope that you managed to contact her […]

With kind regards,
Yours sincerely,
W. H. C. Bailey

British Embassy
Djakarta
25/6

Dear Chris,

It was nice of you to write. Thank you enormously for your letter which I received this morning.

I can't very well say I have 'settled down' in Djakarta as yet. My first week here I spent with Mr. & Mrs. Leland (he is in Maclaine, Watson), and then for 2 weeks I slept in our Military Attaché's flat and took meals with an Embassy couple who have the top half of the house. I'm now completely upstairs until a tiny pavilion becomes vacant in a fortnight's time and then I shall move into it with another girl from our Embassy. How long we shall be allowed to remain there is on the laps of the Gods! I had no idea accommodation was so difficult.

We have just had the Lebaran[164] holidays and have been completely without servants for four days. I hate washing up even in England but in this flat, in this heat, with no running water (the electric pump is broken and will take weeks to mend) it is too ghastly

---

164 Javanese name for the Muslim Eid al-Fitr; a holiday with feasting to celebrate the end of the Ramadan fast.

for words. But we have struggled on, and the floors have not only been swept but given their bi-weekly wash with Dettol. We didn't attempt the laundry, and the electricity ration wouldn't permit an electric iron to be used and these fearful charcoal ones fill me with terror. But you must know all these difficulties…

Lots of people who were planning to go to Bogor and Bandung for the weekend cancelled their trips, as hordes of police and soldiers went there on a much-publicised cleaning-up operation of the bandits there. So far, the only casualties that have been announced were the occupants of a military truck which crashed into a lorry and caught fire when the ammunition exploded. So far as I can see, one is in more danger from the forces of law and order than from the bandits. The military all look thoroughly trigger-happy! Actually though, I'm told the security position is just about the same.

I'm enjoying Djakarta so far, apart from the frustration and difficulties. Compared with non-diplomatic people we are quite well off as far as most things are concerned. We have supplies sent over from Singapore and are exempt from the ridiculous regulations, such as not using the telephone between 8 a.m. and 4. But the Indonesians themselves are the least likeable of any race I have yet met. One can hardly blame them, of course, considering that the Dutch did nothing to make them at all conscious of the duties of citizenship. But the Djakarta natives are a set of rogues. I'm told, though, that in the country they are different.

No, I haven't yet been to Bandung. I gravitate between the office, this flat, and the houses where I'm invited for parties. I'm becoming a member of the Box and went to the St. George's Dance there last Saturday.

I've not yet met any of the people whose names you gave me, as they all seem to be away. I do hope to go up to Bandung soon and shall look forward to meeting the Knights. Both the Misses Kermode I understand have left. One married a B.A.T. man and has gone with him to Kenya; the other married a doctor in England. The Embassy seem a very nice lot of people, but my goodness, we have to work hard!

I think I shall like Java, especially if I can get out into the country and see it. If ever you think of coming here for leave, be sure to let me know well in advance. And thank you again for all you did for me in Singapore. You gave me such a nice time that I hated leaving.

Do write again and give me your news. I shall probably take you up on your offer to send things from Singapore!

Best wishes,
Margaret

Hogan, Adams & Allan
Advocates & Solicitors
4 A. & B. Logan's Building
P.O. Box 263
Penang
Federation of Malaya
1st July 1952

G. C. Repton, Esq.
c/o M/s. Turquand Youngs & Co.
P.O. Box 384
Singapore

Dear Mr. Repton,

I am in receipt of your letter of the 20th June.

Mr. Goh is the solicitor, and I am counsel in the case, so that ordinarily all communications would be addressed to him.

It may be possible to get the bail reduced to $50,000 or possibly less depending upon the status of the bailers. A joint bond would be accepted, and each person would be bound in the sum acceptable to the Court and will be responsible for the appearance of the accused at his trial up to the making of the decision by the Judge. If the accused fails to appear then the sureties are liable to pay to the Court the sum in which they are bound. It is necessary for each surety to satisfy the Court as to his means to support such sum.

It may be possible to get the bond actually signed in Singapore after the Court is satisfied as to the means of the bailers. It may be difficult to do so except by production of title-deeds.

It is going to be very difficult to keep the report out of the papers, but an effort could be made. His wife and family are fortunately out of the country so that there is less likelihood of the details appearing in the Home papers.

I cannot see in what way you can assist but should it arise I will communicate with you.

Yours faithfully,
Claude D. D. Hogan[165]

P.S. I now understand that the Court will only accept cash or Penang landed property as security in the case of bailers in Singapore.

> Harper, Gilfillan & Co. Ltd.
> Hongkong Bank Chambers
> Penang
> 10th July 1952

C. Repton, Esq.
c/o Messrs. Turquand Youngs & Co.
P.O. Box 384
Singapore

Dear Mr. Repton,

Many thanks for your letter of the 8th July, and I was glad to hear from you. Nobody here has had a word from Stella since she arrived in the United Kingdom, other than Roy.

There is absolutely nothing we can do here to hobble the Newspapers. The story of his arrest has already been published and subsequent reports have appeared as he has been brought up for mention. It would not be possible, in this instance, to get the

---

165 According to local press reports, Roy's lawyer, defence counsel Mr C. D. D. Hogan, told the court that Roy had threatened to resign and wanted to report his firm's internal activities to the police prior to his arrest. Hogan added that a company director then offered to pay Roy and his wife's passage to London and to pay him $100 on condition that he signed a statement that the firm did not intend to smuggle, and that their accountant had not given instructions to "sell dead goods at normal prices".

Sessions Court Judge to hold the case 'in camera' as he would rule that the matter is one of public interest.

I am very worried about the whole thing on Stella's behalf, and I think the case is almost certainly bound to go to the Supreme Court eventually.

Yours sincerely,
W. H. C. Bailey

H. & S. B.C.
Penang
10th July '52

Dear Chris,

Thanks for the letter – I have forwarded the enclosure via Goh,[166] who will see Roy as usual on Sat. morning.

Am glad you may be able to get down here – but suggest you will only be able to see him at about 9 a.m. at the court on a Saturday, or before 4 p.m. on the weekday.

I haven't a clue on the publicity – but feel free reporting should be allowed. Everyone in Penang has his own story of the case, founded on rife rumour, and the reported facts only will put that right. I may well be wrong in this but believe Roy would agree.

Once more in a hurry –

Cheerio,
Peter

H. & S. B.C.
Penang
23.7.52

Dear Chris,

I enclose the two cuttings on the case so far.

I met Goh as he came out of court yesterday. He was pleased that

---

166 Hogan's deputy.

some of the 'big guns' were allowed to fire. I saw Roy in the police wagon on the way home and he was in good spirits.

Con mentioned a point which is not reported – that the Dutchman in evidence said that in his own mind the money was given to Roy for his own use.

There still appears to be only one charge that they are using, and the rest are, it seems, being held in reserve. If this one is cleared, I suppose they may re-arrest and try on the others. On the other hand, it looks as if the firm are going to be in such a mess they will try to back out at some point.

Am in a hurry as you can guess.

Regards,
Peter

Dear Pim,

Herewith the letter I mentioned over the phone. I have not referred it to Kirk as I don't know when he gets back from Saigon.

Chris Repton

Dear Chris,

Thanks for the sight of Hogan's letter. I think you have done everything possible and I fear there is nothing more that any of us can do in view of Hogan's remarks. It's very tough luck on R. C.-G. and his family – we can only hope the case will go favourably for him.

P. D.

28th July 1952

Dear Chris,

It is ages since I wrote you, and even longer since I had the last letter from you. And this makes me think that we might both be feeling the same way about things – something went wrong, something that cannot be put right between us. I feel as if the light had suddenly gone out, the contact lost... There is nobody to blame, my Dear; it might have been different if you had not left, but as you did after we had only known each other for such a short time, I suppose this was inevitable.

You are right, it is impossible to keep a flame like this alight merely by conversing in letters, not after such a short acquaintance. I did begin to have doubts and voice them, but somehow, as I said, our letters kept on crossing in mid-air and slowly but surely the distance could not be bridged anymore. Please don't blame me, or yourself; these things happen in life and I am sure you will be as sorry as I am, but there is nothing to be done.

I like you very much, Chris, and I always want to be your friend, and sincerely and with all my heart hope that you feel the same about me. I would like to keep on writing to you, and would like you to write to me; I want to know how you are faring in life etc. Please let's do that and not sulk. If you still have them, I think it might be a good thing if you sent my letters back and I will do the same and we start with a clean sheet as two friends, and I do mean that. Believe me, I am a far better friend than I might ever have been to you as a wife. I only plucked up the courage to write this letter because your long silence indicated to me that you felt similarly, and because I believe that the truth is always less hurtful in the long run than a lie. So please, Darling, become my friend, as I am yours, and forgive whatever may have caused this change as a true Christian.

Yours,
M.

H. & S. B.C.
Penang
11th August '52

Dear Chris,

I would have written before this but there has been no news worthwhile.

Roy is in court today and I will let you have a report as soon as one is available.

I spoke to Roy on Saturday; apparently Hogan has had a heart attack and is out of action. Goh will carry on, however, and I hope is competent enough to do a good job.

Roy also asked me not to send newspaper cuttings to Stella as she gets too worried over odd details which appear true. He suggested that the plain facts in an ordinary letter would be more suitable.

I am wondering whether a definite result will come up today or whether this business will drag on further. Still, one can only hope for the best.

Shall be writing to you again tomorrow, I expect – till then,

Cheerio,
Peter

H. & S. B.C.
Penang
12th August 1952

Dear Chris,

I expect to hear from you by 'phone today but am writing this in case I forget any details.

You know that due to Hogan being out of action the proceedings went badly yesterday, Goh being unfit for the actual work in court. Goh has agreed to carry on as No. 2, acting as solicitor to anyone we can get hold of. Roy was on to me this morning and says that he hoped to get at least a week's extension and he may get more if it should prove necessary.

The other point Roy emphasised was the question of finance re. the new advocate; he will probably require some sort of assurance that he will be paid. Roy requests that you contact Kirk Meyer and ask him for temporary assistance, the whole thing being that in a case of this nature it may give an incorrect impression if funds were introduced from homeside. For this reason, too, besides Roy's natural need to economise, he hopes that the chap you now produce for him does not charge too high a fee.

The first thing the new man will wish to do is to contact Goh, and the details are:-

G. H. Goh
4 Church Street
Penang
Tele. No. 884

You can assure him that all the paperwork, brief etc. is well planned, in good order and merely requires that he acquaint himself with the position as already detailed by Goh and presumably Hogan.

I am enclosing the latest news cutting, and from it you can see that the prosecution had all its own way. In Roy's words, all Goh did was to look at the ceiling!

Am now out of contact with Roy and suggest that if you have to communicate with him you do it through Goh as he is useful in that respect.

Roy, I know, is relying on you and Kirk very strongly in this – there seems to be no alternative if your efforts fail – but I feel that he cannot continue having bad luck and something good will turn up shortly.

All the very best,
Peter

c/o P. & T. Lands
Subang
Java
13th Aug. 1952

Dear Chris,

My apologies for not replying earlier to your letter of the 14th May. When it was received, we were still on the Annual Accounts and what with Sylvia returning and going into hospital, I just have not settled down to anything.

First things first. I was extremely sorry to read about the case of Roy Coulson-Gilmer and do hope he was acquitted. We saw snippets of news in the *Straits Times*, from which it appeared he was 'framed', and after the first two days' hearing we saw nothing further, so I am wondering what happened. Whilst I feel sorry for him, I feel sorrier still for his wife and child.

Sylvia enjoyed herself very much in Australia until the last month, when she got complications internally and rushed back here after a spell in hospital. To add to her troubles, David and Colin contracted measles, so that the whole family went straight into hospital on arrival in Subang, in case of contagion. The two boys were out shortly, but all Subang were too afraid to visit them or Sylvia in hospital. The twins were too young to get it, but Sylvia had to stay in because she had inflammation of the womb. She only came out on Monday and is still very weak. You remember how active she was, and the thought of no tennis or swimming for two/three months is naturally depressing her. We are in the process of running the annual P. & T. tennis tournament. We have a few good players, but the standard is not as high as it was. You can appreciate Sylvia's feelings at seeing the tennis and not being able to play, especially as she should run away with the singles.

You ask me about Reg Boulter and Peter Mullins. Reg Boulter flew to England on leave on the 30th July and it was my intention to write to you to meet him. I think he intends to come back for another term. Peter Mullins is also on leave, catching the *Roma* on the 30th June and sailing to Genoa. He had resigned because there seemed to be no prospects for him as Cammell, as usual, said he was no good. They persuaded him to stay but granted him advanced leave on half pay and I would not be surprised if he returned but married. The Noordijks are still here with their son and heir flourishing. John Churchward arrived back from leave on the same ship as Sylvia travelled on, and his wife Joan arrived back yesterday, complete with two children, a girl and a boy, the latter just over a year old. Ball from Tjilater resigned after the murder of his brother and obtained a very good job as a European salesman for his brother-in-law's firm in Northern Ireland, which deals with tinned foodstuffs. Van Ree and Brunklaus have retired on pension.

We have not done too badly at cricket. We lost to 'Box' twice and beat them (a very weak team) on our ground last week. We have beaten the B.S.C. and the Indians. We have two more matches against the 'Box', and I hope we beat them on their ground. There are a number of new young players and Shaw is the captain, but he has never scored against good opposition like the 'Box'. Lofty is twelfth man, so you can see we have quite a useful team.

317

We have run two swimming galas and an athletic meeting this year, and as I am the Sports Liaison Club Committee member had quite a lot to do with them. We had over 100 entries for the sports.

Conditions are a little more stable, but the Darul Islam people still move about the Sukabumi area and two of our young planters were murdered at Gunong Tjimpaka last week. We have sold Palahlar for a song, as it could not be controlled and the price of rubber there was over the sale price; nor could we dismiss any workers because of the trade union. London Office had refused 10 times the amount a year ago.

Sid has resigned and leaves at the end of December. He wants to leave sometime and get married, so he considers it better to move now at the age of 33, and probably get a good job rather than wait for six years after accumulating some money and then losing the opportunity because of age.

Have you made any enquiries about your local leave in Java? There are certain restrictions about immigration, and I suggest you apply at the Indonesian Consulate in Singapore regarding the possibility of obtaining an entry visa.

If you can find any spare Malayan stamps, send them along.

Kindest regards from us all.

Sincerely,
Paddy Knights

> Hongkong & Shanghai Banking Corp.
> Penang
> 14.8.52

Dear Chris,

I saw Roy yesterday and he appeared quite fit.

The answer to the conversation of the effort to get another lawyer is that he realised the impossibility of obtaining a man in the time even if the postponement could have been extended for a week more. He mentioned that, besides the fact that there are no Europeans available in Penang, he had to have a Singapore man because of Goh. Goh is apparently the senior man here and could only serve under Hogan, who is senior to him.

Anyhow, to get to know the case in one day would have been impossible and Roy is now conducting it himself – which in the circumstances is the wisest thing to do. I haven't mentioned this to Stella as yet but will do so when I can report on today's happenings.

Roy apologises for putting you to needless trouble over the lawyer business; but I think he was a bit het-up over Goh's performance on Monday.

Shall let you have the next cuttings as they appear – till then,

All the best,
Peter

The Clock House
Steyning
Sussex
14th August 1952

My dear Chris,

Thank you so much for your nice long letter and the cuttings, which were very much appreciated. I should also like to have those which will obviously appear during this week's proceedings – that is, if you don't mind.

It really was sweet of you to go all the way up to Penang just to see Roy, and I can never tell you how much both Roy and I appreciated your extreme thoughtfulness and kindness. He wrote and told me what a lovely surprise it was and how awfully pleased he was to see you. I felt so happy to know that in you we have at least one real friend. People are so disappointing – they clamour round you when things are going well and you are able to offer them a drink etc., but as soon as you're in trouble they don't want to know you. Various so-called friends made all sorts of promises when I left Penang that they would look after Roy and make sure everything was O.K. and assured me I hadn't a thing to worry about. I now gather that, apart from you and Peter Briggs, no one has even been near him. The last letter I had from Roy was awfully depressing, although P. B. assures me that he is still full of beans. Just to help things along, Hogan has now had a stroke and is in hospital and it's doubtful whether he'll ever practise again.

I wish to goodness we'd never had anything to do with this firm. They're a lot of crooks! And from the cuttings which you sent me, I see that everyone is lying up to the eyebrows, so what chance poor Roy has against them all I wouldn't know. Van der Meulen's[167] story, of course, is quite fantastic, and in no way resembles the truth. It is dreadful to think that people can stand in court and tell these shocking lies, and if they get away with it this time, then I shall never, as long as I live, have faith in British justice and my heart will always go out to those people whom I see in the newspapers are convicted for various reasons. I shall never believe that they are actually guilty of any crime, because I know now how very easily you can be 'framed'.

I don't remember whether I told you in my last letter or not – I'm expecting another baby in January (around 21st). We're both very thrilled about it, but of course Roy is worried to death about finances if things do not go well. I have only a limited amount, and nothing coming in at all, and obviously I can't get a job for some time. Still, it's no good crossing our bridges before we get to them – but Roy paints such a gloomy picture and is obviously so depressed that all sorts of things run through my mind. He mentions something about any letters he writes to me he will send to you first and get you to forward them. I don't quite know what he's getting at, but I think it's something to do with the fact that all letters from the prison are stamped on the envelope 'H. M. Prisons' and he obviously wouldn't want it to arrive in England so stamped. So, if you receive any letters from Roy, would you be very kind and put them in an ordinary envelope (type the address) and forward to me at […], making absolutely sure that it's addressed to Mrs. Stella Coulson-Gilmer, or it might be a trifle confusing as I'm staying with his people at the moment.

Your godson is growing rapidly and is now running about all over the place. He now has 10 teeth and looks frightfully grown-up!

---

167 Roy's successor as manager of the Penang branch after his arrest.

It's very sad that Roy is missing him at such a lovely age, and he gets more like him every day.

I'd be awfully grateful if you'd do one other thing for me, Chris. I wrote to Kirk ages ago and have had no reply – I was very vague about his address so he may not have even received it. The great thing was, I asked him to let me have his Colonel's address as soon as possible, as I wanted to send her a little present in return for her kindness when I was in Singapore. Would you get in touch with him for me? Of course, he may have been away, or may still be away, in which case there's not much you can do. I also want the correct spelling of his Colonel's surname – d'you mind very much?

This seems to be about all for now. Don't think me round the bend, but on recollection I believe I've answered your letter before which means I've now written you two on the trot! You must think I'm going round the bend but are probably not surprised anyway!!

I do hope you are well, Chris. How's the job going? Do you ever hear anything from the Java people? My very best wishes to Ross and family – do you see them at all?!

Looking forward to hearing from you re. this week's proceedings, and hoping and praying that the news is good. I was so pleased to hear that Father Audet went to see Roy, and also that a priest went to Roy one Sunday to give him Confession and Holy Communion. Should you see Fr. Audet please give him my very best wishes and thanks for visiting Roy, and I do hope, amongst all the other things he has to do, that he'll have time to see him again.

All the very best – and with love,
Stella & Christopher

24th Aug.

Dear Chris,

I am out of action for a few days owing to an infection of the tonsils. If necessary, use Goh at 4 Church St. as a go-between. Can you forward the enclosed to Drooglever? I haven't his address.

Nothing seemed to happen on Saturday; it goes on tomorrow – Tues. I am absolutely clueless on what the result may be. Stella wrote in very excited fashion and mentioned that Roy had written to her and said he did not think much of his chances. On the other hand, Roy spoke to me yesterday and said all was O.K. at his end. I unfortunately had lost my voice.

Shall have to be back in the office over the month's end but will be busy. If I don't contact you don't worry, as it will mean the news is not vital.

Yours,
Peter

The Hongkong & Shanghai Banking Corporation
MEMOPENANG
29.8.52

Dear Chris,

Good News! Roy was acquitted this morning on this charge. He called it the main case and the most important, and he is most pleased.

Another one comes up on 8th – it will be the last and he seems confident of being able to handle this O.K. I hope so. Am enclosing cuttings to date.

Yours,
Peter

British Embassy
Djakarta
18.9.52

Dear Chris,

I've just decided that I need a break from Darkest Djakarta and feel that a short trip to Singapore would improve my temper and well-being. What I want more than anything is a good long wallow in a full-length bath with hot water, and some swimming, neither of which can one do here. (You must have suffered from similar feelings – or did you have swimming and bathing baths in Subang?)

Can you tell me whether there are any reasonably cheap hotels in Singapore, and if so, how much they are likely to cost? And is it a good time of the year to come to Singapore? There are bits of odd shopping that I want to do. I should have to fly over to get the trip in time, as I can't take much leave.

The Dick Shaws are in Djakarta for a spell in somebody's absence and I see them now and again. I played bridge with them – or rather against them – the other evening. They send their best wishes to you. They are one of the nicest couples I have met here. I haven't yet met the Knights, although I heard they came down to Djakarta to play in a cricket match – or rather he did – but I was in Bandung at the time so never met them.

I apologise for this being rather short, but I want to get it off. Can you let me know about a visit to Singapore and so forth?

Best wishes,
Margaret

British Embassy

Djakarta

4/10

Dear Chris,

How very kind of you to write so soon and to find out the details of hotels for me.

A new situation has arisen, however, and it may be two or three weeks before I come over, as there is a possibility that I may be able to get a lift with our Air Attaché when he goes over to Singapore in his own plane. I'll let you know as soon as anything definite is fixed, but if I can't get a free trip soon, I'll just come anyway under my own steam.

Heavens, we've just started a domestic row. The 'boy' is shouting about something and so is my stablemate. I can't help feeling that if I were the 'boy', I wouldn't stay here a minute to be treated as my stablemate treats these servants. Thank God, to be quite snobbish, the British Empire wasn't built by people of her class!

I've just joined the local golf club (have I told you that?) and play almost every day. It's lovely out there – fresh and cool – and it's so nice to walk on soft turf instead of stone floors! I'm due out there now, so must be off. I'll write to you again, if I may, as soon as I know more about my movements.

As ever,
Margaret

Ballaggan
Sherwood Park
Lockerbie
Dumfriesshire
18th November 1952

My dear Christopher,

I'm not very sure how long these things take to reach you, so I'm writing this in good time to wish you a very happy birthday, and success and happiness throughout the year. I look forward to the day when you will once again celebrate your birthday at home.

How have things been going for you during this last year out there? It seems more like two years that you have been away, instead of just over one, and now Christmas is nearly on us again. Will you be going up to Penang again this year? I shall be taking advantage of the cheap winter return fare by B.E.A. Viking from Glasgow to Northolt as it will mean that I shall be able to get home by 10 p.m. on Christmas Eve, instead of 8 a.m. on Christmas Day after a night on the train, and it only costs £3 more than the train fare. It will seem very quiet this year without either you or Gervase, but I expect we'll make the best of it.

From your last letter which Mother sent on to me, I see that you are playing squash and badminton. Have you played much before or is it a new venture? I was wondering whether to take up the latter, as there is no hockey club for miles, and I refuse to play soccer, and am not keen on rugger. It will be alright in the summer as Castlemilk has its own cricket team, and there are tennis courts in Lockerbie.

I was interested to read the reports of *Arms and the Man* in the press cuttings you sent. It must have been good fun after the first night was over. Will you be doing another play with them? Did you know that I was in a production of J. B. Priestley's *They Came to a City*, down in Somerset last March? I thoroughly enjoyed it, and was only in it because the leading man fell ill a month beforehand, and I took his part. It's funny that Gervase should also have taken part in a play this year, isn't it? He seems to be kept occupied one way and another, doesn't he? I often wonder how he is really feeling about things now that he is out there;[168] whether he is settling down at all. Though I suppose he will never cease to worry about the part of the family at Cobham now. Fr. Gamble was asking me whether I thought it would do any good if he went round one day and called on Ma and Pa. In a tactful sort of way, I said it couldn't do any harm.

By the way, how is your 'Minor' going these days? Do you use it much out of Singapore? I passed my test in Dumfries about a month ago.

I still dream about my wonderful holiday and am already making plans for next summer. Well, have a good time on the 3rd, old cock! And come home soon.

Best wishes from your loving brother,
Dickon

Corner Cottage
Old Point
Middleton-on-Sea
Sussex
11.12.52

Dear Chris,

Just to let you know that I arrived home safely a couple of days ago. Stella and Christopher are as well as one could expect, and the house is very nice, if a trifle off the beaten track. I'm sorry I didn't have a chance to really see you alone before you left, but as you saw, the situation was a trifle congested.

I've phoned Connie, and she's fine, and we'll try and have lunch one day when we go to town. I'm absolutely frozen but have some

---

168 In New Zealand.

Scotch to console me, and I may last until Xmas if it doesn't snow. You wouldn't recognise your godson now, he's so huge, but hope to shoot some more snaps off to you one of these days.

Give my regards to Mac, Norman and Stanley, and remember to tell Mac that his records are with Lois.

If you get a moment, drop me a line and tell me all the scandal; it'll certainly help to cheer me up.

Thanks again, Chris, for all you did for me. I really appreciate it; without your hand on my shoulder I'd have been completely lost.

Don't forget, write as soon as you can. Stella sends her love, plus a big X from Christopher.

All the very best,
Roy

TWELVE

He Went Back to His Own Funny Steps

1953–1956

1953

Theresa

In 1953, John Curran joined the firm, followed by Bill Swan, Roly Marks, Trevor Brown and a few others. So, the office was quite full of young assistants, and May Large[169] was also there. She was working in the typing pool, and all the other assistants gave her work to do. I worked in the air-conditioned boardroom next to John Phillips' office, so I was quite isolated, but I felt much happier without any interference from the rest of the office.

After living with Agnes for a while in North Bridge Road, I spent a few years living with Daisy's family, up in Serangoon Road. On Sundays I used to go to the Cathedral of the Good Shepherd and see Christopher at the eight o'clock Mass, but he hardly knew me to give me a lift back.

1954

1954 was not a good year. There were riots between Muslims and Christians in Singapore. A Dutch war orphan called Maria had been adopted by

---

169 May Wong, who later married Graeme Large, one of the accountants.

Christmas 1954 at 16 Dunsfold Drive, '(l to r)
Mrs Kon, Boon Eng, Chris, Song & Miss Pang'

a Malay family who wanted to convert her to Islam, and there was some conflict over this. Somehow it sparked off riots in Singapore, which were quite bad. During some nights we had curfew, and of course nobody was allowed out on the streets.

1955

Christopher went back home on leave after three and a half years in Singapore; I think for six months. So, I didn't see him for that time, and it was touch-and-go whether he wanted to return. But my boss managed to persuade him to return for another contract.

I went on a weekend trip with Mary Boey to Kuala Lumpur, and we stayed with Mary Cheong, the daughter of a friend of mine in Singapore, who was managing a shop in Batu Road, selling Singer sewing machines. On the Sunday, Mary Cheong wanted to visit Port Dickson. She only had a learner's driving licence, and after Mass drove us to Port Dickson – to Travellers' Peak, I think. On the way, halfway between KL and Port Dickson, we had a terrible accident while trying to avoid a motorcyclist. Luckily, the Malay driver, who was sitting next to Mary, managed to pull the steering wheel to the other side of the road, where we landed in a ditch about five feet down. If he hadn't done so, we would have landed in a deep ravine. The car was badly damaged, and the chassis was bent. It was a Sunday morning, and the road was very quiet. Luckily, a passing Malay schoolteacher stopped to help us and drove the driver to get a mechanic from a nearby sawmill. When he came to repair the damage, we needed a heavy lorry to lift the car. By the time it was back on the road it couldn't go fast; only about ten miles per hour. That evening we had to catch a plane back to Singapore. We got to KL just in time to get to the airport and return home. I suffered a bruise on my chest, and we were all quite shocked, but nothing serious. That was quite an experience for us all, as at that time the 'Emergency'[170] was on. There were guerrilla actions along that road – ambushes and that sort of thing – so we were taking risks going that way to Port Dickson.

About 1955, I moved to live at 17 Alnwick Road, Serangoon Gardens. I had a half-share of the house at that time. Dick and Amy had their wedding reception there, and they stayed with me for some months. When they moved out, Agnes and Chai Seng occupied a room for a few years. My mother used to spend a night or two with me during weekends. It was a good area. Mary, Elizabeth and their families were living in Berwick Drive, which was also in Serangoon Gardens. Sometimes I walked to their house for dinner after work, which was convenient for me.

1956

1956 was a very eventful year at Turquand Youngs. On the 7th January Bill Swan and Felicity were married, and I was invited to the reception at Bishopsgate Mess. I think Christopher was also invited, as were other members of staff. My boss was definitely there, as I have a picture taken at the reception, in which I am standing talking to him. After the reception, May, Graeme, Willie Lochhead and I went to have a drink at a restaurant on Orchard Road.

A week after that, Trevor and Jean were married, and the reception was held at Donald Stewart's house in Holland Road. I remember very well that

---

170 The British authorities implemented a state of emergency in Malaya from 1948 to 1960, to suppress the anti-colonial Communist insurgency.

The Swans' wedding at Bishopsgate Mess

my boss John Phillips and his wife were there too. Christopher and Walter Bellam were, I think, involved in the wedding and the reception, but I didn't see Christopher at the reception.

Once again, May and Graeme, Roly Marks, another person and I went on to Cathay Restaurant for a drink and a few dances. The evening ended up being most enjoyable. Bill Swan had completed his first contract and returned to Australia to join his father's practice. He and Felicity were living in Mosman, Sydney, where their children were born. Soon after, Trevor and Jean Brown left TYs and, with the help of Donald Stewart, moved to Jamaica, as Trevor had a post there.

The London office sent out two senior accountants to replace Trevor and Bill, one of whom was called Davidson. He turned out to be an alcoholic. On turning up to work drunk one day, he was dismissed. The following day, he appeared at John Phillips' house and threatened to shoot him. Fortunately, they managed to get the police to arrest him. Soon after that, he was sent home to the UK. I remember very clearly when my boss dictated a letter to me to send to one of the partners, telling him of the incident. I was a bit confused and quite shocked and made a terrible mistake by addressing the letter to Mr. Davidson instead of Robertson, the intended recipient. A few days later the envelope was sent back to my boss, and I realised the

Graeme & May (left), Terry (2nd right), Willie (right)

mistake I'd made. But Phillips was very kind and just laughed about it. I felt so embarrassed!

There was another young assistant called Michael Gurney, whose father was Sir Henry Gurney.[171] While Sir Henry was travelling with a convoy along the Mantin Gap, terrorists ambushed his car and he was killed; a real setback for the British Army in that area. Sir Henry was succeeded by General Templer[172] during the time of the Emergency. Michael Gurney worked in Singapore for only one contract term.

I had my tonsils removed, as they were giving me a lot of trouble every month. To recuperate I went on a sea trip to Hong Kong and Japan with Agnes, Chai Seng and my sixth brother on the P&O ship *Chusan*. It was

---

171 Sir Henry Gurney, a veteran of World War I and former Chief Secretary to Palestine, was appointed British High Commissioner to Malaya in 1948 at the beginning of the Emergency. He was killed in an allegedly random ambush by Communist guerrillas on the Jalan Gap-Bukit Fraser mountain pass on the way up to Fraser's Hill in October 1951. Reportedly mourned by Malayans of all races and classes, he was buried in Kuala Lumpur.

172 General Sir Gerald Templer, a veteran of both world wars, built on Gurney's counter-insurgency work from 1952 to 1954, flushing out Communist guerrillas from the jungle using curfews, food restrictions and Dayak headhunters, while 'winning hearts and minds' by integrating the ethnic Chinese into Malayan society. The Emergency dragged on until 1960, but terrorist attacks were greatly reduced during his term as High Commissioner.

Aberdeen restaurant, HK - 6th Brother (2nd left), Chai Seng,
Agnes, Theresa, CS's niece & her husband

very exciting for me, as it was my first journey abroad. We left about the end of April and arrived in Hong Kong for two days. Agnes and I shared a first-class cabin on the A deck, while Chai Seng and my brother shared accommodation on the economy deck. We used to meet up regularly. Meals on board were wonderful – so much to eat – and there was lots of time to walk around the decks and play games, but I didn't use the pool because I was unable to swim.

We took three days to get to Hong Kong. The ship docked in Kowloon Harbour. We went to Hong Kong Island and did quite a lot of shopping, buying beautiful pieces of silk for my cheongsams, and brocades. It was so cheap in those days. One evening we met up with Chai Seng's niece and husband and they took us to Aberdeen Harbour where we had a meal on a boat. Everything seemed so exciting. The following day we visited the New Territories and were allowed to go back to the ship at night.

After Hong Kong we headed north for Yokohama, which took another three days. The ship was docked in the harbour, and we had to take a taxi to Tokyo, where we stayed for a couple of nights. It was springtime but we

*Chai Seng, Agnes, Theresa & 6th
Brother in Hong Kong*

didn't see any blossom in the city. The crowds were tremendous, crossing the roads especially. We did a bit of shopping there. In the evenings most of us stayed in the hotel because it was too cold to go out, though my brother ventured out on his own. One night we went to a steakhouse, which was run by a British chap, and had a lovely meal. They served the famous Kobe beef, from cattle fed on beer. But it was so costly – US$20 for one fillet steak! Everything – the food, the coffee – seemed so costly in Tokyo then.

After two days we took a taxi back to Yokohama to catch up with the boat. Because of a traffic jam, we nearly missed it! We were just about the last passengers to board. We then sailed north to Kobe. That took another day or two. We docked in Kobe Harbour and took a taxi to Osaka; a beautiful, ancient city where most women and men wore their national costume, the kimono. I remember going out in the evenings among the crowds of people. It was fascinating. The following day we went to Kyoto. There was an old temple in a beautiful setting, with all the cherry blossom still out. One day, we were entertained by some Japanese businessmen, as my brothers' shop in Rochore Road were agents for their chocolates.

After two days in Osaka, we left to join the boat in Kobe. On the way back to Singapore, we stopped off in Hong Kong again for another couple of days, which was delightful. We bought more things, and went sightseeing, up to the Peak and to all the other places of interest. It was another three days' journey back to Singapore. It must have been the third week of May when we reached home.

Our trip was most enjoyable, and for me a ship was the best way to travel. You get to see places, have excellent food and service on board, and it is most relaxing. In those days oil prices were very low, so there were a lot of passenger boats. The most popular lines were the P&O,[173] Blue Funnel and Lloyd Triestino. It was reasonable, and you got to stay on board most of the time, so you didn't have to worry about hotel reservations. The only drawback in Japan was the food, which I didn't like very much. Perhaps we didn't order the right dishes. But the countryside was most beautiful, especially in Kyoto.

When I returned to work after my holiday, to my surprise, my job had been filled by an old classmate of mine called Irma Leembruggen while I was away. I hadn't seen or been in touch with her for a long, long time. It was a real surprise to see her back in Singapore again. The last news I'd had of her, some years before, was that she was in Borneo. It was nice to see her again. She and her sister Mae had been in the same senior class as us when we'd passed the school-leaving exams in 1941, but I never saw Mae again after school.

During the war, all the TYs partners had been interned in Sime Road, except Bridgewood, a very fat man who was interned in Indonesia. They were civilian prisoners, and so were detained in concentration camps and lived on a horrible diet of rice, salted fish, sweet potatoes and tapioca.

When Christopher first arrived in Singapore, he was living in the office Mess at Number 1 Bishopsgate with some of the other assistants like Bill Swan and Roly Marks. A few years later, he and Walter Bellam shared a bungalow in Braddell Heights – Number 16 Dunsfold Drive. Later, they moved to 24 Dunsfold Drive.

Colin Coey was another bachelor who at times shared the house at Number 24. He, Walter and Christopher shared a dinghy. One time, we went out on the boat with Graeme and May for a picnic at Coney Island. The darned boat's outboard motor didn't work, so we had to paddle!

---

173 The Peninsular & Oriental Steam Navigation Company.

Walter playing piano, Chris & Vicky listening

It was fun in those days. We went out all the time. One evening a week we used to go and learn ballroom dancing. Christopher had a funny way of dancing, so we needed to take lessons. We met a professional dancer through Mary Boey; he used to teach cabaret girls and was a very good dancer. I could follow the steps easily. I could do the tango very well, but Christopher had to have notes! Our lessons took place in Mary Boey's aunt's house, somewhere in Katong. Christopher used to come away with bits of paper showing all the steps. But he never really learned the proper ones, and he went back to his own funny steps. I enjoyed the ballroom slow fox most of all, and the tango when it was properly done.

I remember Christmas 1956. Some of the office girls were invited to visit 16 Dunsfold Drive on Christmas morning, and we had a nice morning with some other guests. One of the senior partners, Paul Saunders, retired around then, and we were all invited to his farewell dinner. After that, two new partners were admitted: Gordon Van Hien and Freddy Westworth.[174]

---

174 Freddy Westworth was the only one at Turquand Youngs, apart from Christopher, who had been a prisoner on the Burma-Siam railway.

THIRTEEN

Through the Silvery Olive Grove

1953–1956

P. & T. Lands

Subang

2nd January 1953

Dear Chris,

The seed planted in my mind in Singapore is germinating strongly in these Java conditions, and I find that the few comments dropped by you re. a change of employment have definitely had their effect.

You can imagine what an anti-climax Java is after our happy stay in Singapore – so much so that my wife and I definitely want to get out as soon as possible, provided that it is to our advantage, of course. It is on that point that I ask your help and advice.

Do you honestly think that I could secure a good job with my present qualifications – good enough, that is, to give me a fair standard of living and reasonable savings; and do you feel your firm would be interested in me, semi-qualified as I am? Again, what sort of minimum salary must one have as a married man to exist as a general rule at a reasonable level, one's wife and self being sober-minded types who don't want drinks and parties every other night? From this side, you see, Chris, I haven't a clue about these things.

I don't want to walk out on the P. & T. on the slightest provocation – I have a certain silly sense of loyalty – but really, things stink here after Singapore and one realises that it is subsistence rather than life that one endures here, and I honestly don't think my wife can 'take it' for another 1½–2 years.

For these reasons, then, I would ask you if you would be kind enough to sound the feelings of your people on a possible offer of my services (in the most discreet manner, of course), taking your own time about it. Any news or comments you could give concerning other avenues worth exploring would also be welcomed.

I do hope you don't mind my getting in touch with you about all this, but you're my only hope, and I apologise in advance for the trouble I am causing you. Needless to say, I shall be very grateful indeed, however much or little you are able to do.

Sincerely yours,
Gerald W. Champney

British Embassy
Djakarta
4/1/53

My dear Chris,

Many thanks for your Christmas card and also for your last letter.

I hope you had as good a Christmas as we all did over here. Like us, you probably found it difficult to feel really Christmassy in this heat. Anyway, it was all very amusing, and three weeks of gaiety were wound up on New Year's Eve by a fancy-dress dance at the Box.

And now we are back to normal. It is Sunday morning and I'm trying simultaneously to write letters and listen to a concert on the wireless. The fact that my 'boy' is sweeping the floor and the Minister of Information who lives next door has some native musicians playing, makes it all the more difficult.

I'm doing a lot of driving these days and hope soon to get my licence.

The native musician has just appeared outside my door. It's pure blackmail – they know you will pay them to go away. I merely turned up the wireless and his bamboo pipe couldn't compete with 'The Poet & Peasant' turned up full blast!

Have you any plans for coming over here? I hope to spend a fortnight in Singapore later on in the year, so we mustn't clash.

Andy will be leaving very shortly, as his replacement has finally sailed from the U.K. Did you know John Muriel when you were here? A great cricketer. He's been transferred to Singapore, so you are bound to see him. He's Hongkong & Shanghai Bank.

I've recently acquired a small kampong[175] dog, by name Jennifer. She has practically lived at the vet since she was born but is now in very good condition.

For the first time for days the sun is shining, so all suitcases, shoes, golf clubs are going out in the sun. They all seem to be covered with mildew – the damp, I suppose.

I spent last weekend at a house lent us by the Ministry of Foreign Affairs, hundreds of miles away from Djakarta on the west coast. I have never seen anything so lovely as the coast there. The drive is very pretty. As you say, Java is a beautiful country, where only man is vile!

The very best of good wishes for 1953, Chris, and I hope to see you soon, either here or in Singapore.

Sincerely,
Margaret

The Corner Cottage
Old Point
Middleton-on-Sea
Sussex
January 13th

Dear Chris,

Firstly, big rocket for you for not writing. I wrote to you simply ages ago, without getting any reply, and now Stella tells me that she wrote a long letter (very unusual for her) to you, about three

---

175 Indonesian village.

weeks ago, including a request for some certificates, and likewise, no answer – what goes on, are you dead? Or just don't you talk to us anymore? Shame on you.

What news of

a. You
b. Mac & company
c. Singapore
d. Kirk
e. Penang
f. etc.

Did I tell you that I'd actually had a letter from Kirk? It's absolutely incredible really, as he never writes to anyone, under any conditions. I know that Ross is due to go to Sarawak quite soon but am not too sure exactly when – have you seen anything of him recently or did the christening finish you?!!!

England is so cold that it just isn't true. Yesterday, for the first time since my return – I SAW THE SUN. Yep, it's really true.

Incidentally, you'll be amused to hear that I'm playing rugger again, AND scoring tries, so there must be life in the old man yet!

Stella is very fit, and we have only a week to go before the new infant arrives; big excitement. I have to tell you that the certificates Stella asked for are required in connection with the christening. Incidentally, any suggestions re. godparents? We don't have a clue.

Did you go to Midnight Mass? And where? You'll be pleased to know that the movies of your visit to Penang came out very well. We showed them last night and the colour was quite good – you looked almost handsome!!

I have spoken to Connie on the 'phone, and made a tentative date to natter to her, but it fell through, so have decided to wait until Stella can come too and do it in style.

Nothing more for now. Apart from being freezing and starving, I'm fine.

Lots of love from Roy, Stella, Christopher (he's huge now)

The Corner Cottage
Feb. 10th

My dear Chris,

Many thanks for both your letters, dated 23/1 and 3/2 respectively. Firstly, our big news. In case you haven't already heard, our second son was born on Friday 16th January 1953!! We are calling him Kirk, for very good reasons, and we hope he likes it!!

I have told Kirk that he is expected to be godfather, but naturally, haven't heard a word from him! Naturally, as a non-Catholic, he can't really be Kirk's actual godfather, so we're considering him a sort of 'lay' model!! It sounds rather complicated, so to make it even more so, Stella and I want you to stand up straight and be Kirk's godfather in God, as it were – will you? Please – it'll make it so much easier if we have one person keeping a spiritual eye on our brace! You needn't mention this to Kirk; he'd probably be a little hurt, if he could even make sense out of it!

Now for my 'case' news. I had a letter from Jagjit Singh the other day, letting me know that things had come to a head, and that I had to do something or other at once, but as it was impossible to do anything owing to flap re. Stella, I had to leave the matter. I intended writing to you, but then your letter telling me of your Bangkok trip arrived. Would you please get in touch with J. J. and see what it's all about, and what you can do about it? It's impossible to do anything from here. He seems to have an idea I can just hop on a plane and whizz back to Penang. His address is: Jagjit Singh, P.O. Box 167, Penang. Tel.: 238 (house) or 925 (office).

Stella and babes are all well but yearning already to leave England. This is going to be tough to achieve with two babes, but I'm trying like hell. Even if I get a job locally, it'll be scrape-scrape. No good. Incidentally, to hark back, J. J. does not know my address, but has only this: me, c/o BM/TGTA, London W.C. 1. Which is a Monomark effort. I think it best not to tell him my exact address.

Still haven't managed to get up to see Connie, as it's a bit difficult to get away to town, but I did manage to have lunch with Bill Bailey a few weeks ago.

I haven't space here to reply to all your items in your letters, but by all accounts, you seem to be having a really riotous time – I don't know how you can stand it physically and financially.

Incidentally, my regards to Mac, Stanley and the rest of the gang. Ross, I know, has gone to Borneo, but if you see Bep, our love to her. AND, if you get a chance to see/ring Kirk, give him the 'gen'. Don't let's lose touch with each other, Chris, so write often and let's hear your plans. In the meanwhile,

All love from Stella, Christopher, Kirk & Roy

Look after yourself.

> BM/TGTA
> London W.C. 1
> 9th March '53

Dear Chris,

Firstly, thank you very much for the marriage and baptism certificates, which have safely arrived. I see, too, that I have not yet replied to your letter dated 23rd February, so forthwith. But before I start, will you please write from now on to me c/o the above address? We shall be moving from here at the end of the month, and the above address will cover the transit period.

Another forethought – I've sent you under separate cover, by sea mail, four photos, two of which are for you, and the others for Kirk. Will you pass them on, please? It's very difficult writing to Kirk, as he never writes letters! When you do pass them on, would you do me a very large favour, please? I left a squash racket, press and cover with him, and it would be extremely useful here. Forwarding by sea mail to the accommodation address would do fine.

Now, as regards your being K's godfather in absentia is concerned, I think that it's perfectly O.K. Should there be any snag, I'll let you know at once.

What news of Ross? Has he been in touch with you at all? Or is he too busy in the Borneo long huts?!!

Miss Margaret Ross seems to have had you hopping around

in a big way. Isn't she the one who once arrived in an Anson?[176]

I think I mentioned that I did contact Connie once, and we made a tentative date, but somehow it fell through – due mainly to the arrival of Kirk, I believe. At any rate, I've decided to leave it until Stella can join in, as it were; it'll be more interesting for Connie anyway, I imagine. I certainly remember that when I did speak to her on the 'phone, she seemed to be on great form, and perfectly fit.

The weather is gradually improving, and it means much to everyone here, as you'll well remember. Christopher doesn't seem at all jealous of Kirk, which is a good thing, of course, and before long I anticipate having two huge boys racing around the place. Poor Stella is completely outsexed now: three to one! But just the same she has coped marvellously – I honestly don't know how she does it.

Well, once more, the end of a letter. I'll keep you fully in the picture, Chris, and let you know immediately anything exciting happens.

Stella sends you all her love, as do (does) Christopher, Kirk & Roy

PERMANENT ADDRESS
C/O BM/TGTA
LONDON W.C. 1
Good Friday

My dear Chris,

The briefest of brief notes to check if you're still in the land of the living – as you haven't replied to either mine or Stella's letters, we are, to put it mildly, a trifle distraught.

Your No. 2 godson is blooming, as are we all, and we have a photo of him we would like to despatch to you, once we learn definitely that you still exist. Stella asks me to tell you that Christopher accompanies us to Mass regularly and behaves himself reasonably well.

Write soon.

---

176 The Avro Anson was a British twin-engined aircraft used by the RAF during and after World War II. After the war, the second-generation Anson was also used as a light transport and executive civil airplane.

With love from us all,
Roy

P.S. What of Kirk & Ross? Any news?

H. & S. B.C.

Penang

30.5.53

Dear Chris,

I have intended to write for some time to let you know that I met the couple who passed through here via P. & O. and unfortunately we did not manage more than a "Hallo" in the bank. I have forgotten their names so perhaps you will let me have a chit so that I know them next time.

It seems quite a while since the party at your Mess[177] – a very enjoyable party it was too. I have had the rest of my leave since then and could do with another.

Roy wrote some time ago saying he was O.K. – I don't know what he is doing now, but that is my fault as I haven't written to him as yet.

Coronation celebrations[178] are about to commence with astonishing violence, and I imagine Singapore will be a pretty colourful place in the next week. Most of my time is supposed to be spent in controlling crowds – I still do police work as a pastime.

Should you have some leave and think of coming to Penang, remember there is room in the Mess!

Cheerio for now, and best wishes,
Peter

---

177 Christopher was living in Turquand Youngs Mess (accommodation for expatriate bachelor employees) at No. 1 Bishopsgate, Singapore.

178 Elizabeth II was crowned queen on 2nd June 1953 at Westminster Abbey in London aged 25 after acceding to the throne on the death of her father, King George VI on 6th February 1952. The service was attended by representatives from 129 nations and territories. Malaya and Singapore were among Commonwealth countries taking part in and celebrating the Coronation. Some 30,000 men took part in the procession along the Mall from the armed forces and police, including 2,000 from the Commonwealth and 500 from the 'Colonies'. The Coronation was the first service to be televised by the BBC and was watched by 27 million of the UK's 36 million population.

PERMANENT ADDRESS
C/O BM/TGTA
LONDON W.C. 1
Sunday 7th June '53

My dear Chris,

How very nice to get a letter from you, after all this time. For my part, I was convinced that a) you'd taken over Stanley's duties, and had been ambushed; or b) just didn't want to write anymore. However, I'm so pleased to hear from you again, that you're forgiven your long delay in writing, as you knew you would be, of course!

To answer your letter in good order, I have had a job for some time now, details of which I do not intend entrusting to the post, and I fare well. Stella and both your godsons are in excellent fettle, and all of us, with the occasional absence of Kirk, attend Mass regularly.

Just for the record, Kirk was baptised on Sunday 24th May 1953. His names: Aloysius Kirkwood Royden Coulson-Gilmer. For a breakdown, I would inform you that Aloysius was a last-minute touch, as the local priest looked so shocked when I rolled out his other titles. He will, naturally, always be Kirk, just as Christopher will always be another you. As a matter of fact, both their names were a complete breakaway from the usual family nomenclature, and to my mind, a good thing too! The name of your 'stand-in', by the way, was Minnie!! Kirk was named Royden in order to avoid any invidious comparison with Christopher, later on. No further apology.

I do not intend settling down in England, and intend going abroad just as soon as an opportunity presents itself. As a matter of fact, something of the sort is in the air at the moment, and I will let you know immediately anything materialises.

As far as Jagjit Singh is concerned, I'm afraid that it's all rather late for that. Of course, I fully appreciate that a lot of pressure was put on him by the local Bar Association for giving evidence for me, and I imagine that life for him will be difficult to say the least. I appreciate his actions more than he will ever know, more particularly as I had hardly even spoken to him and wrote to him fairly recently and asked him to keep me in the picture if he would, but if not, not to trouble, and he fully understood. That's it, then.

No news from Kirk of course, since Xmas. I presume that he's still in S'pore. You might ring him for me, and jog his memory, and tell him that his namesake has just been baptised. I find it very difficult waiting and not receiving replies, although I was warned by his slackness in respect to his other correspondents.

I have heard of the decline in trade of course, but then no one expected the slump to be very far off. Bad luck about poor old Mac. Perhaps you'd like to let me have his address. Perhaps I could drop him the odd line.

Of course, all we have had for the last six months is CORONATION, and at last it's all over. By any standards, it seems to have been an overwhelming success, and better perhaps than expected.

You must make a point of writing to me regularly, Chris; it's good for you, and besides, it will keep you out of the 'Worlds'[179] one night a week! How is your car running? (By the way, we've had some snaps taken of the christening; will send you samples later.) What are you doing with yourself now? Playing any cricket? You really should try and keep it up, although you didn't seem very keen last year. You'll be interested to know that I've been to see the Australians, who are touring England *au moment*. Very, very efficient, although I should say, a bit on the old side. By their standards, you've quite a few years of 1st-class cricket left in you, Chris!!

Repeat, I do not get any local gossip, so please act as a broadsheet and give me all the 'gen'. I get the odd line from Ross of course, safe in the heart of Borneo, and rather gather that he now considers his move not altogether a good one. But perhaps you've seen Bep. I believe she's still in S'pore.

Please write soon. Stella particularly stresses this. We were all very happy to hear from you and hope that one way or the other we'll all be together one of these days.

---

179 Before the days of television and shopping malls from the 1930s until the 1960s, Singapore's main nightlife consisted of three huge open-air amusement parks, 'Happy World' (renamed 'Gay World' in 1966, though without today's meaning), 'Great World' and 'New World' which offered a variety of entertainment from sports matches, films, cabaret and nightclubs to fairground rides, shopping and cultural dances.

Lots of love from us all, and take care of yourself.
Stella, Christopher, Kirk and Roy

British Embassy
Djakarta.
19.6.53

Dear Chris,

What an odd thing! I decided last night that I would write to you today to tell you my latest news, and now today your letter arrived. Many thanks. It was good of you to write.

Yes, I have been enjoying poor health for the last few months, in fact most of the time I have been in Djakarta, but I didn't realise just how rotten I felt (and looked!) until I was over in Singapore and enjoying life so much. So I set wheels in motion to get transferred, and the Foreign Office, in the goodness of their hearts, are posting me to Hong Kong at the beginning of July – at least, that seems fairly certain. Funnily enough, the thought never entered my head! Wish I had thought of it earlier… I could have been transferred to Singapore, but for various reasons decided against it. I may pass through S'pore on my way to Hong Kong, and if so, will let you know as soon as possible. I have it very much on my conscience that I still owe you $6. Also, a possibility that our Air Attaché will make a flying visit in his NEW plane and has promised to take one keen passenger!

Yes, I had heard that the Knights had left Subang. But you know how gossip is in these places – I heard it was because of their own domestic troubles.

Lebaran was GHASTLY! My cook went away for a week, and the babu for two days, and my little pavilion (I am now on my own in a microscopic place) got more and more squalid. I had to beg meals off friends, since the first night I tried to cook dinner a rat ran over my foot in the kitchen and I only ever ventured into it again to boil water for my bath and make my morning coffee.

Our Coronation festivities were great fun. I'm told that all the feuds at present in operation in Djakarta are the result of the last Coronation and the feuds made at this one will last well into the next! Nevertheless, it was all great fun. I saw the colour film last night and, in spite of a Dutch commentary, was terribly moved – I felt like knocking down the first *betja*[180] driver out of sheer superiority! What with Everest as well, and Gordon Richards winning the Derby (!), and no Americans in the Open Golf, all we need now are the Ashes…

Eh bien, I hope to see you shortly. I'll try to let you know as soon as I do myself what the exact plans are.

As ever,
Margaret

> 177B Mount Kellett
> The Peak
> Hong Kong
> 17th July

Dear Chris,

I am just getting my breath back! I was whirled out of Singapore at a moment's notice, roared up here in a Cathay Pacific plane which I felt would fall to pieces in the air (the F.O. always do things on the cheap!), and have been moving at high speed ever since in and out of the office. The people here seem very friendly, and I've been in the middle of the usual preliminary entertaining that surrounds a newcomer.

Hong Kong is absolutely lovely. You should try to come up here if you can get leave. I have always heard that it was one of the most beautiful places in the East, but never imagined it to be quite as lovely as this. I'm living in a flat way up on the Peak and the view is absolutely breath-taking. After Djakarta I'm thoroughly enjoying the coolness (an air-conditioned office!) and the cleanness. Also, the baths. I'm sharing this flat with two of the girls from the office. The drive to the office is quite hair-raising, as the hills and bends are terribly steep. I should never dare drive here! I've been down to the

---

180 Indonesian-style rickshaw, a 3-wheeled pedicab with passenger seat. Also known as *becak,* the word originates from *Be Chia,* Chinese Hokkien dialect for 'horse carriage', though the *betja* driver is a man pedalling.

town and looked at the shops, which are full of the most exciting things. I shall have no money when I leave here.

Chris, I'm sorry I didn't see much of you in Singapore. I'm afraid the four days weren't nearly long enough for everything I wanted to do. Do write and tell me all your news.

As ever,
Margaret

PERMANENT ADDRESS
C/O BM/TGTA
LONDON W.C. 1.
July 22nd 1953

My dear Chris,

Many thanks for your letter dated 12th July – we'd almost given you up for good. I am sorry that you've been bothered about the job thing, but it didn't really matter. As a matter of fact, I've given up any idea of taking that particular one, for several reasons. I would like to think, however, that I might use you as a reference in future and hope that it's O.K. by you.

Likewise, I hope that we'll meet up with each other, and am sure that we will, if we both want to sufficiently – it's as simple as that. As you must have gathered, I'm working here, and doing quite well (I think!!), but it is only a stepping stone to other things; perhaps we'll be able to get together on this later on.

I don't really blame you for not wanting to go out to Malaya again. Apart from anything else, I believe things are becoming a little difficult in business these days.

Surprised that you haven't managed to skittle 'em all out at the S.C.C. – you always had a better length than I did (let's face it!!), and I'm doing all rightish still!

The Segamat 'do' sounded fun. Wish I'd been there – I could just about use an occasion like that now!?!

Bluett I remember – good for him! No news on squash request from Kirk. Please pass on my regards and tell him I'm still waiting for his letter – also, of course, the racket! I didn't know about the

Knights – where are they bound for now, and who and what is going on in the P. & T. accounts dept.? What about Cormac?

Your two godsons fare well. K. has 2 teeth; C. is perhaps just a little dickey *au moment* – we hope a little hospitalisation will fix him up shortly. Nothing to worry about, I hope!

I'm glad that Ross contacted you so promptly, and in turn am still waiting to hear from him. No doubt you'll jog his elbow for me, please?

What are your plans for the future? When is your leave due? I can understand your not particularly wanting to go back East, but don't suppose for a moment that you wish to stay in England? There just can't be any comparison as far as money, standard of living and future is concerned. What about Canada? They're going ahead there like a house on fire. You know more about the country than I do – perhaps you've some ideas?

Had a letter from Peter Briggs the other day – big surprise really, I'd almost given him up for lost. Silly, but I was rather hurt, as we'd been quite good pals in Penang, and as you know, he'd helped me a lot when the nonsense was going on.

(Incidentally, I suppose you did pass the photo to Kirk?)

Ross seems to have fallen on his feet, and a very good thing too. It must have been extremely worrying for him, after the Borneo fiasco. It obviously didn't turn out as well as he had hoped and could have been very awkward if he'd fallen out of the frying pan into the fire! Are you seeing anything of him/them these days? And how d'you get on with Bep now?

Referring back to Peter for the moment, he tells me that he had a 'talk' with you at your Mess, when he last saw you. For shame! What I wouldn't give to be there with you now. No more news of 'Mac', I suppose? What about Stanley et al.? P. B. tells me that he was virtually proposed to recently – which brings me to G. C. T. R. What about it, Chris – you're not trying! Still haven't seen Connie, of course.

Time and pages running short. Can we look forward to hearing from you reasonably now? We do hope so. Take good care of yourself, and love from us all.

Yours,
Roy

6/10/1953

Chris, my darling,

How are you? As usual, it's years since I last wrote to you, and since I heard from you… I meant to keep my promise to write to you from Capri, but somehow or other I just didn't, for which my humble apologies.

I have just had a telephone call from your Mr. Phillips, who is here to discuss, among other things, the business about Pifar's tax, payable by Pirelli Holding. This headache has been one which has worried me a good deal as I have been ploughing through old files trying to get out the information TYM in Singapore require. However, we are to see him on Thursday to try to straighten out the knots. I asked him how you were, and he said you were settling in very well and seemed quite happy with the life there.

What is new in Singapore? Here, life seems to jog along much the same as ever; I had a very lovely time in Italy and got brown […] but it has now all worn off, except on my body where some remains. The sun doesn't shine strongly enough in England, although it has been very pleasant here all through last month and even now is quite sunny, although frosty in the mornings and late evenings and quite misty. The leaves are just about beginning to turn colour but there is still a lot of green about and it doesn't seem to be too wintery yet, which is a blessing and certainly different from last year.

I saw Gillie on Saturday when we both went to see the International Club match at the Queen's Club, which was great fun; unfortunately, Pam couldn't come as she went to Finchley to welcome her mother back from a stay in Jersey, where she stayed with Mr. Asgarzadeh.[181] He seems to delight in the life there and has taken a bit more interest in life than he did at Finchley. They are both fairly well […] They have made lots of improvements in their lovely flat (I don't think you have ever seen it, but I'm not sure) and seem to be very happy. Gillie helped Jocelyn the other day over the move from Twynersh; it seems awful to think that those wonderful weekends we used to have there cannot ever be repeated; it was a

---

181 Pam's father.

very pleasant house but I'm sure the new flat is a better proposition and is still near enough to Cobham for Mr. Repton to enjoy the cricket. Gillie said your parents seem to be very content there. It seems to me to be partway to solving one of your difficulties, and I do hope things work out really well, Chris, dear.

We have finished the major redecorations to the inside of Highwood and are now coping with renewing various fixtures; we do miss not having Teddy at home to fix things like the lights which have gone out in two rooms and which are not mended by a fuse – we shall have to get an electrician in to see to them, I fear. Teddy is enormously busy at the moment, working weekends and late at nights on some ship they have to complete quickly, so we see nothing of him, unfortunately […]

Did I tell you that Leo de Stefani is here in London as the Labour Counsellor to the Italian Embassy? He, Gill, Pam and I had a lovely dinner the other evening at Kettner's and had lots of fun. He seems to be happy here but cannot find a suitable flat for himself and his wife.

I have just started to think about Christmas – isn't it awful? But I want to get all the presents before the ghastly rush starts and you have to do everything in a flat spin. Especially where friends abroad are concerned – I can't think what to give Margaret. And you of course are a big problem – do write and tell me if you would like anything particular, because it's so difficult to know what to send you out there – I may be sending coals to Newcastle. Please don't forget, Chris, there's a dear.

Do write soon, darling, and tell me all your news; it seems too long ago that I heard from you, but then we are both pretty ghastly letter-writers, I suppose. I still think about you such a lot and wonder how you are, and ponder about everything – ah me, it seems aeons before you are due to return to England and I shall be able to see you again. I do hope to write to you a longer letter soon, but don't scold me if I don't; it doesn't mean I've forgotten you!

Lots of love, darling.
From Connie
xxx

H.M.A.S. *Sydney*
c/o Fleet Mail Office
Singapore
Sunday 8th Nov.

My dear Chris,

I was extremely glad to hear from you, and very sorry that I was unable to see you. I tried to contact you on the Tuesday via Francis Peek, however they were not at all helpful. Astrid hoped very much that I would see you as she has always had a soft spot for you; so have I for that matter. That awful photograph did serve some purpose after all.

I am on loan to the Australian Navy for one year approximately. As you surmised, *Sydney* is now on her way to Korea. Prior to coming up here I spent five months in Australia, where I looked up Syd Carter. He is very fit and working as an accountant for some big firm. He told me you were still in Singapore. I have his address should you require it. I also ran into Victor Post in Sydney. You may remember him. He was rather a gross Dutchman who worked in the P. & T. Batavia office. Pete de Vries lives in Perth with his son. The son owns a dry-cleaning business and Pete helps. I didn't see the latter, which was a pity.

I do wish I could have seen you as I have a lot to tell you and undoubtedly a lot to hear. Anyway, I should be in Singapore again in about six months so will see you then.

Astrid is very well. We now have a family of three – all boys, worse luck. The last one was born in July this year, so I haven't seen it.

Syd Carter told me that June van der Molen was now in Singapore with her husband. I gather they have a family. I should like to see her again.

I am not quite sure how much P. & T. news you know; you very probably know more than I do. I gather Dick Shaw is Acting Representative in Fletcher's absence, and also that they are closing down this year.

So Roy is back in England! Oddly enough, I met some people from Kenya who had known him out there. Syd actually told me that he had left Singapore or was about to leave.

We arrive in Hong Kong tomorrow, when I'll post this. If you have time let me hear more of yourself. Thank you very much for troubling to write. If you hadn't, I might never have located you, and I do want to see you again.

All the best.

Yours,
Bobby Cox

P.S. My address is Lieut. N. B. Cox, R.N., H.M.A.S. *Sydney*, c/o Fleet Mail Office, Singapore.

PERMANENT ADDRESS
C/O BM/TGTA
LONDON W.C. 1.
November 21st

My dear Chris,

Nice to get a letter from you at long last. You were quite right in assuming that you owed us a letter. Shame on you.

How amusing to see Bobby Cox in a beard. I wonder how Astrid and the babes are getting on?

Frank Warner. No letter from him, in spite of your passing on our address. For old times' sake, we've sent him a card for Xmas, and imagine that he's still at the Johore estate.

You'll pardon my jumping about like a grasshopper, but I'm trying to answer your questions point by point – else, I just won't make it.

Rugger – I've had it really. I'm not quite sure what I'm trying to prove. Talking of which, big day here – Cardiff beat the All Blacks 8–3.

Like yourself, I've not heard from Ross Smith for some time now. Perhaps he'll get around to it now that the festive season's approaching. I suppose he is still in Malaya? What with the retrenching going on, I thought perhaps he might have been 'axed'.

Yes, Kirk was always hard to contact. Try dropping him another note – might work!

My plans are very indefinite. My present job is quite reasonable, and I could carry on with it indefinitely, but frankly, as you know, never having lived in England, I feel very strange here. Of course, there are so many other factors to consider: Stella, your godsons, etc. However, without any doubt, we'll meet up again one of these bright young days – at least we all here hope so.

You shall receive snaps of the C.-G.s *en famille* in due course, but *au moment*, weather etc. is rather against that sort of thing. Talking about paper clippings, I'd appreciate your bundling up some of your used newspapers from time to time and sending them off to us by sea mail. We'd get quite a lot of fun out of reading them.

Christopher, who of course is quite a young man now (still blonde), is now undergoing the 'patch' treatment for his eyes. I suppose you know how it works, and I certainly hope that it does. Kirk is much darker, never stops grinning, and will, we think, be even larger than Christopher! Stella is in great shape, misses her golf, but hopes to return to it when the babes are older.

Having forgotten Stanley's proper name, I can't very well write. However, if you feel like supplying it, in your next letter, I'll drop him a line. What about Mac? Did you ever get his? The old reprobate!! […]

Exactly when are you due for leave, and what will your plans be then? Try and let us know. Your replies are so few and far between that we mostly forget our queries by the time we make contact again. How are things locally, by the way? We gather that generally business is not so good, but only in general terms. And what of the Emergency?

Talking of snaps, how about sending us a few? I don't think we've any of you/us except those taken in Java.

Well, that seems to about cover it, Chris, and to bring you up to date. Try and write a little more often, as we'd like to think that you're still in there swinging.

All our love to you from Stella, Roy, Christopher and Kirk

1954

17 Brandon Road
Fawdon
Newcastle upon Tyne 3
7th January 1954

Dear Chris,

A Happy New Year, and I hope that you have had a merry Xmas. I had a very quiet time at home enjoying the mild weather, which has now deserted us. As I write the ground is covered with snow and more is falling. Everything is very chilly, and I would much prefer to have the long, warm tropical day.

I had an uneventful journey home. The only incident was a diversion from Zurich to Nice on account of fog, which delayed us for two hours. I stayed at the Cumberland in London for a week and found it comfortable but expensive. However, everything in London is expensive. This is the first thing that struck me – I suppose partly because I was paying cash for everything and could actually observe the £ sterling sliding through my hands, but also because prices do compare pretty well with Singapore. Cinemas – 9/– to 12/– for a reasonable seat; whisky soda 2/4d. An ordinary, reasonable meal – 6/– to 10/–. The only commodity that I have so far found to be cheaper is draft (or draught) beer at 1/6d – 1/8d a pint – but this I find disappointing after Anchor and Tiger. It can be drunk in large quantities without any apparent effect. I have stuck to it, though, and am beginning to acquire a taste for it once more, though I prefer bottled Worthington or Bass (2/10d to 3/– a pint).

Whilst in London I had to work at the office for two days on the Shell audits, being interrogated on audit methods and practices adopted […] by a Dutchman called De Younge and a Mr. Cherry of P. & W. & Co. I also had to spend a Sunday morning filling in a large questionnaire. Everything seems to have gone off alright as far as I can tell.

I also spent a day collecting the car, which I find very satisfactory, and another day attempting to drive it to Cambridge through thick fog, which made me abandon the journey halfway.

I hoped to see Stanley, but he was behaving very mysteriously and typically. Garrett, with whom I had a night out, told me that S. had sold his house (and nobody knew his new address), but had promised to ring the office just before my arrival. This he did not do. Then after about four days I received a 'phone message at the Cumberland to say that Mr. Maymon had rung whilst I was out and would ring again, but he did not do so. On the Thursday night before my departure north, T.Y. & Co. had their annual dinner to which I was invited and to which Stanley was supposed to be going, but on the Thursday morning he rang T.Y. & Co. to say that he could not go. So I did not see him. It appears, however, that he now intends to rejoin the firm and is talking about going back to Singapore before his leave expires.

The staff dinner was quite good – tomato soup, turkey and Xmas pudding, with as much white and red wine as you cared to drink. This was followed by a couple of female entertainers, singing a mixture of sentimental and low, but amusing songs. They were followed by a mediocre conjurer and after that there were free drinks until 11 p.m.

I did not go to any shows or hear any music. That I will do when I return to London for three weeks in a month's time. Until then I remain in Newcastle, playing the piano, reading, and drinking beer. I am so far untouched by romance.

Give my regards to the others.

Yours sincerely,
Walter

17 Brandon Road
Newcastle upon Tyne 3
4th April 1954

Dear Chris,

I was pleased to receive your letter, which, it seems, must have been written just before my letter regarding accommodation reached you. Since that subject takes up a fair portion of your letter we may as well deal with it straightaway.

My acceptance of Norman's invitation to share the house in Thiam Siew Avenue was made on the understanding that I would be able to go there as soon as I returned to Singapore. When he wrote and told me that he had meanwhile taken in this other fellow and that I would consequently not be able to go there until Norman went on leave, I replied postponing any possibility of an arrangement until I returned to Singapore. I am therefore free to make any other arrangements that I please, without regard to Thiam Siew Avenue.

You will know from my last letter that what I want is a flat, and that I would be very happy to share one with you. I was pleased to learn from your letter that the same thought was in your mind. Can we, therefore, agree to do this? If so, I suggest that you go ahead with your suggestion of looking round for one, and I am quite ready to trust your judgement should you find one which seems suitable before my return.

As regards expenses, I would be prepared to share rent and servants' wages as from the date of your occupation. The question of a premium would probably arise, and I suggest that the firm might be willing to advance this temporarily on a short repayment basis. If they are not, then we can probably manage to raise the money ourselves, and I would prefer to do that if there were any question of the firm obtaining the lease of the flat in return for an advance of the premium. If the firm want some security, I could probably provide it, if the premium were of a reasonable amount (which I trust it would be). As between ourselves I would suggest that the premium be written off over the term of the lease, so that if you did not return to Singapore after leave (or did so but did not come back to the flat) then you would bear only a proportionate part of any premium.

I think that the foregoing sets out my proposals in sufficient detail at this stage, and I look forward to learning your views in the near future. I should also like to have your confirmation that, if necessary, I shall be able to return temporarily to the Mess when I get back, as I should much prefer that to a boarding house.

Now to deal with the remainder of your letter.

I did not enjoy the cold spell, but it must have done me good for I find that I am now troubled less by cold days than other people seem to be if one can rely on their comments. There is no snow in the N. of England except for small patches on high ground.

On grounds of expense, I have decided not to go to Paris. It is costing me more than my budget in England. My minimum daily expenditure during the three weeks I had in London worked out at £3.12.1 a day and usually exceeded that. Most of the things that one spends money on during leave are at least as expensive as in Singapore and often more, viz:-

Petrol 4/6d a gallon
Cigarettes 3/9d for 20
Tobacco 4/9d an ounce
Decent beer 2/6d a pint (bottled)
Draught beer 1/8d, ditto
Whisky soda 2/6d (average)
Meals (ordinary) 6/–
Meals (good) 10/– to 30/– (oysters 12/6d per ½ dozen!)

Many things which go to make up the cost of living are cheaper, of course; clothing, for example, but you don't consume much clothing in six months. In this connection laundry charges are high, which does affect you.

I am not saying that I find myself hard up, far from it, but the expense is appreciably higher than I expected.

I have not heard anything further from the firm about the Shell audits since I had the session in London, so I assume that in this connection, no news is good news. B. B., I hear, has been to Djakarta in the capacity of inquisitor, which is the more agreeable position to be in.

You all seem to have been very busy in the office. I will not say that I grieve for you – in fact one derives a certain amount of added satisfaction in one's leave from the knowledge, though it is tinged with the foreboding that a similar fate lurks ahead in 2½ months' time.

I am sorry to hear that you have temporarily lost touch with Molly at the Cricket Club. Please give him my regards when you see him next.

I enclose a brief note which you might pass on to G. V. H.

Yours sincerely,
Walter

Farningham
2/6/54

My dearest Chris,

I've been meaning to write to you for ages; Mother forwarded one of your letters on to me in March (I was staying in town for a period) but it never reached me, much to my utter disgust and annoyance. So it really is simply years since I heard from you; I should, of course, write regularly to you anyway, but I fear I don't unless I hear from you!

I had lunch with Margaret Bond yesterday and was very upset to hear you have been ill, and that the long period in the Far East is upsetting you rather. I hope you got the messages I sent out to you via D., although he said he had very little time in Singapore and didn't have much opportunity to see Turquandia except on business with Mr. Phillips. Knowing him, I fear he's quite capable of forgetting everything, and not having heard from you I expect I'm right. Anyway, do try to drop me a line shortly, as I feel awfully worried about how you are. I had a vivid dream about you last night.

As a matter of fact, Dr. and I are shortly coming to a parting of the ways, at least temporarily. He is getting more and more impossible to work for, and as I've had an offer from the young Mr. Pirelli to go to work for him as his secretary in Italy, I think it extremely likely I shall go – probably in October. I am a little sad about it, for it means I shan't have much time with you when you come home on leave next year, but I do hope that you will manage to get a boat coming home via Italy, and perhaps you could somehow or other come to Milan and stay for a few days so that I can see you. Do think it over, Chris, darling; I'll keep you fully posted of my movements and maybe you will let me know what you feel about it.

I haven't seen very much of Pam and Gillie recently; for one thing we had the tragedy in the family – my brother Teddy died in Venezuela whilst on a mission there for Vickers-Armstrongs. You will, I know, be upset to hear about it, and you can imagine what a terrible shock it was for all of us, particularly for Mummy. The period between his death and the funeral at home (he was brought back) was ghastly and I really don't know how we got through it all.

However, the worst feeling has passed, and we are slowly getting back to normal. I felt it more than I had realised at the time, got run-down and had chickenpox, of all things, rather badly. I've now been back at work for just a fortnight and am getting over that awful depression one gets after an illness which was quite nasty, in spite of its childish nature. I hope to see something of Pam and Gillie soon; we had arranged to meet John Shelley for lunch, but Teddy's death put an end to that. However, perhaps we shall manage it soon, and I will send you all the gossip.

The weather here is pretty awful; however, the English countryside (which we both love so much) is looking simply glorious, lush and green, all the summer flowers just coming to perfection. The garden at home is, however, quite a problem and I sometimes wonder how to cope with it all.

Not having seen Pam or Gillie for some time, I don't know how Jocelyn and the family are; I do hope they are well and that your father is still able to enjoy the cricket. Gillie started to play again this season but ricked his knee and so I'm not sure if he is still playing. Do you manage to get any games? And what are you doing? I do long to hear from you and I hope this letter will prompt you to reply by return! Do write, Chris, dear, even if it's only a line; I think about you such a lot and wonder such a lot about things. It seems a whole lifetime ago since I last saw you and I do hope that you will be able to manage to come to see me if and when I go to Milan. Forgive this typewritten letter; I will try very hard to write to you regularly and I hope you will manage to do the same. Do take care of yourself and don't get too tired in that awful climate.

All my love, Chris.
Connie

16th Nov. '54

Dear Christopher,

I have no idea how long this letter will take to reach Singapore now that the Comets are out of action but hope it will arrive before or on Christmas Day. I hope that you will have a good time. I can

360

recollect many very enjoyable anniversaries in my bachelor days in New York, in spite of absence from home and family. I shall be glad to bid goodbye to this departing year. I cannot remember anything so wretched: rain day after day, cricket suffering awful weekends and very few played to a finish.

I find it difficult to know what to write to you as your mother will have given you all the news.

It is sickening that we should have no proper home now that you are coming home so soon. I cannot express to you properly how I am looking forward. Leila's[182] death was a shock that has aged me, and I am getting deafer every day and find a difficulty in taking part in the animated conversations, not to say arguments, at meals. I try to get my own back by telling the members of the family that their diction is abominable.

An interval here owing to various chores which I have to attend to and as I am told that I should hurry up to catch the next plane, so I will finish up this – I am afraid – lugubrious letter, so best love and wishing you a Happy Christmas.

Your loving father,
B.

1955

P. J. T. Repton
Grasmere
High Road
Byfleet
Surrey
4/3/55

My dear Christopher,

Thanks for your letter which arrived last night – also the photographs; our only complaint was that one couldn't see you behind the sunglasses.

---

182 Bernard's sister.

Chris in Bangkok, February 1955, Monument of Democracy behind

It's cold up here this evening in my bedroom. We've had a week of identical days starting from Monday – very cold, frosty nights and clear, sunlit days; sunlit but coldish. There is no snow left. These two hard months we've had seem to promise us a good summer. I hope so.

It's nice to hear that you are now almost on your way, and we all look forward to seeing you again. Now, your car – I'm sorry about the delay but honestly, I don't remember you asking me. I felt that Gillie was going into it thoroughly – I met him for lunch yesterday before I read your letter and so I phoned him today, and he promises he's writing tonight. I've spoken to several car owners and they are all of the opinion that you should bring it back. The resale value is said to be £350–400 and you would have to pay about the same figure to get a reliable second-hand car which wouldn't involve you in heavy repair charges etc. This is based on £230 for sale in Singapore – no, my reasoning is going wrong… Anyway, it seems that if you want a car while you're over here you would be wise to ship it home, and in the long run, you'd be at least £25 better off and probably more. Gillie will corroborate, and probably in more detail.

It's a pity about the question of accommodation but we'll do the best we can. I quite agree with you about sharing a room, and in any case this room is not really big enough for two beds. At weekends with Gareth and other short occasions we make do but for a long spell – no.

Good Lord, it's nine o'clock and supper not ready – chops tonight.

Don't worry about your holiday in Italy as far as Ma and Pa are concerned. After all, two weeks after 3½ years isn't much and the main thing is we know when to expect you. You might pay a courtesy call on Mr. Ellis in Genoa. We also have agents in Bombay, Colombo and Karachi but we'll leave them alone.

I left this last night and worked this morning for a change (Saturday). Since the weekend is here the weather has gone grey again – very strong N.W. wind and snow showers – what a pity. Will post this in Cobham on way to library.

Love from Jocelyn

Saturday
Saw a 1953 Minor for sale, £525; 1952 – £450.

> Food & Agriculture Organisation of the United Nations
> Viale delle Terme di Caracalla
> Rome
> 14 April 1955

Mon cher Christophe,

Just got your letter from Ceylon – nice stamps. I've been waiting to write to Port Said in case anything else happened, but I haven't heard from Connie, nor could I write to her as you didn't put in the street number of her address. Of course we'll put you up, but there's no room for her, and at this time of year in Rome it's practically impossible to find a room. So, it's just as well perhaps that she doesn't materialise. Also, I can take you round on the Lambretta, whereas *en trois…* The thing would be for her to meet you in the northern cities; you certainly should go to Venice… it's a dream one never really believed in, and yet there it is!

Don't phone from Naples (one mightn't be in); send a wire as soon as you know the date and time of your arrival in Rome and I'll meet you at the station. I suppose you'll have some luggage, so I won't come on the Lambretta – don't be scared; Dickon liked it! Tavazzi, Via Riari 46, Roma: for the wire.

Actually, I thought you were coming on the 23rd. The 22nd is Friday and I'll be at the office until six, so it would be best if you were to arrive after that hour or first thing on Saturday. While you're down there, you ought to do a day trip around the Sorrento peninsula: there are sure to be organised tours. Amalfi and Ravello are the plums. Then you should see Pompeii and Herculaneum, and the Naples Museum, so I think you'd really need two days. What a beautiful place Italy is: one only realises at moments like this, when one's thinking for someone else. You say Rome/Florence/Bologna/Venice/Milan. But what about Perugia/Assisi/Siena? Oh well, we'll have to get down to serious operational planning when you arrive. You won't see much of Alberto, I'm afraid, as he's working like a dog on films for the American television with Douglas Fairbanks Jr. – as Art Director, of course. He leaves the house at 6.30 a.m. and gets back between 9 and 10 in the evening!

Best love,
Bianca

I see I've run things too fine and that your boat leaves Port Said on the 17th. (Why didn't I check up before?!) So I'll chance your getting this at Naples; otherwise – *pazienza*.

Via Circo 12
Milan
Tel.: 864092 / Office 2772
19/4/1955

My dearest Christopher,

Thank you so much for your letter from Colombo which reached me, however, only last week; too late to write to you en route. I had hoped so much to be able to come to Naples to welcome you to Italy, but my boss changed his plans to be away so I cannot take off the time I had planned to. However, this weekend is free for you and I want you to let me know as soon as you can what we are to do. I could be in Rome or Naples on Saturday: we could go to visit Capri for the weekend if you are in Naples still, or see Rome if you are there. The first is probably the nicest idea, but we shall spend a lot of time travelling. On the other hand, I could take one extra day off which would mean 2 complete days of holiday. I will try to see if I could travel down from Milan by sleeper on Friday, arriving at Naples about 11ish Saturday morning. Try to send me a wire telling me what you think.

I really am excited at the prospect of seeing you again and am bitterly disappointed that I can't join you on your arrival. However, I will keep the following weekends free and hope to spend them with you. If you are in difficulty contact our people in Naples – Dr. Germano is unfortunately not there, but there is a man I know slightly called Dr. Bruno Grimaldi who would help you willingly: he is at the cable office in Via Arenaccia 236, Tel.: 54284. If you need help, call him up and tell him you know me; I must do so if I go to

Chris & Connie in carozza near Sorrento, April 1955

Naples. I'm longing to hear your news and to see you: do cable or ring me on Thursday at home, or on Wednesday in the office where I shall be until 6.30 or 7. A cable perhaps would be surer, telling me where and when I can call you.

Longing to see you, Chris, dear. Meanwhile,
Love from Connie

Perugia
1st May '55

My dear Sylvia and June (I hope you will forgive me writing to you both on one card),

It is lovely here and at Assisi and the sun never stops shining – is it similar in England at present? Pity you can't come over and meet me in Paris – that'll be about May 9th if I stick to my schedule. Today I move on to Florence – pity, as I love it here. I think there will be a good summer this year, don't you? Have been taking lots of photos, though they've not all come out well.

Looking forward to seeing you all soon.

Love,
Christopher

Terme di Vicarello
Lago in Bracciano
14.5.55

My dear Christopher,

It was so nice to get your postcard from Perugia. I'd meant to write to you in Florence, but two days after you left, I came down with the sort of influenza that's going around (hope you didn't!) and it ruined everything. We came here on May Day – I feeling rotten but hoping the change wd do me good, but on the Tuesday we went back to Rome so that I cd see a doctor. I went back to the office for a couple of days but was too thoroughly run-down and now the doctor – thank heaven – has ordered ten days' complete rest and I've come here with

Lazio,[183] and Alberto is joining us tomorrow for 2 or 3 days. Various restorative medicines, the good air, peace and quiet, and an enormous appetite are already making me feel more myself. Lazio too – thank you for your enquiry! – is full of beans and, I hope, quite recovered.

I wish you cd have seen a little of the Italian countryside as well as the towns. This place is quite lovely. I am sitting on the luscious grass (alright, it hasn't rained for two months) – everything is very green, because we are over hot water springs; hence the *Terme*, dating back to Etruscan and Roman times. In a week the cures will begin, and it'll be full of people crippled with rheumatism and arthritis – we only come in the off season. The place is run by German nuns and it's beautifully clean and orderly, the food excellent. There's a little noisy brook at my feet going on for ever, and Lazio hides in the bracken on the bank and hopelessly dreams of catching the fireflies. Through the silvery olives the lake gleams a deep powder-blue – it's really a dream of a place. Tomorrow it will seem an earthly paradise – when Alberto has arrived! And of course, the birds are singing their heads off all around. There's a coppice behind me and a grotto reproducing Lourdes – full of flowers; very nun-like and soothing!

I'm going on babbling like the brook! I long to hear how the rest of your Italian sojourn went – hope you met some nice people because it's a bit lonely sightseeing by oneself. I know I'm not fond of Perugia because I was stuck there all alone for two days waiting for Alberto and practically lost the use of my tongue. Did you find that restaurant, I wonder?

I'm only sorry Alberto was still working that last week – though an extra £100 isn't to be sniffed at – because he wd have made so much better a guide than I – are you clear now what are Romanesque churches?! […]

Oh dear – we've been surrounded by a herd of buffaloes/bullocks; prehistoric, excessively large animals with enormous horns. Lazio was scared out of his wits and hid in my arms, though I was little less scared than he. Luckily, they were also scared of us, so cantered off like thunder into the hills. Oh dear, oh dear – I feel quite Victorian. Lazio is not going to get off my lap again.

---

183 Bianca's kitten.

Gilly & Chris map-reading before setting off for Devon, June 1955

I'm terribly happy with my brocade and Alberto was delighted too. Thank you again enormously. Some jolly nice stamps you left me too. Do write when you have time – long to hear.

Love to all the family,
Bianca

Via dei Riari 46
Rome
30 August 1955

My dear Christopher,

For the last three months I've been trying to write to you – hard to believe, isn't it? The fact is I never have enough energy when I have the necessary time, and vice versa. So, I've hurried over my lunch and am determined to dash this off from the office, even if it will be a scrawl. This state of things is due to a very satisfactory cause: the expected arrival of a baby at about the end of the year! We couldn't have been more surprised, and realised that when I wasn't feeling too well just after you were here, remember, it must have been due to the beginnings of all this. We're very happy about it, though we are both getting to an age when it would be more suitable to be becoming grandparents! Luckily,

I'm very well, have a nice doctor in whom I feel confident, and the only disadvantage is that I can't do very much in addition to the office.

One effect of this news: it made us decide to buy a car, because one can't obviously keep on with the Lambretta and Rome's public transport is almost as much out of the question. So, we bought a one-year-old Morris Minor, pale grey, looks new, and has been well maintenanced [sic]. It had done just over 15,000 miles and we paid a little over £300 for it: that's not too bad, is it? Of course, no tax on it – we're running on a carnet. The bore about that was, we had to take it immediately to Nice to get the carnet renewed in my name – 850-odd miles there and back. I went up to San Remo by train, where Alberto's sister had a flat for August; then A. and I drove over to Nice, and we came back to Rome by easy stages. A little tiring but quite bearable. Lord, it's bliss to have it now. The Lambretta had three disadvantages: the kick-starter, the difficulty of carrying parcels and things, and rain (when any). However, I hope to go back to it in due course!

So, you see, there have been changes. We even have another kitten: pitch black, male, abandoned at night in our street at five weeks or so, and quite adorable: beloved of Lazio, who we thought might object, but not at all – perhaps he's not normal! We took the two of them to S. Remo in an enormous basket: they quite enjoyed hotel life and behaved perfectly! Looks as though I'm following in Leila and Ina's footsteps and getting dotty about cats.

Please don't give another thought to the Balzac book. I never meant you to take half that trouble – only if our old copy was still lying about; perhaps H. or G. took it at some time. It couldn't matter less. And though I don't deserve it, I hope you will write a short scribble to tell me how you've enjoyed your stay and how the family are. Please ask your mother to forgive me for not having answered her either. She's on my list! I'm writing to you as I feel you can't be for old England much longer. My own mother is the only other person I've written to, but she hasn't replied yet – her first grandchild!

Love to you all,
Bianca

P.S. Love the photo: if you have the neg. still, wd like it.

Outside Smuggler's Inn, Dawlish. Gilly, Pam and Steve
(cricketing friend) 'before partaking of Double Diamonds'

14 St. John's Wood Terrace
London N.W. 8
14.10.55

Dear Christopher,

How I envy you in your lovely hot country. Odette and I, having fed sumptuously off *escalope de veau*, petits pois and *pommes Dauphines*, are literally laid out in front of a roaring fire, the wind whistling outside the windows, the horrid fog seeping through every crack, stealing into our little den. Think I'll be an Eskimo, cover myself with blubber, and hibernate for the entire winter.

Oh, Christopher, it was lovely hearing from you. Please do write very often, if it's not too much trouble.

We are listening to the Danish State Symphony Orchestra, director Eric Coates, playing the *Queen Elizabeth Suite*[184] from Copenhagen.

Newsflashes from the old country. London is agog with the

---

184 June may be referring to *The Three Elizabeths Suite*.

news of Captain Townsend and Princess Margaret.[185] He returned yesterday, and visited Clarence House, where he was literally swamped with reporters. Consequently, an appeal has just been made by the BBC to respect the privacy of the Royal Family in this matter.

The Russians are having a wonderful orgy with the Cadets at Portsmouth, eating and drinking and being very merry. They have just sung your song – the one with all those verses. (The Mrs. Whittaker choice.)

Sylvia stayed with me last weekend. I made the ghastly mistake of asking her the night before to come to Mass the following morning. Of course, she thought that I was trying to start a campaign, and promptly refused to come. You see, it's as I told you in Byfleet. She'll come next time, though, as I'll revert to the old ritual. It was such a pity that she did not come, as we had the most wonderful sermon by a padre – a real preacher, a born one, who came from the East End of London, and who could have stirred even a Pagan, should there have been one amongst the congregation. How marvellous it must be to be able to move a whole mass of people, even to salvation.

Norway is off. Rather shattering, as I was practically there, having got as far as choosing my skis in Oxford Street and gathering together endless leaflets and library books on Norway, all of which now almost reach to the ceiling! I suppose that the next item on the agenda will be a topee, as I shall probably find myself on the Equator.

How frightful for you with all these delays. I do admire the attractive girl on the postcard. Hope that they are not all so lovely.

Hurry up and come back, Christopher. We all miss you so much. Wish you were here. I hated seeing you go at the Airport. Thought of you every hour or so – imagined you over the sea, coast, and then

185 The Queen's twenty-two-year-old younger sister had an affair with her late father's equerry, which became a royal scandal, as he was married. Although Captain Peter Townsend divorced his wife and proposed to Princess Margaret, she had to ask the Queen's permission to marry, but Queen Elizabeth advised Princess Margaret to delay. The Church of England disapproved of marriage to divorcees, and had she married Townsend when she came of age at twenty-five, Margaret would have had to renounce her claim to the throne and her royal allowance. On the 31st October, she issued a statement saying that she had decided not to marry Townsend, due to the Church's teachings about Christian marriage.

[…] Airport. If I find any good detective stories, I'll send you some. Look after yourself, Christopher.

Much love,
June

P.S. Would you like me to knit you a pullover for Christmas?

29 Nov. 1955

Dear Christopher,

'Many Happy Returns.' I cannot write you a long letter as Mother must have given you all the news; moreover, those infernal planes are revving at their worst […] and my eyes are very bad. I went to the eye place in Cobham for an appointment for 4.30 and did not leave until 6, and the gist of the examination was, after a good deal of technical jargon, my age.

You must be wondering why I have not sent you the Family Budget, but while the Expenditure by Theme is easy there is a mass of payments to be analysed. There are so many interruptions for shopping […], etc., involving a break in continuity in pulling together the figures. I will make an effort to finish the job before Christmas. I do hope you will have a festive time.

Your departure has left a sad gap in our daily round. We miss not only your company but the trips in Surrey. Mother and I thoroughly enjoyed them, for Mother especially as she cannot do much walking.

With best wishes for Christmas and the New Year,
Your loving father

1956

Hamburg-Amerika Linie
Penang
18th July 1956

Sylvia above Housel Bay, Cornwall, July 1955

Dear Chris,

This is just a wee note to say thank you to Bill and yourself for waiting so patiently for such a long time in order to wave us off. As we sailed away from the wharf, Trevor remarked that his one and only regret in leaving Singapore was his friendship with you and Walter.

This ship is everything it promised to be – we are sleeping like logs, eating like hogs, and having a wonderful time. The Captain is now trying to make up for lost time and we are batting along at 19 knots; quite a speed. We sailed into Port Swettenham, but as the cargo was not ready, the Captain refused to wait, and we sailed right out again. He also says he is going up the East Coast of Africa "to miss the monsoon" – only a mere 300 miles out of the way, but I gather it actually takes less time than battling the monsoon all the way to Aden in mid-ocean. I guess we'll arrive home sometime, somehow; meanwhile I can take four or five weeks of this life with no trouble at all.

Hope you can read this – have not quite got my sea legs yet, which is as good an excuse as any for my atrocious script.

I will write again when we have more news of our future plans. Meanwhile, thank you for seeing us off on Tuesday.

Very best wishes from T. and me, Jean

S. M. Repton
Grasmere
High Road
Byfleet
Surrey
28th August 1956

My dear Christopher,

You are too wonderful for words and I shouldn't really take advantage of you, but I promise I will return. Thank you very much.

We arrive in Rome 6 a.m. Sunday morning. I'm writing this under great stress at Olympia – I'm at the Food Fair. There's a record at intervals of a chorus singing 'Who Took the Murray Mints?' and there's a tea bar right next to me and people keep leaving their cups on my table and empty beer glasses and I have to get after them […]

Did you know Hilde is expecting a baby in February? I believe you do. (Jocelyn's a hep cat tonight – he's got Nat King Cole on the radio.) Humphry and Hilde are pleased about your talking about marriage. You ought to have your pick. You are God's gift to any woman if you'd only realise it. I don't think you messed things up. You were just unlucky. You ought to try a few more.

I can't concentrate. My head will be in a whirl till Saturday.

Rosamund went up to Yorkshire this morning for a week.

Will write to you from Italy. Thanks again for the money.

All my love,
Sylvia

FOURTEEN

I Miss You Most in the Morning

1957–1959

Theresa

Christopher was involved in the Society of Friends of Singapore, a group trying to preserve all the local monuments and old buildings. So, he gave me quite a bit of typing work to do. One evening, there was a talk by Professor Lim Yew Tan. Christopher invited me to go along to take down the notes for him. From that time onwards, we saw more of each other.

Christopher used to come to tea on Saturdays at 17 Alnwick Road, after I got back from Novena.[186] Also, sometimes in the evenings he would drop in for his whisky soda. When Walter was away, on some evenings he invited me to 24 Dunsfold Drive for dinner. It was he who introduced me to sparkling red burgundy, which I loved. He said his father used to get it at Christmastime for his mother. After dinner, we sat out on the patio, listening to records; mainly Chopin, which was my introduction to the composer. I enjoyed that.

Braddell Heights is not very far from Serangoon Gardens, so sometimes Christopher picked me up and we would go for a drink at the Palm Tree Inn in Bartley Road, which was just at the top of Braddell Road. Then we would go for a drive somewhere on the east coast.

I recollect our first date was on the day when Dick and Amy were married,

---

186   Evening prayers at the Redemptorist Church of St. Alphonsus in Thomson Road.

and in the evening they were having a reception at 17 Alnwick Road. That night I went out instead for dinner and dancing with Christopher. But I did attend the wedding reception in the afternoon, so I didn't feel guilty about not being there for the evening.

Christopher used to take me across the Causeway to Johor Bahru, to a Chinese restaurant called the Hai Suan, where they served delicious crabs – crab claws, especially. We used to have lovely evenings travelling across with no customs problems and out in a couple of hours. He drove a black Morris Minor with a Penang number plate. He also used to take me to Bedok for Chinese food at the Mun Yuen Restaurant. For only S$12, you could have a lovely dinner for two, including Christopher's two whisky sodas.

His salary in those days, when he started at TYs, was S$1,250 per month before tax. He was always running out of money as his rent and expenses were much higher than mine, and I had to foot the bill, but he paid me back a few days later. It was fun, and sometimes we went to Pasir Ris, where there was an open-air dance floor and a band. I think we went there on special occasions: on Chinese New Year night, and on Christmas and New Year for a special celebration. We'd have the band and the whole dance floor to ourselves. It was so far out of town, there were no other people there.

One Chinese New Year – it must have been January or early February – I invited Walter, Christopher and Trevor Brown round to lunch. I managed to serve them a whole cold lobster each, and salad and a dessert. During the few days of the Chinese New Year public holiday, they had no cook. It was nice to have them in the house.

My boss John Phillips retired at the age of fifty-five; the required age of retirement for partners at Turquand Youngs at the time. I was very upset for a while, as I enjoyed working for him, and had asked him for a reference to work in London with him, as he was being transferred to the London office. But he sent me a very nice letter advising me about life in England, adding that it would be impossible for me to commute to work in London, and that he thought the climate would be too cold for me in the winter. So eventually I had to drop the idea. As he was the senior partner his retirement party was a great occasion for all of us, and I had the pleasure of sitting beside him at the dinner table. He made a wonderful speech – something about partnership being like a marriage – and a lot of speeches were made by the other partners. After the dinner we had a group picture taken. I kept a copy of it: Walter Bellam and Christopher, both very tall, are standing right at the back, while

John Phillips' retirement 1957, Terry in front row beside JP, May 2nd left.
Back row 2nd left Colin Coey, on right - Walter, Chris, Graeme, Van Hien

I'm in front, sitting next to my boss. Donald Stewart succeeded him.

Turquand Youngs' office was in Hongkong Bank Chambers, on the third floor. In the '60s they moved to Ocean Building. Hongkong Bank was a very solid colonial building, but the owners decided to add three more storeys. After John Phillips' retirement, we moved up to the sixth floor, where TYs occupied practically the whole floor. Part of the firm was run by Henry Noon's, which Christopher would later take charge of.

On the sixth floor, I had an office to myself, next to Donald Stewart, for whom I worked after Phillips' retirement. Christopher's office was separated from mine only by the library, so I did a lot of work for him, because there was this panic in Singapore. All the big companies wanted to have their head office in Kuala Lumpur, because of the coming merger,[187] so often Christopher and I worked quite late. I had to do a lot of typing and paperwork for him, so I didn't do much for Donald Stewart, who, in any

---

187 The merger between the Federation of Malaya and the former British colonies of Singapore, North Borneo and Sarawak eventually took place on the 16th September 1963, forming Malaysia. But after disagreements between the leaders of Singapore and the federal government, opposition from Indonesia, and race riots, Malaysian Prime Minister Tunku Abdul Rahman expelled Singapore from the Federation. Singapore declared independence on the 9th August 1965 and Lee Kuan Yew became its first Prime Minister. In 1957, Singapore was transitioning towards self-governance from British rule, and held two pivotal elections, causing great uncertainty for business.

Terry with May Wong

case, had retained his previous secretary.

I began to do more private work for Christopher when my boss was on leave, including typing out his itinerary for his 1957 trip with Walter. They planned a trip to France and Spain in Walter's car, which was bigger than Christopher's. I managed to see them off at the airport along with Willie Lochhead, who was sharing the bungalow with them. During their absence, Willie asked me to help him to choose some curtains for the house. So, after lunch at the office, I went along with him, and we selected some fabrics at Robinson's. I remember that very well, even the pattern of the curtains.

They started their holiday in England in the summer of that year. I used to get a postcard or a letter from Christopher from every place where they stopped, so I knew every stop they made. I was so happy on finding those letters and postcards on the floor when I got home from work. I missed Christopher in the months while he was away, but he kept in touch and I did reply to him, care of his parents' house, Grasmere in East Byfleet.

While Christopher and Walter were on holiday, May and Graeme Large were married in the Presbyterian church on Stamford Road. The reception was held in May's friends' house in Raffles Park, where the newlyweds stayed for a short time before moving to England. It was quite an occasion. Most of May's family were there, and quite a number of staff from Turquand Youngs. Graeme Large only had one contract with TYs, and he and May left for England on their long leave, before taking up a post in Nigeria, sometime in the summer of 1959.

May was unhappy in Nigeria because of the living conditions there – rather primitive, she said. After the end of their short contract, Graeme managed to get a job as one of the assistant bursars at the University of Hong Kong.

7B Scotts Lane
Shortlands
Kent
18th May 1957

Dear Christopher,

Once more the sight of a letter from you filled me with a sense of guilt and just a little horror at how the time has passed so quickly since we last met. After all these years it seems quite pointless excusing my ability to correspond at even reasonable intervals, enough to say, 'Please, if possible, could you come within telephoning distance?!'

I should like to deal with your letter in chronological order, but all sorts of thoughts crowd my mind, so once again, indulgence, please.

The new flat – we have just completed a year last Thursday – is a great improvement on the ruin at Norwood, even if only on the count that we can keep it warm. Pamela is indeed very happy, and I might add fitter than I have ever seen her. We cannot admit to an oversight as regards the new address, as Pamela assures me a change of address card was duly sent to you at Dunsfold Drive and presumably not forwarded.

Before going into the whys and wherefores of 'Topsy', may we both thank you for your very kind attention to Tony and June during their stay in Singapore. We duly heard through Mrs. Breden, Tony's mother, what a wonderful reception they had and how much they appreciated your kindness.

The mathematics of the 'Topsy' problem are a little obscure. Once, just recently, a letter was started to you but with the fluctuations of the domestic petrol scene I decided to wait and see how a complete return to normality has hardened the second-hand car market generally, although Minors[188] always seem to keep a good market. To hire a car, as you will see from the enclosed clippings, would be around £12 per week; that is including, I understand, unlimited mileage. If you could obtain a good price in Singapore the thought of a Morris 1000 is very tempting. On the other hand, have you thought of bringing 'Topsy' home and selling after 3 months' use?

---

188 Morris Minors.

Market value	£500+
Less freight one way	–£75
	£425
Less P.T. (which I presume is still payable), say	£125
	£300 towards
	new 1000

Subject to auditing the above, I feel it could be one answer, but it is difficult advising from this distance.

Very much regret not seeing Jocelyn of late – part of the reason being I only officially have ¾ hour for lunch, and also, we get such a good free one. A beer and a sandwich doesn't seem to satisfy my frame, which incidentally has reached the gross proportions of 13 st. 3 lbs!

Nothing much of startling importance to report on the cricket front because the weather hasn't been very kind – too cold for my old bones. Just a few agricultural runs with the 2nds.

Clifford and Suzanne have managed to ride out the storm in Qatar, and both are very well and, I understand, enjoying life. Here again the Brown trait rears up and all I have is information passed on by Mother.

Incidentally, Mother had an accident in November last year, fracturing her femur, and has suffered much the same discomfort as Mrs. Repton a few years back. She is progressing slowly and walking with the aid of crutches.

Have no doubt forgotten many things but will leave them until July – which we are both looking forward to very much.

The Sydenham cricketing fraternity send kind wishes – Steve, David Mason and Ken in particular.

Take care. Lots of 'cheers' to make up for.

Love from us both,
Gillie

P.S. This is just a postscript to you, Christopher, from me, to say that we are both more than looking forward to seeing you again and to showing you our new home – not to mention the garden in which there is plenty to do, but which is enjoyable. All the family are well – Sheyda[189] and her husband are now resident in Haslemere and we spent a happy Easter with them.

Gillie is telling me to hurry, so will have to leave details of all the news until you arrive. Hope Gillie's views on the future of 'Topsy' have been helpful to you.

Love to you,
Pamela

P.P.S. Hope you have avoided the flu!! Today's *Telegraph* reports 56,000 cases in the Federation of Malaya.

G.

> Convent of the Blessed Sacrament
> The Towers
> Upper Beeding
> Steyning
> Sussex
> 2nd June 1957

My dear Chris,

You really are spoiling Christopher! There arrived for him by parcel post during the week a very nice Fuller's parcel. Needless to say, the contents were much appreciated, and he has asked me to thank you and to say how very kind you are.

You will see I have given you our new address – we actually move in on Tuesday next, 4th June, and hope to be there for a few months; unfortunately it cannot be a permanent arrangement as the cottage may eventually be required as a science lab. But as yet there are no plans and we may stay there for six months or so, by which time any number of things could happen to change the course of our lives. One thing seems pretty definite now: there won't be any case for damages – my application for a civil aid certificate

---

189 A sister of Pamela's.

has been turned down on the grounds that 'You have not shown that you have reasonable grounds for taking, defending or being a party to proceedings.' Roy's father hasn't given up hope tho' and has written a very strong letter to my solicitor who put the case to the Law Society, asking him to appeal against their decision. The trouble is, I think, that it was by no means a cut-and-dried case and the coroner was unable to establish who was at fault since there were no reliable witnesses. I will tell you more about it when I see you.[190]

I seem to have endless correspondence with all sorts of people – filling in forms etc., etc. – which so far have got me absolutely nowhere. Sometimes I feel like running away from it all.

Tues. 11th June

I'm so sorry about this letter being written in scraps – but what with the move and one thing and the other, I hardly seem to have had a quiet moment.

We have now been at the Convent a week and are all very happy here. The Mother Superior and the Sisters are so kind, and it is such a wonderfully peaceful atmosphere. It couldn't be better for Christopher, who only has to run through the grounds to school – he may stay until he is eight and the fees are quite reasonable, I think, but that is something about which I must tackle the R.A.F. Benevolent Fund. They have been rather 'cagey' so far and I have been in touch with the R.A.F. Chaplain, who has written me a very nice letter, and will do all he can to help in this respect.

Many thanks for your letter which I received last week. Unfortunately, we're not on the 'phone, but if necessary, you could leave a message for me at the Convent – Steyning 2185. I feel quite sure they wouldn't mind. I came across your Byfleet number the other day in Roy's address book, and so can always contact you.

Must say goodnight now, as it's almost midnight! Our love to you.

Yours ever,
Stella

---

190 Roy sadly died in a car accident in 1956.

Tuesday 9th July 1957

My dear Chris,

Many thanks for your postcard which I found on my doorstep when I got home this evening; I assume this was posted from Milan. The one you sent from Rome must be somewhere in the post and no doubt I shall receive it some day. I have been anxiously waiting to hear from you, and thought this morning that I might write and ask you how you are and whether you had a pleasant flight to Rome and onward train journey to London. Did your eye give you any more trouble after you left Singapore?

I might have been wrong, but you seemed a little troubled that morning at the airport. I, on the other hand, was trying my best to look cheerful. Frankly, Chris, after you said goodbye and walked away, I felt so lost and unhappy I stood there for about five minutes not knowing what to do, then suddenly I realised that the plane was about to take off. When I rushed outside, I was just in time to see you boarding the plane, and I said to myself, *There goes Chris, whom I shall not be seeing for three months.*

I met Joyce's husband at the airport (he has some business connections with C.P.A.)[191] and he gave me a lift to the office. I said 'goodbye' to Kon[192] for you and he remarked that it was very nice of you to remember him. He had to rush off that afternoon to look over No. 2 Swiss Club Road with a prospective buyer, and he was also under the impression that you would be in on Tuesday morning. It may interest you to know that the secretarial department (R. D. S., Kon, Phillips, Kriekenbeek and Chua) worked over the weekend and all yesterday (Hari Raya Haji)[193] to complete the Metal Box bonus issue and dividend. Chua was sent to my house to get the 'seal' key – he turned up at 8.30 on Sunday night just as I was turning in.

We are definitely moving upstairs on the 22nd of this month, and the Singapore Baggage and Transport has been instructed to move the furniture, cabinets etc. on Saturday 20th/Sunday 21st and

---

191 Cathay Pacific Airways.
192 Mr Kon Choon Kooi was Chris's deputy at Henry Noon & Co., a company associated with Turquand Youngs, and took over from him as head when he retired.
193 A Muslim public holiday in Singapore.

possibly the following weekend. I expect we shall finally be able to vacate the old offices by July 28th. I am looking forward very much to the move, as I find it rather distracting working in a crowded room at the moment. Minjoot is back so there are four of us now in the room. What makes it worse is that people keep popping in and out of the room now and again.

Life in the office is very uninteresting without you around and is never the same as it used to be. I miss you most in the morning when you used to look in to wish me "Good morning." I have finished all your work that you left me and have sorted out all the papers in the box file and put them in their proper sections. I have not been very busy during the last few days. Seng, May and the other typists seem to have got over their busy period.

I must thank you once more for the beautiful brooch you gave me. How very thoughtful of you, Chris. Many of the girls have remarked that it is very pretty. I am wearing it to work every day to keep me in good cheer. I want to thank you also, Chris, for your kind attention, thoughtfulness and concern towards me all this time. I now fully realise how helpful and wonderful you have been to me. I'm afraid I relied very much on you for everything, and I find now that I am quite helpless at times. I must have been a nuisance to you sometimes, but you are too nice a person to tell me so.

I went to the evening service at the Cathedral on First Friday and felt I missed you very much in church. On Saturday I went with Mary's sister and brother-in-law to the Novena at six, after which I asked them to take me to Agnes's house at North Bridge Road so that I could go home with her. I was quite pleased on Sunday morning when Agnes suggested that we should all go to church together. I shall try to persuade her to come with me every Sunday. I spent the whole of yesterday (Hari Raya Haji) at my hairdresser's, to have my hair permed. Throughout the long weekend I had to keep myself busy with work when I was all by myself.

The night is getting late, so I had better stop talking, although I feel I have a lot more to tell you. I shall be looking forward to receiving a reply from you quite soon. In the meantime, take good care of yourself, Chris, and don't worry about me because I shall be all right as long as I hear from you.

With love,
Terry

P.S. I am enclosing herewith your bank statement which, I think, requires your immediate attention.

Do you want me to forward the *Accountant, Secretary, Punch* and *Motoring Journal* to you?

Grasmere
High Road
Byfleet
Surrey
10th July 1957

My dear Terry,

No news from you yet but I expect you are waiting to hear from me. I wonder whether you have the postcards which I sent you from Rome and Milan?

I finally arrived at Victoria Station, London about 4.30 on Sunday afternoon and was met by Sylvia and my youngest brother Dickon.

Dickon at Dryfesdale House Hotel, Lockerbie, Scotland, July 1955.

He had his 'Vespa' motor-scooter with him too. Whilst Sylvia and I came down by train, he came on this and was in time to transport us in relays from Weybridge Station to Byfleet. We had a late tea at home and then Dickon helped again by driving me down to Byfleet Church for the 6.45 evening Mass (apparently evening Mass is now fairly general in England too), as I'd not been able to get to morning Mass in France.

I think I've described the earlier parts of my journey on the PCs but in case they're lost here's a summary:

Bangkok on time – short stay where I ran into Mr. Hedberg of Wendt, who was travelling SAS; Calcutta for tea after a cloudy and rather bumpy trip. The monsoon was in full swing at Calcutta and it rained heavily during our rather prolonged stay. The first half of the journey across India was rather bumpy and we had to keep seat belts fastened. It cleared later and we arrived at Karachi about 9.30 p.m. (1½ hours late), having been told earlier on the plane that we were not going on that night as the relief crew had only just arrived and consequently had not had enough rest. So we had quite a comfortable night's rest at the Airport Hotel, then breakfast the next morning at the BOAC hotel and off again about 7.30 a.m. The continual re-setting of one's watch is a little confusing. Going from Singapore to London one gains 6½ hours in the summer, and so on the journey this way the days are longer, and dusk and dawn seem a long time away whilst one is in flight.

Our next stop was Bahrain on the Persian Gulf. Fortunately, we did not stop long as Bahrain was scorchingly hot and even in the inadequate waiting room under the fans there was no relief. Singapore is quite a cool spot compared with Bahrain. After Bahrain, which we left about 10.30 a.m., came our longest 'hop' – 2,100 miles to Athens. We flew up the Persian Gulf over Baghdad and Kirkuk and then, in view of the unsettled political situation in Syria and neighbourhood, we had to make a big detour right across Turkey. In fact, we passed over Istanbul, which is only about an hour's run from Athens. We eventually reached Athens about 7 p.m. local time, where we had a not-very-good dinner. The Athens Airport is some way from the city – it has the mountains on three sides and the sea, a lovely bay with island mountains in the distance, on the other side.

Bianca with Flavia in Rome, January 1957

Despite the fact that we were now in Europe, it was not noticeably cooler, although the air seemed fresh and there was a pleasant breeze.

From Athens it was only 2½ hours' more flying to Rome, which we finally reached about 9.45 p.m. – some 10 hours late. This was unfortunate as it meant that I didn't reach my cousin's till nearly midnight. I rang from the airport – fortunately Bianca had my flight no. so knew about the delay – Alberto was in Rome after all, his Kenya trip having been postponed. As it was so late, they hadn't been able to meet me, so I took the airport bus into the city and a taxi on from there. When I arrived, we just exchanged greetings and then all tumbled into bed. It was so hot at night that I slept without even a sheet – of course the houses are not so well designed for hot weather as they are in Singapore and in a big city like Rome the heat lingers longer.

Bianca's little daughter, Flavia, now just 18 months, is a delightful little girl and she seemed to like the fluffy white rabbit which you may remember we got in Wako Wako's. I left Bianca and Alberto the little white horses, which they preferred to the jade statuette. Rome, as I mentioned in my PCs, was frightfully hot. I don't know what the exact temperature was while I was there, but it must have been at least 95°. At about the same time it was 101° in Vienna and nearly 100° in Venice where many old people died of the heat – so perhaps Singapore isn't so bad after all. The only thing about the Italian heat is that it is much less humid, so perhaps preferable.

I made a fruitless trip to Milan, as I told you in my second PC, and in doing so suffered considerable discomfort as I cancelled my sleeper reservation on the *Rome Express* and instead spent two nights on trains, only on the second night being able to put my feet up! The first lap was Friday night from Rome to Turin and the second night from Milan through Switzerland into France.

Milan was, if anything, hotter than Rome. The only relief there was when I visited for a half-hour the huge and impressive Gothic cathedral. It was much cooler the next day, Sunday, as we trained through France – apparently there had been heavy thunderstorms in the night at Paris and in parts of England and they had ended the 3-week heatwave in England and N. France. Actually, we did not pass through Paris – after leaving Basle in Switzerland it took a route along the N.E. border of France direct to Calais.

I was unlucky with the Customs at Folkestone (nr. Dover) – they seem to have become suddenly tough as I had no trouble 2 years ago. I simply said I was from Singapore on leave and had a few small presents with me, for which I showed the inspector the bills. He wasn't satisfied with this, however, but demanded to see all the items themselves – I was furious. The outcome was that I had to pay £2–17–0 in duty (for purchase tax), say $24, and nearly missed the train to London. A woman next to me fared much worse. She had bought a watch in Switzerland during a holiday there, and was wearing it on her wrist. She failed to declare this, hoping, as she said, to get away with it. However, it was 'spotted', and she had to pay a penalty of £7 for making a false declaration and the watch was confiscated! A nice welcome to England, I don't think!

Since Sunday the weather here has been cool and showery with temperatures 60° to 70° during the day. Here it's now July 12th so I've spread this letter over 3 days. Picked up the new car on Monday – the green upholstery is quite pleasing. She is running well but the gears are very stiff at present. The family seems fairly well and Mother if anything seems better than when I was last here. My father, however, now 87, has aged considerably and his sight is not so good now, so he finds it difficult to keep himself occupied and I'm afraid is rather miserable at times – all very sad. My young brother is planning to get married at the end of August.

Afraid all this long rambling about the journey etc. must be rather boring for you – if you can read my writing? How are you, Terry? What are you doing about your leave, and has Mary changed her mind? I suppose the Metal Box issue is in full swing and the move to the new office imminent. Don't forget you were to tell me how much the loan of the car cost. Did you manage the Novena last Saturday? Sylvia is delighted with the sarong material and asked me to say she'll be writing soon. I look forward to hearing from you soon.

Love from Christopher

Tuesday 16th July 1957

My dear Christopher,

I received your lengthy and interesting letter last night when I got home from Joyce's and it was too late for me to reply. Since you've signed yourself 'Christopher', I shall address you so when writing to you. Your postcard which you posted from Rome did arrive after all – the day after I received the one you sent from Milan. My letter seems to have crossed yours and I imagine you would have received it last week. I'm afraid I wasn't very cheerful when I wrote it, so will you forgive me?

Thank you very much indeed for your lovely basket of orchids which are still as fresh as ever. My neighbour was kind enough to accept them from the florist on my behalf, and when I returned home after the Novena, I was delighted to receive them. It was very nice of you to remember my birthday.

As regards my leave, I doubt I'll be able to persuade Mary to come with me. She is more inclined to spend her holidays in Hong Kong with some friends of hers. I shall let you know if anything crops up.

I'm sorry to learn that you suffered considerable discomfort on your train journey from Rome to Calais, and also about your trouble with the Customs. I'm glad to know that your mother and other members of the family are well, but your description of your father seems rather grim. Does he know that you'll be coming out to the East again? I only hope this will not make him feel any worse. Is Sylvia working at present? Have you been to see Stella and the children, and have you been able to help her in any way?

Are you going ahead with your plans re. your trip to Spain? Do let me know, Christopher, when you expect to leave for Spain. Walter must have contacted you by now to fix things up.

Incidentally, Twentieth Century Fox and the Cathay Organisation sent you an invitation to Cocktails and to a preview of the 'Big Show' presenting Twentieth Century Fox's *March of Progress*[194] at the Odeon Theatre on July the 24th at 9.30 p.m. The card, by the way, was addressed to 'Mr. and Mrs. G. C. T. Repton'. I wonder where they got this information from. Anyway, I sent them a reply yesterday.

As I told you in my previous letter, the Metal Box issue was started last week and apparently the job has not yet been completed, because I still see Mr. Stewart, Kon and Kriekenbeek working on it for a couple of hours each day. We are all busy packing and getting things ready to move up. Everybody has to look after his or her own things so that there should be no question of anything being mislaid. Poor Dollah has to see to a great number of jobs and is working extremely hard. I understand that the junior audit clerks have been asked to help over the weekend. Needless to say, all the peons have also been told to work over this weekend and the next. I can just imagine the chaotic state upstairs during the first few days of the move. Added to this, we shall probably be without telephones for some time, as the Telephone men are on strike since the 6th. Army technicians have been called in to help at the Telephone House to cope with the work there. At this stage there is still no indication of any negotiations between the Telephone Board and the Union.

---

194 Theresa may have been referring to *The March of Time*, an American feature film series with an anti-fascist slant based on newsreels, that was shown in movie theatres from the 1930s to 1950s.

May handed me only two negatives, which are enclosed. I seem to remember there were three – she must have mislaid the third one.

You've only been away a fortnight, but it seems ages to me – weekends especially seem to drag on.

I consulted Dr. Gethin-Jones, a skin specialist of the Federal Dispensary, last week and will have to be under his observation for a little while; otherwise, I am well.

How are you, Christopher? Do write and tell me more about your leave. I shall write again as soon as I hear from you. Please give my regards to Sylvia.

With love,
Terry

Byfleet
27th July 1957

My dear Terry,

Thank you for your letter of 16th which was waiting for me when I got back from Devon at Thursday lunchtime. You had not, when you wrote, received my second letter – posted, I think, last Saturday – which answers many of the questions in your letter. That, I am afraid, is the difficulty when we are writing to each other from such a distance; letters tend to cross each other despite the speed of the air mail.

I was somewhat disturbed to hear that you've had to consult a skin specialist. About the time I left the trouble you'd been having with your face seemed to have cleared up and I was hoping it had gone for good. Do you mean to say it's been really bad again, and has it been giving you more sleepless nights? Please let me know.

I was glad to hear that the postcard from Rome eventually arrived, though it must have been confusing getting the Milan one first. Whilst in Rome I got some good coloured pictures of churches, monuments etc. and others of Bianca, Alberto and Flavia.

Am sorry to hear that Mary is not being very co-operative about your leave. You must take a trip somewhere – Penang would be good if you could make it.

The weather here is still unsettled and inclined to rain. This morning, Saturday, there is a strongish N.W. wind, and bright intervals interspersed with heavy showers of rain. The temperature is in the lower 60°s so you can imagine I am feeling quite chilly. Towards the middle of last week when I was down in Devon it seemed to be getting warmer and more settled, but it seems to have gone to pieces again.

Did you get my postcard of Exeter posted from Newton Abbott, the town next door? I stayed over at Gillie & Pam's flat at Beckenham last Saturday night. Gillie, though not a Catholic, came to the 8 a.m. Mass with me at the Beckenham Catholic Church – unfortunately, as so often happens in England, there was an Irish priest whom G. could not understand properly. We were rather slow with breakfast and at length set off in the car for Devon about 11 a.m. At the start we got lost in the suburbs between London and Croydon and this cost us half an hour. It was another showery day and we nearly got caught in a heavy one just as we were finishing a picnic lunch in a field near the road.

We eventually reached the little inn at which we were staying about 7.30 p.m. – this was a place called Clyst St. Mary, near Exeter. I had originally agreed to come down just for a day or two, principally to see something of Gillie and Pam, and also for the trip and to see

Pam, Jocelyn (standing by car), Gilly, Gareth, Sylvia

Devon again – particularly round Exeter, where it is very pleasant. However, the Shell team had only eleven players and in the Monday game one of them suffered a severe blow from the ball in his face, which broke his nose. Fortunately, I was able to drive him quickly to the little hospital at Totnes, where a doctor set it and put it in splints for him. The next day we took him to Exeter hospital to see the specialist, who said a good job had been done by the Totnes doctor. Anyway, this chap was unable to play for a couple of days, so they asked me to take his place on Tuesday and Wednesday, which I did. Quite enjoyed the two games, though felt rather stiff on the Thursday.

I left Devon after the game on Wednesday, which was at Paignton near Torquay, both seaside resorts. I drove up to Salisbury which is about 100 miles – a little over halfway – and stayed the night with my youngest brother Dickon, travelling on the next morning.

Yes, Sylvia is working for Cook's during the week and for Keith Prowse on Saturday afternoons – I gather she's trying to save for another trip to Rome in September; rather silly really.

The Spanish trip is scheduled to go ahead as planned – starting next Wednesday – we meet at Canterbury on the Tuesday evening. No doubt we shall run into some difficulties but am hoping it will be fun. As I think I told you, I met Walter at Oxford 10 days ago.

Thank you for dealing with my invitation to the 20th Century Fox show – you ought to have gone along yourself. Looking forward to hearing from you how the new office is going. Sorry to hear you have a telephone strike. Here in England, we have at present a strike of porters at Covent Garden (the principal market for fresh fruit and vegetables in London) and a strike of provincial buses (that is, most of the buses other than London Transport). In the latter there have been several ugly incidents involving pickets, which are reminiscent of Singapore. Are you having nice cool weather with lots of rain or is it still as hot as when I left? Sylvia has promised to write you shortly; has she not done so yet? As I mentioned, she was very pleased indeed with the sarong material.

It's Saturday afternoon but unfortunately there's no Novena to go to near here and I miss it very much. You will be in bed and asleep now (4.45 here), as it's 11.15 p.m. your time. May not be able to send much more than postcards whilst we tour in Spain – please overlook this.

Must go to post now.

My love to you,
Chris

Tuesday 30th July 1957

My dear Christopher,

Many thanks for your postcard of the 23rd – you didn't say when you would be returning to Byfleet, but I imagine you should be home by the time this letter reaches you. I wonder whether you've received my two letters (posted 9th and 17th July) addressed to you at Byfleet.

We finally moved to the new offices on the 22nd but could not do any work on that day as we had so much to unpack, and there was no water, no light and no internal or external telephones. As yet I cannot say that we are comfortably settled in. There is only one lift working, the service of which is very uncertain. Last Thursday morning we had to walk all the way up to the 6th floor, which was quite an effort for me. Also, owing to the S.T.B.[195] strike, we have no switchboard or extension lines; merely two direct lines to a central position to which one has to proceed when making or receiving a call. Both lines packed up yesterday morning and poor Mrs. Watts had to run down to the 3rd floor several times to put through some calls. Fortunately, the lines seem to be all right this morning. The minute books and seals are kept in your room, but the secretarial files and tax files are at the other end of the room. My room is reasonably cool and so is yours – there is a constant breeze from the sea, and the views over the harbour are lovely.

Almost one month ago since you left Singapore – it seems such a long time. A lot has happened since then; a Penang Chinese, who is an A.R.A.N.Z.[196] and also a Chartered Secretary, joined the firm a fortnight ago. His name is P. S. Kooi – he will be with us only for a short

---

195 Singapore Telephone Board.
196 An accountancy qualification in Australia and New Zealand.

time as he will be transferred to the KL office sometime next year. Mrs. Turner is leaving us tomorrow as her husband is being transferred to Melbourne. A young girl of 18 has been engaged to take her place.

May has been very discontented ever since we moved upstairs. She is not at all happy at her work as she used to be. I think I know the reason why – she certainly doesn't like where she is sitting. Recently she has been coming in late in the morning and very often returning to the office late after lunch. She told me that Westworth had ticked her off several times. It so happened that she had an appointment with Joan Tookes last Thursday evening at 4.30, so she dashed off without informing Westworth. The next morning, she was called in and as soon as she left his room, she came to see me and burst out crying. I talked to her for more than half an hour and tried to stop her from sending in her resignation. All the same, she wrote to Mr. Stewart asking to be released of her service at the end of July. Mr. Stewart told her to stay on and to think things over. In the meantime, her resignation has not been accepted, but I have no doubt that May will leave us as soon as she gets a good post. Esther Ang has also mentioned that she will resign if she gets another job.

How are you, Christopher? I seem to have lost touch with you since the 10th, except for the postcard from Exeter. Are you enjoying your leave? You must have seen quite a number of your friends and your aunts by now. Have you been able to do anything for Stella and the children – how are they? When are you leaving for Spain?

I might be able to arrange a trip to Penang with Joyce – everything depends on her servant situation as she needs another one to look after her children while she is away. I'll let you know as soon as I hear of any definite plans from her. I am going to a concert with her on Saturday the 3rd, to hear Luigi Infantino – he will be accompanied by Campoli.

I go down to the Library once a fortnight to renew the books – have been reading quite a lot lately. I spent the last weekend with Mary, Joyce and others in town. It has been raining continually for about a week, so the weather here has been quite cool.

Willie came to see Mr. Stewart one morning re. Lewis & Peat, and he was enquiring about you. I told him about your cricket match in Exeter and he was highly amused.

It's getting rather late, so I had better stop writing – long past my bedtime! Give my regards to Sylvia. Hope to hear from you soon.

With love,
Terry

Friday 9th August 1957

My dear Christopher,

I was very happy indeed to receive your letter of 27th July, which sounded rather confusing to me at first, as your second letter (said to have been posted on 20th July) has yet to arrive. I'm quite certain this would have answered most of the queries raised in my first two letters; you must have written something about Stella and the children. I can only hope that it will turn up one day, but I must admit it's a very faint hope. Perhaps the same thing has happened to Sylvia's letter – how unreliable the postal services are these days!

I've received your postcards of Bayeux and Bordeaux – many thanks. Of the two places, Bordeaux looks grander. I managed to send off a letter yesterday morning, hoping that it will reach you on the 12th at Hotel Gran Vía in Madrid. I imagine that you and Walter

Humphry (left), Sylvia & Jocelyn (right) in Cornwall

396

must have seen quite a lot of Spain by now. Do write and tell me all about the tour when you are comfortably settled down once again at home. I wonder when you'll be returning to Byfleet, but I expect you'll be home in time for Dickon's wedding.

The trouble with my skin started a week after you left Singapore and I was quite miserable as I didn't know what to do about it. I decided to see one of the firm's doctors – Dr. W. – and he made matters worse by prescribing some ointment which irritated the skin more. I stopped using it after one application, and it was Boon Eng who recommended Dr. Gethin-Jones to me. He gave me a skin test with a certain type of talcum powder I had been using, which I thought was the cause of it all, but unfortunately there was no reaction to it. In the meantime, he has asked me to stop having facial treatments as he seems to think that this may have been the cause of all the trouble. However, since going to him for treatment there has been no recurrence so far and I hope his assumption is correct.

In my previous letter I told you that I might be able to arrange a trip to Penang with Joyce – I'm afraid our plans have fallen through. I quite appreciate how difficult it is for her to plan a vacation, especially with a family as big as hers. With Merdeka[197] approaching, I don't think I want to take a trip upcountry after August 31st.

Preparations for the Merdeka celebrations are going ahead very quickly. The Sultan of Negri Sembilan has been elected as the Paramount Ruler and the Sultan of Selangor as the Vice Paramount Ruler. The Duke and Duchess of Gloucester, as you know, will represent the Queen; Lady Gurney and Lady Gent[198] have also been invited by the Federation Government.

Graeme tells me that TYs will not be playing against the planters in Johore after all, as the manager of some estate has not been co-

---

197 Malaya's Independence Day. The Federation of Malaya's independence from Britain was declared on the 31st August 1957 in Kuala Lumpur. Tunku Abdul Rahman became Malaya's first Prime Minister.

198 Lady Gent was the widow of Sir Edward Gent, the first Governor of the Malayan Union and first High Commissioner of the Federation of Malaya. Gent was sacked for not eliminating Communist guerrillas attacking plantations at the start of the Emergency in June 1948. He died in a plane crash flying back to Britain. Lady Gurney was the widow of Sir Henry Gurney, Gent's successor.

operative. Graeme has, however, arranged for TYs to play against Evatt's this weekend, and I'll let you know the result in my next letter.

A meeting of Lam Bian was held today, and Lim Bock Lai was again absent. The position regarding debtors has not improved; the total amount collected so far is a little over $9,000.

Mr. and Mrs. Phillips are at present on holiday and Mr. Phillips, I understand, will be starting work in the London Office on October 1st. I've not had a letter from him yet, but I expect to hear from him soon after he settles down to work.

It's Saturday tomorrow and I think I'll take my mother to the Novena again. She was very impressed with what she saw on her last visit. Agnes also came along one Saturday afternoon. Father Myers seems to be back on his work again and I've heard him for two Saturdays. It's a joy listening to him.

On Sundays I usually get down to the Cathedral myself in the morning, and often spend the day at Berwick Drive. Occasionally I go to a show with Agnes, her husband, Amy and Dick. Joyce and I had an enjoyable evening last Saturday, listening to Luigi Infantino.

Do you really think that time flies? I don't. I really wish you were back again – how very selfish of me to say this, but I do miss you, Chris.

With all my love,
Terry

Monday 19th August 1957

My dear Christopher,

Thank you very much indeed for your two picture postcards of Madrid and Ávila; I'm afraid I haven't received the one of Poitiers (France). The buildings in Madrid look colossal, and such wide roads. About the time I received your second card from Spain, I was reading the little book of St. Teresa of Ávila. So, my letter did not reach you in time at Hotel Gran Vía in Madrid.

I imagine you and Walter must be now on your way home, and no doubt wishing to have a quiet holiday in England once again. It must have been rather tiring at times having to drive for long hours. Nevertheless, both of you must have enjoyed the trip.

(Clockwise from back) Terry, Chris, Mr Kon, Esther Ang, Mrs Kon,
Richard Ang, Mrs Rees, Norman Rees, John Curran, Boon Eng

Without you in the game, TYs did not have much chance against Evatt's, who scored 124. TYs, consisting of John Curran, Graeme, Graham-Eagle, Lambert, Ossy and John Wilson, together with 5 outsiders, scored only 84. Ossy, I was told, kept forgetting that he was playing cricket and once or twice wanted to drop his bat after hitting the ball, but checked himself in time. John Curran and Graham-Eagle, I understand, were the only 'stars' of the team.

Scott has just returned from leave; he called in at the office this morning to say that he would not be rejoining TYs as he was going to take up some religious work.

As I anticipated, Westworth asked me the other day if May had confided her troubles to me. Someone told him that she had cried on my shoulder one morning, so he wanted to know the reasons why. I didn't tell him, of course, all that May had said, but merely mentioned the fact that she probably disliked her place among the other typists. He agreed that this could be the reason and said that he had noticed a change in May ever since we started working in the new office. What puzzles me is that he has not made any attempt to persuade her to stay on. He got me to put an advert in the papers and there are two girls coming for an interview tomorrow morning.

So, May will be leaving us at the end of this month; in the meantime, she is still looking for a job. I'm losing another old friend soon.

The Swans have a baby girl; and rumour has it that Bill is contemplating rejoining TYs. Boon Eng was admitted to the General Hospital on the 13th August and I understand he will soon be discharged. Meanwhile Loke has taken over his work.

All three lifts went out of order after lunchtime today and we had to walk up – much to my dislike. Kon and Boon Watt were caught in one of the lifts and it took them some time to get out.

I'm having a cold at the moment, but it isn't all that bad to keep me in bed; I must have caught it from May. I should be all right in a day or so.

I shall probably have to take my leave sometime next month and make the most of it in Singapore. One has to obtain a pass to cross the Johore Causeway after Merdeka.

I managed to get another book by Jane Austen from the library, called *Persuasion* [...]. It should be quite a nice book, judging by the Introduction.

I must get to bed now, as I have to work tomorrow. Do write soon, Chris.

With all my love,
Terry

Byfleet
24th August 1957

My dear Terry,

When I returned to Byfleet yesterday there were your three letters of 31st July, 10th and 20th August waiting, for which I thank you very much. I was most upset to hear that my letter of 20th July had not reached you; as you guessed, this one bridges the gap and answers some of your later questions.

The recurrence of your skin trouble was sad news as I did think it had mended again when I left. I sincerely trust that Dr. Gethin-Jones will be able to find out what is causing it; you must go and see him regularly. This time in six weeks I should be back in Singapore again, all being well, and hope to see your complexion with its natural bloom again.

All of you seem to have had rather a trying time during and after the move to the new office. I hope that the effort of having to climb six sets of stairs did not strain you?

Your news re. May is sad – especially as Mr. Phillips had made particular arrangements for her to carry on with the firm after her marriage. I think you guessed originally that she was going to be upset about the organisation in the new office, and of course you were right. Westworth can be a bit of a 'so-and-so' at times. Please send her my sympathy, although from both her own point of view and Graeme's I think it is a good thing that she gets a job somewhere else. I see no reason why you should lose her as a friend, though of course you will miss her in the office.

I shall have to close this shortly as the Post Office will be closing in a few minutes (5.30). Next week I shall be spending a few days in Cornwall, so afraid it will only be postcards from there. In your last letter you sounded a little fed up with postcards – are you?!

The last PC I sent you was from Paris mentioning that I wasn't well. In fact, I was rotten for three days and then Walter developed some sort of tummy trouble so neither of us were able to enjoy Paris. The evening we got back to Canterbury I began to feel a little better, and yesterday evening I saw the doctor who has given me some penicillin tablets, gargle etc. Sorry to hear about your cold.

Goodbye for now – if there's time I'll write again from Cornwall.

Love from Christopher

Sunday 25th August 1957
8.30 p.m.

My dear Christopher,

I received your postcard of Barcelona last Wednesday and was not at all surprised to learn that the bullfight didn't appeal to you – I wouldn't like to see it myself.

I've been following your trip with the aid of a map and I'm positive you must have taken a different route home and stayed in Paris for a few days.

The weather in England should be nice and cool now, but Singapore seems to get hotter each day as we have had no rain for the last two weeks.

The S.T.B. strike was settled last week, and we shall be having a switchboard very soon. There had been a few instances of sabotage, with the result that most telephones were frequently out of order. Thank goodness, everything is almost back to normal now.

The Singapore Government[199] has been intensively making arrests of the top officials of the P.A.P.[200] in its campaign to stamp out Communist subversives. Only two weeks ago the P.A.P. had elected new executives and Lee Kuan Yew is now no longer its Chief Secretary, so he is still at large. I'm glad that the Government is taking such action in order to preserve peace and order in the Colony.

I'm enclosing an editorial column regarding the proposed introduction of a Causeway[201] pass, which I think will interest you. The Tunku[202] came down to have a talk with the Chief Minister[203] on Friday on this point, but as yet no official statement has been issued.

Song goes on leave tomorrow for a week, so I shall be quite busy while he is away. Just at this moment the office is arranging to have a cocktail party at the new premises on Saturday 7th September, from 11.30 a.m. to 1 p.m. About 50 'outside' guests are being invited – most of them are partners of accountant firms, and no client is being invited. I expect to send out the cards within the next few days. Most of the wives or husbands of members of the staff will be coming, and I estimate that there will be about 180 people attending. Mr. Stewart has not forgotten about Tan Keng Or.

For your information, Hammers will be declaring an interim dividend of 10% on 30th September. Loke Wan Tho was appointed a director of the company last month.

---

199 The British colonial administration.
200 The People's Action Party, then a socialist party, which took power on independence from Britain. Led by Singapore's first Prime Minister, Lee Kuan Yew.
201 The bridge connecting Singapore to Malaya. After Singapore separated from Malaya, customs checks were introduced at the Causeway.
202 Malaya's Prime Minister.
203 Singapore's Chief Minister Lim Yew Hock, who imprisoned Communists and leftists, including P.A.P. members. However, moves were under way to transition Singapore towards self-government.

Mr. Addis returned from leave last week and he told me he had a wonderful holiday. He shares a room with Norman Rees, while the next room is occupied by Macartney and Buckley.

Boon Eng called in to see Mr. Stewart on Saturday morning and he looked quite fit. I understand he will be away from the office for some time.

May has invited me to spend a night with her, as Graeme has gone away to Kluang for a fortnight, but I don't think I like the idea. As you know, she is leaving in a few days' time.

I went to church this morning with Agnes, Amy and Dick, and later spent the rest of the day at Berwick Drive. My eldest sister has just got a baby boy.[204]

I'm keeping well at the moment but am still missing you a lot. I hope you are keeping very fit yourself and having a wonderful holiday. Looking forward to hear from you very soon.

With all my love,
Terry

Friday 30th August 1957

My dear Christopher,

I've received your postcard sent from Paris and your letter of the 24th August, many thanks. I was most disturbed to learn about your illness just before you reached Paris – how unfortunate. I've had quite a lot of experience with tonsillitis and can well imagine what an awful time you must have had. The journey by car must have been quite a strain on you and Walter since you both had to cover so many hundreds of miles in such a short period. However, I'm glad to know that you've reached home safe and sound, and I sincerely hope that you've completely recovered from your tonsillitis and that you've had a wonderful holiday in Cornwall. How's everyone at home? Have you taken your father and mother out for car drives often? How is Sylvia? Give her my regards.

---

204 Sebastian.

I'm terribly sorry if my letter of the 20th August implied that I was a little fed up with postcards – well, I wasn't, so please don't misunderstand me. I'm sure I did express how glad and grateful I was to receive all your various postcards, and I was also aware of the fact that it would have been rather difficult for you to write a proper letter since you had to be on the move most of the time. I must say I'm very proud to have such a nice collection of picture postcards of so many different places, and I'm having these inserted in an album.

Last night Joyce and I went to the St. Joseph's Institution to hear *La Bohème*, and Geoffrey Weeks of Radio Malaya gave a full explanation of the plot before the presentation of each Act, so that the audience could understand and enjoy this work. It is a weekly symphony concert of recorded music presented by the Singapore Recorded Music Society for music lovers. We had quite an enjoyable evening, and it was almost twelve when we got home. Surprisingly, Andrew Peattie and Muggleston were also at the concert.

We are having a holiday tomorrow, but my brother will be coming to take us all to church at 6.30 a.m. to hear a Thanksgiving High Mass. My mother will be seventy-five tomorrow. There will be a procession at Thomson Road on Sunday evening at 5 o'clock in honour of Our Lady of Perpetual Succour. We've been told to write our family names on a piece of paper and drop it in a box which will be placed close to the statue of Our Lady. I intend to place your family name as well before Our Lady's shrine.

Mr. Stewart will be proceeding on leave on the 13th October for two months, by which time Mr. Phillips will have started working in the London Office. I'm just wondering whether to send him a gentle reminder. What do you think, Chris?

Don't forget to let me know the actual date of your arrival in Singapore and the flight number.

I must say goodnight now and hope to hear from you soon. Do take good care of yourself, Chris.

With all my love,
Terry

Gareth 'steering us back to Englefield Green boathouse' on river Thames, June 1955

Byfleet
3rd Sept. 1957

My dear Theresa,

Thank you for your letter of 25th August, which was waiting for me when I got back from Cornwall the following Sunday 1st September. I'm glad to hear the PC from Barcelona has reached you – there should be still one to come from Paris. Then since my return, I wrote you a short letter on 24th August and sent you a PC from Cornwall on 30th August (no time for letters there), all of which should have reached you by now.

I am glad to say that the sudden illness which struck me at Bourges in France and laid me low in Paris has quite left me now. The fine sea air of Cornwall rapidly brought me back to normal. It must have been either a mild attack of Asian flu (which is now spreading to Europe) or tonsillitis. Anyway, I'm glad it's gone.

Whilst in Cornwall, I had a dip in the sea each day from Monday to Friday although the water was pretty chilly for the time of year – I don't think you would have been able to stand it! When you first plunge in you gasp with the cold and it's almost painful, then you come out and go in a second time and it's not quite so bad, and then a third time and it becomes almost bearable. Although the air was rather cool and there was a chill wind at the beginning of the week, we were lucky to have a lot of sunshine and so I got quite sun-tanned; much more so than I do in Singapore. Generally, however, since I have been here the summer weather in England has not been too good – rather a lot of rain and not so warm as usual – so I'm glad we got the sun in Spain.

Sept. 5

Sorry, I was unable to finish this yesterday as I went up to London. Whilst there, I checked in with BOAC about my return passage. Provided the plane is on schedule it's due to leave London Airport about 2.30 p.m. on Wednesday Oct. 2nd. I did not check the time of arrival in Singapore but, if the plane is on time again, I think it's about 10 p.m. on Thursday Oct. 3rd. The flight no. is BA708 (BOAC Britannia). I will write to Mr. Stewart and let him know when I expect to be back in the office, which should be the morning of Friday Oct. 4th, provided I'm not too tired. I will also write to Willie Lochhead to see if he can meet me. I don't want you to try and meet me as it's much too late for you and there's the difficulty of transport etc.

I was interested to hear that you followed our Spanish trip with the aid of a map. As you say, we did make some changes and not all those routes you so kindly typed out for me one evening were used. We started off as planned, with the addition of a day in Bayeux from which we made a tour of the Norman battlefields which Walter remembered. We then went down through Tours, Poitiers and Bordeaux to Bayonne as per route. Then, instead of crossing into Spain by Hendaye, Irun and San Sebastián, we went by a pass through the Pyrenees and our first Spanish town was Pamplona. We got back onto the planned route again at Vitoria and then to Burgos for the first night. After that we went down to Madrid via Aranda de Duero. We did not go south from Madrid to Granada, as previously planned – it would have been too far and much too hot down there; they were having temperatures of over 100°. So we took the alternative route direct to Valencia and then up the coast to Barcelona. It was after re-entering France that we made the main changes. Instead of going up the Rhône valley via Lyons we decided to go via the Central Massif[205] (that is, the mountains in the middle of France). The first night Perpignan was full, so we went back towards Spain and stayed at a little place called Molitg-les-Bains (a sort of spa or watering-place) nestling in the Pyrenees. The next night we stopped at Nîmes, with its Roman amphitheatre, instead of Avignon, which we did not see. The next day we turned N.W. into the mountains and stayed the night at a small town called Saint-Flour – very ancient and medieval – perched on top of a 300-ft. hill which I made Walter climb. The next day we went north to Bourges via Clermont-Ferrand. Finally, Paris, where we stopped a day.

Thus, we arrived in France on 31st July, in Spain on 6th August, returned to France 16th August and returned to England on the evening of 22nd August – stayed the night at Canterbury and reached Byfleet at midday on 23rd. Then left for Cornwall on the evening of 24th and got back here on 1st September. So, saw little of my parents during the whole of August. The only other trip I expect to make is to Scotland over 17th–20th September to see some army friends from Singapore, the Reardons. Walter will probably be coming over from Newcastle too. I was hoping to combine this trip with my brother's wedding, but I fear that has been postponed for the time being – maybe until after I return. Olive, his fiancée, is having difficulties over religion. She is not a Catholic but as it is to be a 'mixed' marriage she has had to have the usual course of instruction, and this has rather unsettled her, I'm afraid, so that she has asked for more time to think about it all. Anyway, I'm hoping it will all turn out well in the end.

Sorry to hear the weather's been so hot in Singapore – let's hope it's cooler by the time I return. October normally has plenty of rain.

Glad to hear that the S.T.B. strike has been settled and that the new office is getting more organised. I'm sorry to be missing the cocktail party, though midday on a Saturday is rather a funny time. Are you going yourself?

From the English newspapers I gather that the Malayan independence celebrations have gone off rather quietly – one reporter mentions a sort of 'apathy' in KL. Anyway, I'm glad there was no trouble.

You have not given me any news regarding the various unfinished jobs of mine, on which I queried you. As you have not done so, I can only assume that everything is all right. The one I'm particularly interested in is the Fielding Brown liquidation. If there were any snags, I could contact Shepherd before my return.

---

205 *Massif Central*

I'm glad to hear that Boon Eng is fit again. Is Ong unhappy about Loke being promoted over him? It's something I would rather had not happened but was, I fear, inevitable as Mr. Stewart had made up his mind to it and I could not have persuaded him otherwise (all this is between you and me of course).

I am very sorry indeed about May and do hope she is not feeling upset about the affair. I cannot quite follow why you did not want to accept her invitation to stay with her? Have you taken sides against her?

Congratulations to your eldest sister on her new baby. Are you to be godmother? I take it that Amy and Dick are still living with you and that you all get on well together?

You say nothing about your leave at all. I expect I shall return to find you still haven't taken it. I haven't been able to contact Mr. Phillips yet but will try and do so before my return.

Sylvia tells me she has written to you – have you received the letter? She is very pleased with the sarong material and is making a dress out of it.

Must close here. Haven't heard from you for some time – what's up? I do hope you are really keeping well and that your skin is quite all right again.

My love to you,
Christopher

Monday 9th September 1957

My dear Christopher,

Thank you very much indeed for your letter of the 3rd which was waiting for me when I got home with Agnes this evening. I was naturally very happy when I first saw the cover on the table and wasted no time to read it. In fact, for the whole of last week, I felt ever so morose, because I did not hear from you. I really can't understand myself why a letter from you should give me such joy and a wonderful feeling. Thank you also for your postcard of Cornwall which I received on the 2nd.

I'm happy to hear that you are well again and enjoying your holiday. I want to see you looking very fit when you return. I shall most certainly meet you at the airport on the 3rd October, regardless of the time, since I know the flight number. I should be able to check on the time of arrival quite easily. I'm already looking forward very much to seeing you in about 3 weeks' time. Mr. Stewart is rather anxious about your return and I think it is only proper that you should write and tell him.

I was interested to read your detailed account of the Spanish trip and I can still picture in my mind the route which you had taken.

So you are making a trip to Scotland to see the Reardons, and I do hope you and Walter will have a wonderful holiday in Scotland. Don't forget to send me a card from there.

I'm sorry to hear about the postponement of Dickon's wedding. I sincerely hope everything will eventually turn out all right.

I'm afraid I haven't received Sylvia's letter at the time of writing. However, I shall write to her in a day or two.

The cocktail party at the office went off quite successfully. Every one of us had to go to work as usual that Saturday morning and we only stopped work when the guests started to arrive. May also came specially for the party, at Mrs. Stewart's request. John Allan and his wife were also there, and he was enquiring about you and Walter Bellam. Oddly enough, he had asked me whether I was serious about going to England. I was rather taken aback, and I still can't understand how he came to know of this. He mentioned the name of the person who had told him, and I don't even know this person, who is also with Hume's. Anyway, I told him I wasn't sure about everything.

You'll be interested to know that I drank a whole glass of champagne for the first time, and quite enjoyed it. I sneaked out of the other entrance before one o'clock, and I learnt this morning that the party went on until after two. It would have been so much nicer if you were there at the party.

I can't understand your reference regarding the various unfinished jobs on which I was supposed to give you a reply. As you know, your second letter of the 20th August has been mislaid, so if I'm not wrong this could be the letter that contained a lot of your queries. Mrs. Elphick's tax was the only unfinished job you left with Kriekenbeek; this has since been properly dealt with. Flaxman's tax is being handled by Ong, and all the other tax matters are being done by Macartney. Nothing has cropped up re. the F. B. & F. liquidation, so I presume everything is all right.

There has been a lot of talk in the office among the old staff, with regard to Loke's taking over from Boon Eng. They are also of the opinion that Ong should be the right person, and I have a feeling that Ong is not looking very happy these days. Incidentally, Boon Eng told me one day that he had recommended Loke to Mr. Phillips and Mr. Stewart when they approached him on the subject of his successor. Ong, he said, is rather slow and slipshod in his work, whereas Loke, though slow, is very careful and keen in his work. Everybody in the office now is well aware of the fact that Loke is taking over from Boon Eng in the near future. I do feel sorry for Ong.

The reason that I had not accepted May's invitation to stay with her was one of transport. Taxis are not always available in her area, and her friend, Mr. Choo, leaves very late for the office. No, Chris, I haven't taken sides against her, as you say. Last Friday they invited me to their house for tea, but I couldn't go because I had to make my First Friday on that evening. Graeme wants me to have a game of badminton with May one day at their house when the court is ready.

Yes, I'm getting on well with Amy and Dick. Dick, I'm afraid, is down with chickenpox at the moment.

The new girl who is supposed to take May's place will not be able to join TYs until October 1st, so in the meantime we are rather hard-pressed, just when I feel like having a leave! Westworth told me last week that he had a special job for me – a 20-page report on S.H.B. (an important Government assignment we have just attained). So, it means the end of my leave, I'm afraid. I can't very well take my leave now – he might think I'm trying to shirk work. It's just my bad luck.

I hope this letter will reach you before your departure for Scotland. My letter of the 30th August will have reached you by now.

I'm keeping quite fit and expect you and everyone at home are keeping well. Must say 'Goodnight' as it's getting quite late. Always looking forward to hear from you.

With all my love,
Terry

Byfleet

Sat 14th Sept. 1957

My dear Terry,

This morning arrived your letter of 9th September, and as I haven't yet answered your previous letter of 30th August you are now, I regret to say, two up on me. As a matter of fact, your letter of 2nd arrived just as I was going out to post mine to you of 3rd–6th – so I did not re-open to acknowledge it. Earlier this week I had written some pages of a letter to you all about the difficulties and problems of our family; but I have since torn this up as I've decided it's not fair to worry you with such things.

I have today written a letter to Mr. Stewart advising him of the date of my return. I had intended to do so before you mentioned it; in fact, earlier this week, I had written a letter which dealt at some length with a meeting I'd had in London with Mr. Hoare and Lord Shepherd. Later I decided to cut out all the detail and so re-wrote the letter. Talking of writing, I must buy myself a typewriter as my handwriting seems to get steadily worse. I haven't overlooked what you say about sending Mr. Phillips a reminder – it might be better to wait until I get back as I will try and see him before 2nd October. I rang the London office yesterday, but D.C. Murphy was on holiday and the acting staff manager said that J.H.P. was still away on holiday. Both, however, are expected back next week. Meanwhile I obtained J.H.P.'s private phone no.

Willie Lochhead and Mac have promised that either both or at least one of them will meet me at Paya Lebar[206] on 3rd, so if the plane is due in in the middle of the night, I don't think you should try and come. However, if the plane is on time and you are still determined to come down, perhaps you could check with Willie.

The weather during September has so far been pretty poor: windy, showery, cool, occasional bright periods, temperatures seldom exceeding 65°. Still, I suppose it's a tonic for me. This morning for instance, as I write at 11 a.m. the temperature is only 53°! We are hoping for some fine days before I return.

---

206 Singapore Airport.

Last week was fairly busy. On Monday I drove up to London, lunched with Mr. Hoare and Mrs. Lund, and later we all saw Lord Shepherd. On Tuesday I drove down to Sussex to see Stella. It wasn't a very nice day, unfortunately. In the afternoon Stella and I, the two boys and one of the nuns there, Sister Teresius, drove over to Burwash (45 miles). Roy is buried there, and I saw his grave. The parish priest gave us a very nice tea and we got back rather late at Steyning (8.15 p.m.). It was dark then and raining, and I was scared we should run out of petrol. However, I got them back safely and then as all the petrol stations seemed to be shut, I stopped at an inn in Steyning and was lucky to find a contractor who sold me some petrol from his private pump. Afterwards I stood him a drink to thank him for his help and didn't leave Steyning till nearly 10 p.m., which meant I didn't get back to Byfleet till about 11.20 p.m. and the family was a little worried.

On the way back I had some trouble with the car. This model has the trafficators and the horn on the same switch. In operating the trafficators, I set the horn off and it wouldn't stop! This is a very noisy horn but luckily, I was a long way from any house. At length I managed to stop it by forcing the switch down; by then the windscreen wipers, petrol gauge, horn and trafficators had all ceased to function! Luckily, I was only a mile from Byfleet so got home all right and had the damage repaired next day.

On Thursday I drove Mother down to Bexhill (70 miles) on the Sussex coast to see a sister of hers now living there. I think she enjoyed the day. Yesterday I was up in London again. This afternoon I go over to Bromley (20 miles) to see some friends of mine there, spend the night with them and return on Sunday morning. Sunday afternoon I plan to go down to Salisbury (70 miles) to see my brother Dickon for tea. The wedding is on again now, I'm glad to say, and may be before I return.

Must close now as I want to go to post. Hope you are really keeping well – will write again soon.

Love from Christopher

Dickon & Olive's wedding

Wednesday 18th September 1957

My dear Christopher,

I had written a letter to you last night but kept it back as I was hoping to hear from you today, and sure enough, your letter of the 14th was waiting for me when I got home from work.

You shouldn't have destroyed that letter which you had written last week, about the difficulties and problems of the family. Anything concerning you or your family will have my interest at heart, and I do hope you'll tell me all about it when you return. I always tell you about my troubles and I never even stopped to think whether it was fair to worry you about my affairs. You are so understanding a person, that is the reason why, I think, I never hesitated to confide my worries to you.

I'm very grateful to you for endeavouring to see Mr. Phillips on my behalf. I hope you'll bring back some good news.

You had indeed had a busy time last week and I was sorry to learn about the trouble you had with your car. I'm so glad that Dickon is getting married after all and I hope they'll both be very happy.

I had a letter from Sylvia last Monday, to which I replied yesterday; I also wrote her on the 12th. She seems to be working extremely hard, trying to save some money for another trip to Rome. I was surprised to learn from her that Gervase went with you to Cornwall – I didn't know he was home also. Sylvia wanted to know if I would be coming

413

to London, and I told her I would let her know as soon as there was news from Mr. Phillips.

No doubt you'll have heard from Walter that he has been asked to return a month earlier. We received a cable from him yesterday saying that he'll return as requested. Mr. Stewart received a 'bombshell' from London last week requiring the Oilfields' audit to be completed and report submitted by November 20th. The Oilfields being such valued and important clients, the firm has to comply with their request – even though it means upsetting Mr. Stewart's plans for leave and cutting short Walter's leave.

Soon after I wrote to you last, there was a query from Lord Shepherd, so I suggested to Ong to write to you about it as he didn't know how to reply.

Ong's youngest son, Danny, is getting married on Sunday 22nd, and I've been invited to attend the wedding reception at 3.30 in the afternoon at the Peking Restaurant. I must try to attend, although it's going to be a little difficult with transport.

Graeme and May took me out to lunch on Monday and I again had lunch with them today. May seems very happy in her new temporary job, and she will be starting on a permanent post on October 1st.

Something happened in the office today which aggravated me very much, so I've decided to take a week's leave from the 23rd and I look forward to a nice quiet holiday – in Singapore of course!

In two weeks' time I shall see you again; the thought of it makes me feel very happy. As you say, I expect to hear from you again soon.

With all my love,
Terry

Grasmere
Byfleet
23rd Sept. 1957

My dear Terry,

Thank you for yours of 18th which arrived this morning (Monday). Today you will be starting your week's leave – it's a pity you could not have got away from Singapore, but I suppose it was difficult to arrange.

I was most disturbed to hear that the immediate reason for your taking leave was some trouble in the office – but why didn't you tell me what it was all about? I can only guess that Westworth must have upset you in some way or other – am I right?

Yes, I must have forgotten to mention that Gervase was at home. Originally, he intended to come by sea from New Zealand (on a cheap passage) and would not have reached England till mid-September. As it turned out, he couldn't get a sea passage so, on the spur of the moment, decided to come by air – thus he was here when I got back from Spain. Coming this way has, of course,

Leila and Gervase

cost him rather a lot and, as he does not get paid passage and leave pay as we do from Singapore, he'll probably have to take a temporary job in England later on in his stay, which may be until next February or so. It's been pleasant having him at home as I'd not seen him for six years and he and I have been able to make a number of trips together.

Last week I went up north and he came with me. We set off on the Tuesday morning in pleasant warm weather down here. We lunched somewhere near Bedford, then got on the Great North Road which runs from London to Edinburgh. The weather deteriorated the further north we got, and by Doncaster it was raining. We intended to spend the night at Harrogate, a pleasant old Yorkshire town which is a watering-place (that is, a place where people come to take the medicinal spring water) and not industrial as are most big Yorkshire towns. However, there was a conference of librarians there (over 1,500 of them!) and so all the hotels were full. Fortunately, we were able to telephone ahead to a little AA[207] hotel some 20 miles further north and they booked us in for the night. We reached there in heavy rain about 10 p.m.

---

207 Automobile Association.

The next morning was cloudy with rain in the offing when we set off at 9 a.m. I took Gervase up to Darlington, where he was to catch a train to Newcastle, spend the night with some friends and come across the next day to Carlisle to meet me again.

We parted there about 10 a.m. in the rain and I then drove west across the Yorkshire and Westmoreland moors to Carlisle, where I lunched. I had decided to get some presents for the Reardons' three children and, being a very bad shopper as you know, I spent nearly 1½ hours wandering round Carlisle trying to get what I wanted. I finally left about 3.45 with 3 hours' driving still ahead of me. I had vaguely promised Olive, Dickon's fiancée, to call in upon her and her family on my way to Airdrie. They live at Lockerbie, which is on the route. However, it was raining so hard and I was so much behind schedule that I decided to leave it to the return journey. As it turned out, I was also late on the return journey and then couldn't find their house, so didn't see them at all, I fear.

Reached Airdrie about 6.30 – the rain had stopped, and it was a clear, rather cold evening. Of course, Airdrie, which is near Glasgow, is about 400 miles north of Byfleet so one must expect it to be colder at this time of year. The Reardons gave us a wonderful welcome – Walter had arrived earlier – and we spent a delightful evening; or rather night as we didn't get to bed till nearly 2 a.m. We were looking at some of the colour photographs that Walter and I had taken in Spain – Walter has some very good ones – rather better than mine, I would say.

Unfortunately, I had to leave the next day (Thursday) – Walter was staying on till Friday. It was a lovely sunny day for a change, and I left Airdrie about 11 a.m. Once you get out of the industrial belt round Glasgow and Airdrie, there's some lovely Scottish country down to Carlisle – the valley of the Clyde with the lowland hills on either side. I kept stopping the car to take colour pictures as it was such a beautiful morning after the rain. Had a very good lunch at Moffat and finally reached Carlisle about 3 p.m., when I met up with Gervase as arranged.

We had got the AA to give us an alternative route back via the Lake District, Lancashire and the Western Midlands. This turned out to be much more interesting than the Gt. North Rd. We wasted no further time and set off south, making a wide detour through the Lake District. This is a unique part of England in the extreme N.W. containing a series of small mountain ranges 2 to 3,000 ft. with steep sides coming down to some beautiful lakes. It is very picturesque and a favourite district for walkers, campers and climbers. We spent the afternoon there and then down to Kendal, where we spent the night.

The next day, Friday, was a long day – 290 miles to Byfleet. We were off at 9.30 a.m. and reached home about 10 p.m. We had to go via part of the industrial district of Lancashire but once through there we had a pleasant, fairly quiet road, not so many of the heavy lorries that you get day and night on the Gt. North Rd. We stopped for tea in Worcester and visited the cathedral. From there I sent you a postcard which I trust has arrived safely. Then we returned through the Cotswolds, Oxford and Henley. A very enjoyable trip – 900 miles in 4 days, so I was a little tired at the end of it.

I have not yet been able to get in touch with Mr. Phillips but hope it may be possible this week. Incidentally, I've just this minute had a telephone call (presumably via our London office) from Mr. Petty of Skoda/Exico who would like to see me before I return – quite friendly. Shall probably try and see them on Wednesday.

Have got a lot to pack into my remaining 9 days so you cannot expect many more letters, I fear. Am glad Sylvia has written to you at last – she mentioned she'd had your reply.

Yes, I heard from Walter about the Shell special audit and the curtailment of his leave. Poor Mr. Stewart – I suppose he won't take any leave now. I had Ong's letter re. F. B. & F. but by that time I'd already seen Lord S. You must try and go to Ong's son's wedding – it's over now of course – did you go? Am glad to hear that May likes her new work.

Hope you are keeping well and no more skin trouble. Goodbye for now.

Love from Christopher

Theresa

Christopher and Walter returned to Singapore after their trip to Europe. Christopher had a nasty flu, while Walter was suffering from tummy trouble. I think it was quite exhausting, that long trip down to France and Spain and

Chris (back row, 2nd right) with St Vincent de Paul group

back by car. Willie Lochhead was still around, and he told me that they were coming home one evening. So, he invited me to 24 Dunsfold Drive for dinner and the cinema afterwards, and on to the airport to meet Walter and Christopher, whose plane landed quite late that night. We were very pleased to see each other again.

We made a retreat together at St. Joseph's Church in Middle Road, next to my old school in town. Christopher used to pick me up about six o'clock in the morning, having given me a call to wake me up at half past five. The retreat lasted a week. Afterwards we ate our breakfast in G. H. Café; just toast and tea.

Christopher was also very much involved in the church's branch of the St. Vincent de Paul Society. He was president of one of their conferences. Apparently, he made weekly visits to families in need, to give them rations of some sort and rent money, and to say prayers with them. He became president of one of the society's conferences. Gordon Van Hien also got him involved in the Singapore Musical Society as their treasurer, and he sometimes had to meet prominent artists from abroad who came to perform in Singapore.

Braddell Heights is not very far from Serangoon Gardens, so sometimes Christopher would pick me up and we would go for a drink at the Palm Tree Inn on Bartley Road. Then we would go for a drive somewhere on the east coast. At other times I took a bus right up to the corner of Bartley Road and Braddell Road. Christopher picked me up from the bus station, and he would bring me a beautiful gardenia from his garden, which I really appreciated.

Christopher, Walter and a couple of other bachelors went to Cameron Highlands to spend Christmas 1957 in the mountains. They made it to the top without much trouble and had a very nice Christmas up there. I think I spent that Christmas with my family in Serangoon Gardens.

1958

At the beginning of 1958, Gervase came to Singapore, and I met him at the Raffles Hotel for tea one afternoon. He was staying at the Cathay Hotel for one night. He complained about earache and the following day was a Sunday, so I arranged for him to see my doctor, Dr. Thompson, before he joined Christopher on a trip to Johor Bahru. Apparently, he felt much better, so he went on the trip without that terrible pain in his ear.

I saw Gervase again with Christopher one evening when we went out to the Happy World to show him the '*wayangs*'[208] and the '*ronggengs*'[209] which they performed nightly at the park. One evening Christopher took him to meet some of his SVP[210] conference members, and he was quite interested. The next night he stayed with Christopher, as there was room in the house for him; somebody was on leave. He soon left for New Zealand to take up a job with Dalgety's. It was my first meeting with one of Christopher's family. Gervase was a lovely person, and I liked him.

31/1/58

Dear Miss Pang,

I acknowledge your letter of 13th January and have not overlooked your request. However, it is not so easy to arrange

---

208 Traditional open-air Chinese opera.
209 Traditional Indonesian dances.
210 St. Vincent de Paul.

these matters in London as it was in Singapore. In the first place, conditions are entirely different. I am not the undisputed No. 1 as I was in Singapore, and have nothing to do with staff matters, which is an entirely different department from mine.

The work here is chiefly auditing and there is not the number of letters to write as we have in Singapore. The girls are in a sort of pool, and not only type the letters but also type the accounts. There would be no question of you therefore working for one person like myself.

I have of course mentioned your request to come to London, but at the moment cannot get a definite decision. Moving to the break with Arthur Andersen, some reorganisation is in progress, and the main problem appears to be a reduction of staff rather than an increase. However, as I said before, this is not my department.

You would find living conditions very strange at first, and it would be essential for you to find suitable accommodation, preferably before you arrived. Also, it would be better to arrive in the summertime, so as to have a chance to acclimatise before the winter. The winters are very cold and grim and take a lot of getting used to. The travelling in buses and tubes is what I find to be the biggest trial. They are always crowded and to get a place is a struggle.

Miss Wylie, one of the girls here, tells me that you would receive at least £10 a week to live in London, and even on that you would have to be careful. Most of the girls in the office of course live with their parents or their husbands.

I regret I cannot let you know definitely in this letter of the decision to employ you in London and think it will be a few months before the present re-organisation is settled. However, as soon as I can get an answer, I will let you know.

I hope you are keeping well, and with this, best wishes from Mrs. Phillips and myself.

Yours sincerely,
J. H. Phillips

Theresa

Christopher and I saw a lot of each other after Gervase left. During Chinese New Year I invited him, May and Graeme to lunch at 17 Alnwick Road. I repeated the same menu by serving them cold lobsters, salad and dessert. After lunch, Christopher took me to 24 Dunsfold Drive for the day and I had tea there. I think that evening we went out to Pasir Ris for dinner and dancing, and this time there were more people around. We really enjoyed going there for a quiet dance. The open air was so lovely in the evening.

One evening we took Joyce out to a musical concert at the community centre or somewhere like that. Other times we took Mary Boey out for dinner on her or my birthday, which was nice. One weekend we took off for Johor Bahru, hoping to find a nice picnic spot for lunch. But we drove on and on, and it was all rubber or palm estates. We managed to find a quiet spot where there were not too many insects around. We enjoyed the trip there and back.

We used to go to cinemas now and again. I remember one time when Christopher picked me up at Agnes's shop in North Bridge Road to see *War and Peace*. He was delayed at a lunch at the Tanglin Club, but the film was so long, we only missed the first part.

My mother became ill about April or May that year, and I took her to see my doctor. It turned out to be very serious: she had cancer of the uterus. I was so upset, wondering what I could do to help. We persuaded her to have an operation. She told me my doctor had to be there with the surgeon. She had a lot of confidence in Dr. Thompson. In June Professor Sheares operated on her at the Kandang Kerbau Hospital, but they found the growth too advanced, and he could not remove it. A few days later she was very ill and wanted to go home to my brother's house, so I was called from the office to the hospital on the day she was discharged. [By the time I got there] she was unconscious and could not speak. Arrangements were made for her to be transported to my second brother's house. That night she died very peacefully, with most of her children around her, along with her grandchildren and my father, of course, who was very upset and saddened by her death. The three-day wake was held at my brother's house. I felt that I had lost somebody so dear and was really traumatised by it all.

Soon after, I took leave to go on a trip with Joyce to Penang, as I was suffering from skin trouble. We stayed in Penang for a few days, then I flew back to Kuala Lumpur on my own and stayed at Joyce's shop, where she had a room upstairs. Joyce remained in Penang with friends. On the Saturday evening Christopher drove up to Kuala Lumpur and picked me up from the shop. We went for a meal, and a nice drive to the Lake Gardens. I spent another night at the shop, while Christopher stayed at the Majestic Hotel. Early the next morning, we went to Mass together, and after breakfast we drove slowly back to Singapore. That was a very memorable trip for me. It did me a lot of good. I felt much happier, and not so lonely.

Christopher bought his first car in Kuala Lumpur, a Morris Minor with a 'P' registration, 7126 – I can still remember that. It was a good car; it didn't give him a lot of trouble. His next car was also a Morris Minor, SS 3289. Christopher was a great comfort to me, and my skin rash gradually got better. I had to see Dr. Gethin-Jones a number of times and he said it was due to nerves.

12th June 1958

Dear Miss Pang,

I have delayed replying to your letter until I had a further chance to speak to Mr. Sillens, who is in charge of staff matters. As you know, he has been travelling quite a lot recently and is rarely in the office.

I regret there is no vacancy in the London office, for which I am sorry as I would like you to work for me once more. I very much appreciate your efficiency and loyalty.

If you are still determined to come to London, then I feel sure you would, with your knowledge, be able to get a decent job. I will of course do all I can to help you. Please, however, remember my previous remarks about conditions in London – they are very different from Singapore. Besides, of course, a job is not 100% guaranteed.

With best wishes from Mrs. Phillips and myself.

Yours sincerely,
J. H. Phillips

Hu Chye Neo
4 Kinfauns Rd.
Tulse Hill
London S.W. 2
2nd July 1958

Dear Theresa,

Your letter was a real shock for me because I never had the idea that you will ever know of my coming to London. Well, as you know, all young girls love to have adventure and leave their loved ones behind like I did. Anyway, I want to thank you for your rather interesting letter. Yes, I am happy that you will perhaps join us one day. Do you think you can give me the answer soon? What of your boss's reply?

The distance from Tulse Hill to Coleman Street, London E.C. 1[211] is almost the same distance as I have to travel daily. Firstly, you will have to catch the electric train from Tulse Hill Station (which is not very walking distance) to London Bridge and then catch a bus to Coleman Street. You need not have to worry about travelling because there are so many buses, trains and underground trains too. We found difficulty in travelling during the last weeks because the bus strike was on, but not at the present moment. If you do desire to have a fresh morning walk, where most of the English people do, you can easily walk but perhaps you shall have to walk for miles before you arrive at your destination. Previously, we had to walk 4 miles to and from the office, i.e. during the strike.

The people of London are of so many nationalities, but you will find the majority of them in the West End – Piccadilly – a very notorious place but as well as a place where all the latest fashions in clothes, hats, etc. and even the Princesses do their shopping there. That is the place where Chinese food can be found, but unfortunately, [it] cannot be compared with our home food.

As for the weather, it is very uncertain. Sometimes you can get the warm sunshine about 70° but sometimes it's as cold as 45° and with very heavy rain. Therefore, you can imagine that we have to take our coats and raincoats along with us every day. The sun is only mild, and you should see how the mad English people rush for the sunshine as soon as they see it shining. They will lie on the grass in the parks and couples will lie embracing each other, kissing and rolling like mad animals! Kisses to them is nothing and you can even see them doing, I mean, petting in

---

211 Location of Turquand Youngs' head office in the City of London.

the trains too. On the whole, if you are ever in difficulty to trace your destination, I am sure that they are always helpful. As for the English food, oh dear, I am fed up of it already. There are no varieties in the courses, and you can expect what is coming up in the next dish.

Well, Theresa, I hope my explanation is clear, but I hope you can join us later on. Frankly speaking, I am so homesick and fed up with this office. Had it not been for my sister-in-law who will be arriving on 11th July, I would have certainly taken a slow boat to Singapore.

Since my arrival, I saw two live acts at the Saville Theatre and the London Coliseum. On the whole, the acts were quite good. I visited Weymouth – a seaport at the southern coast of England – a place where the people spend their summer holidays. Then I visited a friend's house in Kent – i.e. the English countryside, where I saw beautiful roses 4 inches in diameter, daffodils, and oh, many beautiful flowers that are beyond description. Another thing I want to say is, the shopping. The clothes are so well displayed, and they are about the same price as in Singapore if you buy ready-made. Majority of the clothes are ready-made because the tailoring is too expensive.

Theresa, if you wish to come here, do let me have your answer earlier because I shall then be able to arrange accommodation in the same boarding house. As regards the jobs, I am sure you will get one here, but it will be convenient if your boss could arrange one before you leave Singapore. This is the best time to visit England now – summer.

Well, Theresa, if you are still keen, please reply earlier then I shall inform you of what clothes to buy. Don't buy too many woollies, they are cheap here – get only 1 suit, 1 twinset, 1 housecoat (thick), 2 pairs of nylon stockings, and buy a lot of cosmetics (especially American ones). We cannot get American goods easily here. So, hoping to see you soon.

Best wishes.

Yours,
Chye Neo

8th July 1958

Dear Miss Pang,

I was sorry to hear of the death of your mother – please accept my sympathy. I shall of course be pleased to give you a testimonial. Will you let me have your full name (including Chinese one) and the date you started work? I cannot remember the exact particulars now.

I think perhaps it would be better if I delayed writing the testimonial until you arrive in this country. I do not want to upset Mr. Stewart by giving testimonials when you are at present employed by him. In this country people would in any case ring up and refer to me personally.

With best wishes,

Yours sincerely,
J. H. Phillips

152 High Street
Kuala Lumpur
19th August 1958

My dear Christopher,

We arrived here at 7.40 this morning after a pleasant trip. I slept quite peacefully all the night through.

We were met by Joyce's friends at the station and taken straight to the above address. At the moment I am writing this note in an air-conditioned office. We have booked an air-conditioned room for you at the Majestic from Saturday night under your name. I suppose you would much prefer to go directly to the hotel as soon as you arrive and give us a ring from there.

Our train leaves at nine o'clock tonight for Penang, so we have some time to take a look around.

I shall look forward to seeing you on Saturday night, my dear.

With fondest love,
Terry

Theresa

In the late '40s and early '50s, for expatriates who went out to work in Singapore, one of the conditions in their contract of work was that they could not marry local girls, otherwise they could be dismissed instantly. But things began to improve, and in the mid '50s, nothing like that happened. Turquand Youngs never had a condition like that in their contract.

We discussed marriage sometimes, but Christopher was doubtful that it would work. He was thinking of the children of mixed marriages and that sort of thing. He actually consulted one of the Redemptorist priests at the Novena Church, who gave him good advice; namely that his faith and mine were strong enough to build our lives on. So, Christopher wrote to his mother, telling her about our plans. I had a beautiful letter from her.

W. R. Lochhead
c/o Price Waterhouse & Co.
Windsor
Ontario
July 31, 1958

Dear Chris,

If this letter wanders about from subject to subject, please don't think I'm trying to stall. I sincerely hope you decide to marry Terry, not only for your good fortune but for hers. To use an Americanism – it's a natural.

I do think that Canadians would accept your difference in race more readily than Britishers. Obviously, you must be prepared for people to look at you twice, but this will only be natural and not malicious.

As an aside, Canadians tend to be on the defensive with the English in the initial stages of getting to know each other. Frankly, Scots and Irish are made to feel more at home quicker than English. However, knowing your ability at getting along with people there will be no difficulty here, especially with Terry to charm them.

The main difficulty is going to be getting settled in at a job. I honestly believe you will have to come over here yourself and get settled in a job first of all. I do think it would be foolhardy to marry and then both of you come here on spec. The chances of landing a job without having a personal interview are very slender. Bluntly, age is a factor which will hamper you to quite an extent in getting a job. Even I came across it. One C.A.[212] firm I applied for a job with told me bluntly that my age was against me. Some of the partners were 28 years of age, and their supervisors, whom I would work under, would be even less. I think the position with Price Waterhouse is better than that firm, but I know, from the local partner here, that my age was taken into serious consideration, and me a mere 31. That doesn't mean that I think it would be hopeless getting a job.

As you know, the economy of Canada at the moment is certainly not in boom conditions, but this of course will pass fairly quickly, and she'll really grow. Even the little I've seen of Canada has made me envisage the tremendous growth possibilities in Canada, and when she gets going there'll be more jobs than men.

The local partner is due off his vacation on Monday and at the earliest possibility I'll ask him his views on your best chances at getting settled in.

Climate. From what I've heard, Vancouver would probably be better. But I wouldn't be put off too much by that. You go from air-conditioned houses to cars to offices to supermarkets to houses, and frankly I found that the Canadians like the temperature to be hotter than I do. Some of the offices are really stifling. I definitely don't think Terry would find it hard to get used to.

August 6, 1958

I cut off writing this letter for I was feeling I wasn't giving you a very authoritative opinion. My boss is now off his vacation and yesterday I had the opportunity to get his opinion. Bluntly, his opinion is that at the moment you would have difficulty in getting settled in at a job. He said that a Canadian C.A. of your age would have difficulty. Bluntly, he wasn't clear what a Chartered Secretary was. (Of course, I told him about your wide auditing and accounting experience.) In Canada very few big companies do their own secretarial work. This is done by trust companies; the smaller companies have this work done by public accountants. Both pay poorly.

---

212 Chartered accountancy.

My boss particularly emphasised the depressed economic conditions at the moment. Now Windsor is a particularly depressed area and I have no idea what conditions are like in the west.

A shot in the dark. Is it not possible to establish a contact with Catholic universities in North America? What I am thinking of is that perhaps there is an ideal opening as Registrar. It's just a thought.

I hope I don't need to tell you that I'll do anything I can to help you. If you want adverts put in papers or for me to serve as a mailbox, please don't hesitate. I'm sorry I can't be more helpful or hopeful, but it would be stupid of me to give you what I consider to be a wrong picture. The position is obviously not completely hopeless, but you should have your eyes wide open when you come over here. I think you must come over here at some time and have a damn good try, for it is the sort of thing which, if you don't do, may prove food for future regret. Of course, I'll keep my eyes open, and my boss has promised to do so also.

I think I'll leave it at that, just apart from thanking you for remitting the £11.

Aye yours,
Willie

Theresa

Strangely enough, it turned out that Christopher and I both had the same problem. Christopher had been engaged to a non-Catholic English girl way back in 1948. He'd tried to get her to convert, wanting her to join him in Java, where he was working. But things hadn't worked out and she'd refused to be converted, so she'd broken off their engagement. Christopher had been quite upset about that. Later on, he'd tried again once or twice to see her, but she'd stuck to her decision not to marry him.

For my part, I had been very much in love with a Chinese man [before] the war. He was a friend of my brother. As he was the eldest son, his mother had refused to let him become a Catholic; she was a very staunch Buddhist. So, we had never got engaged and the friendship had ended.

1959

Grasmere
High Road
Byfleet
Jan. 6th 1959

My dear, dear Christopher,

By the time you receive this, Dadda will not be here. A week ago, he was up, and now he has got weaker each day, and tonight he seems to be sleeping very peacefully and does not know anyone, and we feel he may not last the night. Nell is here; she came Sunday and is being a great help. Fr. Kerry is very good and has been coming every day since Sat., when he gave him Extreme Unction and anointed him.

Dickon was here today and Leila and Bill last Sunday. It is very late, and must not stop for more as Nell is waiting to settle down in the drawing room so she may be near to help me. Jocelyn has been at home several days to help in lifting etc.

Please forgive short letter.

Very best love from your loving mother

P.S. He is sleeping very peacefully and not suffering.

Theresa

Christopher's father died at the age of eighty-eight in January 1959. Soon after, we were engaged, and I had to make up my mind to resign from my work. According to the company's policy, I was not allowed to work as a confidential secretary after my marriage to Christopher, who was still carrying on working with the firm. I tendered my resignation up to June that year.

Surabaya
Feb. 18th 1959

Dear Chris,

Many thanks for your letter. I enclose a cheque for $500 re. household expenses.

Walter (2nd left) and Chris (3rd right) with friends

The same key unlocks the petrol tank, the boot, the doors and the ignition in my car. The lock on the door does take a bit of fiddling with and I do not think you can unlock the nearside door if it is locked from the inside. However, you should be able to open the door on the driver's side. If the worst comes to the worst could you get Borneo Motors to come up and deal with it, as the car will get into a poor state if not used for a month or so.

I am due to leave here on the 26th and will return to Singapore about the 15th March. I can hardly wait!

Very glad to hear you joined the Island Club, and am looking forward to some golf. Have been playing a bit of tennis here and think I will take it up again when I get back.

Yours,
Colin

Grasmere
High Road
Byfleet
Surrey
June 9th 1959

Dear Terry,

Congratulations to you both on your engagement and we all join in wishing you joy and happiness in the future. Now we are looking forward to meeting you when you come over in August.

With all good wishes from

Yours very sincerely,
Caroline Repton

Theresa

Christopher and I used to drive up to The Gap[213] and look at the ships in the harbour with their lights on at night. We'd also drive right up to the top of Marina Hill to enjoy the fresh air up there, and to see the beautiful view down in Keppel Harbour with all the ships lit up. At times we would drive up to Mount Faber, which is not as high as The Gap. There again you got a beautiful view of the islands. It was a very happy six months before our wedding, and Christopher took me to Mass on Sundays. We did another mission together, this time in the Cathedral of the Good Shepherd after work for about a week.

Walter happened to be on leave at the beginning of that year. Christopher wrote to him, asking him to be his best man. He was delighted to accept. In Newcastle-upon-Tyne he bought us a beautiful painting by Russell Flint[214] as a wedding present. We received it after our wedding.

After our engagement we had no doubt that our marriage was going to work, as we both had very strong faith and we were going to build our life and our family on that.

A general election was held in Singapore about that time, so many of the local companies were rather anxious about their future. So, what they did was make Kuala Lumpur the location of their head office, and there was therefore much restructuring. A lot of work from Christopher was done in the secretarial department, and I was permitted to help with the typing. Often we would work quite late into the evening together. The People's Action Party came to power with very little opposition, though there were two opposition parties. The P.A.P. had a majority and Lee Kuan Yew

---

213 A lookout point at Mount Faber, overlooking Sentosa Island to the south of Singapore Island.

214 A signed print of Sir William Russell Flint's painting, *Festal preparations, Manosque*.

became the first Prime Minister of independent Singapore. A few years later, Singapore became a republic and elected a President. The first President was a Malay, and it worked out very well for the people of Singapore.

We began to make plans for our wedding. Christopher set the date as the 25th July as he was due to go on leave about that time. Father Teixeira of the Portuguese mission at St. Joseph's Church would marry us, since he was involved with the St. Vincent de Paul conference there. Mary Boey was to be my bridesmaid.

I ordered my wedding dress from Mulchan's in High Street, and Freddy Streuss, who used to be my hairdresser, helped to design it. It was made of a beautiful satin material from Holland. On the bodice and on the panels of the skirt there was lovely French lace. It had a very full skirt, with sequins sewn onto the front panels according to Freddy's design, so as to match the headdress which he also designed for me, and which was made by one of his relatives in Serangoon Garden Estate. Mary ordered her bridesmaid dress from Modern Silk Store. I used to get my Montagut suits from there. They have some of the most beautiful fabrics. She looked lovely in a salmon-pink three-quarter-length skirt with a spray of flowers in her hair. Christopher ordered himself a very light grey suit from his usual tailor in Chulia Street.

Peggy McMaster helped me to organise the wedding reception at the Adelphi Hotel. One day she and I went there for lunch. We booked the date and the cake and everything else. The hotel used to be situated at the corner of North Bridge Road and Coleman Street.

Eighty-two-year-old Mr. Pang How Yew, who arrived in Singapore 62 years ago and brought up a total of 74 children and grandchildren, yesterday declared that "arranged" marriages were still the best.[215]

Mr. Pang, today the owner of a prosperous and flourishing provision store in Rochore Road, came to Singapore with nothing more than the clothes on his back. Working as a $3-a-day labourer, Mr. Pang saved enough to start a poultry farm. From this, he progressed to a stage where he found it was cheaper to buy wholesale for the needs of his four farms. Later, he decided that there was more to be made in selling to farmers than in farming, and so he bought out his supplier.

---

215 A Singaporean newspaper article from 1958 or 1959 which was found by Theresa Chua among her mother's (my Aunt Elizabeth's) possessions, with a photograph of our grandfather sporting a long white beard.

Looking back on the marriages of his children and his own marriage, nearly 60 years ago, Mr. Pang said: "Arranged marriages are still the best. They seldom end up in divorces or estrangements."

Asked for his secret for long life, Mr. Pang said: "Abstinence from vices, such as gambling and heavy drinking."

Looking back on the Singapore he had known, Mr. Pang declared: "I am very contented with my life and happy to see the rapid changes which are taking place. I saw Singapore when it was a small fishing village. Today, it is a busy city."

He said the bleakest day in his life was the recent death of his life-long companion and helpmate – his wife.

Mr. Pang How Yew

requests the pleasure of the company of

....

at the marriage of his daughter

Theresa Kim Lui

to

Geoffrey Christopher Tyrwhitt Repton

at St. Joseph's Church,

Victoria Street,

on Saturday 25th July 1959

at 8 a.m., and

at a reception at 9.15 a.m.

at Adelphi Hotel.

R.S.V.P.

17 Alnwick Road,

Serangoon Garden Estate,

Singapore 19.

Theresa

Christopher did meet my father before we were married, and some other members of my family, and they were all very happy to hear of our engagement.

During the last few months before I left Turquand Youngs, my boss, the senior partner Donald Stewart, gave me permission to do a lot of work for Christopher, as he was given a special assignment to transfer many of the head offices of Singapore companies to Kuala Lumpur. So, there was a lot of overtime, a lot of typing, and I thoroughly enjoyed working for him.

At that time, Gordon Van Hien was in charge of the company when Donald Stewart was on leave. He lent us the company's car and driver, Abdullah,[216] for the wedding. My brother-in-law Chai Seng was the official photographer and took some wonderful black-and-white photographs.

The St. Vincent de Paul group at St. Joseph's Church organised a beautiful choir and sung Mass at eight o'clock on the morning of our wedding. Needless to say, Christopher and I were very happy and at the same time a little nervous.

My third brother gave me away, as my second brother couldn't do the honours and my father was at that time quite ill. So, he was also one of the witnesses at the registry. Another sponsor at the registry was Mary Boey's sister Boly. After the wedding a lot of photographs were taken, and we all proceeded to the Adelphi Hotel for the wedding breakfast. There were quite a few friends and relatives at the reception. I wish I had Walter's lovely speech recorded. Everyone was feeling very jolly, and a lot of champagne was drunk. Apparently, after we left for our honeymoon some of the guests proceeded to Walter's house for more celebration. Peggy McMaster did a very good job in arranging the wedding breakfast and the cake. I gave her the job of posting little boxes of cake to various relatives in England.

We set off in our little Morris Minor for the first part of our honeymoon in Cameron Highlands. We stopped in Kuala Lumpur to spend the night at the Federal Hotel, as it was too long a journey to make it in one day. My friend Joyce joined us for dinner at the hotel, which was nice.

The next morning after breakfast we continued our journey to Cameron Highlands, stopping somewhere for lunch and arriving at the Smokehouse Inn about teatime, where we stayed for just over a week. It was really beautiful up there; cool, and the flowers were lovely, especially the roses. It being my first trip up there, I felt very excited. We met some nice people at the Smokehouse Inn. One was the Finance Minister, who was also having a holiday there, and there was another young couple who had just married. I can't remember if he was Swiss or Belgian, but he had married a Singaporean girl. We decided to go with them up to the top of Brinchang.[217] They had a small Fiat and had to travel backwards up the hill! But our little Morris Minor did the trip very well. The owner of the Smokehouse Inn, Mr. Cowley,

---

216 Abdullah was later employed as Walter's driver for many years.
217 The highest peak in Cameron Highlands.

Terry & Chris on honeymoon

took us in his jeep to see the Blue Valley tea plantations. It was interesting to see how tea was processed in the factory. We had some nice walks around the place, especially to the Robinson Waterfall. The air was so relaxing.

On our return journey we stopped one more night at the Federal Hotel and booked in at the York Hotel in Singapore for about a week before setting off on the second stage of our honeymoon. Christopher had to go back to the office to hand over his work. That gave us an opportunity to invite some of my family to a dinner party before we left for the UK.

I was overwhelmed with excitement, it being my first long trip abroad. At the same time, I was apprehensive about meeting Christopher's mother and other members of his family for the first time. In those days, flights from Singapore to the UK were arduous and long. We had three or four stops, like [either] Bangkok or Bombay, Tehran and Rome or Frankfurt, before we got to Heathrow.

We stopped over in Rome on our way to England, to see Bianca, Alberto, and Flavia, who was only three years old. They were living in an apartment in the city centre, and we had a hotel booked near the station. The day after we arrived, we went out to get some lunch before seeing the family. We had such a wonderful lunch. That evening, we took a train and had dinner with Bianca's family near their apartment. The next day they took us to the

Vatican to see St. Peter's Basilica. It was most fascinating for me to see such a huge cathedral for the first time. We were supposed to have a picnic but, as it was raining, we had to eat it at Alberto's little studio in Rome.

I had expressed a desire to see Sorrento, so Christopher organised a trip to Naples, Pompeii and Sorrento. That morning we left at six o'clock and didn't return till midnight, and it was a very exciting trip for me. We didn't see Alberto very much during that trip, as he had just had a very bad accident in Africa during the filming of *Ben-Hur*[218], so he was having frequent headaches and had to take rests in the afternoon. Before our flight to the UK, Bianca, Alberto and Flavia came to say goodbye to us at the terminal.

From Heathrow we took a train to Victoria Station, where we were met by Jocelyn, Sylvia and Humphry, who gave us a very warm welcome. We all went for a drink at a pub somewhere along Bayswater Road; it was rather dimly lit. Later, they helped us to check in at the Carlisle House Hotel in Lancaster Gate, where we stayed for a few days, awaiting delivery of our new car.

The following day Christopher took me to the Tower of London to see the Crown Jewels; seeing London for the first time was most exciting. But when he took me to the zoo I was wearing stiletto heels three and a half inches high, so I felt very tired by the time we got to Aunt Belle and Aunt Mary's place in Westbourne Grove. Aunt Belle had a basin of hot water to bathe my feet, and that really helped. The aunts were very hospitable and kind.

As soon as we took delivery of our car in Holland Park, we left Bayswater and drove down to Grasmere in East Byfleet, where the family was living. Jocelyn had booked us a room in Linatus House in a cul-de-sac opposite their house, which was very convenient. When we arrived, mother and son greeted each other warmly and affectionately, and Christopher introduced me to his mother. Naturally I was a little bit nervous, but after the initial meeting we were more at ease with each other. I found that she was a really lovely woman, very caring and loving.

We didn't see much of the family that year because we were travelling a lot. The summer of 1959 was beautiful and lasted all the while we were in England. Sylvia organised a trip down to Cornwall with Jocelyn. Four of us

---

218 Alberto had been working on the film set as art director.

set off for the Lizard. On the way we stopped at Chard. The clock tower used to strike the hour during the night, which disturbed our sleep. We booked in at a place in Cornwall. At night the foghorn used to go, and it frightened me at first. When the others went to the pub for a drink, I decided not to go with them. We had to climb down steep paths to the beach at the Lizard. I managed to take a dip or two in the sea but found the water too cold and the wind too strong. I was trying to keep away from the wind all the time. We then moved to a hotel in Housel Bay but the light from the lighthouse worried us at night, so we didn't stay very long. On our way back to Byfleet we stopped off at Maidenhead for one night. That was my introduction to Cornwall. I must say I found the climb down to the beach a bit treacherous.

At Grasmere I met Gillie and Pam for the first time, and little Simon was only two years old. Humphry, Hilde and John also came down to see us, and John was a very young boy. We didn't see Rosamund at all that year. Christopher was a bit disappointed. I think she was away at camp picking fruit somewhere. We drove down to Salisbury with Mother to see Dickon and Olive. Joanna was in a pram; she was only two years old, and Olive was expecting Ruth at that time. We also made a trip with Mother down to Hastings to see Aunt Nell, who was staying with a friend. On the way back we stopped at Five Oak Green in Kent to meet Bill and Leila, who had a mini-supermarket. One evening Sylvia and Trevor joined Jocelyn and us for dinner at the Indian Curry Centre. Afterwards, we went to see *The Importance of Being Earnest* in London. That was my first meeting with Trevor, and I didn't see him again until 2000, when I was at Carol's house. I don't remember meeting Gareth that year. He must have been away somewhere. On another evening Humphry and Hilde invited us to their council flat in Camberwell for dinner. Sylvia and Jocelyn were also there, and I met Edda[219] for the first time. She was sitting in a corner, very quiet, not saying a word.

Meanwhile Christopher was planning a car trip to Lourdes, and to stop off at Düsseldorf to see the Reardons. The drive from Byfleet to Dover made me a little ill in the evening, and crossing the Channel was no help at all. By that time, I realised I was having morning sickness. On reaching Abbeville I was very hungry and enjoyed my lunch. I remember those lovely seedless grapes fresh from the fields. In Grenoble, which was rainy the night we got

---

219 Hilde's German daughter from her previous marriage.

there, we stayed in a pension; I was a bit worried when the light in the toilet kept going on and off. Then Béziers, where we had a nice fish soup. By the time we got to Lourdes, the weather was beautiful, and we found the place ever so peaceful. We thoroughly enjoyed our stay there and attended the candlelit rosary parades in the evenings. Lourdes was the highlight of our visit that year, and we loved it so much. A third underground basilica was being built at that time.

Looking back, Christopher was so keen to show me so many places in England and Europe, and it was a wonderful experience seeing so many places in such a short time. I think myself very fortunate.

Leaving Lourdes, we headed for Düsseldorf and stopped off for one night at Karlsruhe. After some time, we managed to find a room; there was a big conference going on. We lost our way looking for the Reardons' house in Düsseldorf. They were expecting us for lunch, but we finally turned up for dinner. We stayed up very late talking, so were up late the following morning, and didn't make our appointment at Eindhoven, where the Philips factory had laid on a lunch for us and wanted to show us round the factory, so the whole thing was cancelled.

On our return to England via Switzerland we stopped in Basle for a while. I loved that country; I thought it was beautiful. We went through France and stopped at various places. The weather was still very good. We visited Tours and Rouen Cathedral.

It must have been late September by the time we got back to England. Christopher was planning another trip, this time up to Scotland, to the Highlands. We didn't see very much of Sylvia after our European trip, but we did see Mother and Jocelyn a few times before we left for the north. We stopped in Yorkshire for a night to see York Minster the following day, which was quite impressive, and met a Singaporean lawyer there. Then we went on to Loughborough to stay the night. In those days the motorway was not yet ready, so it was a long journey up, and we had to stop at various places. In Stockport we went to see May and Graeme, and May laid on a sumptuous Chinese dinner. They were preparing to go to Nigeria the following morning, for Graeme's two-year contract. We met Graeme's mother and his sister Carole, and that night we stayed at a nearby B&B.

Reaching Scotland, we stopped at a place called Tweedsmuir, recommended by May and Graeme. It was a beautiful village by the River Tweed. We passed a huge canyon called the Devil's Beef Tub. I found Scotland very interesting, with its massive mountains and lakes. In Edinburgh we stopped to see the castle, and I stayed in the car while Christopher climbed up to see Arthur's Seat. We also had lunch with a former Turquand Youngs colleague called Mrs. May Watson. It was early October, and most hotels were closing for the winter, but on arrival at the Trossachs in the Highlands we managed to get a room for a night or two.

It was time to return to Byfleet to see the family for the rest of our leave. Dickon came one evening from Salisbury. He, Christopher and Jocelyn went to Laxton for their reunion dinner, while Mother and I stayed at home and played draughts. I won the first game; she was determined to beat me in the second game, and she did. The three men came back rather late, after eleven o'clock. It was getting very cold, so Jocelyn lent me his sheepskin and put it round my shoulders, as we had to walk back to Linatus. Dickon must have stayed at Grasmere.

It was early November when we left Grasmere. Frost was on the ground. We had to say goodbye to Mother and the rest of the family. Jocelyn managed to organise the shipment of our new car to Singapore. We flew back by Qantas in a small version of the Boeing. When we touched down at Karachi Airport, we learned that we were to stop there for a few days, as one of the flaps on the plane had to be replaced. We were there for three and a half days. They put us up in a hotel and everything was on the house. We were taken to a Pakistani wedding, and to see *Some Like It Hot* with Marilyn Monroe, and on a cruise down the harbour. It was a mini holiday, but we were keen to get back to Singapore.

Walter and Colin met us at Singapore Airport and took us to their new place in Jervois Road for breakfast. They had given up 24 Dunsfold Drive for us and left some of the furniture there as well, and organised an amah for us, which was very kind of them.

Our trip to the UK and Europe was so very well planned by Christopher, and I consider myself very fortunate to have seen so many places in that short time.

It took us a while to settle in at 24 Dunsfold Drive and to prepare for our first Christmas in that house.

The Backstory

My mother, Theresa, died on the 23rd February 2020 in the Good Shepherd Loft care home, Singapore, aged ninety-six. This book is dedicated to her and to my father, Christopher, who died in Tunbridge Wells on the 19th June 1998.

My sister Angela read out extracts from this memoir to Mum when she visited her in January 2020. She read the parts based on Mum's life, which Mum, being blind, had recorded onto fourteen cassettes between January and May 2000 while living with Angela and her family in Sydney.

In May 2000, Mum was looking forward to returning to England, to spend the summer with us in our new home in London and visit old friends and relatives. Little did she know that she would have another twenty years to live, in relatively good health, mostly with myself and my daughters, Madeleine and Alice, from 2002 to 2017. We were blessed by and appreciated having her company, support and guidance during those years.

For many years I intended to write about my father's war experiences but procrastinated, uncertain how to approach the subject. There seemed to be inadequate information to start with, since Dad never spoke to me about his past, though Angela and I had heard anecdotes from Mum. Dad was a very dignified, quiet man, and I didn't want to upset his cheerful mood by asking him about the past. Angela says that during the 1990s when our parents visited her and her husband Andrew and their sons, Robin and Thomas, in Australia to escape the British winters, Dad would unwind after a few drinks and talk about his experiences as a prisoner on the Burma-Siam railway.

I remember talking to Dad in his care home in April to June 1998. When I mentioned that the Japanese Emperor was visiting London and that some veterans had turned their backs on him along The Mall, Dad said he wouldn't do that, as the war was over and times had changed. He used to say, "Forgive and forget", though he had long ago forgiven but not forgotten – and I don't think he would want us to forget what he endured either. Most importantly, he always looked on the bright side, gave people the benefit of the doubt and did not dwell on hard times. One thing that cheered him when he was in hospital two months before he died was the news of the Good Friday Agreement that brought peace to Northern Ireland.

After Dad died, while packing up his and Mum's house for sale, I discovered many files crammed with old letters in his wardrobe; business letters and personal ones, dating from the 1940s to the 1970s. Christopher's family and friends were prolific letter-writers, and I think he kept them all for sentimental reasons. So, after their house in Kent was sold, I kept all his letters, and the diaries he wrote for decades. His last diary entry, on the 2nd April 1998 before going into hospital, was lucid, though on the previous two days he had left blank bits down one side of the page, as though he were partially sighted. By that time, the brain tumour which affected the left side of his body was advanced. When my Uncle Jocelyn died in 2004, I also inherited the letters written home to the family dating from the 1930s which, being the self-appointed family archivist, he had kept.

I never met Connie or Dad's POW comrades, though I exchanged letters with Jack Shuttle after Dad died. I knew my Grandma Caroline, who died when I was seven. She had white hair, wore a midi-length blue dress with a cameo brooch at the neck and little ankle boots, sat in an armchair by the fireplace in their flat at 3 Yew Close, Weybridge[220], and used to read to me. Of the great-aunts, her sisters, I remember Aunt Nell, who lived at Yew Close; and Aunts Mary and Belle, who lived in a flat above an antique shop in Notting Hill. I knew all my English uncles and aunts: Uncle Jocelyn, our jovial guardian at boarding school who met us at the airport, drove us to school and back to Weybridge for half-terms and 'visiting weekends', lent me his P. G. Wodehouse books and sent letters enclosing *Peanuts* cartoons;

---

220 Yew Close was a huge, characterful Victorian house divided into three or four apartments with their own gardens and garages, at 50 Oatlands Chase. It was demolished in 1990, as property developers built a new apartment block and renamed it Yew Place.

Aunt Sylvia, who did the cooking and brought up her son Steve on her own; and Rosamund (she refused to be called 'Aunt'), who kept rabbits and cats. They all lived together in Weybridge and later West Byfleet, where Sylvia cooked us delicious Sunday roasts and Christmas dinners every year for twelve years after Dad died.

Uncle Gervase emigrated to New Zealand and had two adopted children with Aunt Joyce, Teresa and Bernard; Uncle Dickon and Aunt Olive had Joanna, Ruth and Chris, and lived in Goodwood, Sussex, then moved to a farm in Scotland; Aunt Leila married Uncle Bill and lived in Camberley with their dog. We used to visit Aunt Bianca, Uncle Alberto and Flavia in Rome and Tuscany; Uncle Humphry, Aunt Hilde and John in Luxembourg and, after Humphry retired as an EEC translator, in Putney; Uncle Gareth and Aunt Janet in Bradford-on-Avon. I also knew some of my parents' friends featured in this book, including Pamela and Gillie Brown, Felicity and Bill Swan, John Curran, Walter Bellam, Willie Lochhead, Colin Coey, Peggy and Alec McMaster, May and Graeme Large, Jean and Trevor Brown, Marion and John Reardon.

Listening to Mum's tapes brought back memories of our Chinese aunts and uncles in Singapore, especially Aunt Agnes and Uncle Chai Seng; Aunt Elizabeth and Uncle Chua Wee Heng; Aunt Mary and Uncle Cheng Yong Nghee; Sixth Uncle Pang Tong Khiam, who was an interpreter during the war and used to chat about politics with Dad; and Sixth Aunt Chew Cheok Eng, who made fresh '*kaya*' (egg jam) – all of whom we knew and whose children we grew up with; Third Uncle Pang Tong Kuan, who used to visit Mum and give us pictures of the Queen; Second Uncle Pang Tong Hak, who was blind and whom we visited in Upper Thomson Road; Eighth Uncle Pang Tong Jin, whom we called 'Bicycle Uncle' as he cycled to our house from Serangoon Gardens, bringing cooked food; and Fourth Uncle Pang Tong Yong and Tenth Uncle Pang Tong Chew, who ran the shop in Rochore Road selling imported chocolates and used an abacus.

When my mother came to live with us in London, she gave me the box of cassettes containing her life story. Life got in the way, and twenty years passed. While I worked full time as a journalist in the City, my mother, despite being blind with retinitis pigmentosa, cooked dinner for us every night, and I brought her to church every Sunday. From 2002 until they left for university, Mum helped me raise my daughters.

Some months before she moved to the care home in Singapore in September 2017, I began listening to her tapes. She spoke very clearly and slowly, so they were easy to transcribe. I realised I could combine my mother's story with my father's, tracing how they had grown up on opposite sides of the world, yet had much in common, particularly their strong Catholic faith and large, close-knit families – and how circumstances conspired to bring them together.

Jocelyn had typed up Dad's 1938 diaries after Dad died, possibly as a form of therapy, as well as wanting to pass on their story to the next generations for posterity. He gave the ninety-two foolscap pages to Angela and me. I also found the original diaries. My Dad's handwriting as a young man was upright and legible; quite different from his tiny, spidery scrawl in later life. For this book I selected extracts from the diaries spanning the whole year, because the seasons, weather and nature meant so much to him.

The problem of how to recount Dad's war experiences diminished after I reread the memoir of Jack Shuttle, who met Dad in a prison camp on the Burma-Siam railway. In 1997 Dad wrote a letter to Jack, recalling his own war experiences, which was invaluable for this book. After Dad died, I wrote to Mr. Shuttle, and he kindly replied and sent me a signed copy of his book. It was very moving to read and striking to see the parallels between some of their experiences. Over the years, I read books and watched films and TV programmes about the war in the Far East. *The War Diaries of Weary Dunlop* also brought my dad's story to life. I realised that the Australian surgeon Sir Edward Dunlop was probably running the two hospital camps where Dad was treated for dysentery and leg ulcers while he was there. Dad told me he had been in a hospital camp in Nakhon Pathom when I returned from holiday in Thailand in 1992 and showed him a photograph of its golden *chedi*. Chungkai was mentioned in Jack's book as the camp where he met Dad. In Lieutenant Dunlop's book a chapter is devoted to each of these camps, with meticulous details including dates, statistics and anecdotes. So Dunlop, as well as other Allied doctors including Dr. de Wardenn, whom Dad mentions, probably contributed to saving his life.

I had glanced at a few of the 1940s letters when I first found them. But once I started to open the envelopes and read them properly, delicate and yellowed with age, it became apparent that this was a precious time capsule from a historic era. My cousin Steve sent me letters addressed to his mother Sylvia, and some of Jocelyn's letters. Angela sent me the letter Dad wrote to Jack Shuttle and others. While decluttering in 2020, I found more letters. Angela also discovered more, including some from Dad's Java interlude and the ones he wrote to Mum while on leave in 1957, the final pieces of the puzzle. I found another cassette Mum had recorded about their wedding and honeymoon.

My cousin Anne Toh started compiling the Pang family tree, from our grandparents onwards, in 2011, and sent me her latest update. I have only used the first two pages, which cover our grandparents' and my mother's generation. The Repton family tree was researched by genealogist Mr. G. Cope-Cartledge from 1964 to 1971, who traced the ancestry of my great-great-great-great-grandfather, landscape gardener Humphry Repton (1752–1818).

While in Singapore for my mother's funeral in February and March 2020, I was given a copy of the press cutting about my maternal grandfather which my cousin Theresa found.

I have let my parents tell their story in their own words, or through the words of their relatives and friends. My notes in italics and footnotes are to explain or provide background. I hope their account will be widely read, because they belonged to an incredibly brave and strong, though modest and selfless generation, who sacrificed the best years of their lives for our freedom.

The Pangs arrive in Singapore, 1897–1926

According to my Chinese cousins, our grandfather, John Pang How Yew, first travelled from China to Singapore alone, aged twenty, to work, then returned to China, married our grandmother, Mary Yeo Kwee Choo, in 1899, and brought her to Singapore to start a family.

Theresa was not taken to hospital, nor to the doctor, when she had her accident aged three, so her scalded fingers, half closed in pain, fused together and remained so for the rest of her life. Her mother, born in nineteenth-century China, had bound feet so was not very mobile, and delegated looking after the children to her eldest daughter, my Aunt Mary (known as 'Big Aunt'). With such a large family and everybody working hard or going to school, nobody was available to take children to the doctor after an accident. Later, Theresa's second brother enrolled her in English-language school, so she was the only daughter of the family to benefit from an English education like her brothers'. She became bilingual, speaking both Teochew, her parents' dialect, and English. This was a life-changing decision taken by her brother.

Christopher grows up before the war, 1918–1939

Christopher was born in Montreal, Canada on the 3rd December 1918, the eldest of Bernard and Caroline's seven children. His parents were married in Montreal on the 31st August 1917, after meeting on the ship crossing from Britain to America. Caroline was a governess before her marriage. They started their family when Bernard was forty-eight and Caroline thirty-three. Christopher's brothers, Jocelyn and Gervase, and sister Sylvia were born in New York while Bernard was working as an accountant for Paramount Pictures. The younger children, Dickon, Leila and Rosamund, were born after the family moved back to England. Christopher and his brothers attended Catholic boarding schools in England from the age of about nine; his sisters went to a day school nearer home. They lived in a succession of rented houses, from Crouch End in London to Surrey.

During the 1930s the family were living at St. Ann's Lodge, Chertsey, a large house with its own tennis court, gardens and orchard, near the park of St. Ann's Hill. Jocelyn saved a press cutting, probably from the 1980s, showing the Lodge, a 'house of immense charm and character; original 19th century; extended to 4 reception rooms; garden room; kitchen; utility; 5 beds; 2 baths; ample parking; over half-acre garden', advertised for sale for £235,000. By 2019, newly renovated to twenty-first-century standards, the Lodge was on the market at around £2 million. Bernard and Caroline were only renting the house, so they had to move to a smaller one during the war for financial reasons.

At that time, many women remained single throughout their lives, since a generation of young men had been killed during the First World War. Bernard's unmarried sisters, Leila and Ina (Regina), lived in the neighbouring Cottage. Ina had been an ambulance driver for British troops in France in the First World War. The two aunts brought up Christopher's cousins, Bianca, Humphry and Gareth, who had been brought to England after their father Philip, Bernard's brother, died aged forty-one in a car accident involving a donkey in Italy in 1917 while working for the Dunlop tyre company, and their Italian mother Maria Musso was moved to a care home. Bianca was just five years old when her father died, while Humphry was seventeen months and Gareth was a three-month-old baby.

Christopher spent two years between leaving school and the start of the Second World War with his siblings and parents at St. Ann's Lodge and his cousins and aunts who lived in the Cottage. In autumn 1938 he attended a business course, and in January 1939 he started a clerical job at an accountancy firm in the City of London. Constantly aware of the seasons and weather, he spent his days gardening, cycling and going for walks with the others in nearby St. Ann's Hill – which they called 'the Park' – and the surrounding countryside. This was in the days before major roads or motorways, when farmland and fields surrounded Chertsey. In the spring, they planted flowers and vegetables from seed, watered the growing plants during the summer, harvested and ate the vegetables, and their mother made jam from the fruit in autumn. They played tennis in the summer and followed the cricket Test matches and Wimbledon tennis tournament on the radio. Throughout the year they went to church every Sunday, where Christopher and his brothers sometimes served as altar boys. They cycled to the public library to borrow books and did a lot of reading. 'Free libraries' were greatly appreciated in those days, having been introduced in 1919.

In the evenings, Christopher would join the others around the fireplace to listen to classical concerts on the 'wireless'. In the summer, they attended Prom concerts in London. Sometimes they performed amateur dramatics or played parlour games, especially at Christmas. They went to the cinema to watch early Hollywood or British black-and-white films and newsreels.

Having started a large family late in life, there was always financial pressure on Bernard, especially as he had to pay school fees for all the children. He continued working to support his family until his mid-seventies, as his adult offspring were away in the armed forces and unable to contribute much to the household budget during the war.

World War II, 1939–1945

In September 1939, war was declared between Britain and Germany. Aged twenty, Christopher joined the army, was assigned to the Queen's Royal Regiment, and moved to Stoughton Barracks for military training. In December he was shipped to India for a year, then to Malaya from late 1940 until December 1941, when the Japanese invaded.

Christopher wrote to his friend and fellow former POW Jack Shuttle in May to June 1997, the year before he died. Unbeknownst to them at the time, Christopher and Jack had both travelled to India in December 1939 on the same troop ship, the *Nevasa*.

In addition to the approximately sixteen thousand Allied troops who died while forced to work on the 'Death Railway', an estimated three hundred thousand Asian labourers had to toil on its construction, of whom more than a hundred thousand are believed to have perished. The death toll among the Asians was proportionately higher, as they had no medical care and the hygiene in their huts was even worse than in the Allied POW camps. The exact numbers who died on the Death Railway will never be known, as the Japanese Army destroyed records at the end of the war. During their three-and-a-half-year ordeal, tens of thousands of physically fit young British men, most of whom had never travelled to the Far East nor engaged in combat before, were reduced to skeletons, dying or desperately clinging on to life.

The prisoners from Changi were transported up the west coast of peninsular Malaya to the far north of Thailand near the border with Burma during 1942. Jack Shuttle recounts in *Destination Kwai* how he and the other POWs were packed so tightly into windowless freight carriages that they had no room to lie down, sweating through five days and nights in a seemingly endless, hellish journey. With no lavatories, and many already suffering from diarrhoea, the men had to relieve themselves through the open door of the moving train, while being held on to by their comrades on either side so that they did not fall out. For the first two days or so, they were only fed and let out of the train about once a day, until they crossed the border into Thailand. Stopovers then became more frequent, and they were able to trade their precious few possessions for food and cigarettes from Thai vendors at the stations where they stopped. Some men were so hungry, they exchanged the shirts off their backs for an egg or a banana, which they later regretted.

Jack Shuttle describes how the POWs were first brought to a flooded transit camp which had been built by a group of prisoners who'd had the 'misfortune' of being sent up earlier than them in June and who had already moved upcountry to start work on the railway. This was near a small town fifty miles west of Bangkok called Ban Pong.

The Supreme Command of the Imperial Japanese Army, defeated by Allied forces in naval battles at Midway and other Pacific Islands after America joined the war in December 1941, decided they needed an alternative route to supply their army in Burma. So, in June 1942 they drew up a plan to build a railway connecting Singapore, Hanoi and Rangoon. The Burma-Siam railway was to be built from Ban Pong in northern Thailand up to Moulmein in southern Burma; a distance of 250 miles, across narrow, deep gorges and rivers, and through fever-infested virgin jungle. A similar project had been surveyed in the early 1900s by the British but had been rejected as too dangerous to construct. The Japanese, however, were not deterred by the inhospitable terrain, as they had what they considered to be an expendable workforce.

Construction of the railway began at both the Burmese and Siamese ends simultaneously using mostly British, but also Dutch, Australian and a few hundred American, Canadian and New Zealander, prisoners of war, in addition to the hundreds of thousands of Asian civilians rounded up in Indonesia, Malaya, Burma, Vietnam and India. Thai Prime Minister Field Marshal Plaek Phibunsongkhram signed a treaty of alliance with the Japanese from the start of the war in Asia in December 1941. Similarly, the French in Indochina came to a 'diplomatic understanding' with the Japanese invaders and were spared the horrors of slaving on the Death Railway.

Christopher recalled that he avoided the worst of the so-called 'Speedo', as he was suffering from dysentery in a hospital tent in Tarkanun from May until about September 1943.

According to an anonymous account compiled by J. P. from POW testimonies, *The True Story of the Death Railway & the Bridge on the River Kwai*, Australian POWs called the five-kilometre stretch of track from Konyu to Hintok 'Hellfire Pass' because, viewed from the top of the rock cutting at night as they worked by candlelight, 'it looked like the jaws of hell'. Construction of the cutting began on the 25th April 1943, using four hundred Australian POWs. By June the work was behind their accelerated schedule, so in July an additional six hundred POWs, Australians and some British, were drafted in to work twelve– to eighteen-hour shifts around the clock, without a rest day, for the next six weeks until mid-August. The cutting was in two sections. The first was approximately 450 metres long and seven metres deep. The second, main section was approximately seventy-five metres long and twenty-five metres deep. The prisoners had to excavate the soil and rock by hand using eight-pound hammers, steel tap drills, explosives, pinch bars, picks, shovels and '*chunkels*' (wide hoes). They removed the waste rock manually, carrying two cane baskets or rice sacks slung on a pole on their shoulders. The Konyu section cost the lives of at least seven hundred of the thousand-strong workforce, including sixty-nine men beaten to death by Japanese engineers or Korean guards.

Jack Shuttle replied to my letter a year after my father died:

Yes, I did see the Timewatch film[221] with some sadness. The whole party left from our camp at Chungkai and we saw them off with a certain envy – they were in buoyant mood and pleased to be leaving the jungle camps and horrors of the railway.

Many of them were my friends and all comrades working on the same sections of the railway, having all gone up to Thailand from Changi together.

It was only because Chris and I were down with amoebic dysentery that we did not go with them!

After the prisoners finished building the railway in October 1943, the Japanese split the survivors into three groups. The fittest, probably including those Jack recalls leaving Chungkai, were shipped to Japan to work in coal mines. But of the ten thousand men sent to Japan, some three thousand are believed to have drowned when their ships were torpedoed by US and British submarines. Those in the second group were deemed fit enough to stay on the railway as maintenance workers. About a hundred of them were killed in Allied bombing raids on the railway and bridges across the River Kwai. The third group were considered too sick to work and were sent back to Changi Prison in Singapore. Those, like Jack and Chris, who were too ill to move, stayed in the hospital camps and did maintenance work on the railway when they recovered, until the Japanese surrender.

According to Australian surgeon Sir Edward 'Weary' Dunlop's[222] war diaries, amoebic dysentery was the most common disease at Chungkai when he arrived there in January 1944, with 714 cases in the camp at the time. Ulcers were the next most common ailment, with 459 cases, possibly including Christopher. Dunlop recorded fifty-five POWs as being 'limbless', and as the camp's chief medical officer performed operations including skin grafts and leg amputations on prisoners with aggravated ulcers, where the flesh was eaten away down to the bone. Owing to a lack of medical instruments, Dunlop (who, in his early thirties, was only ten years older than his patients) had to use handmade tools and containers fashioned from bamboo, bits of rubber, oil drums, or whatever materials could be salvaged.

---

221 A BBC documentary about the Death Railway.
222 The POWs affectionately nicknamed him 'Weary' based on a pun on 'Dunlop tyres' and 'tired' as he was always exhausted.

There was an acute shortage of medications, and amputations often had to be performed without anaesthetic. Rare Red Cross parcels were confiscated by the Japanese and not distributed until 1944.

Dunlop continually went beyond the call of duty to protect his sick and dying patients. When the Japanese were forcing severely ill men to go to work on the railway – a daily occurrence – he pleaded with them to send the less ill prisoners instead. When the Japanese ignored him or there were not enough able-bodied prisoners, Dunlop, a very tall man, told a few of the seriously ill men to pretend to faint; then he would pick them up and carry them to the sick bay on his back. Like other medical orderlies who had to give the daily list of sick to the Japanese, Dunlop was frequently beaten by the Japanese guards. He was even tortured for refusing to kowtow to them. However, Dunlop carried on fearlessly and without complaint, performing operations, looking after his patients and recording everything in his diaries.

Throughout their captivity, a heroic Thai river trader, Boon Pong Sirivajchaphan, smuggled drugs, food, cash and radio batteries to POW camps by boat along the Khwae Noi River, at risk to his life from the Japanese military police. According to Boon Pong's obituary in the British press after the war, in September 1942, K. G. Gairdner, a civilian internee in Bangkok, heard about the terrible conditions in POW camps upcountry. He started the clandestine 'V' organisation by asking fellow internees R. D. Hempson and E. P. Heath to organise help, which they did through Nai Clarn, who contacted his friend Nai Boon Pong in Kanchanaburi. From then on, since he had a contract with the Japanese to supply food to the camps, Boon Pong smuggled cash and life-saving drugs such as morphia for anaesthetic and pain relief, emetine to treat dysentery, iodoform and phenol as ulcer treatments, into the camps, hidden among the food. After the war Boon Pong was awarded an MBE, and welcomed former prisoners who visited him in Bangkok, where he ran a successful bus company.

In an article in the British press, a Captain Durnford said:

Boon Pong (the Thai river trader) was also the first to let us know the war was nearly over. On August 10, 1945, a working party of prisoners passed his shop in the high street at Kanchanaburi. They heard his gramophone playing 'God Save the King'.

Historical Notes

The Fall of Singapore, 1941–1944

After Japanese kamikaze pilots bombed the US Navy fleet at Pearl Harbor, Hawaii in a surprise attack on the 7th December 1941, US President Franklin D. Roosevelt declared war on Japan and Germany, and British Prime Minister Winston Churchill announced that Britain was at war with Japan. The Japanese military immediately started multi-pronged attacks across South-East Asia. On the 8th December, Japanese forces attacked Malaya from the north and bombed Singapore; the Japanese bombed airbases in the Philippines and invaded the north of Luzon island, but American troops defended the archipelago until May; the Japanese started attacking Guam and Wake Island in the Pacific, and Hong Kong. Allied troops and local forces in Hong Kong and Wake Island fought on until the 25th December when they surrendered. On the 10th December, Japanese aircraft bombed and sank the British Royal Navy battleships *Prince of Wales* and *Repulse* off the east coast of peninsular Malaya. By mid-December Japanese troops started invading Sarawak in East Malaya. In late December they started bombing Rangoon in Burma. In January 1942, the Japanese invaded Borneo and the Celebes in Indonesia. By February, they started launching major air raids on Java and Sumatra. On the 13th February Singapore began evacuating foreigners. On the 15th February British forces surrendered Singapore island to Japan.

In an article in the British press after the war, titled *Fall and Rise of Singapore*, journalist Richard West wrote:

> *The fall of Singapore to the Japanese on February 15, 1942, was described by Sir Winston Churchill as "the worst disaster and largest capitulation in British history". Later it came to be seen as the moment when Britain's subject people scented their chance to rid themselves of the Empire.*

Japan launched further attacks on Burma in January 1942, where they fought against British, American, Chinese and Burmese troops until the latter capitulated in mid-May.

In Singapore in mid-February 1942, an inexperienced, poorly equipped British force of almost eighty-five thousand men surrendered to some twenty-five thousand Japanese veterans of the war in China, where they had been fighting for ten years and captured Manchuria.

The British Army, although their troops far outnumbered the Japanese, were forced to surrender Singapore Island within only a week. This was ultimately because, under Lieutenant General Arthur E. Percival, GOC Malaya, their guns were pointing towards the south, from where they were expecting a naval attack, leaving the north of the island defenceless. Percival did not heed the warnings of his chief engineer that the Japanese were advancing fast from the north, down the Malayan peninsula on bicycles and in tanks, after landing at Kota Bharu, north-east Malaya on the 8th December 1941. Percival arguably had no choice but to surrender to Lieutenant General Tomoyuki Yamashita, given that Churchill had provided no tanks for the British Army in the Far East and fewer than two hundred aircraft, of which most were obsolete, so the two British warships had no air cover against Japanese fighter planes. In fact, Percival's decision was possibly the lesser of two evils, for if he had not surrendered but followed Churchill's instructions to "fight to the last man", the Japanese could have subjected not only the Allied troops but Singapore's civilian population to even more savage massacres than they did in order to subdue the island.

West explains that the people who should have told Churchill about the imminent Japanese threat from the hinterland, particularly General Percival, failed to do so until it was too late, so that by the time Churchill ordered the two battleships to be sent up the east coast of Malaya off Kuantan, the Japanese were able to destroy them from the air within hours. By late December 1941, the Japanese Army, battle-hardened from fighting in China for a decade, had advanced most of the way down peninsular Malaya and were approaching the Straits of Johore; they had also captured another British island colony, Hong Kong. On Boxing Day, Percival's chief engineer Brigadier Ivan Simson urged him to defend Singapore's north shore by setting up anti-tank devices, underwater obstacles, fire traps, mines, floating barbed wire, and searchlights against a night attack. But Percival reportedly refused, saying, "I believe that defences of the sort you want to throw up are bad for the morale of troops and civilians." Some weeks later, when Churchill had seen Simson's plea and ordered Percival to defend the north coast, he still refused to do so. At the last minute, when the Japanese had reached the Straits of Johore, a short distance across the Causeway bridge from Singapore, Percival ordered the defences to be put on the north-east, instead of the north-west from where he was being warned the attack would come.

Hong Kong, which had fewer troops and a lack of water, defended itself for longer than Singapore, despite the latter's massive army and plentiful food and water supplies. The island of Singapore, the so-called jewel in the crown of the British Empire in South-East Asia, fell because the British colonial government was caught unawares. Complacent, sorely lacking in leadership or any coherent strategy, the British seriously underestimated the forward planning, aggression and superior firepower of the Japanese military machine. The British government failed to supply sufficient or up-to-date fighter planes or any armoured vehicles; nor did it warn its own armed forces or prepare the citizens of the island for an imminent invasion. The British authorities did not even order civilians to evacuate until two days before the surrender, apparently for fear of dampening morale. This resulted in many expatriate civilians missing their chance to escape on ships that were offering to take them to safety in other countries like Australia, though some of those ships were also torpedoed by the Japanese. Many expatriates ended up trapped in Singapore when the Japanese invaded and were detained in prison camps by them throughout the war. Meanwhile, the majority ethnic Chinese population were subjected to the most brutal treatment.

The Burma Campaign, 1942–1945

After the Japanese Army invaded Burma in January 1942, they pushed the joint British and Indian forces back towards India and threatened Britain's colonies of Burma and India. General William Slim, a veteran of World

War I, was put in charge of taking back control of Burma and arrived there in March 1942, initially leading the Burma Corps to stem the Japanese advance, together with American General Joseph Stilwell, who was leading Chiang Kai-shek's Chinese troops in north-east Burma along the so-called 'Burma Road' from Rangoon to Kunming which was China's only outlet to the outside world. At that time, morale was very poor among the mixture of British and Indian soldiers and their Burmese comrades, who had little in the way of skills or training and had faced a formidable, hardened enemy in the Japanese veterans of their war in China during the 1930s.

General Slim personally met the troops in the paddy fields and jungle, talked to them about how they could beat the Japanese and boosted their morale. He made sure the soldiers on the ground were adequately supplied with food, armour and ammunition. Mules were brought in to carry their equipment through dense jungle, though the animals struggled to carry heavy loads uphill in the mud of the monsoon rains and the men ended up carrying seventy-five-pound backpacks while climbing through treacherously steep jungle in single file. In 1943, the 14th Army was formed and given military training. It comprised combined British and Indian Army brigades and divisions, the notoriously fierce Gurkha fighters from Nepal, and troops brought in from the Commonwealth, notably from West and East Africa. The soldiers spoke different languages, but all were united in the fight against the Japanese Imperial Army. The Allied forces gradually grew stronger.

Major General Orde Wingate's Chindits played a crucial role in the Allied victory over the Japanese. Wingate pioneered the strategy of dropping food, arms and ammunition supplies into the jungle from small, light RAF and USAAF[223] airplanes by parachute or by landing on purpose-built airstrips. Specially trained agents from the clandestine Force 136, the Asian arm of Britain's Special Operations Executive, also parachuted into Burma behind enemy lines and played a key role in defeating the Japanese, fighting alongside Burmese forces on the ground. British and American pilots flew injured soldiers to hospital in India. There was an airstrip on the Imphal plain in northern India, which, following Slim's plan, became one of the main battlefields. After securing the support of Churchill and British and US armed forces chiefs of staff at the Quebec Conference in August 1943,

---

223 United States Army Air Forces, the US air force during WWII.

Wingate became commander of the Chindits, and trained soldiers who followed his strategy of penetrating deep behind enemy lines and sabotaging the Japanese supply lines, with air support. By the end of the fighting, the Japanese troops were starving in their bunkers, as their generals did not provide them with sufficient food. Unfortunately, Wingate was killed in an air crash in March 1944 while visiting troops on the front line.

In mid-1944, in the decisive Battles of Imphal and Kohima in the mountainous Nagaland in the far north-east of India just across from the Burmese north-western border, General Slim's 14th Army defeated the Japanese in fierce, strategic fighting in which the latter lost eighty-five thousand men. However, the Allies' victory over the Japanese at Kohima in early June coincided with the D-Day Normandy landings, so what was arguably the most significant victory of the war was barely reported in the European press.

By March 1945 the Allies had captured Mandalay and the Japanese headquarters of Meiktila, forcing the Japanese troops to retreat to Rangoon. Then General Slim led a land attack on Rangoon, while the Chindits attacked from the air and sea. Rangoon was recaptured by the Allies in May 1945, which coincided with the defeat of the Nazis and Victory in Europe on the 8th May, so again the Allies' ultimate victory in Burma, after three and a half years of persistent fighting against the Japanese, was hardly reported in the British press. The Burma Campaign, though one of the most brutal and longest-running battles of World War II, became a forgotten victory back in Britain.

Churchill did say at the time, "We may allow ourselves a brief period of rejoicing but let us not forget for a moment the toil and efforts that lie ahead", reminding the nation that while the war in Europe was won, the world war was not yet over, as the Japanese had still not conceded defeat and the future was at that point uncertain.

An estimated seventy-one thousand soldiers from Britain and the Commonwealth were killed in the war against Japan, including up to sixteen thousand POWs who died in Japanese prison camps in the Far East. After the end of the fighting in Europe in May 1945, Japan was given a deadline of the 28th July to surrender. But the deadline passed, and it was not until after US forces dropped atomic bombs on Hiroshima and Nagasaki on the 6th and 9th August that Japan's Emperor Hirohito finally surrendered. After the surrender of Japan on the 14th August 1945, two days of national holidays were declared for celebrations in Britain, the United States and Australia. Japan officially signed the surrender documents on the 2nd September on board the USS *Missouri* in Tokyo Bay.

General Slim told his men, "When you go home, don't worry about what to tell your loved ones and friends about service in Asia. No one will know where you were, or where it is if you do. You are and will remain 'The Forgotten Army.'" Nevertheless, a lasting tribute to the brave men who fought in the Burma Campaign is inscribed at the Kohima War Cemetery:

When you go home, tell them of us and say,
"For your tomorrow, we gave our today."[224]

---

224 John Maxwell Edmonds, a Cambridge classicist and wartime codebreaker, composed this epitaph for unknown soldiers at the end of World War I.

Epilogue

Chris and Terry lived for twenty happy years in Braddell Heights, first in the bungalow he had shared with Walter at 24 Dunsfold Drive, and then at 4 Muswell Hill, the house they bought in 1964. Throughout the 1960s and '70s they had a wide circle of friends in Singapore, both locals and expatriates, and were close to Terry's large extended family.

Chris retired from Turquand Youngs in 1979, and he and Terry moved to a bungalow in Pembury near Tunbridge Wells, where they lived contentedly for another nineteen years until Christopher died from a brain tumour on the 19th June 1998, aged seventy-nine.

It was appropriate that they retired to Kent, the 'Garden of England', because Chris loved gardening, growing a colourful array of hardy annuals every year – daffodils, crocuses and tulips in spring; and in the summer, fuchsias, delphiniums, lupins, sweet williams, nicotiana and roses; tomatoes in the greenhouse; runner beans, spinach, redcurrants and blackcurrants behind the apple trees in the back garden. He played golf regularly with the 'veterans' at the Nevill Club in Tunbridge Wells. Terry enjoyed cooking both English and Chinese cuisine, particularly when visitors came and for the traditional Christmas and Boxing Day Repton family reunions. In the 1990s Chris and Terry made frequent trips to Singapore, Hong Kong and Sydney to visit Angela and her family and Terry's relatives, staying with Aunt Mary's youngest daughter Rosalina and her husband Richard in Seletar, or her eldest daughter Lucy and her husband Khiow Mong in Serangoon Gardens.

After Chris died, Terry moved to Sydney to live with Angela, Andrew, Robin and Thomas. Being blind, she could not live by herself, so the house in Pembury had to be sold. In 2002, she moved back to England to live with me and my daughters, Madeleine and Alice. In January 2010 Terry flew to Singapore to stay with her sister Agnes and her maid Linda for a year and a half. In autumn 2011, she moved back to London and lived with us again until September 2017. Then, aged ninety-four, she decided it was time to move back to her roots, as she could no longer climb the stairs. Sebastian, Aunt Mary's younger son, found a place for Terry at the Good Shepherd Loft, a small, Catholic senior citizens' home run by Dr. Joseph and Dr. Belinda Wee, friends of his sister Lucy. Terry spent the last two and a half years of her life back in her birthplace, where she was well cared for and often visited by her many nieces and nephews and their families, who took her out on special occasions.

Mum used to reminisce about Dad and the old days, being the last surviving member of her generation of the Pang family. She was one of the republic's 'pioneer generation', who saw Singapore transition from a British colony to a thriving, independent country and are revered as the founders of modern Singapore.

Bibliography

E. E. Dunlop, *The War Diaries of Weary Dunlop: Java and the Burma-Thailand Railway, 1942–1945*. Penguin Books (Australia), 2009.

Otto Kreefft, *Burma Railway: A Visual Recollection*. Museum Bronbeek; first English edition 2004.

Eric Lomax, *The Railway Man*. Vintage, 1995.

Donald and Joanna Moore, *The First 150 Years of Singapore*. Donald Moore Press Ltd., Singapore, in association with the Singapore International Chamber of Commerce, 1969.

F. T. Palgrave (ed.), *The Golden Treasury of the Best Songs and Lyrical Poems in the English Language*. First published by Oxford University Press in 1861, reprinted in 1959 and 1960.

David Rooney, *Burma Victory: Imphal and Kohima, March 1944 to May 1945*. Cassell Military Paperbacks, 1992.

Christopher Shores and Brian Cull with Yasuho Izawa, *Bloody Shambles – The First Comprehensive Account of Air Operations Over South-East Asia, December 1941-May 1942 Volume 2: The Defence of Sumatra to the Fall of Burma*. Published by Grub Street, London, 1993.

Jack Shuttle, *Destination Kwai: A 1939/45 Far Eastern War Memoir*. Self-published, first edition 1988.

Julie Summers, *The Colonel of Tamarkan: Philip Toosey & the Bridge on the River Kwai*. Pocket Books, Simon & Schuster UK Ltd., 2006.

Alvin Tan, *Singapore: A Very Short History from Temasek to Tomorrow*. Talisman Publishing Pte. Ltd., 2020.

Tan Chong Tee, *Force 136: Story of a WWII Resistance Fighter*. Translated by Lee Watt Sim and Clara Show. Asiapac Books (Singapore), 1995.

Acknowledgements

Thank you to everyone who helped bring this book to fruition. Firstly, thanks to Dad for leaving us his letters, diaries and photographs; to Mum for recording her life story on tape for us, and for her photographs; and to Uncle Jocelyn for keeping all the family correspondence and archives and typing up Dad's 1938 diaries.

Jack Shuttle corresponded with me after my father's death in 1998, sent me his war memoir and encouraged me to write my own book.

Deirbhile O'Grady sent me the inspirational *War Diaries of Weary Dunlop*.

My sister Angela in Sydney read through and helped me edit countless drafts of the manuscript from the beginning onwards and found and typed up Mum's letters as well as digging up other letters of Dad's and documents that helped fill in the missing links.

My partner Christopher Anderson helped me shape and format later drafts as the book progressed, mostly on the technical side but also giving objective editorial advice.

In Singapore, my cousin Anne Toh let me use the Pang family tree which she started compiling in 2005. Both family trees have had to be edited down for reasons of space. Bernadette Toh took me to the Changi WWII Museum back in 2001, and shared Pang family photos.

Theresa Chua shared the press cutting about our grandfather and accompanied me and my daughters on a tour of the Fort Canning Battlebox Museum in Singapore in 2020. Lucy Lim answered my questions about the Pang family photos. Elizabeth Chua, Robin Jordan and Jonathan Anderson read and gave feedback on the manuscript.

Flavia Tavazzi answered questions about her side of the family and shared photos of them in Rome in the 1950s. Steve Repton sent letters, postcards and press cuttings that belonged to Sylvia and Jocelyn and answered my questions. Joanna, Ruth and Chris Repton let me use their father's letters and photographs of their parents. Janet Repton answered questions about her husband Gareth. John Repton let me use letters from and photos of his father and helped with the family tree. Teresa McEvoy answered questions on her branch of the family.

Pamela Brown answered my questions and let me use letters from herself and her husband Gillie, and photographs of them.

The Coulson-Gilmer family kindly agreed to let me use Roy and Stella's letters and photographs of them. Chris Coulson-Gilmer showed me his maps of the plantations in Java.

John Curran identified people in the photograph at a Turquand Youngs dinner in a Chinese restaurant in the late 1950s.

In Sydney, Felicity Swan let me use a photo of her wedding, and John Yee a photo of his mother Boly and Aunt Mary Boey (Yoke Chee).

Purcell Press publisher Alice Wickham and her creative writing group in Twickenham critiqued the very first draft in 2017 and encouraged me to continue.

Jeremy Thompson of the Book Guild saw the potential in *Lotus-Eating Days* and agreed to publish it. Rosie Lowe at Troubador steered the production of the book, Hayley Russell did a meticulous copy edit and Philippa Iliffe organised the marketing.

My daughter Madeleine Carter gave early feedback and helped me find long-lost friends and relatives. Both Madeleine and Alice accompanied me on a journey of discovery, a fateful trip from the 1930s art deco Tanjong Pagar station in Singapore[225] via Gemas to Kota Bharu on the Jungle Railway in April 2011. Rosalina and Richard Kho and Zhang Su Li came to the rescue when things went disastrously wrong – but that is another story!

---

225 The railway station's land and tracks were owned by the Malaysian rail operator until the 30th June 2011, when they reverted to Singapore and the station was moved to Woodlands. The historic building has been retained.